Ellery's Protest

ELLERY'S PROTEST

How One Young Man Defied
Tradition & Sparked the Battle
over School Prayer

STEPHEN D. SOLOMON

THE UNIVERSITY OF MICHIGAN PRESS *Ann Arbor*

Published in the United States of America by
The University of Michigan Press
Manufactured in the United States of America
⊚ Printed on acid-free paper

2010   2009   2008   2007   4   3   2   1

A CIP catalog record for this book is available from the British Library.

Library of Congress Cataloging-in-Publication Data

Solomon, Stephen D.
    Ellery's protest : how one young man defied tradition and sparked
the battle over school prayer / Stephen D. Solomon.
        p.   cm.
    Includes bibliographical references and index.
    ISBN-13: 978-0-472-10837-4 (cloth : alk. paper)
    ISBN-10: 0-472-10837-9 (cloth : alk. paper)
    1. Abington Township School District (Abington, Pa.)—Trials,
litigation, etc.   2. Schempp, Edward—Trials, litigation, etc.
3. Prayer in the public schools—Law and legislation—United States.
4. Church and state—United States.   I. Title.

KF228.A25S65   2007
344.73'0796—dc22   2006102220

For Sarah and Brian

I think that tradition is not to be scoffed at, but let me say this very candidly: I think it is the final arrogance to talk constantly about the religious tradition in this country and equate it with this Bible. Sure, religious tradition. Whose religious tradition? It isn't any part of the religious tradition of a substantial number of Americans. . . . And it's just, to me, a little bit easy and I say arrogant to keep talking about our religious tradition. It suggests that the public schools, at least of Pennsylvania, are a kind of Protestant institution to which others are cordially invited.

—Henry W. Sawyer III, argument before the
U.S. Supreme Court, February 28, 1963

Acknowledgments

Although research and writing require countless hours of working alone, the process of taking a book from idea to published work involves many helpful people. I am indebted to all those who assisted me at every stage of this endeavor.

Special thanks go to Ellery Schempp, who spent many hours recalling for me the circumstances of his protest against Bible reading and recitation of the Lord's Prayer at Abington High School. Ellery made available his family papers, which contained, among other things, correspondence, clippings, and photographs. I also conducted valuable interviews with Ellery's siblings, Donna and Roger, as well as his parents, Sidney and Edward. I am grateful as well to many other people who shared their recollections of the case and of the times in which it was litigated.

I worked in some of the nation's finest research libraries and greatly benefited from their comprehensive collections of letters, manuscripts, and legal materials. To the extent that this book contains original scholarship, thanks go to these libraries for maintaining such valuable repositories of American history and to their knowledgeable and helpful staffs. At the Manuscript Division of the Library of Congress in Washington, D.C., I studied the files of many of the justices who decided the *Schempp*, *Murray*, and *Engel* cases. The National Archives in Philadelphia had case files from the *Schempp* trial. The Syracuse University Library made available its extensive files from the Leo Pfeffer Papers. The Tarleton Law Library at the University of Texas School of Law provided access to its collection on Justice Tom C. Clark, and the library deserves special commendation for making available online an extensive array of Justice Clark's drafts and many court documents relating to the *Schempp* case. The Princeton University Library welcomed me to research the papers of Justice John Marshall Harlan as well as the American Civil Liberties Union Archives. Temple University's Urban Archives provided access to the files of the Philadelphia ACLU chapter as well as the papers of Spencer Coxe. The ACLU's Philadelphia chapter gave me permission to quote from ACLU materials. The American Jewish Historical Society, in New York, had useful information on Shad Polier. The Old York Road Historical Society in Jenkintown, Pennsylvania, gave me access to historical material about Abington Township and the surrounding area. Thanks also go to Hugo L. Black, Jr., son of the justice of the same name, who gave me permission to look through the justice's files. Finally, I thank the staff at New York University's Elmer Holmes Bobst Library, where I found many books that proved important in my research.

Robert M. O'Neil, professor of law at the University of Virginia School of Law and director of the Thomas Jefferson Center for the Protection of Free Expression, gave graciously of his time and expertise. Professor O'Neil, who, as a clerk to Justice William J. Brennan, Jr., worked on the *Schempp* case in 1962–63, provided recollections of the case as well as scholarly critiques of my work at several important junctures in the creation of the manuscript.

Special thanks go to Jim Reische, my editor at the University of Michigan Press, and to Phil Pochoda, the editorial director. Both saw value in this work and gave me encouragement and invaluable guidance along the way. I am indebted to Kevin Rennells, senior copyediting coordinator, and to Jill Butler Wilson, both of whose careful editing improved my writing. Deborah Patton deserves my appreciation for her valuable work in indexing the book. My thanks go also to many people at the University of Michigan Press whose work behind the scenes was so important to the development and production of this book.

A number of student research assistants helped me find important documents and run down needed details. They include Lisa Miller, Esta Tanenbaum, Jonathan Nabavi, Sachin Gandhi, Michael Schimel, and Brian Solomon. I appreciate their diligence and dedication in adding to the depth of this book.

Finally, I owe so much to Debbi Dunn Solomon, my most enthusiastic supporter. In so many ways, she made it possible for me to write this book.

Contents

1. Ellery's Protest

Ellery[1] Frank Schempp closed the door of his house behind him at ten minutes before eight in the morning and felt the chill November air on his cheeks. The date was November 26, 1956, a Monday, and high school was resuming after a long Thanksgiving weekend. Ellery felt a little different this morning, a little nervous. He fingered his leather binder, zippered up with a notebook and a few books inside. They were a substantial weight to carry every day, but now the weight itself was a little reassuring, a little steadying. Usually he took only textbooks between home and school. Today, though, he also had a book that he had borrowed over the weekend from the father of a friend. It was the Koran, the holy book of Islam. It made his heart race a little to think of what he planned to do with it in school.

His plans for the beginning of the day in his homeroom class would surely cause a stir—he was quite certain of that. But he didn't know exactly what the trouble would be. What could the teachers and administrators do to him, anyway? He wasn't a troublemaker. He was an A student enrolled in all the advanced college preparatory classes in the eleventh grade.

Since second grade, Ellery had lived with his parents and two siblings in a white stucco cape-style house at 2457 Susquehanna Road in the Roslyn section of Abington Township, a suburb north of Philadelphia. Situated perpendicular to Susquehanna, the house presented a rather stark silhouette to the street, with no shutters on the windows and no dormers on the second floor. There was no sidewalk in front of the house, and no curb lined the street. The roof was constructed of aluminum sheeting. It looked like a house built in a big hurry, with much that might soften its appearance left to do later but never done.

Ellery's younger brother and sister were still at home preparing for their day in junior high school. It had been a relaxing enough weekend, with lots of family time and a Thanksgiving turkey at Grandmother's house. This four-day holiday was a much-needed break after a long stretch of school. Sixteen years old and nearing the halfway point of his junior year, Ellery had to think not only of school but also of the college applications that would be coming up soon. Neither of his parents had studied beyond high school, and the knowledge that he would surely be heading off to a top-flight university gave him feelings of both accomplishment and anticipation.

He walked down Susquehanna Road. Traffic was busy already on the road that separated his house from a cemetery of rolling hills across the street. Here in Abington Township, the estates and farmland were falling fast to developers, who carved them into small plots and quickly threw up houses for middle-class families, like his own, that wanted to escape the city for some room to breathe. Just this year, about a mile and a quarter from the Schempp house, the township had opened a sprawling new high school to accommodate all the children who arrived traveling with their parents in Chevys and Dodges up the Old York Road into town.

He enjoyed the brisk fifteen-minute walk to school, which took him east on Susquehanna, over railroad tracks, and through a field to the front entrance. When the air was bitter enough—that would happen in another month—his damp hair would freeze and stiffen by the time he entered the high school lobby. Built on a hill at the end of a long and steep driveway, the new school was nicely appointed with some of the niftiest technology of the 1950s. A public address system enabled administrators to reach all the classrooms in the school at once with announcements, and the school even boasted a media center for students interested in radio and television production. But for all the advantages brought by a new facility, the school still greeted students with standard-issue cinder block walls and linoleum tiles, a design meant to deny the scuffs and markings that record the passage of human activity. Ellery thought that perhaps that was the point. A scuff mark is evidence that an individual has passed by, and in Ellery's judgment, the notion of an individual making his or her mark outside of the accepted social covenants of the school merited no celebration at Abington Senior High School. In the conformist fifties, all of the pressure at school—from students, from teachers, from administrators—was to swim entirely within the lane of the pool that the powers that be had assigned.

Ellery, however, was not in the mood to conform. He came to school that day with an idea to express. He was unhappy that each school day started with a reading of ten verses from the King James Version of the Protestant Bible, followed by recitation of the Lord's Prayer. Ellery was himself a Protestant, though from the Unitarian denomination, which is relatively liberal theologically. But the King James Version expressed religious lessons that Ellery and his family did not accept, and Ellery's understanding of the First Amendment of the U.S. Constitution led him to conclude that the religious ceremony imposed by the state of Pennsylvania through the Abington public schools violated his rights to religious freedom. So on this day, Ellery planned to protest in the most effective way he knew—by using the morning devotionals to read the holy book from a different religious tradition.

The corridors were busy with students hustling to their rooms. Up the stairway he went to the second floor, and then down the hallway to Elmer Carroll's homeroom class. Homeroom is where the school day started, with about fifteen minutes filled with administrative details, the morning devotionals, and the Pledge of Allegiance. As was his usual custom, Carroll took attendance and then asked the students to clear their desks. For once, Ellery did not comply. The public address system came to life with a few bars of music. Then, as he heard a student's voice begin reciting a verse from the Bible, he opened up his Koran and began reading silently. Ellery Frank

Schempp didn't know it at the time, but he had just started his journey that chilly November morning to the Supreme Court of the
United States.[2]

꒜

Ellery finally arrived at the door of the Supreme Court early in 1963.
In its ruling, the Court supported his view that Bible reading and
recitation of the Lord's Prayer in Abington Senior High and in other
public schools throughout the United States violated the First
Amendment's guarantee of religious freedom.[3] But that, in a sense,
only begins the story.

The *Schempp* decision inflamed passions in 1963 and still does so
today. Virtually all of the Court's opinions, even ones that were controversial at the time they were decided, eventually become woven
into the fabric of American life. The *Schempp* decision has proved
otherwise. Perhaps it was inevitable that the decision would not age
well, since it involved two of the things Americans are most passionate about: their religious beliefs and the education of their children.
But *Schempp* has become one of the decisions most often cited by
political conservatives and the religious Right as an example of the
activist legacy of the Warren Court and as a decision that warrants
reversal either by the Court itself or by constitutional amendment. It
has remained a target of Christian conservatives and many politicians
who have argued that America's public schools have become havens
of secularism.

History, though, does not support the constant rhetoric that the
Supreme Court tossed God out of the public schools. In fact, as the
story told in this book makes clear, the American people themselves
accomplished most of that through voluntary agreement among
themselves. Schools in the American colonies began as private institutions whose mission was to teach children to read so that they
could study Scripture. That mission worked well enough in colonies
that boasted mostly homogeneous populations of Anglicans and
Congregationalists. Children spent most of their day in essentially

religious learning, as teachers drilled them in prayer and in the catechism, the Bible, and the Ten Commandments. They used readers
and textbooks dominated by religious references, and often their
teachers were ministers.

The nation's growing religious diversity changed all of that in a
gradual process that stretched over several centuries. A religious curriculum could not last for long under the stress of an increasingly
pluralistic nation and the conversion of the schools into public institutions. The Anglican and Congregationalist monopolies melted
away into an increasingly diverse society. Scores of new Protestant
denominations flourished in the United States—Baptists and
Methodists and Presbyterians and others—the result both of immigration and of the spontaneous splintering of existing churches into
wholly new ones. Unable anymore to teach the dogma of any one
denomination, Protestants settled among themselves on a common
public school that taught a common Protestantism, centered on
Bible reading and recitation of the Lord's Prayer.

Even that compromise was doomed to collapse, as the ships dock-
ing on American shores brought Roman Catholics, Jews, and eventually millions more people of non-Christian persuasions. Riots in
Philadelphia heralded religious strife in many large cities, as
Catholics rebelled against the exposure of their children to the
Protestant King James Bible. Many school systems dropped their
Protestantism so that people of diverse backgrounds could live
together without conflict, and others compromised by allowing religious minorities to excuse their children from participation. Americans themselves negotiated an end of most religion in the public
schools because they wanted to do so. They judged that living peaceably with their neighbors was important and that what religion they
removed from the schools could be taught at home and in houses of
worship. By the early 1960s, what religious practices in the schools
were left for the Supreme Court to consider? Many schools still held
holiday celebrations. But the most significant remnant of the past, by
then practiced in less than half the public schools in the country, was
a five-minute devotional exercise at the beginning of the school

day—readings from the Protestant King James Bible and recitation of the Lord's Prayer.

The choice of which Bible and which prayers to use in the public schools involved government in the kind of sectarian conflict that the framers of the First Amendment wished to avoid. Although it was a distant cousin to the sectarian bloodletting in Europe over more than a millennium, Americans suffered more than a century of riots, prejudice, and persecution relating to the choice of religious material in the public schools. Whose version of the Bible should be read? Whose prayers should be recited? If it was school boards and principals making the choice for public school pupils, then the government was in fact endorsing one tradition over another and forcing children of minority religions to either join in the majority's devotionals or find the strength—unusual in a schoolchild—to resist the gravitational force of peer pressure. The conservative justice Felix Frankfurter, concurring in *McCollum v. Board of Education*, wrote that any devotional activity that "sharpens the consciousness of religious differences" among children in the public schools causes "precisely the consequences against which the Constitution was directed when it prohibited the government common to all from becoming embroiled, however innocently, in the destructive religious conflicts of which the history of even this country records some dark pages."[4]

An important fact seems lost in the history of the last half century. *Schempp* was not a difficult decision—at least not among the eight justices who voted to ban Bible reading and prayer as a violation of the First Amendment. Among them were three of the four conservative justices then sitting on the Court—John Harlan, Tom Clark, and Byron White. Clark, a Democrat from Texas who served as U.S. attorney general under President Truman, was the author of the Court's opinion. Justice Harlan, a conservative intellectual leader on the Court for many years, voted to take prayer and Bible reading out of the schools. His personal notes, on file at the Library of Congress, indicate his strong support of the decision. Harlan even joined a concurrence by Arthur Goldberg, a liberal, in which the two of them said that the government had involved itself in divisive sectarian practices. In that judgment, Harlan was following the precedent of leading conservatives before him, such as Felix Frankfurter and Robert Jackson, both of whom strongly endorsed separation of church and state in earlier cases.

All of these justices, in the decades leading up to and including *Schempp,* recognized the dangers of excessive religious zeal in the most religiously diverse nation on earth, one that had dedicated itself to respecting each individual's freedom of conscience. As a matter of law, however, none of the justices could act until plaintiffs brought cases before them, braving anger and retaliations within their own community. Ellery Frank Schempp, sixteen years old, was one of those plaintiffs.

2. The Making of a Rebel

Ellery Schempp's act of civil disobedience was extraordinary, a teenager challenging the authority of school administrators on a matter as serious as religious exercises in the classroom. During the 1950s, such behavior was shocking, even mystifying. It upset the natural order of things, as if the earth had tired of the sun and had gone off to circle a different star.

Protest and youthful rebellion—in fact, rebellion of any kind by anyone—never gained any footing in the fifties. It would be another ten years before society would roil with Vietnam War protests and the civil rights movement, with changing roles and opportunities for women, and with challenges to prevailing norms on sex, drugs, and grooming. The conformist fifties during which Ellery was in school brought the silent generation and its pursuit of normalcy after the exhaustion of World War II and the Korean War. The priorities of the broad middle swath of Americans were clear enough: buy a house in a suburban subdivision and achieve financial security inside a big corporation. No bigger issues bothered them.

Two fictional members of the silent generation had attempted to do exactly that. Tom and Betsy Rath, the protagonists in Sloan Wilson's novel *The Man in the Gray Flannel Suit*, brought the struggle against conformity into sharper focus for Ellery.[1] The Raths had three kids and strived for the good life offered by an increasingly consumer society. Tom Rath, thirty-three years old, commuted from the suburbs into Manhattan every day to work for a foundation. His salary of seven thousand dollars was good for a man at his stage of his career, but of course not nearly enough to fulfill his aspirations.

In fact, the Raths were in debt. Betsy stayed home, as wives in the fifties did, raising the kids and deciding which bills to pay each month so that the bank wouldn't cut off their credit. What did they most desire? They wanted a bigger house, a more upscale neighborhood, and a new car. How could they feel even remotely successful if the moving vans kept taking their neighbors away to fancier digs, leaving them behind? "I don't know what's the matter with us," Betsy said to Tom. "Your job is plenty good enough. We've got three nice kids, and lots of people would be glad to have a house like this. We shouldn't be so *discontented* all the time."[2] But discontented they were.

Two other iconic fictional characters of the time, Ozzie and Harriet Nelson, displayed on their television series all the antiseptic qualities of the idealized fifties family. There was no serious dissent within this household. How could there be? Mom and Dad loved each other and never seriously disagreed. Children were well behaved and respectful of their elders. In this America, nobody divorced, nobody drank too much, and nobody slept wrapped in blankets on the sidewalk. In fact, nobody seemed to seriously disagree with anyone else about anything. Historian William Manchester characterized the silent generation as follows: "Its members could not be disillusioned because they had no illusions. They kept their mouths shut, avoided serious discussions, and eschewed reformers as 'bleeding hearts.' In the conflict between independence and the system, they came down hard on the side of the system."[3]

That was true enough, but the 1960s would not be long in arriving, a hurricane ripping and rearranging a placid landscape. For those who were watching closely, however, there were signs even in the fifties of what was to come. Most noticeable was the civil rights movement, beginning its legal confrontation with segregated facilities around the country. The U.S. Supreme Court threw out segregation by law in its 1954 decision *Brown v. Board of Education*, but change came slowly or not at all. On September 23, 1957, nine black youths tried to integrate Little Rock Central High School and were met by an angry white mob. It took more than one thousand soldiers to enforce an order from President Eisenhower himself to enroll the children. Meanwhile, Rosa Parks, who worked as a seamstress in a department store in Montgomery, Alabama, refused to give up her seat in a whites-only section of a public bus and was arrested.

While tempers flared in Montgomery, a small group of writers, led by Jack Kerouac and Allen Ginsberg, started a bohemian movement on the West Coast that spread eastward. The beatniks were not revolutionaries, though they certainly were different enough in their rejection of the materialism of the era and their embrace of marijuana, folk ballads, and Oriental mysticism. Perhaps the worst nightmare for fifties parents was for their son or daughter to slide into the beatnik lifestyle. "Eisenhower's America was horrified," wrote Manchester.[4]

If fifties society did not want its young to become beatniks, neither did it want its women to step outside the narrow circle that defined their role. A woman's role in the fifties was to take care of the children—to make sure they did not become beatniks, presumably—and to support their husbands as they jockeyed for the best corporate jobs that provided the fattest paychecks. Women who were consigned to day after day at home were avid consumers for the washers, dryers, refrigerators, televisions, and newfangled cleaning supplies and cooking equipment that America's factories churned out. The message for women with higher aspirations was obvious: just keep baking brownies and helping the kids with their homework.

Change, however, was coming to the woman's role, too. In 1957, Betty Friedan, then a little-known writer, began researching an article on the fifteenth college reunion of the Smith College class of 1942. She discovered a group of women who, once fired by intellectual challenges as college students, now felt despair at not having a meaningful life outside the home. Her book *The Feminine Mystique*, published in 1963, was the seminal work that helped launch the feminist movement and a complete rethinking of women's role in society.[5]

In Washington, meanwhile, a conservative U.S. Supreme Court began its migration toward a far more protective stance on the rights and liberties guaranteed to all Americans by the Constitution. President Dwight D. Eisenhower, a conservative Republican, appointed Earl Warren as chief justice in 1953 and William J. Brennan, Jr., as associate justice in 1956. Both men would play key roles as Ellery Schempp's protest reached the Supreme Court.

Protesting a perceived wrong was certainly not part of the teenage subculture of the fifties, at Abington Senior High School or elsewhere. If conformity was highly prized in society at large, it was the same or more so in the schools. Dress codes tightly regulated student attire and produced a universal clean-cut look. Only decades later would many schools give casual acceptance to cutoff jeans, low-cut blouses, and long scruffy hair.

In Ellery's time, curly hair was in for girls, achieved with a perm or through time-consuming pin curling and rolling. Boys typically sported a crew cut or a flattop. The Abington schools banned the ducktail haircut—also known as the DA (i.e., "duck's ass") cut, because of the way the hair was swept to the back of the head and then parted in the middle. Without blow-dryers to help, it took a lot of grease to hold the DA in place. Girls wore dresses, boys slacks and a shirt. Ellery remembers that Abington also prohibited students from wearing peg pants, which tapered to a tight fit around the ankles. "Everything was black and white," says Ellery. "If you wore peg pants, then by definition you were evil. You probably took drugs. You were unchristian, chewed gum, smoked in the restrooms. [The principal, W. Eugene Stull,] categorized people: there were the good people and there were the bad people. He was clearly against the bad people. And you could identify the bad people. Clearly they had DA haircuts and peg pants. These were banned as a symbol of all that was evil." His father kidded Ellery about it: "As my father would say, if you wore peg pants you would spit in church," says Ellery.[6]

Peg pants and ducktail haircuts marked the frontiers of rebellion, but a tamer way for teenagers to show their differences with the adult world was with their own idiom. "Cool" now meant something pretty neat. You certainly didn't want to be a "spaz," or even a "drag," because that would make you "bad news." Some "nice threads" were more than okay, but they might cost a "cat" a lot of "bread."

"Square" was one term that teenagers would certainly never use to describe Elvis Presley, who burst onto the scene in the midfifties and soon became the king of rock. He took the stage with a raw sexuality that shocked adults but sent teenagers into an ecstasy of screaming and fainting. Had he performed in the Azores in August, his gyrating hips would have stirred the air enough to cause a tropical depression.

For the first time, in a nation of sharply increasing wealth, teenagers had the wherewithal to embrace music as part of their own separate culture. Technology was on their side, with record players and small transistor radios enabling the newest in pop culture to spread quickly. David Halberstam observed: "The young formed their own community. For the first time in American life they were becoming a separate, defined part of the culture: As they had money, they were a market, and as they were a market they were listened to and catered to."[7]

Centrifugal forces would soon begin to spin the nation's youth into an orbit farther from traditional authority. But this process was only just beginning. As with Elvis's gyrating hips, its context was more cultural than political. There was not yet a direct challenge that reverberated through society's power structure. For most people, any outright challenge to authority still lay a decade away.

But this was not true for Ellery. His home life was far from most of the stereotypes of the fifties. The lessons he absorbed at home taught him that questioning authority was an honorable thing to do. In fact, the Abington school officials found that the Schempps were not a family to easily shrug off a perceived injustice.

☙

For Ellery Schempp, life in the suburb of Abington Township was already splintering from its moorings. His home was far from the Tom and Betsy Rath model of middle-class ennui. The strongest influence in his life was his father, Edward, a small, wiry man with the punch of a prizefighter when it came to the issues he passionately believed in. Ed was born in Philadelphia in 1908 to German immigrant parents. He worked in the family business, the Schempp Brothers Hardware Store in the Kensington section of Philadelphia, which was run by his father and uncles. When Ed was nineteen, his father died, and Ed inherited an ownership stake in the store. He had to assume much of the responsibility of caring for his family.[8]

Ed grew up in the Lutheran Church and, as a young man, rebelled against its teachings. What troubled him was "the endless sermons about the blood of the Lamb. It sounded dreadfully gory," Ellery explains. "We were supposed to be talking about goodness and decency. But this went on and on about being washed in the blood of the Lamb, the terrible sufferings of Christ on the cross."[9] Ed preferred to believe in a merciful God who encouraged human goodness without threats or acts of vengeance. He very early concluded that he should look beyond the Bible—to other religious traditions, to moral philosophers, to a variety of thinkers—for ideas about religion. "The idea that the Bible should be taken literally as the sole authority in human life was for him an unacceptable point of view," says Ellery.[10]

Ed's view of the Bible as conveying inappropriate moral lessons became one of his core beliefs. Years later, it became critical to his son's legal case challenging morning devotionals in the public schools. When Ellery challenged the practice of Bible reading at Abington Senior High, Ed cited the bloody stories of the Bible as representative of the kind of religious doctrine to which he didn't want his children exposed.

Because he could no longer tolerate thunderous pronouncements from the pulpit about human sin and redemption, it was inevitable that Ed would leave the Lutheran Church for something different. "I think the big break," says Ellery, "came when he was traveling on the West Coast and ran into my mom [Sidney], who had been raised a freethinker." Born in Oregon and raised in several cities on the West Coast, Sidney had grown up without strong ties to any denomination. "I think that's part of why they hit it off," says Ellery. "Dad was questioning to what degree he had already made a break with traditional upbringing. My mom was a kindred spirit in this regard. It was one of the bonds that led to their initial attraction."[11]

After he and Sidney married, Ed determined that it was time to break from the family hardware store. Young, without children, and free of any pressing responsibilities, the newlyweds decided to take an extended trip out West. Unable to afford hotel bills, they bought a Dodge truck and built living quarters atop the flatbed chassis in the back. It was a kind of hobbyist forerunner of today's recreational vehicle. For about five years in the 1930s, they traveled throughout the West, living in the back of the truck and earning their spending money by selling advertising space in small-town newspapers. "It was the Depression years," says Ellery. "Dad would go in and say, 'I'd like to buy four pages of advertising.' The editor would of course faint dead away. He hadn't sold four pages of advertising in the last month." Ed and Sidney would then subdivide the space and sell the pieces to local businesses, in turn filling the space with advertising articles extolling each company's product or service. "They'd make enough money to move on to the next town and repeat it," Ellery says.[12]

When Ed and Sidney returned to Philadelphia, it was time to start a family. Ellery was born in 1940, followed by Roger in 1943 and Donna in 1945. Ed had resumed his work at Schempp Hardware, but it was long past time for a change. He had been an electronics hobbyist throughout his life, reading electronics magazines and teaching himself about tubes and circuits. He built ham radios from parts he picked up here and there. Leaving the hardware store, he got a job at RCA and, during World War II, worked on electronics for radar systems.

The family lived in a row house in Philadelphia. Ed opened an electronics surplus store in 1946 and sold communications equipment and parts to other hobbyists. The business flourished there, and by the time he sold out two years later, he had enough money to build a house in the suburbs without the burden of a mortgage. Ed wanted nothing to do with the builders who were just then beginning to buy up large farms and convert them into housing developments, so he purchased a parcel of land across from a cemetery in the Roslyn section of Abington Township. He found some published blueprints and handed them over to a builder. The house went up as unadorned and as beautifully efficient as the electronic circuits that he loved. Ed just didn't care much about the aesthetics. He covered his house with an aluminum roof because he heard that it would last longer than one made of shingles. It didn't matter to him that others in town might think a metal roof belonged on a warehouse.

Upon moving to Abington, Ed started working for an electronics company that soon became part of Sylvania Electric Products, Inc. During the day, he worked with Sylvania's equipment that tested vacuum tubes before shipment. At night, he ran his own electronics company out of his garage. Two or three men would come by around six every evening during the week, and for the next three or four hours, Ed and his helpers would build electronic testing equipment by hand for a variety of corporate customers throughout the United States.

Ed found stability in his spiritual life as well. There was no going back to the Lutheran Church. Uncomfortable with traditional Christian theology, Ed and Sidney joined the Unitarian Church—later to become the Unitarian Universalist Church, in 1961—one of the most theologically liberal of all the Protestant denominations. Unitarian Universalists believe in no creed; they look to no book or institution to carry one acceptable vision of religious truth but, rather, seek it through the continuous unfolding of ideas from many sources. Their congregations govern themselves rather than answering to a hierarchy, and they typically emphasize social action and service to the community.

This orientation appealed to the Schempps, for religious dogma was as foreign as some Paleolithic language. The idea of social action and the encouragement of thinking for oneself profoundly affected Ellery as he grew up. His parents "set a tone in which you were free to question," says Ellery. "If one of my mates at school told me that Jesus died for my sins and I'd say, 'What does this mean?' and it didn't make any sense, Dad would say, 'Well, it never made any sense to me either.' They emphasized that it was perfectly all right if you did your own thinking and came to your own conclusions if you could support them. If you want to believe in little green men hiding under your bed, the question would be, 'We're not sure if your belief is right or wrong, but do you have some evidence to back it up?' That same attitude would come towards conventional religious ideas: 'Do you want to believe that God listens to every prayer and doesn't have anything better to do with the universe? Fine, but maybe you ought to think if that's a basis for building a life faith on. Maybe there are some alternative possibilities.' So the idea was that you could think things through and you weren't going to be condemned for coming up with an idea that was unconventional."[13]

Every Sunday morning, the five Schempps went off to the Unitarian church on Lincoln drive in the Germantown section of Philadelphia. An imposing gray stone building, it held a particular fascination for Ellery because major intellectual figures showed up there on a regular basis to deliver the sermon. Even as a preteen, he listened intently to Reinhold Niebuhr, Norman Thomas, and Paul Tillich, as well as a raft of rabbis and ministers, each of them there to challenge the congregants on a broad array of issues. Ellery remembered years later that the underlying context of all their talks was the need to make a difference in this life, not positioning oneself for the hereafter. For Ellery, already encouraged at home to think for himself, the Sunday sermons provided ways to look at the world through many different—and at times unconventional—prisms.

Apart from involvement in Sunday services and religious school, the Schempps showed little interest in religious observance at home. They celebrated all the holidays, but Ellery remembers Christmas and Easter as primarily family-oriented holidays rather than times of spiritual commitment. In fact, there was little religious tradition in the Schempp household, but much talk—in fact, constant talk—of religion and of issues surrounding it.

The Schempps often discussed these concerns around the dinner table. When religion came up, it was often in the context of Ed's increasingly intense belief in the separation of church and state. He did not believe in religious dogma, and he believed fiercely that the government had no business supporting any particular religion or religious idea. Ellery sometimes brought up some Bible passages they had listened to in school that day. Ed didn't think it right that Christian teachings be forced on children in public school.

Around the dinner table, the Schempps also discussed religion in the Unitarian tradition of social activism. "There was a liberal intellectual political bent that was part of the family," says Ellery. "It was closely tied to the social justice concepts of the Unitarian Church. You were expected to care about equal rights for blacks and minorities. You were expected to care about First Amendment freedoms. So these things meshed together in a seamless fashion." While neither Ed nor Sidney had gone to college, Ed had become self-educated on the social and political issues of the day through his extensive reading. He felt strongly enough about individual rights and liberties to join the American Civil Liberties Union, and he closely read the ACLU publications that came to the house. He also subscribed to the *New Republic,* the weekly political journal. Ellery read all of these materials himself. "My father was the dominant member of our household, no doubt about it," says Ellery. "He defined— intellectually and, to a large degree, emotionally—the character of the family."[14]

Although Sidney deferred to her husband on the political issues he served up at the dinner table, she was not uninterested in them. "She was not a crusader," says Ellery. "She would never have gone out and started a war, but she was prepared to realize when a war was worthwhile, and she also had a strong sense of social justice. I don't think she had an antiauthority or antiauthoritarian attitude the same as my dad's, but she went along with it."[15] Ellery's younger siblings, Donna and Roger, showed interest in the political issues but never approached either Ellery's intensity of feeling or his increasing commitment to aggressively protest what he found wrong.

One morning when he was in eighth grade, Ellery's homeroom teacher, Irvin A. Karam, who also served as the assistant principal, was lecturing the students on obeying school regulations. Ellery remembers: "He was making some peroration in homeroom one morning after Bible reading about showing respect and following the school rules. And [he was saying] that you kids are in charge of your own destiny. I sat there smirking, thinking to myself, we know perfectly well that the kids don't have any authority here, and that these edicts come down from above. He became very offended by my smirk. He said, and pointed to me, 'Hey there you, with that smile on your face. You're a leech and a parasite. You don't participate in any of the school activities. You don't wear the school colors on football days.' It was a little bit shocking to be singled out like that."[16]

Incensed at this attack on his son, Ed Schempp wrote a letter to the school demanding an apology. Both Eugene Stull, the principal, and Karam came out to the house. "Dad was adamant and said, look, if you guys don't give an apology, there's going to be a lawsuit here," says Ellery. A few days later, Karam apologized. "That kind of incident may have in some vague way influenced later things," Ellery remembers. "I certainly got the idea that you could protest something the school did and live to tell the tale."[17]

Ellery got into some mild trouble once more. Clothes were occasionally a sore point in the Schempp household (as they tend to be in many homes), because Ellery didn't always agree with what his mother brought home from the store. "My mother wasn't always good at this," he says. "I didn't want to stand out. But I remember once she bought me pants that were chartreuse." Apparently unaware of the school dress code, she also bought him a pair of peg pants, and he wore them to school. "It wasn't long before I got into trouble for breaking the school rules," Ellery says. "But they didn't know what to do with me, because I hadn't been in trouble with them before. I wasn't a disruptive student and therefore didn't fit the model." He was told not to wear the peg pants again but was not suspended.

"We had a student council," says Ellery. "I thought, why doesn't the student council take some position on this in terms of individual freedoms? Why do these guys have the right to send out an edict like this? I quickly learned that the student council were a bunch of mice and wouldn't stand up to the school administration. That was a big disappointment to me. At that time, I was full of fervor. This is a democracy, and [remember] Thomas Paine and Thomas Jefferson! To the battlefronts! I do remember typing up, with carbon paper in those days, a passage from Thomas Jefferson to the effect . . . 'I have sworn eternal hostility against every form of tyranny over the mind of man.' I typed [it] seven times on a piece of paper, carbon paper, and cut each one out on little slips and left them around in various class-rooms."[18]

If that small protest seemed sophomoric, it was nonetheless important in moving Ellery toward a position where he could more openly stand up to authority. His junior year, which began in the fall of 1956, coincided with the opening of Abington's new high school on fifty-seven acres of land off Highland Avenue in the center of the township. Built for just under six million dollars, the school served a burgeoning suburban population.[19] Between 1950 and 1958, the student population of the Abington school district exploded from 4,700 to 9,033,[20] with the new high school serving 1,830 students.[21]

The new high school's two senior administrators were familiar to Ellery. W. Eugene Stull, the new high school principal, had been promoted at every major step along Ellery's path through Abington's secondary schools, serving as principal of the elementary school and then of the junior high school where Ellery was a student. Irvin A. Karam, the assistant principal, had held the same position at the junior high while Ellery was there. Both men knew the Schempps from their disagreement a few years earlier over Karam's criticisms of Ellery in class.[22] That squabble was nothing, however, compared to what was soon to transpire.

※

The Schempps spent the summer of 1956 touring the country by car, visiting the national parks and sleeping in campgrounds. When Ellery returned to Abington Senior High for his junior year in the fall, he looked forward to his final two years of school and the process of applying for college. Though a serious student, there was time for some fun, too.

Ellery often went over to one of his friends' houses to talk or play games. He was sixteen and driving now, freeing him to go with his friends to a local drive-in, the popular car restaurants of the fifties. He also could drive a girlfriend under cover of darkness to a hot spot in town for necking—the huge cemetery across Susquehanna Road from the Schempp house. Like a lot of other kids in town, Ellery would drive down one of the winding cemetery roads and pull over on the side. Given the surroundings, practical jokes were irresistible. He and his friends would occasionally climb atop a mausoleum in the dark and scare a couple kissing in a car below. Once, he and his friends rigged a contraption that made a ghost figure pop up when a car tripped a string held taut across the road. "We scared bloody hell out of people," he says.[23]

Back at home, he did his math homework while watching *I Love Lucy,* and on some nights, he skipped down to the garage to help his father and his employees assemble electronic equipment. Unlike most other kids, he wasn't a great fan of Elvis or of rock and roll, favoring instead symphonic music that he heard on a local classical station or that he brought home on forty-five records or on reel-to-reel tapes. One of his great loves arrived late every fall, when he unpacked his Lionel trains and took over the living room, setting up the tracks and scenery on four-by-eight plywood boards mounted on sawhorses. It was never finished until Christmas Eve.[24]

Ellery was all business in school, and his junior year provided him with the most formative of all his school experiences. An excellent student, he took the high school's most advanced classes in English, math, and science, and his circle of friends comprised about twenty-five other students from these classes. Ellery ran on the track team, but he was not a particularly gifted athlete and took his self-identity from his academic prowess.

His honors English class with Allan Glatthorn helped provide the intellectual framework for what had until then been a somewhat scattered sense of youthful rebellion. Glatthorn, who would later become principal of the high school and then a professor at East Carolina University, required his students to hand in a five-hundred-word essay every Monday, an exercise that disciplined Ellery's thinking. Glatthorn demanded that students argue logically and be able to find flaws and weaknesses in their own and others' analyses.[25] Readings included Plato's dialogues, Emerson's "Self-Reliance," and Thoreau's "Civil Disobedience." "As Thoreau indicated, a person needs to take a stand at a certain point, even in opposition to the state," says Glatthorn. "In contrast, Plato's point of view, through Socrates, was the state was supreme and you had to kowtow when necessary to what the state wanted. Ellery was very much on the side of those who rebelled and challenged and questioned."[26]

Glatthorn provided another, even more important forum in which his students could learn. On Thursday nights, he invited all the students from his honors English class to join him at his house for refreshments and an extended discussion of issues that concerned them. "I just saw a need to build some sense of an intellectual community with the students, and the school hampered that in some ways, so we found a way to extend it by coming to my house and being more informal, with light refreshments and student leadership," says Glatthorn.[27]

After a while, Glatthorn mostly dropped out, and the two-hour sessions rotated to the students' homes. About half of the honors English students—about ten or so—became regulars at the sessions. Royal Brown, who would later become a professor of music at the City University of New York, was then one of Ellery's closest friends. Like Ellery, he felt that the class and the evening sessions were critical in providing what the high school generally lacked—an atmosphere of intellectual questioning. "I really think that Allan Glatthorn gave me my mind," says Brown. "Not that I didn't think before that. But to be able to think in those kinds of ways and to write in those kinds of ways, to not be humiliated for mistakes, was just a whole different experience. We'd discuss everything from the existence of God to the existence of conscience to the political situation. So they were bull sessions, but sophisticated bull sessions."[28]

Ellery adds: "It was very stimulating. You'd throw out an idea and find it attacked. It made you go home and think about it." Ellery was thinking particularly about the strictures that the school placed on students. He had absorbed his father's questioning attitude toward authority. Now, such works as Thoreau's essay on civil disobedience stimulated him to think about his own role in accepting what the school authorities dished out. "It led," he remembers, "to lots and lots of questions about the role of individuals in our society, where their social rights begin and end, where individual rights begin and end, and [whether] it [is] true that one man with courage makes a majority."[29] These were large, exciting questions for a boy of sixteen, questions that provided a way to probe and understand better his own conflicts with authority. It also enabled him to see more clearly where the small, petty conflicts over peg pants differed from truly major challenges to an individual's conscience.

～

It was in the Thursday night sessions that Ellery began discussing with his classmates a practice that increasingly bothered him—the school's requirement that everyone participate in morning devotionals comprising both Bible reading and recitation of the Lord's Prayer. Following a long tradition in Pennsylvania, the state legislature directed, through a law enacted in 1949, that the public schools provide children with a Bible-reading exercise each day. The Abington school district conveyed this requirement to its teachers through a publication, the "Employees' Handbook and Administrative Guide," that was distributed to all employees. On page 37, under "Teachers—Professional Obligations," the handbook specified: "No. 1. Comply with the state regulation in reading at least ten verses of Scripture each morning without comment. This is to be followed by the Lord's Prayer."[30] Recitation of the Lord's Prayer was not required by law, as was Bible reading, but school administrators had added this requirement to the handbook. All throughout the years, the only Bible purchased with school funds was the King James Version, accepted by most Protestant denominations. Public funds were never used to buy the Catholic Douay Version or the Jewish Old Testament, although students who led the readings sometimes brought in their own Bible from home.[31]

The morning devotionals, as they were called in school, assumed a slightly different form throughout the school district. At the high school, where Ellery was studying, the devotionals emanated from the radio and television room and were broadcast over the public address system to the entire school, beginning at 8:15 a.m. The program started with a few bars of music to attract everyone's attention. The Bible reading and Lord's Prayer recitation took five minutes or less and was followed by the flag salute and school announcements. William Young, the radio and television teacher, ran the program and utilized his thirty students to perform the broadcast, with each student taking up to five turns throughout the year. Students could read ten Bible verses of their own choosing. About half of them, however, chose verses based on suggestions contained in a roll book that Young made available to the students. The roll book, whose main function was for the recording of student grades, also contained a section titled "Suggested Scripture Selections for Use in Public Schools." The roll book was not supplied by the state of Pennsylvania; rather, it was purchased directly from the publisher, Alva M. Squibb, of McKeesport, Pennsylvania.[32]

Morning devotionals were different in the district's other schools, none of which had a public address system at the time. At Huntingdon Junior High School, where Ellery's siblings were among the one thousand students, each teacher conducted a devotional period during the eight-minute homeroom session. Teachers read the verses themselves in some homeroom classes. In others, students either volunteered to read or took turns through a system of moving up and down the rows of desks until everyone had an opportunity. Readers chose any passages they fancied most.[33]

Reading the Bible and reciting the Lord's Prayer in school seemed wrong to Ellery. He felt that he was forced to participate in a religious ceremony that was foreign to his own beliefs. Although he had never formally studied First Amendment law, he had read related articles in magazines, such as the *New Republic*, and had seen his father's materials from the American Civil Liberties Union. He understood that the Constitution prohibited the federal and state governments from establishing a religion or interfering with an individual's practice of religion. The school's requirement that everyone listen to readings from the Bible—in practice, virtually always the Protestant King James Version—and engage in a Christian prayer certainly felt to him like state sponsorship of religion. Every student was required to participate, no matter their religious affiliation or whether they even believed in God. Although, as a Unitarian, Ellery was himself a member of a Protestant denomination, the King James Bible contained many ideas that were foreign to what he had been taught. "Traditionally, although it's very hard to speak for all Unitarians because there's no creed, traditionally Unitarians do not take the Bible literally," he explained to a CBS interviewer in 1963. "Many Unitarians do not take Jesus as divinity. So these points, and perhaps the concept of an anthropomorphic God as revealed in the Old Testament, were at particular odds, but by no means were all the objections that I had."[34]

Ellery looked beyond his own objections to the King James Bible. If its teachings were objectionable to him, a Protestant, they must be worse still for Catholic students, whose Bible was the Douay Version, and they must be particularly unacceptable for the non-Christians in the school. "It was the establishment of the Christian religion or the Judeo-Christian religion," he says.

That was not the only religion in the world. There were Buddhists, Muslims, freethinkers, and whatever else, and so to my mind it was crystal clear.

I had a very keen sense of the position of minorities. I sort of rooted for the underdog. I was aware that a number of my friends were Jewish and I had in my imagination sort of elevated them to an oppressed minority. I thought that there was something very unfair about the majority using its power in this way, running roughshod over the interests of minority groups.

I also had the unwritten assumption in my mind that to some degree this whole thing must have been some silly mistake. The Bible-reading exercise and the First Amendment were so obviously in conflict that it must have happened more or less by inadvertence rather than deliberately, and that if I only pointed out the error of their ways, they would see that the First Amendment took precedence.[35]

Four or five friends in the Thursday night group agreed with Ellery's ideas on Bible reading and loosely agreed to join him in some kind of protest. "We didn't want to have people ramming religion, patriotism, anything down our throats," says Royal Brown. "It was a homogenized spirituality that was being rammed down our throats."[36]

Nobody knew in the beginning how to show their opposition to the morning devotionals. "We tried to work out some way to make a protest or to object," says Ellery. "Some of the ideas from Thoreau's essay on civil disobedience were floating around in the air because we'd read it. Some of the ideas of the founding fathers, they were all floating in this mix. It was a rich soup."[37] In the fifties, there were few contemporary models for student protest. "It was not an era of protest," says Brown. "The thought of organizing a mass protest against this never occurred to us."[38] As Ellery saw it, simply complaining to the school authorities was too weak and would yield nothing positive. They certainly wouldn't listen. After all, state law required the Bible-reading exercise, and although the law did not require recitation of the Lord's Prayer, it had long been part of the morning devotionals; how could anyone imagine Eugene Stull simply acquiescing to a request to end these practices? Disruption was also not an option; it was impossible to defend as a strategy and would enable school authorities to focus on the tactics and not the message.

Ellery thought a quiet protest during the devotionals themselves seemed much more powerful. "I suggested some civil disobedience," Ellery recalls. "I wasn't sure what it would be, like refusing to come into the classroom until the verses were over, or getting up and walking out."[39] As he and his buddies discussed the options during that fall of 1956, however, support for an active protest slowly vanished. Some of his friends were concerned about getting into trouble, either with their parents or with the school. Ellery knew of one student who had been punished for inattention during recitation of the Lord's Prayer, having to stay after school one day to write the prayer fifty times as penance.[40] But some of the students in Ellery's group feared consequences considerably worse. "The school authorities had enormous authority, more then than even now," says Ellery. "They were pretty terrifying. [One student] raised the issue, what would happen about college applications? They were legitimate concerns."[41]

Ellery wasn't worried that a protest against morning devotionals would hurt his college aspirations. "All of my classmates were very worried about what this would mean in terms of college." he says. "I wasn't very worried about that. I knew I was going to go to college. It was all a bit of an abstraction in my family because my parents had not gone to college. Also, I was very confident. I had good grades. I had As and couldn't imagine there would be no college that would accept me. It wasn't something I was scared about. I wasn't fearing punishment, because what kind of punishment would have been appropriate for this sort of thing? They didn't know either, as it turned out."[42] Ellery added, "The school emphasized, in terms of behavior, not chewing gum, not smoking, not talking in class. I wasn't guilty of any of these sins. In many ways, I didn't think the school had anything to hold against me. I think I'd only been to detention once in my life as a punishment."[43]

To his buddies, however, a protest that must have sounded noble and heroic in the beginning started looking distinctly fraught with peril. "As soon as we came down to some practicalities, I discovered that my comrades in arms were considerably less enthusiastic," he says. "Within a fairly short time, I came to realize that if there was ever going to be a protest, it was going to be me and no one else." The prospect of protesting alone never was a major deterrent to going forward. "It was first of all something that affected me directly, and it was also something I felt confident I could make a difference about," he says. "I felt articulate on this topic. I felt confident that I could defend myself on this. I had tested my ideas against my peers."[44]

Glatthorn remembers agreeing with Ellery that the morning devotionals were divisive and inappropriate for a public school. Though he provided Ellery with many of the intellectual tools as well as the forum for testing his ideas, he declined to back his student in any public way. Years later, he regretted that decision. "I do recall one evening receiving a call from his attorney, who asked me if I would join in Ellery's suit," says Glatthorn. "The attorney said, 'I should warn you, if you do you'll be targeted by the conservatives, and there will be a backlash against you, and you might even lose your job.' After much thought and discussion with my family I decided not to. I think I made a very bad decision in doing so. It was a concern that I might lose my job. At the time, I was trying to provide for a family of five kids. But as I said, I think I should have had more guts and stood there with him."[45] Ellery was alone.

༄

By late November, Ellery felt ready to act. The four-day Thanksgiving holiday arrived, a short breather before the monthlong sprint to the end-of-year vacation time. On Thanksgiving Day, November 22, the whole family had dinner at Ellery's grandmother's house in the Olney section of Philadelphia. On the way home, while sitting in the back of the car, Ellery brought up his plans to protest the school's reading of the Bible and the Lord's Prayer. He still didn't know exactly what form his protest would take. But he explained to his parents his belief that the morning devotionals violated his religious freedom. It was a short discussion—the general matter had come up before—and Ed Schempp agreed with Ellery that the schools shouldn't be sponsoring what Ed and Ellery agreed were religious ceremonies. "I got the clear message that my parents weren't going to object to my protest," he remembers. "Nobody told me, 'Don't do that.' So to my mind, I had a green light."[46]

Ellery spent the next day thinking about it. By Saturday, he knew how he would protest the morning devotionals. He drove to the house of a friend, George Tappert, who was a member of Glatthorn's class. Ellery borrowed a copy of the Koran from George's father's library. "This was my particular way," he says, "of showing that there is another religious tradition and another holy book that is respected by zillions of people around the world, and it has equal status in the global perspective with the Christian Bible."[47]

On Sunday, Ellery mentioned to his parents that he planned to read the Koran the next morning during the devotionals. Ellery remembers that there wasn't much discussion at that point. "I don't think they had thought through what all this might mean," he says.[48] Indeed, they had not. For Ed Schempp, it was a matter of some pride that his son was challenging what he regarded as the wrongful teaching of religious doctrine. "Ellery was forced to listen to a religious ceremony that was antithetical to what he had been taught in his own home," he said.[49]

When Ellery went off to school the next morning, there wasn't much time to worry about his plan. He reported to his homeroom, where he sat in the middle of the class, and the exercises started immediately. The order came from Elmer Carroll, the homeroom teacher, for all students to clear their desks—there were to be no distractions during morning devotionals. Ellery took the Koran out of his book bag just a moment before he heard a student's voice over the public address system reading the first of ten verses of the Bible. He opened up the Koran to a random place and began reading silently. "I couldn't possibly tell you what I read," he says. "My mind was racing."[50]

The Bible reading was finished in a few minutes and everyone rose for recitation of the Lord's Prayer—everyone, that is, except Ellery. "That was very noticeable," he says. The prayer was over in a moment, and Ellery then jumped to his feet for the Pledge of Allegiance. When that was done, Carroll beckoned him to the side of the room. "He said, 'This [participation in the devotionals] is a school rule.' I said, well, I'd been thinking about it, and I could no longer in conscience participate. That left him gasping for words. I think he said, 'Are you going to obey the rule in the future?' I repeated that as a matter of conscience I couldn't. So then he decided he had a disciplinary problem on his hands and sent me to the principal."[51]

Ellery walked alone down the long corridors to the front of the new high school building. Eugene Stull was not in his office, so Ellery sat with Irvin Karam, the assistant principal. "He saw the whole matter as one of respect," Ellery says. "With a sweep of his hand he could point to a whole wing of the building and say, 'All those other students, thousand, three thousand students, they're all doing it, and why can't you?' I said it was a matter of religious freedom."[52] After fifteen minutes or so and without making any progress with Ellery, Karam sent him off to see Evelyn W. Brehm, a guidance counselor. The two of them had what Ellery remembers as a pleasant conversation for almost an hour. Brehm tried to understand Ellery's objections, says Ellery, "as well as to satisfy herself that I wasn't psychologically disturbed, at least not in a socially threatening way." Ellery thought that she was friendly and perhaps even vaguely sympathetic to what he had done—at least that was the impression she left with him: "I thought that if she was in a different context she might have said, 'Good for you.' But she wouldn't dare say it." Finally, the two of them discussed what Ellery planned to do the next day. Would he continue his protest by reading from the Koran during the morning devotionals, or had he made his point, and was he ready to cooperate? "I repeated that this was religious conscience, and I don't believe this, and I don't think I should be forced to believe it," Ellery says.[53] After their discussion, he went to class.

Later in the day, Ellery was called back to Brehm's office for another talk. By then, Brehm had apparently conferred with others in the administration. "She said, 'Well, what you should do tomorrow morning is go to your homeroom, check in for attendance purposes, and then come down and sit here, and we'll talk again," Ellery remembers. "And that's what we should continue doing for the next period of time, which was undefined. I'm pretty sure that she and others thought that, well, Schempp will do this for a couple weeks and then give it up and the problem will go away."[54]

The problem for the Abington school district did not, of course, go away. Back at home that evening, Ellery decided to carry his protest to the American Civil Liberties Union; he was familiar with the organization through his father's membership. He took a piece of stationary from his father's home business—it had *"Research Electronics* LABORATORY" centered at the top—and typed out a message addressed to "Gentlemen" at the ACLU's Philadelphia office. He signed the letter "Ellory F. Schempp," using a spelling of his first name that he would change to "Ellery" in adulthood. The letter read in full:

> As a student in my junior year at Abington Senior High School, I would very greatly appreciate any information that you might send regarding possible Union action and/or aid in testing the constitutionality of Pennsylvania law which arbitrarily (and seemingly unrighteously and unconstitutionally) compels the Bible to be read in our public school system. I thank you for any help you might offer in freeing American youth in Pennsylvania from this gross violation of their religious rights as guaranteed in the first and foremost Amendment in our United States' Constitution.[55]

When he mailed off the letter the next day, including with it a small donation by check, Ellery had no idea what lay ahead. "I didn't have the vaguest notion that this would result in a Supreme Court decision," he says. "I just didn't have the vaguest notion."[56]

3. Byse Breaks the Deadlock

Ellery Schempp's letter arrived within a few days on the desk of Spencer Coxe, executive director of the ACLU's chapter in Philadelphia. It wasn't difficult to reach Coxe in those days, because the chapter consisted only of a small office manned by Coxe and a secretary. Coxe himself had not been trained in law. Then in his late thirties, he had graduated from Yale and then earned a master's degree in history at Harvard. A Quaker, Coxe received conscientious objector status in World War II. He worked in China and Austria for the American Friends Service Committee and became executive director of the ACLU's Philadelphia chapter in 1952, a post he would hold until his retirement in 1981.[1]

Coxe's office was the nerve center of civil liberties activities in the Delaware Valley, coordinating a network of volunteers who carried out the chapter's projects. Setting policy and priorities for the chapter was a board of directors comprised of forty-six individuals, the majority of whom were lawyers and sixteen of whom served on the executive committee.[2] When the chapter decided to file a lawsuit, it called on a local member, often a board member, to represent the client. ACLU lawyers typically received no fee.

For the ACLU chapter, though, these were perilous times. Even with a network of lawyers who took cases pro bono, a chronic lack of resources constrained the chapter's activities and, in the coming months, would raise serious concerns about challenging Bible-reading practices in Abington. In July 1956, less than six months before Ellery Schempp's protest, Coxe called a special meeting of the chapter's finance committee, a move he said indicated "the seriousness of the present crisis."[3] In October, Coxe wrote to Clark Byse, the chapter president, outlining the dire financial picture. Coxe anticipated monthly expenditures of $1,312, including salaries, to keep the office running during the next year. But the chapter's debt stood at $2,266, not including $400 in rent that the chapter had not paid. "It [the rent owed] is not included," Coxe wrote, "because Mr. Fagan indicated he would not press us for it in view of our financial difficulties."[4] Trying to balance the chapter's budget, Coxe wrote with alarm to the national office in December. He noted "the poor showing throughout the country in November"—most likely a downdraft in new memberships—and that the national office planned a 7 percent cut of allocations to local affiliates, such as the Philadelphia chapter. "I can quite appreciate that the November performance called for some drastic action," he wrote. "I am writing now mainly to inquire what the precise consequences will be for this affiliate."[5] One consequence was the necessity of turning away some civil liberties conflicts that the Philadelphia ACLU would otherwise like to have litigated.

༄

Coxe wrote back to Ellery a week after receiving his letter, thanking him for "the generous check" and assuring him, prematurely as it turned out, that the ACLU "was most definitely interested in working with you on the problem of bible reading in the public schools."[6] Coxe contacted Bernard Wolfman to begin researching the legal issues. Wolfman, who had embarked on what would become a distinguished legal career, served on the ACLU chapter's Freedom of Expression Committee and was a lawyer at a leading Philadelphia law firm, Wolf, Block, Schorr and Solis-Cohen. A graduate of the University of Pennsylvania Law School, Wolfman would later return to his alma mater to teach law and become dean of the law school from 1970 to 1975, when he left to teach at Harvard Law School.

Wolfman's early research raised doubts in his mind about whether a challenge in court would prove successful. On February 8, 1957,

Coxe wrote again to Ellery, to inform him that Wolfman had presented his preliminary report to the Freedom of Expression Committee. Coxe explained that on the basis of Wolfman's "analysis on the chances of winning, and other considerations," the committee was "disinclined to recommend ACLU involvement in a court test." Coxe added, though, that "the Committee fully recognizes the existence of a civil liberties problem here."[7] When interviewed six years later in a *CBS News* report, Coxe said that the committee "at that time decided that we should not get involved on behalf of Ellery Schempp on the grounds that the issue was not a very important one."[8] The term *important* was used here in a relative sense. As the name of the committee suggested, the ACLU chapter had long dealt with First Amendment speech controversies, not religion battles.

Three weeks later, the news for Ellery looked a bit brighter. After the question of ACLU representation went to the board of directors of the Philadelphia chapter, Coxe wrote that the directors had decided that Wolfman "should make a thorough investigation of the chances of winning a test case, as a real constitutional issue is involved." Coxe, however, noted a serious concern voiced by the directors: Ellery was then a junior in high school, and by the time his case reached an appellate court, he "would have graduated, and the court would consider the case moot."[9] Courts generally dismiss cases for mootness when a litigant no longer has a personal stake in the outcome of the proceedings. Given the years required for a trial and appeals, the plaintiff in a case of this kind would ideally be an elementary school or middle school student. Ellery, of course, had younger siblings who could carry on the case, but the ACLU did not know this at the time.

⤳

Although they had exchanged letters over a three-month period, Coxe had not actually met Ellery or his family. Neither had Wolfman. From his correspondence, Ellery appeared to be a serious and thoughtful young man, but he was, after all, only sixteen years old.

Both men had to assess his demeanor and whether he had the strength of conviction to present a credible account of himself in court, especially under hostile questioning. Did the Schempp family understand the depth of hostility that awaited them in their community after filing a lawsuit to strike down Bible reading?

Coxe drove out to Abington on the weekend of March 9 and 10, 1957, to talk with the Schempps. "I spent an hour with the Schempp family over the weekend," he wrote in a memo on Monday morning, adding: "They are all apparently very keen mentally, and seem to understand very clearly what ACLU's interest is. They are attractive, well-balanced people, and from this point of view would make good litigants. They have lived in the community (Roslyn) for eight years. They are all ready and willing to bring action, and fully understand that it would involve them in considerable notoriety and possible obloquoy [sic] and would go on for years."[10]

Wolfman also called on the Schempp household. "It was important to find out how serious they were," he says, "whether they were sincere, whether this was a fleeting thing." "And also," he explains, "I wanted to find out whether, if we brought litigation, they and their parents would understand that they might be the objects of horrendous, nonphysical, but horrendous harassment and ostracism and outrage. I needed to know whether they would withstand that."[11]

Wolfman made the short drive to Abington one evening from his home in Elkins Park, an adjoining suburban community of stately homes. Ed and Sidney Schempp greeted Wolfman at the door, and what he saw upon entering was "a modest home, modestly furnished but adequate."[12] They introduced him to their three children and then left the four of them alone to talk in the living room. Wolfman learned that the high school had by then accommodated Ellery to the extent of excusing him from homeroom each morning—but still not from hearing the morning devotionals. "I'd go to my homeroom, say, 'Hello,' 'I'm here,' 'Present,' and go down and sit in [guidance counselor] Miss Brehm's office," Ellery recalls. "Sometimes we'd talk, and sometimes I just sat there during morning devotions and then went off [to class]."[13] That arrangement continued from his protest in late

November until he finished his junior year in June. While sitting in Brehm's office, he still heard the morning devotionals over the public address system each morning.

Wolfman wanted to hear Ellery articulate why he objected to the Bible-reading exercises at Abington. "He said that aspects of the King James Version of the Bible just don't sit with some of their perspectives as Unitarians," Wolfman says. "He didn't go into any theological discussion as to what those differences were. I didn't think that appropriate, and he didn't volunteer it. It was just clear that he felt and his siblings felt that they shouldn't have to have lectured to them daily a religious perspective that was so different from theirs."[14]

Wolfman remembers that all three children agreed: "They said they think it would be a good thing if they and others of like mind didn't have the school system constantly telling them something they didn't believe in, and didn't see why the schools were in a sense trying to indoctrinate them. That was their point of view, and they held it firmly. It was clear to me that it was deeply felt." At one point, Wolfman asked Donna, who was eleven years old, if she could tell him anything about the Unitarian faith: "She said, 'Mr. Wolfman, you're Jewish, aren't you?' I said, 'Yes, I am.' And she said, 'Well, all I can say is that like the Jews, we have a very individualistic relationship with God.' I just thought that was extraordinary. By making reference to me and my religion, she thought I could gain an understanding. First, that she speculated a guess, correctly, that I was Jewish was interesting; and second, that she saw the analogue was to me extraordinary. So you can imagine that this whole evening with them endeared them to me."[15]

Wolfman talked with Ed and Sidney before he left, emphasizing that many people in the community would be likely to express outrage at the entire family for bringing such a case. He asked whether they and their children were prepared for an ugly reaction. Wolfman recalls: "They looked at each other, and one of them, I guess it was the father, I'm not sure, it could have been both, said to me . . . 'The children feel very strongly about this. If you say that there's a case, they want to go ahead, and we'll support it to the end.'"[16] Then one of them asked what the costs would be, not understanding that the ACLU would handle the case pro bono, with the Schempp's paying only some costs, such as the filing fee.

As he left the Schempp house that evening, Wolfman reflected on his own experience with Bible reading. "I was very familiar with that because I was a product of the Philadelphia public schools and always had the Bible read to me," says Wolfman. "I always felt uncomfortable when it was read to me, but I, as a kid, accepted it as part of what happens." Even so, he wasn't prepared for the surprise that awaited him at home. In the kitchen the next morning, Wolfman discovered that his own son, then in first grade, could recite a Christian prayer. Wolfman had explained what had taken place the night before and described the devotionals at Abington. He recalls: "Whereupon my son said, 'I know the Lord's Prayer.' And he started to recite it. And so I learned for the first time that the schools in Elkins Park did the same thing, and that he, a first grader, had been sufficiently indoctrinated that he already knew the Lord's Prayer by heart."[17]

In their resolve to challenge the morning devotionals in the Abington schools, the Schempps were actually less unified than they revealed to the ACLU people who visited them. Ed Schempp was solidly behind Ellery and was quite proud that his son had absorbed the lessons presented to him at home and at the Germantown Unitarian church. Sidney also agreed with Ellery, but she worried that taking the matter to the courts would create problems for her children in school and for the family in the Abington community. Ellery's two siblings shared neither his level of passion for the protest nor his lack of concern for the fallout that might accompany a lawsuit with the Schempp name attached to it. Donna and Roger were too young to share Ellery's political sophistication, although they understood the principle involved. The family discussed around the dinner table the question of whether to pursue a lawsuit.

Donna wavered between supporting and opposing a lawsuit. In

opposing it, she worried about the same thing that would concern most other youngsters—whether her family's action would affect her status with friends and acquaintances. "I remember saying, 'Why are you rocking the boat?'" says Donna. "I liked reading the Bible. I was still in elementary school. Different kids took turns reading the Bible. I looked forward to the chance to do that. Being a Unitarian was different. I wanted to be like everyone else. I didn't have anything against Bible reading."[18]

Ellery remembers that Donna was ambivalent but primarily focused on the social consequences for her. "She was embarrassed," says Ellery. "To her, the idea that she would lose the respect and support of all of her girlfriends was of cosmic importance. If the family was doing things to embarrass her in front of her friends, that was about the worst thing imaginable. Donna was the only champion for the idea that we were making a big mistake. She was able to recognize the intellectual position. But she could also very well support the view that, well, millions of Americans have been putting up with Bible reading and it hasn't hurt them and nobody has died early as a result of it. It doesn't really make that much of a difference. But it was clear it was driven by her, and she was very honest about it—my God, what would her friends think about this?"[19]

Roger, too, wavered because he worried about his status in school. "I wasn't terribly happy about the idea," he says. "I was in junior high. I wasn't too happy about it because I was pretty much of a loner at the time myself, and I really didn't want to feel more isolated than I already was."[20]

༄

Wolfman returned to his research to see if the Schempp's cause looked promising enough to warrant ACLU representation. There were not enough religion cases decided by the U.S. Supreme Court by that time to provide him with much reliable guidance, but he did find signs that the Court was moving toward enforcing greater separation between church and state. Yet some state courts had upheld devotional practices under their own constitutions; they had declared that the states could require Bible readings as a way of teaching morality. "I found nothing to assure me that a requirement to include Bible reading, as a book, and without comment, would breach that wall," says Wolfman. "They [the U.S. Supreme Court] might have concluded that it's within the province of the legislature to include, in a broad education, readings from an important book and without any comment that would suggest that you should follow it."[21]

With his research in hand, Wolfman wrote a memorandum for the Philadelphia chapter's Freedom of Expression Committee. In it, he recommended that the ACLU bring suit to enjoin enforcement of the Pennsylvania law requiring Bible reading, as a violation of the establishment clause of the First Amendment. The issue, he said, was "an extremely close one."[22] So, too, as it turned out, was the ACLU's decision about whether to take on such a case.

The ACLU's meager resources had been concentrated throughout the 1950s on issues of free speech as they related to McCarthyism. Historian Samuel Eliot Morison said of Joseph McCarthy, the Republican senator from Wisconsin, "For success in dividing a country by sowing suspicion of treason in high places, there has been no one to equal Joe McCarthy since Marat in the French Revolution."[23] Perhaps the fifties provided a perfect seedbed for such a reckless provocateur as McCarthy. Despite victory in World War II, the world looked to millions of Americans like a dangerous place. The Soviet Union and godless communism seemed to threaten the United States on many fronts, and China had been lost to the Communists. Into this arena of disappointment came McCarthy, waving documents that he said contained names of card-carrying Communists in the Department of State. McCarthy's witch hunt enveloped the entertainment industry, academia, and the U.S. Army. McCarthy's influence began to wane after thirty-five days of televised hearings in 1954, and he died four years later. Morrison called him a man of "diabolical cunning."[24]

During the fifties, the ACLU was busy protecting individuals from the attacks of McCarthyism. By the time the Schempp matter came before the ACLU's Philadelphia chapter in 1957, the country had reached the ebbing stage of McCarthyism, but the local chapter did not fully realize that at the time. Wolfman says, "It was discussed in the Freedom of Expression Committee—should we divert resources from these terrible issues to this interesting but, some people would say, fringe issue? We'd never had a church-state issue in the Philadelphia ACLU in anybody's memory that we had litigated."[25] Nonetheless, the committee voted overwhelmingly to support taking the matter to the chapter's board with a recommendation to litigate.

Before the full board, however, the recommendation ran into immediate trouble. The president of the Philadelphia chapter and chairman of its board was Clark Byse, a professor at the University of Pennsylvania Law School. Byse would leave later that year to teach at Harvard Law School, where he became regarded by many as the model for Charles Kingsfield, the fearsome law professor played by John Houseman in the movie *The Paper Chase*.[26] Wolfman and Byse brought a strong personal connection to the meeting, Wolfman having been a student in Byse's course on contract law at Penn. After Wolfman's graduation, Byse had asked Wolfman to represent him when he bought a house and, later, when he drafted his will—perhaps as large a compliment a professor ever pays a former student.

Now, however, the two men disagreed. Wolfman, who was not at the time a member of the board and therefore could not vote, remembers that there were about twenty people at the meeting, with feelings running strong on both sides: "It was clear to me that this was not going to be a pushover by any means."[27] Many people argued, as Wolfman had in his memo, that the Bible-reading issue was a cause worth fighting for. Others—including Byse—replied that the chapter had to continue using its scarce funds to fight McCarthyism and should not open new fronts that would siphon resources. "My sympathy was in fighting McCarthyism," says Byse. He says of the Schempp case, "We didn't have much in the way of resources to put to it."[28]

When Byse finally called the question, the vote among the directors split exactly down the middle. Everyone looked to Byse. As chairman, he had not participated in the vote, but now it was his responsibility to break the tie. People in the room knew exactly where Byse stood—against taking on the case. "I was there wanting this case to be accepted, and I hung onto his every word," says Wolfman. "I knew enough of Clark Byse that I wouldn't know his vote until he finally said it."[29] There was silence in the room as Byse started to speak.

Wolfman remembers that Byse made it sound clearly as if he would reject any ACLU involvement. "I am a Roman Catholic," Wolfman remembers Byse telling his colleagues. "I believe that the Bible is the embodiment of morality. I believe it's a good thing that the Bible is read to the children every day." Byse paused, then added, "However, because half of the board believes that the issue is important enough for us to litigate, I'm going to vote in favor of litigation so that the matter can be brought before the courts." Thus, Ellery Schempp would have his day in court. "It's clear that Clark was on the other side," says Wolfman. "If he had just voted his feelings, that case would never have been brought by the Philadelphia ACLU."[30]

⁂

Even the greatest battles can turn on small acts of selflessness that few people can see or celebrate. So it was with Ellery's protest. Had Clark Byse voted according to his own views, the Schempp matter would have ended right there, with the ACLU declining to litigate. Ellery Schempp would have received a polite letter from Spencer Coxe, and that would certainly have been the end of the matter. The Schempps could not have financed the litigation themselves. Without an attorney working on a pro bono basis, the matter would have been dead.

Byse's vote, however, moved the issue to the next step. Now the ACLU had to settle on a lawyer to represent the Schempps and develop a legal strategy for pursuing the case. Then would come the drafting and filing of a complaint to initiate the case. All of these steps were complicated, especially the legal strategy. When it came to challenging religious practices, such as Bible reading, in the schools, there wasn't much First Amendment precedent on which to rely. This was legal frontier in the fifties—comprised of dense forest, little light, and fearful hazards all around. The ACLU had little more than a compass pointing it in the right direction. The maps, if any, were primitive and unreliable.

Which ACLU lawyer was going to represent the Schempps? The obvious choice would have been Bernard Wolfman, who was excited about the case, believed in the cause, and had already done a considerable amount of research for the memorandum he wrote for the ACLU directors. But after Wolfman called the Schempps to let them know that the ACLU would bring their case, he began having second thoughts. It didn't take long for him to decide to step aside. Wolfman went to see Spencer Coxe at the chapter's office. Wolfman reports: "I said, 'There's going to be an enormous outcry about bringing this case. There will be enough to defend on the merits. There will be those who would say I was motivated because I'm Jewish and don't like the fact that the King James Bible is being read. It's not true, but we don't need that side issue.' I said, 'We need to have somebody for whom there will be no foreseeable side issues. The one I just mentioned is not just foreseeable; it will be there and right up and on the table.' So Spencer said, 'I feel terrible. Somebody is not able to do a case because of his religion.' I said, 'Yes, I agree with you, but that's the fact. I don't think I should do it.'"[31]

Although he accepted Wolfman's resignation from the case, Coxe was not convinced that a lawyer of the Jewish faith should not represent Ellery Schempp. He called next on Theodore R. Mann, a twenty-nine-year-old lawyer who was already litigating civil liberties cases through both the ACLU and the American Jewish Congress. Mann would later serve as the president of the AJ Congress, become the founding chairman of the charitable organization Mazon: A Jewish Response to Hunger, and argue a religious liberty case before the U.S. Supreme Court.

Mann accepted the case and took about three weeks to research and write the complaint, the document that initiated the lawsuit. As Wolfman had done, he met with Ellery Schempp to size up what kind of plaintiff he had, getting together with him in Mann's office on Chestnut Street in Philadelphia. "There aren't many kids around who would litigate the issue of his entitlement to be in a public school free of the atmosphere of religion," Mann says. "But other than that he could have been any kid. There was nothing different about him at all."[32]

When he finished drafting the complaint, Mann sent it on for review to two men whom he describes as "my heroes at the time,"[33] Leo Pfeffer and Shad Polier. Both were colleagues—they were the top lawyers for the AJ Congress in New York. Mann was not prepared for what happened next.

⁓

Leo Pfeffer was at the time perhaps the country's preeminent scholar on the First Amendment religion clauses and one of the most influential strategists on bringing legal challenges on religious freedom issues to the courts. Born in Hungary in 1909, the son of an Orthodox rabbi, Pfeffer arrived with his family two years later on the Lower East Side of Manhattan, teeming then with Jewish immigrants. His father began working at a local synagogue but enrolled Leo in a public school instead of a yeshiva. Leo remembered hearing daily recitations from the King James Bible before his parents finally enrolled him in Jewish schools. Later, he earned a bachelor's degree from the City College of New York and then a law degree in 1933 from New York University. Pfeffer joined the legal staff of the AJ Congress in 1945 and soon took over as chief strategist on religious freedom issues.[34]

Although the field was by no means unoccupied, there were relatively few constitutional experts on religion at the midcentury point, and scholarly activity on the subject was barely visible by the standards of fifty years later. That was because it was state and local laws that instigated controversies over religion in public life, and such measures had not even been subject to federal constitutional review for most of the nation's history. Not until the 1940s did the U.S. Supreme Court rule that the First Amendment guarantees of religious freedom could be applied as restrictions against the states.[35] With the field thus open to intellectual leadership, Leo Pfeffer saw the opportunity and grasped it. By 1953, he had established his scholarly credentials with his groundbreaking book *Church, State, and Freedom,* which examined the history of church-state relations. The last line of that book—declaring that "complete separation of church and state is best for church and best for state, and secures freedom for both"—forcefully summarized his stance for more than four decades.[36] More books and articles by Pfeffer followed, broadening his influence, as did his successful arguments before the U.S. Supreme Court in a number of religious freedom cases.

It was part of Pfeffer's genius to understand how to frame church-state issues to move the Supreme Court in the direction he wanted. He could have attacked state sponsorship of religious practices in many different contexts, but he focused on sectarian practices in the public schools no doubt because the vulnerability of minority non-Christian children provided the most compelling case. Pfeffer would play a crucial role in the upcoming litigation over devotional exercises in the schools, even in cases he didn't litigate himself. Behind the scenes and unknown to Mann at the time, he already was using his considerable clout to influence which cases would be filed and which would be appealed to the U.S. Supreme Court. Pfeffer wasn't confident that the justices would support the removal of Bible reading and prayer from the public schools, and he wanted to personally choose the test case and the timing for the litigation. Intervening in some legal disputes he thought too weak to win, he lobbied hard and sometimes successfully with plaintiffs' lawyers to convince them to drop their plans to litigate. Part of the reason for his effort was no doubt his competitive drive to personally develop and argue the case that would make landmark law in church-state relations. As confident as any lawyer who ever walked into a courtroom, Pfeffer certainly couldn't imagine that anyone else stood a better chance than he did of convincing the justices of the fundamental constitutional violation represented by devotional exercises in the public schools. But he had to find the right case, a horse he could run to the finish line with such singular speed that the justices would nod knowingly among themselves and quietly close their books. He could find such a case, but could he hold off all the less-qualified and impatient lawyers ready to run any lame plow horse of a case to the justices? In the end, Pfeffer would find his case in Miami and would compete mightily with *Schempp* to reach the Supreme Court first.

Mann's other hero at the time was Pfeffer's colleague Shad Polier, a lawyer and First Amendment expert and a son-in-law of Rabbi Stephen Wise, founder of the AJ Congress and one of the most influential rabbis of the twentieth century. At Wise's death in 1949, Polier was already a prominent lawyer in New York and a lay leader of the AJ Congress. Mann describes Polier as "obstreperous, brilliant, a pain in the neck, and the kind of person who had the nerve or the gall to stand in front of a trial court judge sitting on the bench and put his feet up on the table as though he were talking to an associate in his office. And he got away with it. Shad was that kind of a person. But he was absolutely brilliant."[37]

Pfeffer and Polier were primarily responsible for pushing segments of the Jewish community toward a far more aggressive attitude toward issues concerning church and state. After their massive immigration to American shores around the turn of the twentieth century, Jews generally felt constrained from organizing politically to make demands on the government. They remembered the persecution in Europe and feared, from what they heard and saw in everyday life in America, that a fierce anti-Semitism might live just below the surface in their new land as well. Even the three major national Jewish organizations—the American Jewish Committee, the AJ Congress, and the Anti-Defamation League of B'nai B'rith—consciously took a low profile in a nation that was predominantly Christian. Instead of directly challenging sectarian religious practices in the schools with litigation that might anger and offend the majority, these organizations worked behind the scenes to advance their

agenda of religious equality for Jewish citizens. They pursued a strategy of public relations and interfaith negotiations. If that approach
was not successful, they pursued legislative initiatives that required
building a consensus in the community.

People of the Jewish faith did not move easily to a more activist
stance of litigating their religious rights. When *Everson v. Board of
Education* reached the Supreme Court for argument in 1946—raising
the issue of whether school districts could reimburse parents of
parochial school students the cost of bus transportation—Pfeffer was
a young staff attorney at the AJ Congress. He recommended that the
AJ Congress submit a brief against the issue from the position of
amicus curiae (or "friend of the court"). But it could do so only with
the consent of the National Community Relations Advisory Council
(NCRAC), the umbrella committee of major Jewish organizations.
The council did not consent. Jewish leaders worried that their public
opposition to aid of this kind to parochial school parents would win
the enmity of Roman Catholics.[38]

The Court articulated a strong commitment in *Everson* to the separation of church and state but ruled that reimbursing parochial
school parents the cost of bus transportation did not breach the wall.
Pfeffer soon got another opportunity for his cause, however. After
Everson, attitudes began to change within the Jewish community, at
least with the AJ Congress, thanks in large part to Pfeffer's constant
pushing. The next important religion-related case to come before the
Court was *McCollum v. Board of Education* in 1948.[39] *McCollum* tested
the widespread use across the country of released-time programs,
through which students were dismissed from regular instruction during the public school day in order to attend religious classes held by
clergy, within their own school. Despite initial objections from the
two other Jewish groups, all of them agreed to join Pfeffer in an amicus brief to the U.S. Supreme Court.[40]

This time, the Court's ruling did not disappoint Pfeffer. The justices declared that released-time programs violated the First Amendment. After the *McCollum* decision, the American Jewish Committee and the Anti-Defamation League favored careful negotiations

with the Christian community to disassemble released-time programs. But Pfeffer insisted that, alone or in concert with the two sister organizations, the AJ Congress should push on with the next attack, this one against dismissed-time programs. These were similar to the released-time programs that had been litigated in *McCollum* but did not involve use of public school classrooms for religious instruction. Schools organized an early dismissal for all students who wanted to attend religious classes away from the public school.

By the time that *Zorach v. Clauson* reached the U.S. Supreme Court, however, Pfeffer sounded downbeat about the potential outcome. On March 21, 1952, five weeks before announcement of the decision, Pfeffer wrote to the director of the NCRAC: "I am not too optimistic about the outcome. My guess is that the decision will be 5 to 4 or 6 to 3 and I am afraid it is more likely that we will (*sic*) on the short end."[41] Pfeffer was correct. The Court declined, in a six-to-three ruling, to extend the *McCollum* decision to off-campus classrooms. (The McCollum and Zorach decisions are explored more fully in chapter 9.)[42]

Zorach was a bitter defeat for Pfeffer. The decision also ended the brief alliance among the three leading Jewish organizations. The other two organizations returned to their model of working for change through community action, thereby freeing Pfeffer to lead the AJ Congress's litigation strategy unconstrained by his more conservative colleagues. A year later, in 1953, his publication of *Church, State, and Freedom* boosted him into a higher orbit still—a role nationwide as both the leading academic scholar and most influential legal strategist on religious freedom issues.

Yet Pfeffer's newfound stature did not push him into a broad new attack on religious practices in the schools. In fact, he seemed chastened by *Zorach,* fearing that the Court was retrenching on the issue of the separation of church and state. His fears were certainly reasonable at the time. The Court had enunciated strong language on separation but had not seemed to follow through in all of its rulings.

The defeat in *Zorach* made Pfeffer a far more cautious man. He remained fiercely dedicated to litigating church-state issues, but now he hesitated to move forward unless he felt he had in hand what amounted to almost a perfect test case. In the meantime, he opposed bringing new cases or appealing decisions that he believed did not offer a compelling enough set of facts. Negotiating to reach a community consensus against a religious practice in the schools was now a more attractive alternative until the right case came along. In regard to one church-state matter, Pfeffer wrote to Sidney Vincent, assistant director of the Jewish Community Federation of Cleveland, "It may seem strange to you that I should be the one to raise so-called community relations implications in a matter such as this." He added, "Perhaps I have grown fat and conservative in my old age."[43] The matter involved the recognition of Good Friday as a holiday in a United Steel Workers contract—a far different legal situation than government sponsorship of religious exercises in the schools. Nonetheless, Pfeffer's statement showed remarkable self-awareness. As the lion of church-state litigation, his roar was sounding a little weak even to him.

༄

In the fifties, Pfeffer was stepping hard on the brakes, and his caution would exert a major effect on litigation of church-state matters over the next decade. He felt that several critical issues involving religious practices in the public school required the U.S. Supreme Court's attention, but he feared a loss if these issues were litigated now. Where did the justices really stand? Pfeffer didn't know, and neither did anyone else. A decision by the justices on any of the religious practices in the public schools would become bedrock principles of constitutional law. For Pfeffer, it was worth waiting for the right time and the right case. The result is that he worked actively to stop a number of cases that came up in the fifties, either opposing the filing of a lawsuit or attempting to prevent a case already decided in a state court from being appealed to the U.S. Supreme Court.

Pfeffer had several concerns. For one, he worried that the justices would pull back further because the *McCollum* released-time decision had met with intense criticism by a large segment of the public and the religious community. To be sure, the justices enjoy life tenure on the bench to help insulate them from just such pressures. But justices are nonetheless human: they read the papers; they live in their communities. Perhaps most significant of all, many were men to whom religion was an important part of their own personal lives. So Pfeffer worried about the criticism heaped on the *McCollum* decision by Christian groups. "What is needed," he wrote to Polier, "is a real public relations campaign to counteract the terribly effective job the Catholic church has done in making the McCollum decision unpopular."[44]

Beyond his concern for the atmosphere surrounding the Court, Pfeffer's correspondence during the fifties shows strong feelings regarding the kind of case he felt would provide the best chance to succeed. He feared that the Court would decide major questions about religion in the schools based on cases he felt were weak. Although he was most concerned about Bible reading and prayer in public schools, he felt the strongest case would be one involving a school district with a wide array of religious practices, such as holiday programs, religious displays, and passion plays. A short Bible-reading exercise might seem to some justices to be a traditional exposure to religion, perhaps justified by an expressed goal of teaching lessons in morality. But a large number of religious practices would show unmistakably just how broadly the state was utilizing the schools to send a sectarian religious message to children.

In addition, Pfeffer wanted to employ both the establishment clause and the free exercise clause in his attack on religious exercises in public schools. The establishment clause banned government support for religion—such as, presumably, the state running devotional exercises in public schools. The free exercise clause focused on individuals and their freedom to practice their religion or no religion at all, free of coercion by the state. Identifying extensive religious practices in the schools would provide a strong basis from which Pfeffer could argue that individuals, regardless of their beliefs, were being coerced to participate, either through an outright requirement or through peer pressure.

Pfeffer wanted to create a deep and detailed trial record. He didn't like cases in which just a few witnesses testified that a morning devotional violated their religious freedom. Worse still, Pfeffer believed, were cases in which a school board simply filed a demurrer to the plaintiff's complaint. In such cases, the board would argue that even if all the facts alleged by the plaintiff were true, they were insufficient to establish a violation of the First Amendment. Without facts in dispute, the matter could be argued to a judge entirely on the basis of how the First Amendment applied to the facts. By contrast, Pfeffer wanted an extensive trial that explored in detail all the religious practices in the schools and how they were carried out and that provided wide-ranging testimony from people in the community who felt that the schools were trampling on their right to freely exercise their religion. Such a full trial record, he felt, would create overwhelming evidence for the appellate judges who would ultimately decide whether these practices violated the First Amendment.

As the leading scholar and strategist on religious freedom issues, Pfeffer exercised great influence over the litigation community. But he was, in the end, still only one person representing one organization. He didn't control the ACLU, which brought some cases without his blessing, and he certainly had no control over the independent lawyers around the country who were approached by an increasing number of litigants interested in challenging religious practices in public schools. When a case went ahead despite his recommendation to the contrary, Pfeffer often entered the case at the end by filing an amicus brief with the court. But, however wise it may have seemed at the time, Pfeffer's studied caution enabled more aggressive litigators to exert far greater influence over events than they would have done otherwise.

꒰꒱

One of the early cases that Pfeffer didn't like arose in New Jersey— and it looked a great deal like the situation involving Ellery Schempp that would come later in Pennsylvania. A state statute required that public school teachers read, without comment, at least five verses of the Holy Bible at the opening of school each day. The law also authorized, but did not require, recitation of the Lord's Prayer. Two taxpayers sued the board of education of the borough of Hawthorne, New Jersey, arguing that the schools were engaging in religious education and services in violation of the First Amendment. There was no trial on the allegations. The judge upheld the practices on the basis of the legal pleadings and a pretrial conference. On appeal, the New Jersey Supreme Court agreed with the trial court and declared that both practices were permissible because "the Old Testament and the Lord's Prayer, pronounced without comment, are not sectarian." The state court ruled "that the short exercise provided by the statute does not constitute sectarian instruction or sectarian worship but is a simple recognition of the Supreme Ruler of the Universe and a deference to His majesty."[45]

Pfeffer, along with his colleagues Shad Polier and Will Maslow, had filed an amicus brief on behalf of one of the plaintiffs in the New Jersey case, Donald R. Doremus. Now, Pfeffer vigorously opposed appealing the case to the U.S. Supreme Court. In a letter on December 13, 1950, to Polier, Pfeffer noted that Doremus's lawyer, Heyman Zimel, agreed with Pfeffer's analysis that either the justices would refuse to hear the case or "would take the case for the purpose of retreating from the *McCollum* decision, which would be worse." Pfeffer added, "My conviction is that an application for certiorari would be a very serious mistake and we may possibly through various sources influence either Zimmel [*sic*] or his clients to withdraw."[46]

Doremus insisted that his case be appealed, and Zimel did so. Even after the Supreme Court agreed to hear the case, Pfeffer worked behind the scenes to convince key people to withdraw the appeal. On March 14, 1951, Pfeffer wrote to Polier of his "extreme pessimism regarding the outcome of this case, basically because of the tremendous propaganda led by the Catholic Church which has been unleashed against the Supreme Court for its *McCollum* decision."[47] Pfeffer and Polier then tried to put outside pressure on Doremus to withdraw his appeal, suggesting a meeting with the lead litigant from the earlier *McCollum* case. On June 7, 1951, Pfeffer wrote of a meeting at which "Shad Polier made the suggestion that I go to Champaigne [*sic*], Illinois to speak to Mrs. McCollum and induce her to speak to Doremus to obtain his withdrawal of the appeal."[48] Instead, Pfeffer and others met with Vashti McCollum in New York. Afterward, he reported, "the ACLU was categorically opposed to the withdrawal of the Doremus case,"[49] and so the matter was dropped. On March 13, Pfeffer wrote that he had "heard over the radio last night that the Supreme Court had agreed to hear arguments on the merits." He lamented: "I couldn't sleep all night. I am sure that the Court will not invalidate Bible reading of the innocuous type presented in the Doremus case."[50]

The U.S. Supreme Court's decision on March 3, 1952, sidestepped the contentious issues at the center of the dispute. The Court dismissed the case without reaching the merits. The child had graduated from the public schools before the case reached the Court, so no decision by the justices could affect her rights. Doremus had lost, but, to Pfeffer's relief, not in a way that created a national precedent on any of the issues.[51]

Four years after the *Doremus* case, yet another Bible-reading case bubbled to the top as a prime candidate for a major U.S. Supreme Court ruling in the area of church-state relations. John W. Carden was a student at East Nashville Junior High School and objected to Bible reading and a few other religious practices conducted in the Nashville, Tennessee, public schools. A state law required each teacher to read or supervise the reading of a selection from the Bible every day. In addition, students recited the Lord's Prayer. Those practices were not so unusual around the country for the time, but one additional practice was: on Monday mornings, John Carden's teacher asked the students whether they had attended Sunday religious school the day before. Those who had not attended were in effect penalized—they were required to copy verses from the Bible by hand. John's father, Phillip M. Carden, argued that these practices were contrary to their religious beliefs and were violations of both the Tennessee Constitution and the First Amendment. At some point during the litigation, the practice of inquiring about Sunday school attendance stopped, and the trial court judge upheld the other religious exercises.

In early January 1956, as the *Carden* case moved on to the Tennessee Supreme Court, Pfeffer took a swing through three Southern states for a series of meetings. On January 12, he arrived in Nashville specifically to talk about the *Carden* case. In a meeting with leaders of the Jewish community. Pfeffer explained "that a suit based on bible reading from the Old Testament was ill-advised at the present time and was not likely to succeed and that I would so advise counsel in the case." He added, "On the other hand, if the suit involved other sectarian practices, it should be prosecuted." The next day, Pfeffer met with Carden's attorney, C. Vernon Hines, who told him that the school district had discontinued all the religious practices except the Bible reading required by law. That was enough of a victory for Pfeffer. "Under the circumstances," reported Pfeffer, "I advised him to try to get a stipulation from the counsel of the Board of Education that the other practices would not be resumed and that upon obtaining such a stipulation, to be made part of the record, the appeal ought to be dropped."[52] However, Carden refused to drop the appeal.

Pfeffer's worries came to fruition on March 9, when Tennessee's highest court upheld the state's Bible-reading statute.[53] After the decision, Pfeffer worried that a further appeal to the U.S. Supreme Court would bring a similar ruling and a devastating blow to his conception of religious freedom. Pfeffer believed that after the setback in *Zorach*, it was "an inopportune time to bring such a suit." He conceded that a lawsuit on Bible reading would eventually reach the U.S. Supreme Court, but he felt that a case based simply on Bible reading and not on more extensive religious practices would be a loser. "It is therefore my advice that Carden and Hines should be discouraged from prosecuting this matter any further," he wrote on March 23.[54] Two weeks later, he wrote directly to Hines, Carden's lawyer: "We do not think that a petition for certiorari should be filed in the Supreme Court of the United States. It is improbable that the Supreme Court would today invalidate Bible reading statutes."[55] Pfeffer was successful; the case was not appealed.

∽

Theodore Mann was convinced he had a winning case with Ellery Schempp. "It was the post–World War II generation," he said. "A lot of young people got married by the mid-1950s. Loads of Jewish kids were being educated in the public schools all over the United States. Their parents were very upset by the readings of the King James Version of the Bible, because they themselves were trying to remain Jewish while at the same time assimilating into the general society, and this was a very difficult thing that they had to confront: meetings with teachers and principals throughout the big cities of America about what was happening in the public schools, not only Bible reading but also Christmas celebrations, Christmas trees, singing of Christmas carols (very religious Christmas carols)—matters of that sort that they didn't want their kids to have to endure."[56]

Mann needed some experts to read the draft of his complaint and provide him with feedback. Two obvious choices were Pfeffer and Polier—the former of whom he regarded as the preeminent scholar on religious freedom issues. In fact, Mann had read Pfeffer's *Church, State, and Freedom* and regarded it as the leading work in the field. So Mann, not yet thirty years old and only four years out of law school, was eager for Pfeffer's and Polier's reaction to his draft, unaware of Pfeffer's strong opposition to cases similar to *Schempp* in the recent past. "I sent both of them a copy of the complaint for their review before I filed it," says Mann, who felt very good about his work on the document. He received a call back from Polier, who clearly was speaking for both himself and Pfeffer. "What I remember so clearly," says Mann, "was getting a phone call from Shad, who said, 'Who is the schmuck who prepared this complaint?' I said, 'You're talking to him.'"[57]

4. The Sage and the Upstart

Polier's telephone call took Mann's breath away. He knew Polier's reputation—brilliant at law, but combative, obstreperous, and direct sometimes to the point of offending people. Knowing that, however, didn't lessen the pain of hearing Polier's denigrating remark. "I remember most clearly trying to figure out at that fairly young age— I was twenty-nine—why did these two people with whom I agreed so much disagree with me," Mann says. "Was it me or was it them?"[1]

Both Polier and Pfeffer were by then familiar with Mann's work in Philadelphia on the upcoming Schempp lawsuit. Polier already knew that Mann had drafted the complaint he had just read; his testy response wasn't so much a question about authorship as it was a contemptuous slap at Mann and the ACLU for continuing to move forward toward the filing of the lawsuit in the first place. For Pfeffer and Polier, the Schempp matter looked like a loser, and perhaps a serious loser that would damage irreparably the cause of removing religious observances from the public schools. Behind the scenes, in meetings and in telephone calls, Pfeffer, Polier, Mann, and the ACLU were locked in a battle over whether a lawsuit should be filed at all and, if one were filed, what strategy would enhance the chances of success— or at least limit the losses if the case went the other way. Pfeffer wielded no veto power over ACLU initiatives on religious freedom issues, but he did enjoy considerable influence, and he tried his best to exert it here.

In fact, Pfeffer had already been asked about the Pennsylvania law requiring Bible reading, as early as February 1956, about nine months before Ellery Schempp staged his protest in the Abington schools. When asked about the validity of Bible reading in the Pennsylvania public schools, Pfeffer wrote that a practice of reading from the Old Testament without comment was most likely consistent with Pennsylvania law but that the addition of hymns, prayers, or other sectarian practices would probably make it illegal. That was not a startling conclusion, given the fact that the state law expressly required Bible reading and no other devotional practice. Pfeffer, however, said that it was "a more difficult question" whether Bible reading was consistent with the First Amendment and that "we do not think it advisable to litigate that issue at the present time." Instead, he advised that "a quiet approach be made by the leaders of the Jewish community to the public school authorities urging a de-emphasis on the sectarian aspects of these activities." If that approach didn't resolve the problem, he recommended consideration of an appeal to the Pennsylvania education commissioner and then, lastly, a lawsuit.[2]

When Ellery Schempp's protest finally raised a real possibility of a lawsuit, the nation's leading expert on church-state relations was cooperative but not at all encouraging. After Clark Byse's vote broke the tie at the ACLU's Philadelphia chapter in May 1957, enabling the ACLU to represent Schempp, Mann met with Pfeffer on several occasions during the summer.[3] Mann wanted his advice, and he, Pfeffer, and Polier spoke on the phone during the fall as well.[4]

For several reasons, Pfeffer didn't like the Abington situation as a test case for religious practices in the schools, and he worked hard over the summer to persuade Mann to his point of view. His objections were by now familiar, having been conveyed to lawyers and litigants in other cases, including *Doremus* and *Carden*. Pfeffer thought Bible reading and recitation of the Lord's Prayer clearly violated the First Amendment's establishment clause, but he was not convinced the courts would agree. The Abington situation lacked the wide-ranging religious practices—including holiday observances, nativity scenes, and religious hymns—that could provide Pfeffer with the additional argument, under the free exercise clause, that non-Christians and nonbelievers were not free to practice their own religion.

Pfeffer also worried that with such a slim set of allegations in play, the Abington school district would simply admit that the devotional practices were held, avoiding the necessity of a trial that would establish a deep well of evidence and testimony. Pfeffer complained in a memorandum the following year, after the lawsuit had been filed, "The complaint in the ACLU's case sets forth no facts requiring a trial and will probably go up on the pleadings." Pfeffer worried that the trial court's record going up on appeal would likely consist of nothing more than the basic complaint, answer, briefs, and judge's opinion. He referred to another First Amendment case he had won some years earlier, saying he was "certain that we would have never won . . . if we would have gone up on the pleadings alone."[5]

Mann appreciated Pfeffer's point about creating a deep trial record. Especially in such an uncharted and controversial legal area as religious practices in the schools, the slow and deliberate creation of a rich record helps to educate the trial judge as well as those who will hear the case on appeal. Mann told Pfeffer that he didn't intend to go up on the pleadings alone and that he would produce Ellery Schempp and his family at the trial to describe their objections to the morning devotionals, as well as an expert witness to establish that the Bible and the Lord's Prayer were sectarian religious observances. "I don't know what further record you would want," Mann would say years later.[6]

If Mann and the ACLU were adamant about litigating the Abington situation, Pfeffer at least wanted the case filed in a Pennsylvania state court, not in a federal court. The choice of courts was a momentous decision in the litigation strategy for the *Schempp* case, for it potentially would affect not only the chances of winning but also the potential impact of the decision. Ideally, the ACLU lawyers wanted a court decision that would strike down not only the Pennsylvania Bible-reading statute but also all similar statutes nationwide. For that to happen, they needed to challenge the Pennsylvania statute under the First Amendment, by eventually arguing before the nine justices sitting in Washington. Only the U.S. Supreme Court interpreting the U.S. Constitution can declare the meaning of the First Amendment nationwide. Pennsylvania's highest court cannot make national law, whether it is interpreting its own state constitution or the U.S. Constitution.

The U.S. Supreme Court normally controls its own docket, accepting for argument only a small fraction of the cases appealed to it from lower courts. Typically, that might be only 75 to 150 cases out of the thousands that lawyers file with the Supreme Court each year. But the *Schempp* case would enjoy a clear path to Supreme Court review if it were filed in federal court. A provision of federal law, later repealed by Congress, would have required the U.S. Supreme Court to hear the *Schempp* case if it was initially filed in a federal court.[7] Under federal law at the time, any case filed in federal court that tested the validity of a state law under the U.S. Constitution would be heard not by a single trial judge, as is typical, but by a three-judge panel. The decision of the panel could then go up to the justices in Washington on a direct appeal, meaning that if one of the parties asked it to, the Court was required to hear the case.

There were ways for the Supreme Court justices to dodge making a decision on the merits even after a case was argued before them, but the chances were certainly high that they would take on the case's central question. So if the ACLU filed the *Schempp* matter in federal court, it was signing on for a major decision on religious observances in the public schools that would affect the entire country. If the ACLU lawyers filed the case initially in state court and then lost in the Pennsylvania Supreme Court, the decision would affect practices only in Pennsylvania. They could assess the risks and rewards again at that time and decide whether to appeal. If they did ask the justices to review it on a writ of certiorari, the justices retained the discretion to decline the case.

Did the ACLU lawyers have the confidence to go forward in federal court? Taking that step required an assessment of risks and rewards that was difficult to make with any feeling of confidence.

After all, the U.S. Supreme Court had never considered a constitutional challenge to Bible reading in the public schools under the First Amendment. Nor had the Pennsylvania Supreme Court ever considered a similar challenge under the state constitution. Certainly, the federal courts looked more promising. Federal judges are often considered to be more sensitive to claims involving individual rights and liberties, and many observers consider most of them to be of generally higher quality than their counterparts on the state level. But the Supreme Court's retreat only a few years earlier in the *Zorach* case was troubling, to say the least, and made it difficult to predict how the *Schempp* case might turn out.

Behind closed doors in the spring of 1957, the ACLU lawyers debated the choice of courts and whether to attack the Pennsylvania Bible-reading statute under the state constitution or the First Amendment. Three ACLU lawyers from the local chapter met in Philadelphia on May 15 to discuss the point. They considered filing in the state courts. But the next day, Spencer Coxe wrote to ACLU staff counsel Rowland Watts (who worked in the national office in New York): "One danger of this latter course is that in case we won in the state courts the issue might be decided only as regards the Pennsylvania constitution, if the state courts decide to ignore the federal constitutional question. Further research is being done by our lawyers on this question, and another meeting is scheduled for Wednesday, May 22."[8]

Meanwhile, Pfeffer, at the American Jewish Congress, knew exactly where he stood on the question. He wanted the case filed in the Pennsylvania courts if it was going to be filed at all, thus avoiding the near certainty of an eventual decision by the U.S. Supreme Court and, he thought, the likelihood of a disastrous loss. That strategy made sense for someone who thought that the case would most likely result in a defeat and thus wanted to limit the losses to Pennsylvania alone. "Both Shad and Leo worked very hard at trying to stop us from filing the complaint," says Mann. "Short of stopping us from filing the complaint, they [Pfeffer and Polier] pressed very hard that if we had to file, it should be filed in the Pennsylvania state courts and not the federal courts, so that the loss, when it would inevitably come, would perhaps be limited to Pennsylvania, and they could take another crack at the issue years later in some other state courts or the federal court. [They said that] the timing was not right to bring this case in the federal court and lose disastrously on a nationwide basis."9 But Mann rejected the advice of the two men he admired so much. "I couldn't see a clear way in the state court that I would be assured we would win," Mann says. "The quality of the judges was not as good. The chance of getting a good judge was not great."10

᠅

On August 1, Mann wrote to Polier that the decision was firm: "There is no question but that ACLU is proceeding with the case, and the initial pleading will be filed by September."11 (Mann was off by six months—the complaint was actually filed the following February.) The fact that Mann and the ACLU held to their original course—to not only file the case but to do so in federal court, with the intention of taking it to the U.S. Supreme Court—reflected not only their different assessment of the legal situation but also a somewhat different worldview. Pfeffer, once the brash young lawyer trying to move Jewish organizations into litigation, had become cautious in trying to find just the right case to litigate. Now, some of the younger activists he had spawned were moving forward aggressively, without his blessing.

"I'm sure that his being so certain that we'd lose and my being so certain that we'd win had everything to do with how old we were respectively," says Mann. "They [Pfeffer and Polier] had been raised in the twenties and thirties. There was really very serious discrimination, societal discrimination, against Jews. Henry Ford was the primary anti-Semite in America. At the same time, he was the most trusted man in America. But at the same time, he was massively distributing the *Protocols of the Elders of Zion* throughout America. That kind of society, where Protestant America was the establishment and must have appeared to them to likely remain the establishment in America for many years into the future—I could see where they would come to the conclusion that there was no chance at all, that the time had not yet come when the Supreme Court or our lower courts might declare unconstitutional statutes that required the reading of the Protestant Bible every morning in our public schools."[12] Mann explains: "Leo did not realize how successful he had been in terms of development of the law. I was much more satisfied than he was that it was so."[13]

Mann also disagreed with Pfeffer on how broad the test case needed to be. Mann believed that they stood at least as good a chance of winning a case on Bible reading alone in the public schools as one that involved additional practices, such as hymns, Christmas trees, and holiday celebrations. "In my mind, all of those other practices in the public schools could be explained away on some basis," says Mann. "It could be something other than religion. Music was culture. The Christmas tree was part of Americana. It did not originate as a religious symbol. People who were not religious had Christmas trees. But if you were talking about the required reading of ten verses of the King James Bible every morning in public schools, no one could ever say that that was anything but a purely religious practice, and the religious practice of only one denomination. So it seemed to me that, confronted with the issue, we would have lost all those other cases complaining about other things in the public schools, but we would surely win this case."[14]

Mann also felt compelled to act for young Ellery Schempp, who had impressed him by carrying out his protest in school and risking the ostracism of both teachers and fellow students. "When a guy like Ellery Schempp comes into your office and talks about what happened to him, it's not a manufactured case as so many of these cases can be, when you're out looking for a client," says Mann. "Nobody was out looking for Ellery Schempp. He was looking for us. When that happens, and he feels he's been hurt, and you look at the case and you think there's probably no way, absent simply ducking the issue, that the courts are going to be able to avoid the unquestionably religious practice by a government that this case represents, then let's do it. Then you look for the downside. What happens if you lose? You figure the only way you're really going to lose is if the courts find a way to duck it. And that's not really a loss."[15]

⌘

As a new school year arrived in the fall of 1957, Ellery Schempp returned to Abington Senior High School for his senior year. For more than half of the previous school year (from the time of his protest on November 26 until school ended in June 1957), Ellery had reached a kind of détente with the Abington school authorities. Each day, he reported to his usual homeroom class so that his teacher, Elmer Carroll, could mark him present for the day. Then he hurried down the long corridors to the office of his guidance counselor, Evelyn W. Brehm. There, he sat for the fifteen minutes or so that it took for the homeroom period to finish. Although he no longer had to take part in the morning devotionals, there was no avoiding them either. Ellery could hear the Bible recitation as it was broadcast to the entire school over the public address system. In practical terms, his excusal from participation in the devotionals meant little in terms of sheltering him from the religious practices he found offensive.

Even this arrangement, however lacking in sensitivity to Ellery's needs, would not survive into the new academic year. It's doubtful that, during the summer, Abington officials had any idea of the legal storm clouds gathering over the horizon. So far, no legal papers had been filed; it had been less than four months since the ACLU voted to represent Ellery, and Ted Mann was still going back and forth with Leo Pfeffer about the direction of the complaint that would initiate the lawsuit. So it's likely that the school officials thought that they had little more than a recalcitrant student on their hands as they tried to figure out how to deal with him during the fall semester.

When Ellery returned to high school in September, a confrontation was not long in coming. On Friday, September 13, Ellery told his homeroom teacher that he wanted to be excused from the morning devotionals during his senior year. He ended up spending an hour and a half with Irvin A. Karam, the assistant principal, who told him that he could sit in the school auditorium during the homeroom class. He would hear the Bible readings there, but he would not have to participate in any formal way. By Monday, however, Karam's position had hardened, possibly after he had spoken with his own boss, the principal, Eugene Stull. Now, according to a memorandum that Ellery wrote to record the reaction of school officials, Karam told Ellery that he "must stay in homeroom and stand and 'show respect.'"[16] On Wednesday, September 18, the homeroom teacher reported to Karam that Ellery wasn't paying attention during the devotionals, so back he went to Karam. "Karam insisted it is no matter of conscience or religion, I must show respect," Ellery wrote.[17]

When the two met, Karam held firm. There would be no accommodation to Ellery's views, as there had been the previous year when he was permitted to sit in the guidance counselor's office. It was a matter of respecting a school rule obeyed by sixteen hundred other students. He had to attend the homeroom class and participate in the Bible reading and Lord's Prayer. "They absolutely compelled me to do what I told them in good conscience I didn't want to do, and it was a violation of my religious liberty," says Ellery.[18] So Ellery, who had been told that the ACLU would represent him, reluctantly agreed to return to his homeroom class each morning.

჻

On November 21, Mann sent another draft of his complaint on to Pfeffer, for a final look. Although Pfeffer wasn't happy with the lawsuit, the litigation was going ahead, and his practice was to help out behind the scenes to ensure that litigation had the best chance to succeed. Mann told him that the ACLU, contrary to Pfeffer's wishes, would go forward with a lawsuit in federal court and not in the Pennsylvania state courts. The ACLU had, however, taken up Pfeffer's suggestion to look for a Catholic and a Jewish plaintiff to add to the lawsuit. Pfeffer and Mann both felt that additional plaintiffs beyond the Schempps would broaden and strengthen the lawsuit. The Schempps were Unitarians, and the King James Version—the Bible used in the Abington schools—was at least nominally their own. A Catholic and a Jewish plaintiff would sharpen the point that state-mandated Bible reading was a sectarian religious practice. Catholicism and Judaism each had its own Bible (the Douay Version and the Old Testament, respectively), and neither one accepted the King James Version. So plaintiffs from those faiths would be able to argue that the morning devotionals at Abington were truly alien to the most fundamental tenets of their faiths. But the ACLU failed to find anyone else to join the suit.[19] Many Jews were concerned about an anti-Semitic backlash, and the Catholic Church hierarchy supported religious practices in the schools.

Mann also sent a copy of the draft complaint to Henry W. Sawyer III, a vice president of the ACLU's Philadelphia chapter and head of its Freedom of Expression Committee. In a note indicating his own due diligence, Mann said that the complaint would "be reviewed by several colleagues who have had experience in suits against school boards, for the purpose of determining whether we have named all of the required defendants."[20] Within a month (by the end of December), however, Mann stepped aside as ACLU counsel on the case. Unlike Bernard Wolfman before him, Mann was not concerned that his Jewish faith would bring attacks from some supporters of religious practices in the public schools. Instead, Mann worried that he didn't yet have the experience to litigate a case that would probably reach the U.S. Supreme Court. By then, Mann had been practicing law for only four years.

The logical choice to take the case was Henry Sawyer. He was yet another University of Pennsylvania Law School graduate who would figure prominently in the case. "He was," says Spencer Coxe, who gave him the assignment, "the brightest man I've ever known. He had a tremendous intellect. He had a marvelous capacity for analyzing law."[21] Mann had similar respect for Sawyer: "He was a very fine litigator with an enormous amount of courage to undertake actions that the general population would be very unhappy about."[22]

Sawyer was only thirty-nine years old when the *Schempp* case came knocking, but by then he had practically lived a lifetime. He had served in two wars, five years as a lieutenant commander in the navy during World War II and then as a commander in the naval arctic expedition during the Korean War. After working in the Department of State for a few years, he returned to private law practice at a prominent Philadelphia law firm, Drinker Biddle and Reath, where he would spend the rest of his career building a reputation as one of the most skilled litigators of his generation. Most of his practice involved complex civil litigation concerning corporations, but he devoted enormous time in pro bono work for causes in which he believed.[23]

Although he came from a privileged background (he graduated from Chestnut Hill Academy in Philadelphia and earned two degrees at the University of Pennsylvania), Sawyer's sympathies were for minorities whose rights had been systematically violated. That's why he joined the ACLU and became, by the time of Ellery Schempp's protest, a vice president of the Philadelphia chapter and chairman of the Free Expression Committee. By 1958, when the suit was filed, he had risen to president of the chapter.

Sawyer was well known in the Philadelphia legal community in the midfifties, not only for his work as a lawyer but also for the fact that he served on Philadelphia's city council. His acceptance of the assignment as lead counsel in the *Schempp* case, however, marked his emergence on the national stage. After arguing the *Schempp* case in federal court in Philadelphia in 1958, Sawyer went to Washington a few years later to make his first appearance before the U.S. Supreme Court. Bernhard Deutch, a physics graduate student at Penn, had appeared before a subcommittee of the House Un-American Activities Committee and refused to answer a series of questions that involved informing on other people. The congressmen voted to hold him in criminal contempt. After Sawyer's argument in *Deutch v. U.S.*, the Supreme Court reversed the conviction.[24] Sawyer was back before the Court three years later to argue the *Schempp* case, then again in 1971 in another landmark church-state case, *Lemon v. Kurtz-*

man.[25] Sawyer also didn't hesitate to leave his firm's well-appointed law offices and head for the streets during the civil rights clashes of the mid-1960s. He went to the South to defend black people who were registering to vote and others who were being prosecuted for allegedly violating a variety of local laws.[26]

Mann was out of the impending Schempp lawsuit as ACLU legal counsel, having handed it off to Sawyer. But Mann also wore another hat, working as an officer for the local chapter of the American Jewish Congress. Although he had batted the Schempp matter back and forth with Pfeffer and Polier, he still thought it possible to enlist the AJ Congress's help. Now that the ACLU had definitely decided to proceed in federal court, Mann thought Pfeffer might want to affiliate the AJ Congress with this cause so that he could maintain some influence. So Mann wrote to Polier in August 1957, noting that the local chapter had voted to support the litigation. "It would seem to me that we should have a voice in the direction of the suit from the very beginning," he wrote.[27] Not having received an answer, he followed up with Pfeffer in November.[28] On December 27, as he put the final touches on the Schempp complaint, Mann wrote once again to Pfeffer, asking him for any legal briefs and memos that might be helpful. "Both Henry Sawyer and Wayland Elsbree consider you the foremost authority on the subject and would greatly respect any material prepared by you," he wrote.[29] Elsbree, an attorney, a member of the local ACLU's Freedom of Expression Committee, and the editor of the *Legal Intelligencer* (a local legal publication), was assisting Sawyer on the case.

Finally, on March 27, more than a month after Sawyer filed the lawsuit, Pfeffer announced that the AJ Congress would not become involved in the case either by cosponsoring the suit or by submitting an amicus brief. Pfeffer conceded, "I was, however, authorized to render my personal assistance in an informal and unpublicized way if I should be so requested by the attorneys."[30] On April 15, Pfeffer wrote to Polier expressing his disappointment with the *Schempp* case. "I am happy," he wrote, "to see that the gravamen of the complaint is not merely Bible reading but also recitation of the Lord's Prayer.

Nevertheless, I still think it was a serious mistake (a) to bring this suit in the Federal courts and (b) to bring it in behalf of a Unitarian. I think it would be highly desirable if a similar suit sponsored by AJ Congress in behalf of a Jewish parent and, if possible, also a Catholic parent, could be brought in a Pennsylvania State court."[31]

↝

As 1957 ended and 1958 rolled around, the complaint that would initiate the lawsuit against the Abington school district was finally ready to go. Any evidence of Theodore Mann's authorship of the legal papers disappeared from the final documents submitted to the court. The lawyers of record, those who signed the complaint, were Sawyer and Elsbree. Of the two, Sawyer was entirely in control of the case, formulating the litigation strategy and making all the arguments in court. In fact, many years later, participants in the case don't remember Elsbree well, if at all.

The complaint was filed on February 14, 1958, almost fifteen months after Ellery Schempp had protested in his homeroom class. Ellery was by then finishing up his senior year, and it appeared almost certain that he would be gone from the high school before the case even reached trial. Had Ellery been the sole plaintiff, the fact of his graduation would almost certainly have caused the judge to dismiss the case for mootness. In order for a court to proceed with a case, including a challenge to the constitutionality of a state statute, there must be a controversy that affects the rights of the parties. Once Ellery graduated from Abington Senior High, the controversy as to his right to be free from religious practices in the public schools would certainly have ended, and no ruling by the court could have affected his constitutional rights or provided him with any specific relief. Thus, Ellery's siblings became critical to the lawsuit. Donna was then in seventh grade, and Roger was in eighth, and they would remain in the Abington schools while the lawsuit slowly spun through a typical course of three to five years in the court system. So, when the papers were filed, the plaintiffs of record were Edward and

Sidney Schempp, who were suing both individually and as the parents of Ellery and his two younger siblings. The defendants named in the lawsuit were the Abington school district and several officers of the district, including the principal, Eugene Stull, and the school superintendent, O. H. English.

By carrying out the mandate of Pennsylvania's 1949 statute requiring Bible reading, Sawyer complained, the Abington school authorities deprived Ellery and his siblings of "certain rights, privileges and immunities secured by the Constitution of the United States." More specifically, Sawyer alleged that the school district officials "have violated and continue to violate the religious conscience and liberties" of Ellery Schempp and his siblings. Mann made the same complaint concerning the school district's requirement that students recite the Lord's Prayer, although no Pennsylvania law mandated this practice. As for Edward and Sidney Schempp, the complaint charged that the devotional practices "interfere with their right to give their children a religious education of their own choosing and according to their own beliefs, and that certain beliefs are fostered by such practices which are contradictory to what they have taught and intend to teach their children."[32]

The complaint then asked that the court declare the Pennsylvania statue and the devotional practices to be unconstitutional in violation of the Fourteenth Amendment to the U.S. Constitution. Alleging a violation of the Fourteenth Amendment was necessary because the religious freedom guarantees of the First Amendment originally applied only to actions by the federal government. It was the Fourteenth Amendment that eventually made the religion clauses applicable to Pennsylvania and the other states. Finally, the complaint asked the judges to stop the Abington schools from carrying out the religious exercises.[33]

୫

Once the complaint was filed in court, marshals delivered it to the individual defendants. Percival R. Rieder, an Abington lawyer who served the school board, understood that this case involved quite a bit more than the everyday questions of contracts, wage negotiations, and other matters that engage school board counsel on a weekly basis. Before Ellery Schempp came along, a lawsuit alleging violation of First Amendment religious freedoms must have seemed to Rieder about as likely an event as the earth opening up and swallowing Abington's new high school. But Ellery Schempp was there, and now the lawsuit was as well. Rieder, then, had to call in lawyers with the depth, experience, and resources to fight such a battle.

Rieder turned the case over to C. Brewster Rhoads, a senior partner in the old patrician Philadelphia law firm Montgomery, McCracken, Walker and Rhoads. Then sixty-five years old and nearing the end of a career of more than four decades, Rhoads not only was one of the brightest lights of the local bar but also enjoyed a national reputation. He was a graduate of the University of Pennsylvania and Harvard Law School and had been awarded four battle stars for his service abroad as a lieutenant in a field artillery unit during World War I. He had served a term as president of the Union League of Philadelphia, a private club for the city's elite in law, business, and other fields. An Episcopalian, he had already served as chancellor of the Philadelphia Bar Association. After the *Schempp* case, he would become president of the state bar association.

Assisting Rhoads on the case was a younger partner, Philip H. Ward III, then thirty-seven years old. Despite the nearly thirty years that separated them, the two men had much in common. Both had graduated from the William Penn Charter School, one of the private secondary academies long known for educating the children of Philadelphia's elite. Both were Ivy League in their undergraduate and law degrees. Ward had graduated from Princeton University and then, like Rhoads, had earned his law degree from Harvard. Also like Rhoads, Ward was a much-decorated veteran, having served in World War II as an artillery officer in the Pacific, where he was awarded the Silver Star, the Bronze Star, and the Purple Heart. Both Rhoads and Ward were Episcopalians, and both were Republicans. Ward followed his mentor to membership in the Union League of

Philadelphia and then went a step further, becoming, by the time the *Schempp* case reached the U.S. Supreme Court, chairman of the Committee of Seventy, a nonpartisan watchdog group that focused on good government issues in Philadelphia and surrounding towns.

Abington's lawyers went to work, for every legal complaint must be met within a specified period of time by an answer, the legal document in which the defendants respond to every numbered paragraph of the complaint, either admitting or denying the facts and allegations as presented by the plaintiff. On April 25, about ten weeks after Sawyer filed the complaint, Rhoads submitted his papers for the defendants. The filings in most lawsuits reveal serious disagreement between the parties on key factual matters, and the lawyers may spend weeks at trial trying to establish a record, through witnesses and documents, that will convince the jury of facts favorable to their case. But in this case, Rhoads admitted the critical facts of the complaint but disputed the legal allegations and conclusions that Sawyer had drawn from them. Yes, Rhoads admitted on behalf of the school district, the students heard ten verses of the King James Bible read without comment each morning before the commencement of classes. Yes, after the Bible reading, the students rose from the seats and recited the Lord's Prayer, although Rhoads said that they were not compelled to do so. Rhoads fundamentally disagreed, however, with Sawyer's complaint on the larger issue raised by the religious observances in the Abington public schools, and it was on this larger issue that the battle was joined. To Sawyer's charge that the Abington school district had violated the rights to religious freedom of Ellery Schempp and his siblings under the Constitution of the United States, Rhoads emphatically gave his answer: "Denied."[34]

5. The Colonists Unite Church and State

With the complaint and answer filed in the U.S. district court, Ellery Schempp's protest had started its long way through the American judicial system. Ultimately, it would end up, as with many disputes that divide American society, before the nine justices of the Supreme Court of the United States. They would have to decide how the First Amendment applied to two of the things that citizens hold most dear, their religion and their public schools.

The First Amendment's terse language said nothing at all about Bible reading in the schools, and the Supreme Court had never before spoken on the question. The *Schempp* case, though, did not arrive unannounced, like a meteor burning brightly through the atmosphere. Just as the *Brown* case a few years earlier had bound critical threads of the nation's history of race relations, so Ellery's protest promised to tie historical strands that were there if one knew where to look.

The first strand was the nation's guarantees of religious freedom. It was not so obvious in the 1950s how the guarantees might apply in specific conflicts—the Court had heard only a few religion cases. But it was clear that the framers of the Constitution had regarded the guarantees as a kind of antidote to the excessive zeal that had plunged Europe for more than a millennium into bloody religious conflict. The new nation had experienced its own instances of religious persecution, including riots and death. By the time of *Schempp*, the prospect of sectarian fights over the public schools was on the minds of many, including the justices.

Another strand concerned the nature of the public schools themselves. They had started centuries earlier as private institutions that taught colonial children a religious curriculum. But they had evolved into public institutions with usually little more than Bible reading and the Lord's Prayer to remind people of the way things had been done in the past.

Finally, and perhaps most important of all, religious pluralism had placed its foot heavily on the scale of American history, changing everything. If the schools had moved away from their roots in religious teaching, it was because the nation had evolved from homogeneous Anglican and Congregationalist colonies to a rich mix of hundreds of Christian and non-Christian denominations. Pluralism had brought conflict over whose religious tradition should be taught in the schools. Many Americans had learned since the mid-nineteenth century that the only way to live together peaceably in their communities was to employ democratic processes that removed devotional practices from the public schools and transformed them into secular institutions whose "religion" was citizenship and civic responsibility. At Abington Senior High School and most other public schools in America, Bible readings, recitation of the Lord's Prayer, and holiday celebrations were about all that was left of a bygone era.

For those who pushed for ratification of the Bill of Rights, the religion guarantees of the First Amendment would help prevent the evils of excessive religious zeal, a concept that would reverberate in the *Schempp* case centuries later. European states had enforced religious conformity by fire and sword. For more than three centuries following the birth of Jesus, followers of the new Christian religion surrendered their lives to martyrdom. Eusebius, the bishop of Caesarea who lived from about 260 to 339 AD, described the horrendous deaths suffered by Christians in cities throughout the Mediterranean region. Eusebius wrote that people were beheaded, crucified, starved to death, and thrown into the sea. "Need I rekindle the memory of the martyrs at Antioch," he asked, "who were roasted over lighted braziers, not roasted to death but subjected to prolonged torture?" Their torturers put eyes out, pierced their nails with sharp reeds, and poured molten lead down their backs. Eusebius continued: "Others again were tied to trees and stumps and died horribly; for with the aid of machinery they drew together the very stoutest boughs, fastened one of the martyr's legs to each, and then let the boughs fly back to their normal position; thus they managed to tear apart the limbs of their victims in a moment." That wasn't all, Eusebius reported: "Some of the victims suffered death by beheading, others punishment by fire. So many were killed on a single day that the axe, blunted and worn out by the slaughter, was broken in pieces, while the exhausted executioners had to be periodically relieved."[1]

In Rome, Nero played the death of Christians as a blood sport, ordering them slaughtered in the arena and often set afire, "so that when darkness fell they burned like torches in the night."[2] Finally, history changed forever for the Christians when Constantine conquered Rome in 312 AD and proclaimed a year later that Christians and others could worship freely.[3] By 380, Christianity had become the preferred or established faith of the empire. That year, three emperors proclaimed, in what became part of the Theodosian Code, that the people should "practice that religion which the divine apostle Peter transmitted to the Romans."[4]

Thus Christianity and the state were joined for the first time in a marriage of faith to secular power. But the special privileges that might come from this union—financial support, for example, or exemptions from various public duties—proved too poor a reward. Christians wanted more than privilege; they believed their faith was the only true way and that it was right and wise to use the power of the state to punish those who raised their voices to a different God. Christians would do unto others what had been done to them. The new union of the state and Christianity, adopted all over Europe, unleashed a fury of intolerance on those who dared worship by their own conscience. Now it was time to root out heretics. On his consecration as bishop of Constantinople in 428, Nestorius made it clear that the newly ascendant church welcomed the assistance of the state. He directed his sermon at Emperor Theodosius II: "Give me, my Prince, the earth purged of heretics, and I will give you heaven as a recompense. Assist me in destroying heretics, and I will assist you in vanquishing the Persians."[5]

The pagans and Jews suffered first under the new union of church and state. Under the Theodosian Code, those who did not become Christians were adjudged "demented and insane." The Roman government denied all privileges to "heretics and schismatics."[6] If the persecution of heretics had been lethal but haphazard through the twelfth century, it became a relentless and systematic pursuit early in the thirteenth, with the start of the Inquisition. Most medieval European states provided in their penal code for the burning alive of criminals. Until then, the church had officially frowned on executions as a punishment for heretics. But it would soon itself slide into the abyss of capital punishment, for what it defined as breaches of faith as the Catholic Church itself defined faith. In 1231, Pope Gregory IX expanded the definition of heresy to include opposition to papal declaration, blasphemy, and sacrilege. Finally, Innocent IV declared in 1252 his approval of torture. In his empowerment of the Inquisition judges, he said that "bodily torture has ever been found the most salutary and efficient means of leading to spiritual repentance."[7]

Heretics, though, were not the biggest problem for the church. It was the distribution of copies of the Scriptures to the common man, a new challenge to the pope's and the clergy's grip on exclusive possession of God's word. These copies, wrote historian Brian Moynahan, "were profoundly dangerous weapons" that revealed the gap between the actual text and the interpretation provided by church leaders—interpretations used to validate persecutions. With a Bible in their hands, literate people could look for meaning in the text themselves without having to accept the interpretation of church elders. What readers found missing from the Scriptures was any provision for the existence of a church hierarchy, for the papal treasures, or even for the papacy itself.[8]

When Martin Luther nailed his ninety-five theses to the church door at Wittenberg in 1517, the Reformation was under way in earnest. The ideas of Luther, John Calvin, and other reformers spread throughout Europe, gaining millions of adherents as they challenged the church at every turn. As Protestants and Catholics faced off against each other, religious wars and persecutions swept Europe with a ferocity that put religion, the state, and intolerance in a fatal embrace. In Germany, the forces of Catholicism and Lutheranism reached a temporary truce with the Peace of Augsburg in 1555. Each of the German princes assumed the right to declare which of the two faiths would become the religion established by his state.[9]

The lethal cocktail of religious intolerance and political machinations continued unabated elsewhere and indeed returned later to Germany. Centuries of conflict devastated the continent of Europe. The madness reached its peak in the Thirty Years' War, fought from 1618 until the Peace of Westphalia in 1648. Armies roamed Europe like a plague of locusts, exacting some of the worst destruction—pillaging, raping, and killing—not on opposing armies but on innocent civilians. The population of some cities and countries declined by a third or more by war, disease, and deprivation. In the end, as Europe bled to exhaustion, the secular princes were left to decide which religion would reign supreme in their land.[10] The rulers of France and Spain chose Roman Catholicism. The rest chose a denomination of Protestantism: Germany and the countries of Scandinavia chose the Lutheran Church; and Scotland, Switzerland, and the Low Countries officially adopted Reformed Protestantism.[11]

England under King Henry VIII rejected the papacy by law in 1534 in favor of the Church of England and later adopted the Book of Common Prayer, which everyone in the country was bound to follow. Eventually, Parliament declared that no Catholic could ever ascend to the English throne.[12] Meanwhile, however, for many religious dissenters, especially Protestants who felt that England had not fully divorced itself from the Catholic Church, memories of burnings and beheadings hung too heavily in the air. They feared that they would persist indefinitely as a persecuted religious minority under the thumb of an established national church whose doctrine and ceremonies they could not tolerate.

While the Puritans had always tried to reform the Anglican Church from within, another group wanted to start all over by building their own church from the ground up. These Separatists, or Pilgrims, felt that the Anglican Church would never fully purify itself. In 1620, Separatists boarded the Mayflower and set sail for northern Virginia. Their boats caught a wind that carried them instead to the rocky shores of Plymouth, Massachusetts, and to the freedom they required to build their own church, safe from persecution by any civil authority. So began the American story of church and state. America's founding generation would feel the tremors of European intolerance underfoot many years later and half a world away.

ᢙ

When the Puritans themselves settled north of Plymouth and started the Massachusetts Bay Colony a decade later, they modified the Anglican faith to forge something different enough to become their own Congregationalist Church. The power of the church lay, they believed, in its congregation and ministers, not in an archbishop and king. They rejected the Book of Common Prayer and subscribed to a rigid piety taken, they said, from God as revealed in the Bible. They believed in a strict observance of the Sabbath and a moral discipline that tolerated weakness neither of the flesh nor of the mind.[13]

The framers of the First Amendment understood that the dissenters from the Church of England founded the Massachusetts Bay Colony for their own religious liberty, not for anyone else's. Their frontier colony, like England and the rest of Europe, united church and state and attempted to impose religious uniformity on all its citizens. Looking unfortunately backward toward the land they had left, the Puritans even hanged a few of their own dissenters on the Boston Common. One Quaker, Mary Dyer, was expelled from

Boston and told she would be executed if she returned. When she returned in 1660, she was hanged for both her impertinence and her apostasy.[14]

This zeal that marked the union of church and state in Europe now followed most of the colonists who settled up and down the Atlantic seaboard. Five of the thirteen colonies—Maryland, Virginia, Georgia, North Carolina, and South Carolina—grew from the genetic rootstock of European unions of church and state, which involved elevating one denomination to the status of official church within their realm and requiring citizens to belong to that church and to support it. In the same way, each of the five colonies established the Anglican Church as its exclusive state church, discriminating against citizens of all other faiths. Maryland, at least, did pass its Act of Toleration of 1649, possibly the first law protecting religious freedom—at least religious freedom for all Christians. But an Anglican establishment soon followed.

In the other eight American colonies, though, citizens and politicians chose a more diverse approach to church and state. Leonard W. Levy, one of the most prominent First Amendment historians, has pointed out that rather than elevating one religious denomination to the status of state church, four colonies gave preferred status to multiple churches or even to Protestantism in general, and four others provided broad religious freedom.[15]

Though overwhelmingly Congregationalist, Massachusetts was one of the colonies with a complex relationship between church and state. In 1692, an act of the General Court did not formally establish the Congregationalist Church as the official church of the colony. Instead, it required each town's voters to choose a minister who would be supported by all taxpayers—the local town option. Theoretically, at least, this local option could produce government support for a minister of whatever faith controlled each town and, thus, was potentially an establishment of multiple churches throughout the colony. In fact, as Leonard Levy found, Baptists formed the majority in the small town of Swansea and thus established their two Baptist churches as the recipients of taxpayer money there. Since Congregationalists dominated the colony, though, they knew that the practical consequence of the law's passage would be widespread state support of their faith. The state's largest city, Boston, stood exempt from the law, so minority faiths there did not have to support the dominant Congregationalist Church.[16]

In neighboring Connecticut, the Congregationalists also dominated politics and religion. A 1697 law provided, as in Massachusetts, a local town option for using taxes to support the leading church. In 1727, though, the legislature created a dual establishment by enabling Anglicans to have their taxes rebated to support their own clergy under certain conditions. The expanding Anglican population built fourteen churches by the middle of the century. This dual establishment of religion by the state, a departure from the experience in Europe, nonetheless carried forward some of the key characteristics of European establishments—mandatory attendance at services and mandatory taxes to support the churches themselves. New Hampshire, too, enacted a law in 1693 that put into place the local town option, enabling Protestants of whatever denomination to establish the town church. Congregationalists dominated the colony, but eventually the Presbyterians established their church in Bedford and Londonderry. In several other towns, there were dual establishments.[17]

Colonial New York was another colony with multiple establishments of religion. After their conquest in 1664, the English ended the exclusive establishment of the Dutch Reformed Church and empowered townships to support any Protestant church. Instructions from the English crown that only the Church of England be established began decades of bickering between Anglicans and other Protestants over taxpayer support of churches. In the end, a provincial court ruled in a dispute in 1731 that the Presbyterians could raise taxpayer money for their own church and minister in Jamaica, Queens, thereby confirming the multiple-establishment model by judicial fiat.[18]

The other four of the original thirteen colonies—Rhode Island, Pennsylvania, New Jersey, and Delaware—separated church and state and extended religious liberty to their inhabitants from the beginning. These colonies thus embraced a model that, if not perfect in its protection of the liberty of conscience, at least foreshadowed the religious liberty that would spread in the years ahead.[19]

With the Puritans of the Massachusetts Bay Colony cracking down hard on religious dissenters, the most significant exile from Boston was Roger Williams. A Puritan minister who arrived in Boston in 1631, Williams became one of the first to challenge Puritan authority in the Massachusetts Bay Colony. Williams had many complaints about the Puritan way. He believed that the Puritans had diverged too sharply from the Church of England to remain within its ambit and that it was unwise to repeat the mother country's union of church and state that had unleashed so much misery for so long. The reward for Williams's dissent was his banishment from the colony in 1635 by the General Court. So Williams walked south from his home in the dead of winter to what would become Rhode Island and there founded the city of Providence.

The banishment of Williams proved to be one of the great turning points for religious freedom in America. Unlike almost all of the dissenting Protestants who came before him both in Europe and the New World, Williams actually believed in religious freedom not only for himself but also for others. In his treatment of other dissenters was a glimpse of a new idea about church and state that would help define liberty in a new nation.

Williams started a new church in Providence, apart from the Church of England, and initiated a "livelie experiment" in religious freedom that involved the separation of church and state. Williams believed that Christians breached their faith if they persecuted others for their religious beliefs. In 1644, he published his *Bloudy Tenent of Persecution*, baldly stating that "the blood of so many hundred thousand souls of Protestants and Papists, spilt in the wars of present and former ages, for their respective consciences, is not required nor accepted by Jesus Christ the Prince of Peace."[20]

Like Rhode Island, Pennsylvania was another haven of religious liberty. William Penn joined the Society of Friends, or Quakers, in 1667 and became a minister, preaching for converts and attacking the

Anglican Church. Imprisoned for his beliefs, Penn developed a deep commitment to religious freedom and wrote a treatise on the subject in 1670. He negotiated for a large tract of land west of the Delaware River (in discharge of a debt that King Charles II owed to his father) and established a colony there in 1682. Not only did Penn's colony immediately become a refuge for Quakers; he pledged freedom for all in matters of faith.[21]

Immigrants of many persuasions soon accepted Penn's invitation to enjoy the liberty of conscience. Nowhere else in colonial America was there such quick development of the diversity of faiths and cultures that would later indelibly mark the entire nation. In addition to the Quakers, German Lutherans and German Reformed Protestants poured into Philadelphia and the surrounding area. The Amish and Mennonite people settled Lancaster County. Moravians, Scotch-Irish Presbyterians, Seventh-day Baptists, and Welsh Baptists found refuge there. Into this Protestant mix came Jews and Roman Catholics as well.[22] America had planted the seeds for a future much different than Europe's.

6. How Religious Diversity Changed America

On the eve of the Revolutionary War, most of the colonies boasted churches supported by law and thus had not broken free of their European past on matters of conscience. Nine of the colonies had elevated one or more denominations to be the established church within their realm. These churches were supported by taxes raised specifically for that purpose and by discrimination of various kinds against those who worshiped differently or not at all.

Throughout the colonies, though, and often below the surface, a swift current already was moving. New waves of immigrants were coming ashore with different ways of worshiping God. The Anglicans and the Congregationalists soon had to share the land with many others of different faiths. As immigration increased diversity, so, too, did growing factionalism among the groups already in America. Groups broke off from the older churches to start their own denominations, adding to religious pluralism.

The growing diversity of the colonies and, later, the nation itself would profoundly shape the direction of religious freedom and of the religious curriculum of the early schools. The great melting pot, just getting under way in the colonial period, would eventually consist of so much diversity of belief that no denomination would be strong enough to sustain an establishment of its faith as either a state or a national church. The new faiths in America needed religious freedom in order to throw off the established churches and grow their own denominations. Their alliance with such constitutional framers as

Madison and Jefferson helped realize religious liberty in Virginia and then helped in ratification of the First Amendment guarantees. Religious freedom, in turn, encouraged broader diversity. This broader diversity would eventually make it inevitable that people of different faiths would have to agree to remove religion from the public schools or else remain in perpetual conflict over whose prayers, whose Bibles, and whose symbols would reach impressionable children.

‍‍

Neither of the two dominant groups, the Congregationalists in New England and the Anglicans in the South, could turn back the strong tide of diversity that began to engulf their religious establishments. Pennsylvania and Rhode Island, the two colonies that most openly proclaimed religious freedom, were not alone in seeing an onrush of people of various faiths. The Anglicans enjoyed an established church and some sixty parishes in Virginia by 1700, with restrictive laws against dissenters, yet a variety of other denominations still made inroads into the colony. Baptists, Methodists, and Presbyterians all entered the state, settling largely on the western frontier.[1] Maryland, although an Anglican royal colony, had originally been settled under the proprietorship of a Catholic family and remained the center of Catholicism in the colonial period up to the Revolutionary War. Maryland was also home to about half of all the Methodists in colonial America by the time of the war.[2]

Farther south, the Anglican establishments in the Carolinas and Georgia tolerated many other denominations. Huguenots, or French Protestants, fled to South Carolina by 1700 and were joined there by Baptists, Congregationalists, and Presbyterians. In North Carolina, other denominations overwhelmed the officially established Anglican Church. There were more Baptist churches than Anglican in North Carolina by midcentury, and the colony also boasted ample numbers of Moravians, Quakers, Presbyterians, and German Reformed Protestants.[3] In Georgia, Lutherans, Jews, Scottish Presbyterians, and Moravians coexisted with the established Church of England.[4]

Diversity also came through the birth of new denominations. By 1740, the Congregationalists had more than four hundred churches and dominated the religious life of New England, but their power had reached its peak. What challenged the old Puritan hegemony in New England was a strong movement of religious revival. The Great Awakening swept through New England and all the colonies from around 1730 to the Revolution, forever changing the course of faith in America. Church worship had long since assumed a passive formalism, but with the Great Awakening came a resurgence of personal piety. Jonathan Edwards, a New England theologian, argued that an emotional commitment from the heart would bring a person to a spiritual transformation.[5]

With this birth of evangelicalism in America, preachers traveled the countryside delivering emotional sermons at outdoor revivals, reminding the faithful that they teetered on the edge of an abyss marked by fire and eternal damnation. Faith became an intense personal experience, far removed from the quiet solemnity of the church pew, as preachers brought fire and brimstone down on fearful parishioners who shrieked in response and sometimes fainted outright.

Although the Great Awakening renewed the spiritual commitment of many people, it sharply divided the Anglican churches in New England and eventually helped to dissipate their monopoly of religious power. It was through the evangelical movement that the Baptist and Methodist denominations flourished throughout the colonies, soon enough overwhelming—with their number of adherents—both of the old-line Anglican and Congregationalist traditions. Gospel preaching reached the South and brought enormous growth to the Baptist and Methodist faiths. Many Congregationalist churches in New England saw revivalism as a return to traditional Puritan practice and actually migrated to Baptist affiliation. The Great Awakening was, according to historian Sydney E. Ahlstrom, "an apocalyptic outburst within the standing order, a challenge to established authority."[6]

With so many religious denominations afoot in the land, support for religious freedom came of necessity. Many sects vied to recruit people for conversion to their faith, while others simply wanted to practice their traditions without harassment by the state. Whatever their goals, the one thing that all the nonestablished denominations had in common was the need for the liberty of conscience that would enable them to worship their god as they saw fit. Sidney Mead argues that the various churches "all were practically unanimous on one point: each wanted freedom for itself." Mead explains that "by this time it had become clear that the only way to get it for themselves was to grant it to all others."[7]

The evangelical sects that helped bring religious diversity to the colonies aided America's thrust toward religious freedom. It was an odd coupling indeed that brought the evangelical sects of the Great Awakening into alliance with deist statesmen, such as Thomas Jefferson and James Madison. Though all of them were Christians, miles of difficult ground separated the evangelicals from the deists. On the issue of freedom of conscience, however, they found a common purpose.

Products of the Enlightenment (i.e., followers of Locke and the concept of natural law), the deists believed that God ruled the universe and the affairs of humans, but they thought that creeds, dogmas, and ecclesiastical authority were the source of much of the world's mischief. Deists generally believed, in opposition to many Christian denominations, that humans received salvation through their deeds, virtue, and benevolence, rather than through faith in God and Scriptures alone.

Madison, Jefferson, and other deists gathered their strength from John Locke and other great moral philosophers of the Enlightenment. In 1688, Locke, a theologian and political theorist, wrote his influential *A Letter concerning Toleration,* in which he clearly grasped the dual nature of religious freedom—the separation of church and state into separate realms and the right of all to practice their beliefs free of state control. "I esteem it above all things necessary to distinguish exactly the business of civil government from that of religion and to settle the just bounds that lie between the one and the other," Locke wrote. "If this not be done, there can be no end put to the controversies that will be always arising between those that have, or at least pretend to have, on the one side, a concernment for the interest of men's souls, and, on the other side, a care of the commonwealth." What was the proper role of civil authority? Locke argued that the government had no power to compel the use of any ceremonies of worship: "The only business of the Church is the salvation of souls, and it no way concerns the commonwealth, or any member of it, that this or the other ceremony be there made use of."[8]

Locke was very much on the minds of Jefferson and Madison during a critical decade in which Virginia became the first state to end its official church. With its established Anglican Church and its repressive measures against religious dissenters, Virginia looked to many citizens like it was subject to much of the same kind of excessive religious zeal that had repressed Europe for an age. Although more than half of the colony's population was comprised of dissenters of various sects, they were required by law to attend Anglican services. Baptist ministers suffered imprisonment and whippings.

Then began a peaceful revolution that created religious liberty in Virginia and provided the model for the similar guarantees written into the First Amendment just a few years later. In 1776, Virginia adopted its Declaration of Rights as part of its new constitution, a provision of which stated that "all men are equally entitled to the free exercise of religion according to the dictates of conscience; and that it is the mutual duty of all to practice Christian forbearance, love, and charity towards each other." In December 1776, with Baptists, Lutherans, and Presbyterians lobbying hard for an official end to the establishment, the legislature ended all punishment of heresy and no longer required the dissenters to pay taxes in support of the Episcopalian Church, which had succeeded the Anglican Church of England after ties with England were broken by the Revolution.[9]

Although a major step, it wasn't enough to completely sever state support of religion. The dissenters wanted the end of forced taxation in support of any religion, including their own. The showdown over freedom of conscience in Virginia came in 1784, when Patrick Henry introduced his bill for a general assessment of Virginia taxpayers for support of teachers of the "Christian religion." In the preamble, Henry justified his bill without reference to religious doctrine of any kind; his bill was justified, he wrote, because "the general diffusion of Christian knowledge hath a natural tendency to correct the morals of men, restrain their vices, and preserve the peace of society; which cannot be effected without a competent provision for learned teachers."

Making handwritten notes as he prepared to oppose the bill, James Madison wondered how judges would resolve the myriad theological questions that would arise under Henry's bill if it became law. His concerns eerily foreshadowed the questions that would be asked two centuries later when judges grappled with Ellery Schempp's challenge to Bible reading in the public schools. Which version of the Bible should be used, and whose interpretation should be conveyed? "What clue is to guide Judge thro' this labyrinth?" Madison asked.[10]

Henry's bill had expressly included all Christian sects and said that all were equal before the law. His bill would have amounted to a multiple establishment of religion in the state of Virginia— specifically, the establishment of all the Christian denominations through the support of taxation. Although the dissenters against the old Anglican establishment would have been included in this new order, most of them, including the Baptists and Presbyterians, vociferously opposed it.

Madison's legal maneuvering and political arguments eventually carried the day. He managed to delay consideration of the bill until late 1785 and helped Henry get elected governor, thus removing him from the very place where he could be at the greatest advantage in advancing his bill.[11] But Madison's greatest contribution to the defeat of the general assessment was his authorship of what would become recognized as one of the most influential documents for religious liberty in world history. His *Memorial and Remonstrance against Religious Assessments* articulated the dual nature of religious liberty that would soon be guaranteed not only in Virginia but also in the First Amendment.

In his *Remonstrance,* Madison referred several times to the "free exercise of religion"—the same phrase as would appear in the First Amendment—and argued that each person's religion "must be left to the conviction and conscience of every man; and it is the right of every man to exercise it as these may dictate. This right is in its nature an unalienable right." The entire *Remonstrance* was a rejection of the establishment of religion. As to civil society, Madison argued, "Religion is wholly exempt from its cognizance." Madison said that the verdict of history backed his assertions on establishment of religion: "During almost fifteen centuries has the legal establishment of Christianity been on trial. What have been its fruits? More or less in all places, pride and indolence in the Clergy, ignorance and servility in the laity, in both, superstition, bigotry and persecution."[12]

The opposition to Henry's assessment bill produced a stunning victory for religious freedom. The Virginia legislature refused to pass Henry's bill. Instead, it enacted Thomas Jefferson's Bill for Establishing Religious Freedom. The new law guaranteed that Virginians would not be required to support any religious group and would not otherwise endure any burdens because of their beliefs. Rather, they would be able to maintain their religious beliefs, which would "in no wise diminish, enlarge, or affect their civil capacities."[13] Virginians now enjoyed religious liberties that would soon be written into the First Amendment.

One by one, all of the states that had maintained establishments of religion began doing away with them in the years after the Revolution. But political battles raged in many of the states. As Leonard Levy has pointed out, six states replaced their earlier single or dual establishments of religion with multiple establishments before doing away with them altogether.[14] The growth of dissident Protestant sects that opposed the existing Anglican and Congregationalist establishments—and, in fact, any establishments at all—doomed the possibility of any continued union between church and state. Massachusetts, the home of the Puritans, became the last state to end its religious establishment, when its voters approved an amendment to the state constitution in 1833.[15]

ᘐᖚᐧ

The delegates to the U.S. Constitutional Convention were men from the Roman Catholic Church and from all the major Protestant sects then in the country, except for the Baptist sect. So diverse was the assembly and so far into the process of disestablishment were most of the states, argues historian Anson Phelps Stokes, that there was no chance of the convention ever elevating one denomination to the status of national church. That "is one reason why the First Amendment must be interpreted more broadly than merely as preventing the state establishment of religion which had already been made almost impossible," writes Stokes.[16]

This diverse assemblage wrote only a few references to religion into the U.S. Constitution in 1787. On August 20 of that year, Charles Pinckney of South Carolina, a state that had endured an Anglican establishment, moved to ban any religious tests or qualifications as a condition of holding federal office. The delegates unanimously passed his proposal, and it became part of Article VI of the Constitution.[17] In his *Commentaries on the Constitution*, Joseph Story, a leading constitutional scholar of the nineteenth century, wrote that the ban reflected more than opposition to religious tests: "It had a higher object: to cut off forever every pretense of any alliance between church and state in the national government."[18]

In the same paragraph of Article VI, the delegates also required officeholders to take an oath or an affirmation to support the Constitution. Oaths normally made reference to the deity, but affirmations did not. The delegates weren't concerned about showing sensitivity to atheists or agnostics but did understand that there were then some Protestant sects in the country—Quakers, Mennonites, and Moravians—who objected to oaths as violations of biblical requirements.[19]

The absence of religion in the Constitution had a much deeper political meaning. The Constitution established a national government with certain specific powers enumerated in the document itself; in the absence of a specific grant, the new federal government lacked the power to legislate or otherwise act. Because the Constitution made no positive grant of power to the national government to act in matters of religion, the government could not constitutionally legislate any establishments or any religious assessments, nor could it enact any disabilities against particular sects or against religion in general. It was devoid of any such authority.

The proposed U.S. Constitution endured gale force winds when it landed in many of the thirteen state legislatures for ratification. Debate raged over the relative power of the national and state governments. The Anti-Federalists argued that the Constitution would bring on a tyranny reminiscent of the one they had just thrown off—that a strong central government would usurp state functions and that the failure of the Constitutional Convention to include a bill of rights within the document would inevitably lead to violations of individual rights and liberties. Madison did not oppose a bill of rights, but he thought, as did most Federalist leaders, that the federal government had not been granted the power to legislate on such matters as the freedoms of speech, press, and religion and so could not threaten individual liberty. In the end, a promise by Madison and other Federalists to produce a bill of rights soon after the new Congress assembled pushed some reluctant states to ratify the new Constitution, bringing the government into being. Massachusetts, New York, Virginia, and three other states of the original thirteen ratified the Constitution with calls for amendments, many protecting individual rights.[20]

Good to his word, Madison introduced amendments to the Constitution on June 8, 1789, at the first session of the nation's First Congress. As consideration of the amendments continued during the summer and into the fall, some committee work was shrouded in secrecy, while other deliberations were poorly reported—a situation that would plague the Supreme Court centuries later as it tried to interpret the constitutional provisions. Congress approved amendments to the Constitution, collectively known as the Bill of Rights, and ratification was completed in 1791.

The First Amendment—originally the third amendment, before the first two failed passage—provided two protections for religious liberty: "Congress shall make no law respecting an establishment of religion, or prohibiting the free exercise thereof." While the First Amendment left each state free to act as it wished subject to its own constitution, the federal government was prohibited from supporting religion or from interfering with a person's right to exercise his or her own religious beliefs. It would be more than a century and a half before the U.S. Supreme Court would begin to say what those two guarantees for the liberty of conscience actually meant.

꒱

The diversity of religious sects and their demand for the end of established churches propelled Virginia and then the country toward a fateful decision on religious freedom. In turn, the constitutional guarantees themselves sparked a further expansion of religious pluralism that in the future would profoundly affect every aspect of American life, most especially religion in the nation's schools. It would be hard to exaggerate the significance of this break from the past.

In Europe and in nine of the thirteen colonies, the government and one or more religious denominations had allied themselves for mutual benefit. The government enjoyed the unity and stability that came with the majority of its citizens subscribing to the same set of beliefs and a single source of moral values. For its part, the church gained the power of the state's sword. It did not have to proselytize for adherents, because all citizens were compelled to belong. It did not have to urge attendance on Sunday, because the state required all to attend. It did not have to worry about raising funds, because the state taxed everyone on its behalf. Perhaps most significant, it did not have to worry about competitors, because the state persecuted dissenters.

When the United States adopted religious freedom, it set every denomination within its borders adrift from the state and required them to rely on their own wits for survival. This choice proved a seminal one in history, for it unleashed a torrent of energy that would remake the religious landscape of the young nation. At the time of the American Revolution, only 17 percent of the country's population had membership in a church.[21] The enormous number of unchurched people represented a major opportunity to spread the Gospel and to grow individual sects in size and influence. Without the government to help them, all the denominations were left to gain new adherents solely through the power of persuasion. So the denominations set about competing with each other to grow their churches and expand their influence. What emerged in the new nation was a free marketplace of religion, such as Western civilization had never seen.

Adam Smith, the great political economist, commented in *The Wealth of Nations* in 1776 that religious establishments and commercial monopolies of the eighteenth century shared many of the same characteristics. In countries with established churches, he said, the clergy need not compete to gain adherents, so they were "apt gradually to lose the qualities, both good and bad, which gave them authority and influence with the inferior ranks of people, and which had perhaps been the original causes of the success and establishment of their religion." These clergy were "perfectly defenceless" against the preaching of the new and more vigorous religious dissenters who learned to move aggressively to gain followers. "Such a clergy, upon such an emergency, have commonly no other resource than to call upon the civil magistrate to persecute, destroy, or drive out their adversaries, as disturbers of the public peace," wrote Smith. "It was thus that the Roman catholic clergy called upon the civil magistrate to persecute the protestants; and the church of England, to persecute the dissenters; and that in general every religious sect, when it has once enjoyed for a century or two the security of a legal establishment, has found itself incapable of making any vigorous defence against any new sect which chose to attack its doctrine or discipline." Had government and religion not united in the European countries, there was "no doubt" that there would be "a great multitude of religious sects," Smith argued. Each sect would compete for adherents instead of holding a monopoly in which the state compelled its citizens to fill the pews on Sundays.[22]

Once ingrained in the culture, vigorous competition among religious denominations seemed itself the best possible guarantee that the state would continue to respect the free marketplace of religion. With so many sects in competition, surely they would not allow the government to favor any one of them. James Madison believed that the wealth of religious denominations in America was the greatest guarantee of religious liberty. In Federalist Paper No. 51, published on February 6, 1788, Madison set out his ideas on how the new nation could avoid a tyranny of the majority and an abuse of rights. One answer lay in institutional design—in the checks and balances of the three branches of government and in the division of power between the states and the national government.

Madison believed that the structure of American society provided another potent safeguard. A variety of interests would check each other's power. He wrote, "Whilst all authority in it will be derived from, and dependent on the society, the society itself will be broken into so many parts, interests and classes of citizens, that the rights of individuals or of the minority, will be in little danger from interested combinations of the majority." Madison continued:

> In a free government, the security for civil rights must be the same as that for religious rights. It consists in the one case in the multiplicity of interests, and in the other, in the multiplicity of sects. The degree of security in both cases will depend on the number of interests and sects; and this may be presumed to depend on the extent of country and number of people comprehended under the same government.[23]

The number of sects continued to increase. As the Second Great Awakening began in the beginning of the nineteenth century, the evangelical sects that had fought for a place at the table next to the established Anglican Church and Congregationalist Church knew best how to convert the unaffiliated masses. The old established churches, long supported by state governments before the Revolution, proved little competition for the evangelicals. In Adam Smith's terms, the Anglican Church and the Congregationalist Church were state monopolies that knew little about how to compete against the upstart evangelical sects once deregulation came to the vast market of souls waiting to be saved.

The Second Great Awakening brought another wave of revivalism to America. To teach creed to the masses would have required too much patience at a time when the greatest priority was winning the largest number of people to God. So revivalists chose not to teach the complexities of doctrine to the common folk without faith. They depended instead on emotional appeals that painted a stark choice between heaven and hell.[24]

The Baptists and the Methodists led the expansion of Protestantism in America, especially throughout the South and the frontiers to the West. People converted in large numbers and then built churches for themselves. In 1780, there were only about thirty Methodist churches in America; the number of Methodist churches reached 2,700 by 1820 and 19,883 by 1861.[25] With religious freedom providing a strong tailwind, Protestant denominations spawned entirely new sects in the first half of the nineteenth century. Among these new sects were the Adventist Church (now the Seventh-day Adventists), the Disciples of Christ, the Church of Jesus Christ of Latter-day Saints, and the Universalists.[26]

At the same time, immigration continued to add to the religious diversity of the young nation. Unlike many of the first colonists, most of the immigrants in the nineteenth century and beyond were not so much seeking religious freedom as they were economic opportunity. The new nation offered immigrants, especially the poor of Europe, the chance to reinvent themselves, either in the growing cities or on the vast tracts of land as yet untouched by a plow. While the opportunity for religious freedom may not have been the primary motivation sending most immigrants to America, it's still true that their faiths flourished in the new land and that their presence there enlarged the scope of American religious diversity.

Immigration was relatively modest for the first thirty years after ratification of the First Amendment. About half a million people arrived in the United States from 1790 through 1820.[27] Shortly after that, though, the emigration from Ireland started, quickly bring a massive infusion of Catholicism to what had been primarily a Protestant population. Only 54,338 Irish came to America in the decade of 1820 to 1830, and 207,381 arrived in the following decade. Then came the potato blight. Although it had struck Ireland many times before, it returned in full fury in 1845 and for a few years thereafter. In the famine that followed, more than a million people perished. Many others emigrated—780,719 to the United States from 1841 to 1850, comprising 45.6 percent of the total immigration to the United States during that time; 914,119 people in the following decade, comprising 35.2 percent of the total of new arrivals. They kept coming in subsequent years, 4.5 million Irish in all from 1820 to 1930.[28]

Nothing challenged the ascendancy of Protestantism in America more than the rush of Irish Catholics. Once religiously homogeneous in Calvinist beliefs, New England—and Boston in particular—absorbed large numbers of Irish Catholics. By 1850, more than a third of Boston's population of 136,881 had been born abroad, and three-quarters of those people had come from Ireland. One-third of the city's working population in 1850 was Irish. A tiny sect of twenty-five thousand people in 1790, Roman Catholics grew into the largest denomination in the United States seventy years later, with about 3.5 million adherents.[29] The large number of Catholics who settled in New York, Philadelphia, and Cincinnati would, by midcentury and beyond, fight hard against Protestant influence in the public schools. Their pressure on the system would eventually force political compromises or, failing that, court cases that would in many instances remove religious ceremony from the schools. Catholic strength only increased with the start of a major emigration of Catholics from Italy. More than four million Italian immigrants arrived between 1880 and 1920.[30]

Another enormous tide of immigrants came from the areas that would become unified as Germany in 1871. Nearly six million people came from Germany to the United States between 1820 and 1924, with about two-thirds of them arriving in the four decades between 1851 and 1890. Although there were many Catholics among them, the predominant group was Lutheran. Many of these Lutherans,

though, found the existing Lutheran churches not to their liking—
English had replaced German in much or all of the service, and doctrine had been liberalized. So many of the new arrivals who preferred
a more conservative style dissented from the American Lutheranism
then in existence and formed the Missouri Synod.[31]

The great German emigration also included many people of the
Jewish faith. By late in the century, the origin of Jewish emigration
shifted largely from Germany to eastern European states, such as
Poland and Russia, as Jews scrambled to the United States to escape
persecution and poverty. From a quarter of a million Jews living in
the United States in 1880, the total swelled to about four million in
the 1920s, about three-fourths of them of eastern European origin.[32]
Few Jews were farmers, so most settled in the nation's largest cities,
adding diversity to the burgeoning public school population and
eventually putting Jews, along with Catholics, directly in conflict
with the Protestant orientation in the schools.

Religious diversity came from all directions. The Shakers moved
to America two years before the outbreak of the Revolution, with a
message that the Kingdom of God was at hand.[33] The Scandinavian
countries contributed more Lutherans to the United States. Armenian immigrants set up their first Armenian Apostolic parish in 1891 in
Massachusetts.[34] Greek immigrants came in large numbers in the
first two decades of the twentieth century—more than 350,000 in
all—and established their Orthodox churches.[35] From the East came
the first immigrants from China and Japan, bringing with them the
Taoist, Confucian, and Buddhist traditions, harbingers of a vast new
broadening of American cultural and religious diversity that would
flower much later.

If America was indeed becoming a religious melting pot, the
ingredients of this stew were becoming more complex by the year.
The old order was losing its primacy in American religious life. Once
dominant in colonial America, the Anglican and Congregationalist
denominations had slid well down the list, replaced by Catholics and
evangelicals. Even some of the new Protestant faiths that had grown
spontaneously in the new nation—for example, the Disciples and the

Mormons—had pushed into the top ten denominations in terms of membership. By 1850, the most dominant sect in terms of number of adherents was the Catholic Church, followed by the Methodists, Baptists, Presbyterians, Congregationalists, Lutherans, Disciples, Episcopalians, and Mormons.[36]

Fifty years later, at the turn of the century, the Episcopalian and Congregationalist churches had slid to seventh and eighth. Their memberships measured just a fraction of the size of some of the other sects that had aggressively grown through immigration or evangelicalism. At about 600,000 members each, they were far behind the Roman Catholics at 8 million, the Methodists at 5.5 million, the Baptists at 4 million, and the Presbyterians and Lutherans at 1.5 million each.[37]

A nation that had bet everything on religious freedom was already reaping the rewards. America had proved that a religious environment free of government sponsorship or support could be the most vigorous in the world. If, at most, 17 percent of the population belonged to a church in the days of the colonial establishments, that percentage had grown to more than a third of the population by 1900—about twenty-six million out of seventy-six million people. As the twentieth century got under way, yet another explosion of religious denominations and church membership was about to take place.[38]

7. Diversity Forces Religion from the Schools

The nation's religious diversity, expanding as a result of both immigration and the founding of new sects on American soil, was a current powerful enough to carry several vessels on its surge. The new denominations demanded religious liberty that would free them from the oppression of state establishments of religion and enable their followers to exercise their beliefs without penalty. Eventually, too, they demanded and won the same liberty for their children within the nation's educational system, removing the vast majority of devotional exercises from classrooms long before Ellery Schempp opened his copy of the Koran in protest of Bible-reading exercises at Abington Senior High School.

All throughout colonial America, the influence of faith reached beyond the steeple. Settling in the new land, within the boundaries of growing cities or on the forested frontier, colonists struggled to devise a system to educate their children. Having built their churches as the centerpiece of the community, the colonists constructed their schools to serve their faith as well. Americans of those times didn't build schools so that their children could become scholars of math and history. Faith informed all that colonial children learned in school. Children learned to read so that they could study the Scriptures.

Several periods mark the history of religion in American public schools, periods that correspond to the increasing religious diversity throughout the land. The first period, from colonial times through the first part of the nineteenth century and during the ascendancy of the Anglicans and Congregationalists, was a time of aggressively sectarian practices in the schools. Teachers used the Bible, the Psalter, and the Ten Commandments and drilled their students in the catechism. Textbooks had heavily religious overtones. The second period, starting early in the nineteenth century, marked the founding of public school systems. As the Anglican and Congregationalist establishments dissipated amid the proliferation of other Protestant sects, many sectarian teachings would no longer be tolerated. Protestants agreed to remove the most sectarian teaching from the schools and replace it with a common Christian religion consisting of the Bible reading and prayers that most Protestants shared.

Finally, in the third period, beginning in the second half of the nineteenth century and continuing to the *Schempp* case, religious pluralism expanded beyond Protestantism to include Roman Catholicism and people of non-Christian faiths. With broader diversity of religion, even the common Protestantism of the public schools became controversial. Many communities began removing religion from the schools themselves simply because the alternative looked much worse—the promise of the kind of religious conflict that many in the founding generation had warned against. Those that didn't remove these vestiges of religious practices from their schools faced conflict and litigation.

It's doubtful that the framers of the U.S. Constitution gave even a passing thought to the questions that bothered Ellery Schempp. Their fight centered on the seminal issue of state recognition and support of official churches. There were devotional exercises in the schools of the day, but these schools were virtually all private institutions, which even in the twenty-first century retain the unquestioned right to provide a religious education. The founding generation did not know the public school systems that would come later, nor did they know the full flowering of religious diversity that had just started in their day and that would change the very fabric of both the nation and the school system.

In colonial times and into the early nineteenth century, education was largely under local control and was primarily on the elementary school level. Except in New England, where lawmakers in some cases mandated the formation of schools, the people were on their own. Practices varied widely. Few schools were funded by taxpayers. Instead, many churches built schools on their own grounds for the education of children in their community. Parents in some places pooled their resources and opened their own schools. Attendance was typically voluntary. What these early schools had in common almost without exception was their vigorous focus on providing religious instruction.[1]

The Massachusetts Bay Colony did require by statute that towns provide schooling. In 1647, legislators enacted the so-called Old Deluder Satan Act, a name that indicated how the Puritans viewed education. "It being one chief project of the old deluder, Satan, to keep man from the knowledge of the Scriptures," said the law, every township of more than fifty householders was required to appoint someone to teach the children how to read and write. When the number of householders reached one hundred, the town had to establish a grammar school.[2]

Early America was largely a rural society, with 95 percent of the population in 1790 living in small towns and farming communities of fewer than twenty-five hundred people. In the Middle Atlantic colonies, which had the largest population and the greatest religious diversity, towns, churches, and parents started schools. As in New England, schools in small towns and rural areas were typically one-room cabins, often poorly situated—near sawmills or blacksmith shops or sometimes out in a field—because people who had to walk or ride a horse a long distance found it difficult to agree on a convenient location. Parents supported these so-called district schools through tuition, taxes, or even contributions of fuel. Into these schools came forty to seventy youngsters from the ages of about four to fourteen, crowded into one room with one teacher for up to six hours at a time. The room itself seemed designed to torture children. Built-in desks faced the walls, and the children sat on backless benches that were usually too high for their feet to touch the floor. If it weren't bad enough to sit slumped for hours, feet dangling, children also had to contend with winter drafts or, if they were sitting close enough, intense heat from the stove.[3]

In the cities, children attended independent schools that charged quarterly tuition fees or dame schools, run by women out of their own homes. Poorer students who couldn't afford tuition might go to a church charity school or apprentice to a tradesman. In the South, meanwhile, the relatively small population spread over large areas sometimes called for different arrangements. Many plantation owners hired private tutors who came to their home. As in the North, children of small farmers typically gathered before schoolmasters who taught them in a small log cabin.[4]

Most of the colonial and early nineteenth-century schools recognized religion as a primary goal of learning. At the very least, children had to become literate in order to read the Bible and learn their prayers. The mission of the schools was not just to educate the sons and daughters of Christians; it was to make Christians out of the children, able to read and understand Scripture and appreciate God's hand in creation. A few states followed the Massachusetts Bay Colony's lead. In 1665, New York passed a law similar to the Old Deluder Act; Pennsylvania enacted a statute mandating that children learn to read so that they would be able to learn from the Bible.[5] In South Carolina in 1710, lawmakers passed a statute creating a free school, listing as its purposes the teaching of grammar, arts and sciences, and the Christian religion.[6] Virginia passed a law in 1643 providing for the education of orphans, requiring guardians "to educate and instruct them according to their best endeavors in Christian religion and in the rudiments of learning and to provide for their necessaries according to the competents of their estate."[7]

Some laws of the colonial period mandated that all teachers be adherents of a specific denomination.[8] Teachers in the colonies were frequently ministers and thus able to convey the religious lessons well. In New England, teaching candidates often had to meet with the local minister, who would satisfy himself that the candidate was sufficiently religious and knowledgeable about doctrine.[9] In Massachusetts and many other states, supervision of the district school fell to a committee of local ministers and officials. When they visited the schools, they listened to the children read and recite from the Bible, the Psalter, and textbooks, such as a primer.[10]

꒜

Recitation of prayers, readings from the Bible and the Psalter, drilling in the catechism, discussion of the Sabbath, appreciation of creation—all these things and more formed much of the heart of the school experience for colonial children. "The children were perpetually enveloped, weekdays and Sundays, in an atmosphere saturated with religious forms, services, ideas, and language," wrote school historian Clifton Johnson in his *Old-Time Schools and School-Books*. Johnson quoted the 1645 school rules of Dorchester, Massachusetts, that required the schoolmasters to "take notice of any misdemeanor or outrage that any of his scholars shall have committed on the Sabbath, to the end that at some convenient time due admonition and correction may be administered." The rules continued:

> Every day of the week at two of the clock in the afternoon, he shall catechise his scholars in the principles of the Christian religion. . . . It is to be a chief part of the schoolmaster's religious care to commend his scholars and his labors amongst them unto God by prayer morning and evening taking care that his scholars do reverently attend during the same.[11]

School rules commanding the teaching of religion were common. In New Amsterdam in 1661, officials required one schoolmaster— and probably others—to "teach the children and pupils the Christian Prayers, commandments, baptism, Lord's supper, and the questions with answers of the catechism, which are taught here every Sunday afternoon in the church." Each schoolmaster was further instructed: "Before school closes he shall let the children sing some verses and a psalm."[12] Connecticut schools carried out the requirements of a state law of 1650 that required teaching of the catechism. "Not only was the catechism of the Westminster divines taught in the schools, but every church and town had some other one adapted to their especial needs," according to one historical account. Later, in 1815, the town of Farmington, Connecticut, published rules on religious teaching. Teachers were required to teach schoolchildren to "revere the ministers of the gospel; to respect the aged and all their superiors; to reverence the Sabbath, the word and worship of God." Teachers were also to remind students "of their dependence on God, of their accountability to him [*sic*], of their mortality, and of the importance of religion both as a preparation for death, and the only means of true peace, comfort, and usefulness in this world." Teachers had to profess their personal belief in the Bible.[13]

Before the Revolution, schools throughout the South also existed chiefly to teach religion. Historian Thomas J. Wertenbaker wrote: "[F]ew of the schools taught more than the most elementary subjects. All that was expected of them was to give the pupil a good knowledge of reading, writing, and arithmetic, and to drill him thoroughly in the Ten Commandments, the Lord's Prayer, and the Catechism."[14] In North Carolina, a teacher who had started a school advertised for students in a local paper in 1822. The purpose of his school, he said, was "to better the religious, moral, and social condition of society, by teaching those who attend not only to read and write, &c. but what is infinitely of more moment, the fear of the Lord, veneration for his holy word—for the ordinances of the Lord's house, and a due observance of the Lord's day."[15]

॰৵

The experience of religion in the early schools was no different in Abington, where the Schempps would eventually settle. The land that became Abington was part of William Penn's charter from King

George, so its development as an area of religious freedom mirrored that of the rest of Pennsylvania. The early years brought mostly Protestant denominations that sponsored their own schools. Schools adopted the same kind of devotionals and religious readings as schools elsewhere.

At the time, the area was called Hill's Township, named after the leading landowner, Philip Hill.[16] Quakers moved into the area, and they established the first Friends Meeting in 1683. Fourteen years later, they established their first meetinghouse in Abington, on 120 acres deeded by one of their members.[17] They renamed the area Abington after several parishes they knew in Northampton and Cambridgeshire, England.[18]

New settlers soon joined the Quakers in this dense woodland just a dozen miles north of Philadelphia. Welsh, Dutch, Scots, and some Puritans from New England came to Abington and gathered for services in each other's homes. At a meeting in the summer of 1714, seventy of them signed a covenant to form the Abington Presbyterian Church. They selected as their pastor Malachi Jones, a Welshman in his early sixties, who had purchased a parcel of land at the intersection of Old York Road and Susquehanna—as it turned out, just down the road from where Edward Schempp would build his house more than two centuries later. In 1719, Jones sold a half acre of his land to the congregation for ten shillings, and the township's first Presbyterian church and burial ground were soon built.[19]

Diversity was on its way, and the Quakers and Presbyterians didn't have Abington to themselves for long. What opened up the area for settlement was construction of Old York Road in 1712 from Broad Street in downtown Philadelphia to the Delaware River above New Hope. Now farms and mills could get their goods to urban markets that were difficult to reach before, and entrepreneurs built taverns to service the increasing traffic that traversed the area on the trip between Philadelphia and New York.[20]

As in many other areas in colonial America, local churches and meetinghouses established schools in the Abington area. In fact, the first school in the area was probably the Abington Friends School, started in 1697 and run by the Abington Friends Meeting. One of the earliest teachers was Daniel Boone's uncle George Boone, who apparently was schoolmaster from 1716 to 1720 and enforced rules that admonished students to "manifest a becoming deportment towards your teacher" and not to "indulge in the dangerous practice of climbing trees."[21] Imagine that—a Boone telling kids not to climb trees.

By then, the second assembly of the province had already enacted an education law, coupling it—as many other colonies did—to a religious purpose. In 1683, the assembly required every parent to see that their children were educated in reading and writing "so that they may be able to read the Scriptures and write by the time they attain to the age of twelve years."[22] Without a system of public education, parents usually fulfilled their legal obligation by sending their children to the schools that the churches built, usually close to or on church grounds. The minister in the church usually doubled as the school's primary teacher.[23] A historical account of schools in the Abington area reports: "The Old and New Testament constituted the reading books. Saturday was devoted to spelling, committing and reciting arithmetic tables, and reciting from the catechism."[24]

Beyond curriculum plans, perhaps the best indication of the extent of religion in the early American schools is the books that students read regularly for their assignments. John Nietz taught at the University of Pittsburgh and created a library there of thousands of early American textbooks. Nietz and other scholars, many of whom studied with him, published books and dissertations analyzing the content of American schoolbooks of past centuries. Nietz wrote that "an analysis of the actual textbooks used in the past will reveal a truer history of what was actually taught in the schools than a study of the educational theories."[25] Charles Kenneth Shannon, who studied history textbooks after 1865, adds, "Nineteenth-century schools were heavily dependent upon textbooks for content and methodology."[26]

Scholars found that schoolbooks of the colonial period and early nineteenth century were laden with religion. For example, R. R. Robinson, who read and analyzed 1,422 readers published during two centuries, found that fully 85 percent of the content of school readers before 1775 was religious in nature.[27] Some books were explicitly religious texts. "When I was young," wrote Noah Webster of his schooling in Connecticut just before the Revolution, "the books used were chiefly or wholly Dilworth's Spelling Books, the Psalter, Testament, and Bible."[28] Teachers drilled students incessantly in the catechism. Virtually all other books the students read—including hornbooks, spellers, primers, and textbooks—had extensive religious references.

The hornbook was a kind of thin wooden paddle. A printed sheet was attached to the board and was protected from rips and smudges by transparent horn. A hole in the handle of the paddle permitted teachers to attach a string so that young students could hang the hornbook around their neck. The hornbooks varied a bit, but they were the most basic of learning tools. They typically contained the English alphabet and some common syllables. About half of the printed sheet was set aside for something every bit as important in those times as the alphabet—the Lord's Prayer.[29] Spellers, also basic texts, were intended to help children spell and read. Dating from 1762, *The Youth's Instructor in the English Tongue: or, The Art of Spelling Improved* contained many reading exercises with religious messages. Other spellers followed, including several that were published by religious groups and found their way into Sunday schools established to educate poor children.[30]

No book was as important in colonial education as the primer. In New England, Puritan education focused on teaching children to read the Bible and on instructing them in the faith. According to prominent school historian Lawrence A. Cremin, the Puritan education required "indoctrinating the Calvinist creed along with granting of the ability to read." He added: "The means of its fulfillment was embodied in the *New England Primer*, which was for a hundred years, beyond any other, the principal text of American schools."[31]

The Puritans brought primers to America with them from

England, but what may have been the first *New England Primer* was dated 1691 and was rich with religion. It instructed students in reading by presenting them with the alphabet, common syllables, and rhyming couplets with illustrations for twenty-four of the letters of the alphabet. Many of the couplets, which might change from edition to edition, had religious overtones: for the letter *A,* the rhyme was "In Adam's fall, we sinned all"; for *C,* it was "Christ crucified, for sinners died."

Beyond the alphabet, the bulk of the *New England Primer* was dedicated to prose and verse readings teaching students the important tenets of Calvinism. The book had sections on the Lord's Prayer, the Ten Commandments, the catechism, the Apostles' Creed, and more. One illustration showed John Rogers burning at the stake in London during Queen Mary's reign; this grisly illustration for children was, for the true believers, a lesson in the strength of faith. Even the filler material between readings presented religious content, as in the admonition "Good children must: Fear God all day, parents obey, no false thing say, by no sin stray." Over the years, about three million copies of the *New England Primer* were sold throughout the colonies, a phenomenal number considering population figures of the day. As historian Clifton Johnson concluded: "No other way could have been devised to mould the religious thoughts of the people so effectively." He added: "In short, this humble little primer was a chief tool for making sure that the children, or, as Jonathan Edwards called them, 'young vipers and infinitely more hateful than vipers to God,' should grow up into sober and Christian men and women."[32]

Equally famous as the *New England Primer* was the McGuffey series of readers, which were published later. William Holmes McGuffey brought out his *First Reader* in 1836, followed by additional readers for older and more advanced schoolchildren. The various McGuffey series were updated regularly and became almost as popular in sales as the Bible itself. Schools and parents bought about 60 million copies of McGuffey readers in the 1870s and 1880s alone, about 122 million copies in all by 1920.[33]

The early McGuffey readers had a heavy religious orientation. Religious material comprised 31 percent of the 1837 edition of the *Fourth Reader* and held at about 24 percent for editions in 1857 and 1866. One entry, the Sermon on the Mount, was published in editions through 1901.[34] Results were similar for the *Fifth Reader;* 22 percent of its material was religious in nature in the 1857 and 1866 editions.[35]

Although not as popular as the McGuffey readers or the *New England Primer,* there were many other reading books during the colonial period, often brought from England. These early schoolbooks served the same religious purposes as the *New England Primer.* One book published in 1635, *The English School Master,* gave as its purpose that "any unskilled person may easily understand any hard English word which they shall in the scripture, sermons, and elsewhere hear or read."[36] In his study of the content of four readers that were published before 1775, Robinson found that 85 percent of the material in the books was religious in nature and that 8 percent more concerned morals and conduct, which was related to religion. "This can only be expected," wrote Robinson, "since the school is practically under the control of the church."[37]

From the Revolution to 1825, Robinson found religious material diminishing in volume but still dominant. During this period, religious material comprised 22 percent of eighty-five readers surveyed by Robinson, with an additional 28 percent given over to morals and conduct. By comparison, spelling comprised only 10 percent of the content, history 2 percent, and science none at all.[38]

Like the primers and readers, history textbooks routinely injected religious references and causes into discussion of the past. According to a doctoral dissertation by Charles Kenneth Shannon, nearly 60 percent of history textbooks from this period referred to the role of divine providence in history, and 48 percent asserted it as a major factor in American history. "They credited Divine Providence with being the ultimate cause of historical events and with blessing the United States because it was a Christian nation," wrote Shannon.[39]

As to Pocahontas, one history text writer asserted: "[W]e may hope that she truly embraced the faith of the Lord Jesus Christ into which she was baptized."[40] A world history textbook published in 1818 had as its main purpose to "show that Martin Luther was the angel of the gospel for the age in which he lived, and will continue to be the angel of the gospel until the millennial day." Another history textbook, written by the Reverend Royal Robbins and published in 1835, discussed creation as described in the Bible and assured students that the flood had taken place.[41] History textbooks attributed the greatness of George Washington, Abraham Lincoln, and even the U.S. Constitution to the hand of God.[42]

Even geography textbooks didn't leave out religion. References to religious doctrine found their way into discussions of the earth's beginnings. There was no doubt, according to the textbooks, that God created the world. Ruth Miller Elson, who conducted a major study of nineteenth-century schoolbooks, concluded: "[S]choolbooks before the Civil War accept without question the Biblical history of the world and the creation of man. The Garden of Eden and its inhabitants are as real as the Appalachians."[43] Of the six major geography textbooks of this period, Jedidiah Morse, a Protestant minister, wrote three of them. "You will be safe in making the Bible your rule," he exhorted his young readers.[44]

Evidently, for Morse, loving thy neighbor did not apply to Catholic neighbors. In one edition, Morse continued the age-old animosities between Catholicism and Protestantism by saying that Catholicism in Spain was "of most bigoted, superstitious, and tyrannical character." Such sentiments were all too typical of authors who felt no restraint in presenting strident anti-Catholic sentiments in their texts.[45] Another textbook writer launched an attack on what he felt was the immorality of Catholic clergy: "The monks and ecclesiastics themselves, who today will pardon our sins for a groat, tonight will become defiled with your bosom-companion in her marriage-bed. And the daughter on whom you dote, while saying her mass, will become debauched by a pretending saint!"[46]

As people of many different faiths came to America, the intense focus on teaching Calvinist and Anglican doctrine in the schools could not last. Schooling that began in the colonies under heavy religious influence and frequently under private auspices finally gave way, in the nineteenth century, to common schools funded by taxpayers. These public schools gradually lost most of their religious teaching. Historian Sidney Mead has written, "Perhaps the most striking power that the churches surrendered under religious freedom was control over public education which traditionally had been considered an essential aspect of the work of an established church if it was to perform its proper function of disseminating and inculcating the necessary foundational religious beliefs."[47]

Over time, as the diversity of faith throughout the nation broadened, people began to look at religious practices in the schools as someone else's practices and therefore not appropriate for children from diverse backgrounds. That brought strife to the schools and to numerous communities. Sectarian religious practices slowly left the public schools, the result of political compromise among people of various religious sects. But reformers defined the term *sectarian* in a narrow sense, within the Protestant context. Those in control of the schools eliminated only doctrinal teaching that would cause squabbles among the different Protestant sects. A "common religion" acceptable to Protestants, a kind of Pan-Protestantism, would become the norm in education.

Growing uneasiness about teaching doctrinal religion in the schools coincided, in the early 1800s, with the emergence of strong sentiment about universal education. Throughout the United States, there was a growing consensus that education was generally of low quality and required drastic improvement if the nation were to grow and prosper. Left to the whims of local communities, most schools were poorly funded. By the 1830s, however, the economy of the nation was growing quickly, and recognition spread that the country needed both a workforce able to handle industrialization and a citizenry more capable of supporting democracy.

The solution seemed to be the creation of common schools that would ensure that all children could read, do basic mathematics, and learn about their country. The most influential figure in the common school movement that swept the country was Horace Mann, a state school official in Massachusetts from 1837 to 1848. That the idea of common religion should emanate from Massachusetts was noteworthy in itself, for no place in colonial America had matched the Massachusetts Bay Colony in the passions of its narrow and uncompromising Puritan beliefs.

Religious diversity, though, had hit Massachusetts with the force of a nor'easter in January. It tore apart the old order and pushed the state on a one-way path toward religious liberty, with a profound impact on education. The changes that diversity would bring to the public school classrooms of Massachusetts would set in motion important educational changes throughout the entire country. By the early nineteenth century, theological arguments had split the old Congregationalist Church, with many congregations veering toward Unitarian beliefs. By 1825, Unitarianism dominated the established church, and Puritan orthodoxy was no longer ascendant. Meanwhile, the Baptist, Methodist, Universalist, and other sects were growing in size—another direct challenge to the old order. The state swept away its establishment of religion by constitutional amendment in 1833, making it the last state to embrace religious liberty by separating church and state in its civil laws.

Even six years before the disestablishment of religion, the state revised its school laws in an attempt not only to improve the quality of education but also to end the bickering among Protestant sects. Puritan dogma could no longer be taught in the schools without invoking the ire of competing sects, so practices that were obviously sectarian had to end in order for Protestants of different sects to coexist. The rising number of Roman Catholics arriving in the state provided another unifying theme for Protestants. As a practical matter, Protestants had to lay aside their stridency over doctrinal differences in order to rally against what seemed to them a more threatening development, the growing influence of Roman Catholicism.

In 1827, the state enacted a law that conferred on local school committees the power to select school texts, excepting books that would favor any specific denomination or any specific belief. Removing sectarianism from the schools, though, was far different from removing religion itself. As the law said, the purpose of education was to provide "the principles of piety, justice, and sacred regard to truth, love to their country, humanity, and universal benevolence, sobriety, industry, and frugality, chastity, moderation, and temperance."[48] To teach piety and other virtues, the state still favored the inclusion of religious practices in the public schools, but it was to be religion stripped of the most sectarian influences.

This idea of teaching a common religion in the common school had no stronger champion than Mann, secretary to the Massachusetts Board of Education. Mann was born into a Calvinist household in Franklin, Massachusetts, in 1796 but later embraced Unitarianism. He became a lawyer and served in the Massachusetts House of Representatives and then in the Massachusetts Senate. When he became the first secretary of the new state board of education, he was committed to the ideal of a common school that would offer youngsters the essential learning they needed in life. That included not only reading, math, and civics but also, notably, a core of religious values that would provide them with spiritual guidance.

The secretary of the school board believed firmly in the value not only of education but of a Christian education. "He who is ignorant is almost necessarily superstitious," Mann wrote. "But a Christian education lifts off the whole, black, iron firmament of superstition from the soul, and brings life and immortality to light."[49] Mann maintained that he could think of no man who "can be willing to have his name mentioned while he is living, or remembered when he is dead, as opposed to religious instruction, and Bible instruction for the young."[50]

For Mann, the Bible was the key to religious education. It contained all the lessons a child needed for a virtuous life, and its narratives on creation, the life and crucifixion of Christ, and other matters laid the foundation of a common Protestantism. For Mann, though, biblical instruction had to be free of commentary. Massachusetts law banned sectarian influences in the new common schools, a stance Mann firmly supported. If commentary were permitted in a religiously diverse community, whose commentary would it be?

Mann concluded that if the Bible were read in school without comment and therefore without any doctrinal interpretation and proselytizing, children could absorb a kind of common Christianity—more specifically, a common Protestantism, since only the King James Version would be utilized. Much of Mann's dozen years in office were spent defending his concept of a common religion for the common schools, against the dying cries of Puritan fundamentalists. His vast writings on the subject, done in response to his critics and as part of his annual report on the Massachusetts schools, became a blueprint for spreading the new gospel on Pan-Protestantism in the common schools of the United States.

Mann got into frequent public spats with clergy who resisted the thinner religious offerings in the classroom. In some cases, he justified his position with long written papers. In one, he wrote about the excessive religious zeal that he felt would inevitably poison local school boards as various sects jockeyed for control—a concern echoed by several Supreme Court justices in the *Schempp* case more than a century later.

> If the question, "What theology shall be taught in school?" is to be decided by districts or towns, then all the prudential and the superintending school committees must be chosen with express reference to their faith; the creed of every candidate for teaching must be investigated; and when litigations arise—and such a system will breed them in swarms—an ecclesiastical tribunal, some star chamber, or high commission court must be created to decide them.[51]

Mann's conception of a common religion was a major milestone in the history of religion in schools. Based on Mann's arguments, democratic processes had led to the elimination of the most egregious sectarian practices in what was once the epicenter of Puritanism in America. Mann's concept of sectarianism was, of course, rather narrow and much different than the concept Americans have in the twenty-first century. Mann's common religion was a common Protestantism—one that excluded other Christians, such as Roman Catholics, as well as non-Christians, who were then few in number but whose numbers would swell in the coming century. Of course, it excluded atheists and agnostics.

Mann's concept of common religion for the new common schools spread throughout the country during the next fifty years. Legislators, education officials, and most Christian leaders confirmed Mann's belief that a generalized Protestantism in a nation newly rich in Protestant sects was the only way to retain religious observance in the public schools without destructive conflict. State after state enacted statutes or constitutional provisions that created new public school systems and required that they be free of sectarian teaching.

The experience in Pennsylvania, where the *Schempp* case would arise, was similar. Starting around 1820, people increasingly agitated for creation of a system of common, or public, schools. Sherman Day, a historian of Pennsylvania, wrote, "The number of people who could neither read nor write had increased to an alarming extent, and Pennsylvanians became an object of ridicule to the people of other States, who had been more careful to provide a proper system of education."[52]

In 1834, Governor George Wolf signed the Common School Law to provide a system of public education for all of Pennsylvania.[53] The law brought severe opposition, in large part because of concerns that religion would inevitably leave the schools. One historian commented:

This hostility was not inspired by a disinclination to support educational institutions, but it was foreseen that the law would completely secularize the common schools of the land, and this was sincerely

believed by many, and by a large proportion of the clergy and ministers of the gospel, to be inimical to the church, and hence to society.
. . . Parents and pastors were unwilling to trust the training of children
to those who were strangers to their religious creeds.[54]

The pastors' foreboding had been correct. The new public schools
sought to prepare students for jobs and citizenship in a rapidly growing country. With an increasingly diverse mix of Protestant denominations represented among the schoolchildren, overtly sectarian
influences could no longer survive. As in Massachusetts, Bible reading emerged as the predominant religious practice in the public
schools. No law in Pennsylvania required Bible reading and prayer at
the time, but school districts, acting on their own, adopted the practice or continued it as a tradition inherited from colonial times. In
1861, about 60 percent of the public schools in Pennsylvania reported
that they used the Bible.[55]

The common school movement became a federal concern as well.
In 1875, President Ulysses S. Grant urged adoption of the common
school system, "unmixed with sectarian, pagan, or atheistic dogmas,"
in states that still relied on the old haphazard and poorly funded system of secondary schools.[56] In that same year, Representative James
G. Blaine introduced a constitutional amendment that would have
forbidden any public support of schools "wherein the particular creed
or tenets shall be read or taught"—although the proposal permitted
reading of the Bible. The proposal didn't pass, but Congress by then
favored common schools free from the beliefs of individual sects.[57]
Lawmakers did enact a statute requiring that all states entering the
Union after 1876 had to maintain public schools open to all. The federal law and most of the state laws banned sectarian control or
influence.[58]

༄

Through compromises among competing Protestant sects, the most
sectarian religious practices left the schools throughout America.

Mann's genius was his recognition that common schools could not survive in a pluralistic nation by teaching the doctrines of Calvinists, Baptists, Methodists, or other Protestant denominations. What was acceptable to the majority of Protestants was a common religion of the schools that included daily readings from their King James Version, recitation of the Lord's Prayer and other common supplications, the singing of hymns, and the celebration of Christian holidays.

Protestants had found a rapprochement among themselves. They had yet to reckon, though, with the fact that American religious pluralism was even then beginning to extend well beyond their own Protestantism. The compromise reached by Horace Mann in the 1840s had been a kind of treaty among Protestants, meant to prevent any one Protestant sect from dominating religious practices in the public schools.

What was acceptable among Protestants, however, was worse than the roughest sandpaper against the cheeks of those who practiced other faiths. Catholics became the largest denomination in America less than a decade after Mann's compromise, and the arrival of a large number of Jews and other people of non-Christian faiths was soon to come. America was changing rapidly, and this next wave of diversity would remake religion in the schools in profound ways once again, opening a path to Ellery's protest.

8. Excessive Religious Zeal

When musket fire broke out at the Nanny Goat Market in Philadelphia on Monday, May 6, 1844, George Schiffler was hit immediately. The eighteen-year-old apprentice leather worker died from his wound. About three thousand Protestants had been listening to anti-Catholic speeches in the middle of an Irish Catholic neighborhood. Now they ran from the market or hid behind the long line of food stalls, trying to avoid the rain of Catholic fire coming from houses all along Cadwalader Street. Joseph Cox had sought shelter by a food stall when he was mortally wounded. Two other men were also shot.[1]

A three-day religious war had broken out, brought on by hatred between Catholics and Protestants and ignited by conflict over Bible reading in Philadelphia's public schools. For a few days, violence gripped the city where the framers had written the Constitution and debated the necessity of a Bill of Rights, and not far from where Edward Schemmp would later build his suburban home. This violence was, in very graphic terms, a reminder that denominational control of the schools carried with it the excessive Old World religious zeal that the framers had tried to avoid. Even in a school system where most sectarian practices had been banished, Bible reading alone released passions fraught with death. The question of whose Bible should be used reached deep into religious sensitivities.

For those willing to listen, this week of violence in Philadelphia provided graphic evidence that Horace Mann's concept of a common religion for the common school—put in place that same decade in

Massachusetts—was unlikely to work for very long in a religious culture that was becoming increasingly diverse. Other ugly incidents would also follow—a Catholic priest was tarred and feathered in Maine, and a student was beaten by a teacher in Massachusetts—as Protestant sects in some communities tried to continue their dominance in the schools against those who argued for their own right of conscience. Catholics saw common religion for what it was—a common Protestantism. They didn't want their children reading the King James Version, and even Bible reading without comment offended them. Catholics, after all, were not free to read even their own Douay Version without textual interpretation supplied by Rome. For their part, Protestants couldn't imagine their children reading the Catholic Douay. Meanwhile, non-Christians wanted no part of either tradition. Religion historian Robert Michaelsen wrote: "By now Protestantism itself, with its King James Bible, its prayers, and its hymn singing, had become sectarian—particular, distinctive, different from Catholicism or Judaism or unbelief."[2]

By 1844, the year of the riots that started at the Nanny Goat Market, immigration from Ireland had pushed the number of Irish in Philadelphia to about 10 percent of the population. In a largely Protestant city, even one built on religious freedom, old animosities returned with a fury. In his book *The Philadelphia Riots of 1844*, historian Michael Feldberg recounted that nativist groups gained strength, railing against all immigrants—who tended to be poor and badly educated—but especially against the Catholics. A severe economic downturn in the late 1830s only exacerbated animosity between the groups, as they both tried to protect their jobs. Religion in the schools, though, provided the spark that set off mob violence.

Protestants controlled the public schools in Philadelphia and required that schoolchildren begin each day with Protestant prayers and hymns. Students took their reading lessons from the King James Bible. Some of the textbooks contained strongly anti-Catholic passages.[3] The Catholic bishop of Philadelphia, Francis Patrick Kenrick, objected to the Protestant flavor of the schools, fearing that impressionable Catholic children would learn principles antithetical to their faith. A Catholic teacher was dismissed in 1842 for refusing to read from the King James Version. Then the school board compromised by allowing Catholic children to excuse themselves from the Bible exercises. That ruling incensed nativist Protestants, who rallied in support of their own King James Version.[4]

The school board's excusal of Catholic children foreshadowed a strategy that Protestants would follow for the next century in an attempt to save the presence of their devotionals in the public schools. As America became more religiously diverse, Protestants would have trouble holding on to their devotionals in the face of dissenters of other faiths who found these exercises offensive. Even when cases—like *Schempp*—were litigated to the U.S. Supreme Court, those defending devotional exercises would argue that excusal provisions saved the devotionals from constitutional attack because they erased any coercive state action against children of minority faiths.

The skirmish at the Nanny Goat Market on May 6, 1844, marked only the opening of broader violence in the city. The next day, nativists again marched to Kensington and came under musket fire. John Wesley Rhinedollar, an apprentice cordwainer (shoemaker), died immediately. Then a ship carpenter, a marble mason, and a rope maker were killed. Eleven others were wounded. Striking back, nativist gangs set fire to the Cadwalader Street houses from which the Irish Catholics had been firing, then they shot at people as they tried to escape the flames. Finally, militia companies arrived and stopped the rioting.[5]

The nativist gangs returned the next morning, and the third day of violence began. Having found their best weapon in arson, they torched St. Michael's Church and stayed to cheer as the steeple collapsed, bringing a cross to the ground with it. Then they burned the seminary of the Sisters of Charity and sacked homes and stores, making a bonfire of books in the street. Later that day, Mayor John M. Scott stood atop the steps at another church, St. Augustine's, and asked the crowd to disperse. A nativist answered with a stone that hit him in the chest. A fire broke out as people attended to the mayor.

With firemen afraid to intervene, the church burned to the ground in half an hour. Finally, the militia enforced martial law, and the violence subsided.[6]

Tensions rose again with the coming of the July 4 holiday, two months after the school skirmish. Fearing more violence, Catholics stored muskets in a church in the Southwark section of the city. As the situation deteriorated over the coming days, the militia took position in front of the church. Once again, violence flared. The militia opened fire on an angry crowd, killing two people and wounding four others. Nativists commandeered two cannons and set them up on Christian Street at two corners, firing up the street and killing two people. The militia fired back with a cannon of its own. For hours, cannon and musket fire echoed throughout a city at war over what version of the Bible to read to schoolchildren. Before it was all over, there were two dead and twenty-three wounded militiamen and about ten dead and twenty wounded nativists. To keep order, two thousand troops occupied Philadelphia. Feeling that Protestant control of the schools could not be resolved any time soon, Bishop Kenrick began building a new system of Catholic parochial schools.[7]

෨

A decade later, violence marred the quiet city of Ellsworth, Maine. There, the school committee selected the King James Version for its schoolchildren to read. In 1854, John Bapst, the Jesuit priest for the local parish, recommended that Catholic parents refuse to cooperate and instead litigate. The Donahoe family agreed; fifteen-year-old Bridget refused to participate in Bible reading and received a suspension.[8]

Bridget said that she would read the Catholic Douay but not the King James Bible. Her lawyer said that the school required her "to take part in a religious exercise from which her conscience shrunk, because, as she believed, God's word was perverted in its meaning."[9]

The Maine Supreme Judicial Court acknowledged that Catholics disputed the King James Version, that Protestants denied the Douay, and that various other Protestant sects disliked both. But the court refused to follow its observation to its logical conclusion—that Bridget was required by the school to participate in a sectarian exercise. The court ruled instead that the school committee had the power to choose any version it wanted and that its choice of the King James Version did not constitute a preference for Protestantism that would violate the Maine Constitution. The court said that the sect representing the majority of citizens in any school district could choose its own religious texts. "The choice is left entirely to the popular will," said the court. "One set of town officers may make one selection, and another may make an entirely different one."[10] Meanwhile, a mob of Protestants attacked Father Bapst one evening as he heard confessions. The mob tarred and feathered him, but none of the perpetrators were arrested.[11]

Five years later, things weren't much better for Thomas Wall in Massachusetts. He was only eleven years old when he refused to read the Lord's Prayer and the Ten Commandments in class during the weekly exercises on March 14, 1859—in a protest similar to the one that Ellery Schempp would make ninety-seven years later. Wall's teacher, McLaurin F. Cooke, whipped Wall's hands with a rattan stick that was three feet long and three-eighths of an inch thick, pausing from time to time to see if Wall would begin his recitations. The beating continued for thirty minutes, until Wall finally agreed to cooperate.

A Massachusetts law required the daily reading of the Protestant Bible. In addition, Boston school regulations recommended that students recite the Lord's Prayer and the Ten Commandments. Both Wall's father and his priest had pushed young Thomas, a Roman Catholic, into his protest. According to the Boston court that heard the case, Wall's father had "told him for his life" not to repeat the Ten Commandments from the Protestant Bible. The priest threatened embarrassment to Thomas and nine hundred other Catholic children. Admonishing them "not to be cowards to their religion, and not to read or repeat the Commandments in school," he threatened that "if they did he would read their names from the altar."[12]

Wall's protest on March 14 emboldened sixty of his classmates to join him. The Wall family lodged a criminal complaint against Cooke for the beating, and the matter landed in Boston's police court, where the case was decided a month after the incident. The court was not impressed with the Catholic family's assertion that Cooke had violated Thomas's religious liberty. The judge said that the Bible exercises had been placed in the schools to teach, among other things, "humanity, and a universal benevolence, sobriety, moderation and temperance"—he evidently saw no conflict between those values and the thirty minutes that the teacher had spent hitting a child. "To read the Bible in school for these and like purposes, or to require it to be read without sectarian explanations, is no interference with religious liberty," he ruled.[13] Oblivious to the fact that the devotional exercises came from the Protestant tradition, the judge blamed the Wall family for making trouble by requesting that the Catholic Douay Bible be used in school. He said that such a specific request, if granted, would bind church and state in a sectarian alliance. The judge concluded that it was the boy's fault that Cooke's blows with the stick lasted thirty minutes; after all, young Thomas had it "in his power to make every one the last." The judge discharged Cooke from the complaint.[14]

⁓

Controversies in New York and Cincinnati showed the futility of the Protestants' hope that they could indefinitely continue to require their own devotional exercises in the public schools. In both cities, protests against Protestant practices in the schools brought new measures that eroded Mann's ideal of a common religion. In New York, Bishop John Hughes put armed guards around Catholic churches when he heard about the violence in Philadelphia, but the situation in New York remained calm.[15] By then, Hughes had been fighting Bible-reading exercises for several years. The Catholic population of New York had been growing steadily since the turn of the century, from only about 1,300 out of 60,000 New Yorkers in 1800 to as many as 80,000 out of 312,710 by 1840.[16]

With that growth came increasing restiveness regarding the public schools, which had a heavy Protestant accent and an anti-Catholic bias. Bishop Hughes actually preferred to leave the Protestant-dominated schools entirely and create a system of Catholic parochial schools. So he lobbied hard for the distribution of tax money to fund Catholic parochial education. After all, in his view, tax money paid by Catholics was going to public schools that were openly hostile to the Catholic faith. In a formal petition for tax money, he complained that textbooks used by children in public schools contained insulting references to Catholicism.[17] In 1842, the state legislature tried to resolve the impasse by creating a new board of education for New York City and prohibiting sectarian exercises. Even so, the first superintendent under the new board, William Stone, ruled that Bible reading would continue. Political compromise, though, had moved the public schools another step away from outright sectarian practice, a gradual process that would continue in New York for the next century.[18]

In Cincinnati, meanwhile, political negotiation over several decades resulted in the school board voluntarily ending Bible reading in the schools. Some Protestant clergy served as school examiners and even principals, positions from which they tested the children on the religious lessons they learned, judged the competence of the teachers, and set school policy.[19] As a result, the public schools utilized Protestant prayers and hymns as well as the King James Bible. Many teachers were Protestant ministers or former ministers.[20] As the *Catholic Telegraph*, the weekly paper for the diocese, railed against Protestantism in the schools, Archbishop John B. Purcell set about building a Catholic parochial school system. Purcell argued: "[T]he fountains of spiritual life are poisoned and those unsuspecting children have tracts placed in their hands, insinuating the vilest and most malicious slanders of our real principles and thus literally received, for bread, a serpent. Knowledge purchased at so dear a rate reminds us of the price first paid for it in Eden."[21]

Bishop Purcell raised his concerns before the school board in 1842. In response, the board passed a resolution allowing children to be excused from the Bible exercises, but teachers routinely ignored it, and the Bible practices continued.[22] Inevitably, tensions continued to mount over the next few decades, as Cincinnati was growing into one of the most religiously diverse cities in the country. Its population by 1869 stood at about a quarter of a million, with all major Protestant denominations represented alongside Catholics, Jews, and free-thinkers. Roman Catholics constituted the largest denomination in the city. The school board was just as religiously diverse: among forty members were eighteen Protestants, ten Catholics, two Jews, and ten people of unidentified religion.[23]

The fate of the schools became a consuming issue in the late 1860s, nearly a century before Ellery Schempp's protest. As the controversy grew and Archbishop Purcell argued in favor of taxpayer support of the parochial school system, one of the school board members suggested a solution: he submitted a proposal to end the reading of the Bible, other religious texts, and religious hymns in the public schools. That proposal set the ground shaking in Cincinnati. Thousands of people signed petitions against the proposal, and ministers railed against taking the Bible and Protestantism out of the schools. Others talked darkly of an alliance of Catholics and nonbelievers against common spiritual and moral values. In the end, though, the school board passed the resolution on November 1, 1869, with a vote of twenty-two to fifteen.[24]

Immediately, a group of citizens sued the school board in the Cincinnati Superior Court. In a two-to-one decision, the court issued an injunction against the school board's plan. Judge Alphonso Taft, the father of future president and chief justice William Howard Taft, wrote a dissenting opinion arguing that sectarian teaching in the public schools violated religious freedom. "No sect can, because it includes a majority of a community or a majority of the citizens of the State, claim any preference whatever," he wrote. "It can not claim that its mode of worship or its religion shall prevail in the common schools."[25] Taft argued that the schools of Cincinnati did not practice the required neutrality: "I cannot doubt . . . that the use of the Bible with appropriate singing, provided for by the old rule, and as practiced under it, was and is sectarian. It is Protestant worship. And its use is a symbol of Protestant supremacy in the schools, and as such offensive to Catholics and to Jews."[26]

Several years later, in 1872, the Ohio Supreme Court agreed with Taft's dissent and backed the school board. The court said that if the board wanted to eliminate Bible reading, the judges had no right to interfere.[27] In Ohio, at least, church and state were separate. "The great bulk of human affairs and human interests is left by any free government to individual enterprise and individual action," the court said. "Religion is eminently one of these interests, lying outside the true and legitimate province of government."[28] The court went on to dispute the contention—made then and continually for the next century—that schools that taught no religion were, by that very reason, in the control of people hostile to religion. "This is by no means so," said the court. "To teach the doctrines of infidelity, and thereby teach that Christianity is false, is one thing; and to give no instructions on the subject is quite another thing."[29]

The 1872 resolution of the Cincinnati dispute was certainly one of the most significant developments up to that time concerning religion in the schools. In a very public way, the city, through its school board, had used the processes of representative government to remove devotional exercises from the schools, in recognition of the diversity of religious practice in the community. The Ohio Supreme Court's ruling that devotional exercises in the schools violated religious freedom was the first major judicial ruling in that direction and would ring even louder in the years ahead.

∽

The Cincinnati experience in removing religion from the schools proved a harbinger of the future. Many school officials around the country agreed to compromise on Pan-Protestantism under the intense pressure of religious pluralism. Compromise brought about increased secularization of the schools, but not enough to keep Catholics from vigorously building their own system of parochial schools to avoid the King James Bible.

Although they were in the minority, even some Protestant religious leaders of the day supported reducing religious practices in the public schools. Some said it was possible to separate the teaching of morality from the teaching of religion, and some opposed even the reading of any version of the Bible. Henry Ward Beecher, one of the most famous Protestant preachers of the nineteenth century, argued that Bible reading should be stopped in schools where religious pluralism made it impossible for people to agree on a version.[30]

With immigration increasing diversity, the pressure to ease common school Protestantism was felt in school districts throughout the country. "In some communities," wrote school historian Carl F. Kaestle, "there was a process of give-and-take that softened the native Protestant emphasis of common schooling during the critical mid-nineteenth century decades of immigration." Kaestle explained, "As part of this process, nineteenth-century schoolmen sometimes made concessions, allowing scriptural choice, restricting prayer, or expurgating offensive religious and ethnic slurs from textbooks."[31]

Education officials of the day noticed that many local school boards within their state were shedding the trappings of religious practice. William Dunn, a historian of the public schools, examined reports released in 1861 by state superintendents and local education officials for eight of the original thirteen states in the Union. Most of these officials declared the importance of religious teaching in the schools, and many then lamented the absence of the religious content they thought was needed. As the education commissioner in one New Hampshire county wrote: "The great want in our schools is moral and religious training—not in any sectarian sense—but a real and thorough training in those duties which pertain to a Christian citizen. We must, if we would succeed, give the Bible a prominent place among the textbooks in our schools, and allow it to remain clothed with the sanctions of the Divine Authority."[32] A school official from Melrose, Massachusetts, wrote: "If there exists any important error in the education of the present day, it seems to be found in a lack of systematic, moral and Christian training.[33]

By then, religious pluralism was not the only force pushing religion from the schools. By the second half of the nineteenth century, Americans promoted different goals for their schools than they had when the Puritan fires burned hot. In a sense, public schools began taking on a different "religion"—that of American nationhood, democracy, and capitalism. Most everyone agreed that the common schools had to educate children in American values of self-governance. To accomplish this goal, lawmakers enacted compulsory attendance laws and, in many states, required the teaching of certain subjects, such as history. A critical task was creating a sense of community amid a hodgepodge of cultures. In thirty-seven large cities, almost 58 percent of schoolchildren had been born of new arrivals, posing the severe challenge of bringing into the mainstream millions of kids with a wide variety of customs and languages.[34] At the same time, factories of all kinds were opening like daffodils in May. They required that workers have higher levels of literacy and discipline, in order to run newfangled machinery that turned out everything from textiles to timber products. An educated workforce was a key ingredient for the growth of the nation's economy.

As the sun rose on the twentieth century, America's public schools had entered a new era. Far behind them, barely visible now on the receding horizon, were the schools of old, in which teachers taught from the Bible, drilled students in the catechism, and read from textbooks full of sectarian religious doctrine. The nation's religious pluralism had made it impossible to continue this regime of sectarian teaching, and even Horace Mann's compromise of teaching a common religion was in retreat.

Textbooks clearly signaled the change. In the second half of the nineteenth century, editors dropped virtually all of the old religious materials, to make room for literary writings and other content. Historian R. R. Robinson, who studied more than fourteen hundred

readers used in schoolrooms from colonial times through 1925, found
that religious content declined precipitously after the colonial period.
Religious content consumed 85 percent of all the material in readers
in the period ending in 1775. In fact, Robinson found of that period
that "it would have been altogether impossible to find a school reader
in which the religious element did not predominate."[35]

The decline of religious material came quickly. From 1775 to 1825,
it comprised only 22 percent of all material in readers.[36] Then religious content plunged to 7.5 percent in readers published from 1825 to
1875. Whereas ministers sometimes doubled as authors during the
earlier periods, Robinson found not a single minister who edited a
reader by the end of this period.[37]

From that point forward, religion all but vanished from the readers—it comprised just 1.5 percent of content from 1875 through 1915.
Robinson found that the readers contained an increase of literary
content, material culled from the works of prominent writers.[38]
Finally, the period from 1915 to 1926 showed no appreciable change,
with religious content remaining at 1.5 percent.[39]

Religious content left the popular McGuffey readers as well. It
comprised 31 percent of the content of McGuffey's *Fourth Reader* in
1837 but fell to about 3 percent in 1901.[40] The *Fifth Reader* carried less
than 8 percent religious content in 1901, down from 22 percent in
1857.[41] Religion evaporated from a wide variety of textbooks, too.

Historian William Dunn concluded that aside from readings from
the Bible, "there was little in the textbook content by the time of the
Civil War to give the public school child an understanding of natural
theology, and even less of Christianity itself."[42] Dunn said that "a child
in the school of 1861 knew nothing of the doctrinal instruction and little or nothing of the religious formation which were part and parcel of
his grandfather's and, to a great degree, his father's curriculum."[43]

⁓

The pluralism that had come to define America in so many ways,
forever changing its schools and communities, only increased late in

the nineteenth century. From the early 1880s to 1930, about twenty-seven million immigrants entered the United States, mostly from southern and eastern Europe. Italians and Poles came in large numbers, escaping economic deprivation. More than two million Jews arrived from eastern Europe, the vast majority of them from Russia. There were also plenty of Greeks, Czechs, Basques, Portuguese, Armenians, Japanese, and Magyars. Arabs arrived from Syria and Lebanon.[44] Meanwhile, from 1925 to 1930, the country welcomed half a million Canadians and a quarter million Mexicans.[45]

Immigration dropped sharply during the Depression and world wars but then picked up again. In time, massive immigration from many Asian nations and countries south of the border broadened American diversity well beyond the traditional European stock. Citizens of Spanish origin numbered around 14.6 million in 1980.[46] The numbers of Hispanics reached 21.9 million in 1990 and 35.2 million in 2000.[47] Meanwhile, immigration from Asia skyrocketed. In the 1940s, only 3 percent of immigrants came from Asia; that percentage increased to almost half in the eighties.[48] By 2000, 11.9 million people identified themselves as Asian, with the most recent immigrants coming from Laos, Vietnam, and Cambodia.[49]

All these new Americans brought with them religious faiths that, in many instances, had been relatively rare in the United States until then. Early in the twenty-first century, Muslims in the United States outnumbered the country's Episcopalians and Presbyterians. Buddhists counted as many as four million members.[50] Sikhs and Jains arrived, as did Hindus and Zoroastrians. Merely putting a census number to a particular faith does an injustice to the true extent of diversity, for adherents of the same faith from different cultures often brought their own particular traditions. In her book *A New Religious America*, Harvard religion professor Diana L. Eck writes:

The face of American Christianity has also changed with large Latino, Filipino, and Vietnamese Catholic communities; Chinese, Haitian, and Brazilian Pentecostal communities; Korean Presbyterians, Indian Mar Thomas, and Egyptian Copts. In every city in the land church signboards display the meeting times of Korean or Latino congregations that nest within the walls of old urban Protestant and Catholic churches.[51]

As religious pluralism continued its growth, those who still wanted faith observed in the public schools clung to the remnants of practices from earlier centuries. In the twentieth century, about all that was left of daily classroom religious practice was a devotional exercise not more than a few minutes long at the beginning of the day. In most places, a short daily reading of Scripture and perhaps the Lord's Prayer—as Ellery Schempp experienced in Abington— marked the extent of religious exercises. In many schools, there was a celebration of Christmas and Easter, typically with hymn singing and holiday decorations.

To make sure they kept at least that much religion, some states passed statutes permitting or requiring Bible reading. Massachusetts in 1855 became the first state—and the only one before the end of the nineteenth century—to enact a law that required public schools to conduct Bible-reading exercises.[52] In 1913 Pennsylvania passed a law requiring that ten verses of the Bible be read to children in the public schools each day. At the time, 89.7 percent of the public schools in the state reported that they engaged in Bible reading. A widespread practice in Pennsylvania since colonial days, Bible reading was on an upswing even in the absence of any legal requirement. In 1861, 60.2 percent of the public schools reported that they had Bible readings, a number that rose to 80.2 percent in 1871 and 84.5 percent in 1881. In Montgomery County, which included Abington Township, 96 percent of the public schools reported that they provided Bible reading in 1865, and that percentage remained nearly the same until 1913.[53]

That trend pleased James Wickersham, who became the state's superintendent of public instruction in 1866. "I would like to have a copy of the Bible upon the desk of every teacher, in the sight of all the children in the land," he wrote in one of his annual reports. "If never opened, it would still be God's book, ever teaching its silent lessons and imposing something of self-reflection and reverence for the sacred things upon the character of youth . . ."[54] Nearly a century later at the *Schempp* trial, contrary to Wickersham's focus on the sacred, the state and the Abington schools would defend Bible reading by arguing that it imparted only moral and not religious lessons.

Bible proponents in Pennsylvania fought to preserve at least this last remnant of religion in the schools against the tide of immigrants from eastern and southern Europe, many of whom were Catholics and Jews. The backers of the 1913 bill were six patriotic societies whose members, fearing loss of both jobs and Protestant hegemony, were anti-Catholic, anti-Jewish, and anti-immigrant.[55] The only major religious group pushing for the law was the National Reform Association, a Protestant organization that was anti-Catholic and anti-Jewish and favored a constitutional amendment that would declare the United States a Christian nation with allegiance to Jesus Christ.[56]

When a version of the bill came up before the Pennsylvania House in 1911, Representative David Speer argued that he "cannot possibly think for a moment that we could close the doors in Christian America against this book [the Bible] in the public schools where our children are to read the wisdom and guidance of a Higher Power."[57] Opposing the bill, perhaps recalling the Philadelphia riots of the prior century, Representative A. C. Stein argued that requiring Bible reading "can do absolutely no good at all, but will work injury and harm throughout this Commonwealth—differences that have been sleeping for hundreds of years and years. Why arouse them?"[58] There was no great enthusiasm for the Bible law in Pennsylvania, and it would not have passed without heavy lobbying by the patriotic societies and the National Reform Association.[59] In 1913, the bill became law and the relatively few Pennsylvania public schools that did not offer Bible reading fell into line. The Bible provision was incorporated into a revised school code in 1949.

After Pennsylvania passed its Bible-reading law, many other states followed the same path, attempting to enshrine the practice in law before local school boards could do away with it under the pressure of religious diversity. By 1962, twelve states and the District of

Columbia had enacted laws requiring Bible reading in the public schools, and twenty-five others either permitted it by law or court decision or allowed it to go on through official silence on the subject. Eleven states had prohibited Bible reading entirely. (Alaska and Hawaii are not included in this analysis.)[60]

In surveys of major cities in 1896 and 1903, the U.S. Office of Education found that about 75 percent of the public schools engaged in Bible reading.[61] But that percentage dropped sharply from then until Ellery Schempp's day. In 1962, an education professor from Macalester College, Richard B. Dierenfield, published a comprehensive study that provided a clear view of religious practices in the public schools at the time of Ellery's protest. By the middle of the twentieth century, what religious practices remained in the public schools were concentrated in the South and the Northeast and were relatively rare elsewhere. Reading of Scripture took place in almost 42 percent of the nation's school systems but varied dramatically by region. About 77 percent of school systems in the South and 68 percent of systems in the Northeast conducted readings, compared to only 18 percent in the Midwest and 11 percent in the West. The King James Version clearly predominated, adopted by 71 percent of school systems. Sixty percent did not allow excusal of students who preferred not to participate.[62]

As Dierenfield pointed out, Bible reading was often part of a broader devotional service, typically short in duration and held at the beginning of the day. The service might also include prayer, devotional talks, and the singing of hymns. In a separate survey of these practices, he found that about half of all school districts in the country held devotional services in all or some of their schools. Unsurprisingly, the pattern looked the same as for Bible reading. About 80 percent of school districts in the East and 89 percent in the South held devotionals in some or all of their schools. In the rest of the country, devotional practices were less frequent. Only 26 percent of school districts in the Midwest and 9 percent in the West held them in the classroom.[63]

The Abington school district was among those that had retained devotional practices in the schools, required to do so by Pennsylvania law. Two devotional practices—Bible reading and the Lord's Prayer—were about all that were left of the expansive school religion of years past, but both exercises lived at the very core of Christianity. So, when Ellery Schempp brought his protest against these exercises to the U.S. district court, both Abington and the state of Pennsylvania were preparing a vigorous fight to keep them.

9. "Mr. Schempp, Do You Believe in the Divinity of Christ?"

Six months after Henry Sawyer filed the Schempps' lawsuit against the Abington school district, Judge John Biggs, Jr,. rapped his gavel to start the trial that would test Ellery Schempp's challenge to prayer and Bible reading. It was August 5, 1958—a Thursday. Biggs's courtroom was inside a large building, on the west side of Ninth Street, four blocks east of William Penn's statue atop City Hall and within easy walking distance to Independence Hall.

The Ninth Street courthouse looked perfectly cast for its role in the case that was about to unfold. Constructed of white limestone in the art deco style, it was built in the late thirties. Bas-relief sculptures entitled *The Law* and *Justice* ornamented two of the facades. Another facade displayed reliefs of the seals of the original thirteen states and inscriptions about law. On the second floor, six trial courtrooms lined a long corridor that ran the length of the building. When the courts were in session, the corridor buzzed with lawyers talking among themselves and conferring with parties and witnesses. As only federal cases were heard here, often raising significant issues of national law, the best and brightest of the Philadelphia bar often did their work at the federal courthouse.

Philadelphia was the home of the U.S. Court of Appeals for the Third Circuit, one of the nation's federal appellate courts. Congress had carved the nation into judicial circuits that heard cases arising within their borders. The Third Circuit comprised Pennsylvania, New Jersey, Delaware, and the Virgin Islands. Lawsuits raising issues of federal law or the Constitution typically went to trial in a federal district court. It was there that the trial would take place, with lawyers examining witnesses and introducing evidence. At the conclusion of the trial, the court would make factual findings—critically important since typically there is conflicting testimony—and then apply the law to the facts in order to decide the case. The loser in district court could appeal by right to the U.S. court of appeals for that judicial circuit, whose job was to decide if the law had been correctly applied to the findings of fact. Beyond that, appeal lay only with the U.S. Supreme Court, through what is called a writ of certiorari. But the Supreme Court exercises discretionary review in most cases, choosing perhaps a hundred cases to hear among the thousands of petitions that come to it each year. At the time of *Schempp*, the chances of convincing the justices to hear a case was at best four or five in one hundred.

The *Schempp* case, however, arrived in court under special dispensation. It was a suit testing whether a state law violated a provision of the federal Constitution. So important a legal challenge—involving both individual rights and liberties and the relationship between the state and federal governments—deserved a speedy and sure process. So a federal law in effect at the time required that any such lawsuit be tried in an expedited process before a special three-judge panel comprised of one appeals court judge and two district court judges. These three judges would sit as the federal district court, hearing the case without a jury. From there, the appeals process skipped the U.S. court of appeals and went directly to the Supreme Court, which was required to hear the case; the only way the justices in Washington could dodge a ruling on the merits was through the finding of some irregularity that required dismissal or a rehearing by the three-judge panel.

Henry Sawyer and the ACLU could have followed Leo Pfeffer's advice and filed the suit in a Pennsylvania state court. There, the process to the Supreme Court would have been much longer and entirely uncertain—moving up through the state court system and finally over to the U.S. Supreme Court, which could decide to hear the case or not. Sawyer, though, was confident in his case, and he welcomed the fact that a filing in federal court all but guaranteed him a date in Washington.

When Sawyer filed the suit, it was assigned to district court judge C. William Kraft, Jr. Because of the constitutional issues it raised, the case triggered the law requiring a three-judge court and expedited review. Under the law, the chief judge of the Third Circuit, John Biggs, had to appoint two additional judges to the panel—an appeals court judge and a district court judge. Biggs, who saw the significance of the case, which raised a new issue under the First Amendment religion clauses, appointed himself to the panel. He also appointed U.S. district judge William H. Kirkpatrick.

It was an impressive panel. Like so many other major figures involved in the *Schempp* case, both Kraft and Kirkpatrick were alumni of the University of Pennsylvania Law School. Kraft, who was fifty-four years old as the trial opened, had been district attorney of a suburban Philadelphia county for eight years and in private practice for two decades. Kraft had taken his seat only three years earlier, after having been nominated by President Eisenhower. Kirkpatrick, seventy-two years old, had been nominated by President Calvin Coolidge and had already served as a district court judge for thirty-one years. He had served one term as a U.S. congressman and had been in a private law practice for almost two decades.

The star of the panel, however, was clearly John Biggs, who would eventually write the court's opinion. As chief judge of the Third Circuit and one of the most important judicial figures in Philadelphia, he commanded wide respect not just for the power he wielded but also equally for his legal knowledge. A personal friend of F. Scott Fitzgerald and a published novelist himself, John Biggs was certainly one of the most unusual persons to have served on the federal judiciary. Biggs was born in 1895 to a wealthy and prominent Delaware family firmly entrenched in the establishment—white and Presbyterian, with old money and a Princeton University legacy.[1] Biggs's paternal grandfather had been governor of the state and had served in Congress, and his father had been the state's attorney general and the presiding officer of Delaware's constitutional convention in 1896. Much was expected of boys born to such privilege, and young John did not disappoint.

Biggs arrived at Princeton in 1914, where he wore the traditional tie, jacket, starched collar, and cap. He majored in literature and befriended both Edmund Wilson and Fitzgerald, who became his roommate. Fitzgerald got such poor grades that he left Princeton during his junior year. Biggs later wrote that his friend "was an exceedingly busy man, and had very little time to devote to the courses so generously made available by the University."[2] When Fitzgerald returned to school the following fall, he was a more serious student. Arthur Mizener, a Fitzgerald biographer, said that Biggs, Wilson, and a few other friends gave Fitzgerald "the only education he ever got" and "a respect for literature which was more responsible than anything else for making him a serious man."[3] Biggs himself had serious literary ambitions, editing Princeton's student journal, *The Nassau Literary Magazine,* where he published both Fitzgerald's and his own writing. Biggs and Fitzgerald, wrote Mizener, "sometimes produced whole issues of *The Tiger* [the student humor magazine] between darkness and dawn and wrote a great deal of the *Lit.*"[4] When Biggs entered Harvard Law School in 1919, he admittedly spent more time writing a novel than he did in classes, barely even attending a course taught by Felix Frankfurter, the eminent Harvard professor who would receive an appointment to the Supreme Court in 1939.

Biggs joined his father's law practice in Wilmington and, during the twenties, wrote two novels edited by Maxwell Perkins, a famous editor at Scribner's. Those two novels marked the peak of Biggs's literary career, for he soon became involved in Democratic state politics and even ran unsuccessfully for the office his father had held, attorney general of the state. In 1937, having received an appointment from President Franklin Roosevelt, Biggs was sworn in as a judge on the U.S. Court of Appeals for the Third Circuit in Philadelphia. Within two years, with the retirement of all four of the judges who had been there on his arrival, Biggs had become the senior judge of the circuit. In 1940, upon the death of his friend Fitzgerald, he became executor and trustee for Fitzgerald's estate, taking responsibility for his literary properties and for the financial security of Zelda, Fitzgerald's wife.

During his tenure on the Third Circuit, Biggs would write about fifteen hundred opinions in more than four thousand cases. Many of them, including *Abington School District v. Schempp*, were cases with far-reaching consequences. He ordered that Delaware's public schools be desegregated, required reapportionment of the Delaware General Assembly, and ordered fifty thousand steelworkers to return to work under the Taft-Hartley Act.[5]

By the time the *Schempp* case reached his court, Biggs was a twenty-year veteran of the federal bench. At times brilliant, Biggs was a highly respected judge, with a deep baritone voice, an acerbic manner, and little evident patience for lawyers who were either unprepared or unconvincing. One lawyer who argued before him, Joseph S. Lord III (who later became a judge in the federal district court), told the story of an argument he presented before Biggs and two of his colleagues on a Third Circuit panel. As Lord droned on and on, Biggs whispered to his two colleagues and then interrupted Lord. "Mr. Lord," he said, "we find ourselves singularly unimpressed with your argument. But, if you care to persist, we will sit here and listen." Biggs wasn't any happier with lawyers who he felt wasted his time describing facts that he had previously read in their briefs. "If counsel began argument with a needless recitation of the facts of a case, Biggs arched from slump to upright position as if he had been released from a Roman catapult," wrote his biographer, Seymour I. Toll. Biggs would inform him that they had read the record."[6]

Biggs was at his best with attorneys who were as skilled and as learned as he, and he enjoyed exactly that situation in the *Schempp* case. Both C. Brewster Rhoads and Henry W. Sawyer III were Philadelphia Brahmins—men educated, as was Biggs, in the finest private academies and Ivy League universities. Both Rhoads and Sawyer boasted extensive military experience and a wide-ranging intellect. These attorneys differed from one another in manner, however. Rhoads, the attorney for the Abington school district, was a courtly gentleman nearing retirement; Sawyer was a tall, redheaded man in whom the fires burned especially bright for civil liberties cases.

꒛

Sawyer and the other lawyers in the courtroom that morning had worked hard to prepare themselves for this moment. At the time (the late 1950s), though, there existed little case law on the First Amendment religion clauses. The Supreme Court had only rarely spoken on the subject up to then. The reason had to do with the reach of the First Amendment.

When the First Amendment was ratified in 1791, it operated—as did all of the Bill of Rights—as a restraint only on actions of the federal government. The states were free to deal with religion any way they pleased—subject, of course, to restrictions in their own laws and constitution. This is the way things remained for a century and a half. Since the states controlled virtually all legislation concerning religion (most notably, the laws requiring or permitting Bible reading), plaintiffs had to challenge the statutes under their state constitutions, not under the First Amendment. Thus, the state courts, not the federal courts, adjudicated most religion cases, and their rulings applied only within their own borders.

All this changed with two cases that reached the Supreme Court in the middle of the twentieth century and made state laws on religion subject—for the first time—to review under the First Amendment. The Fourteenth Amendment, which had been ratified in 1868, said, among other things, that the states could not "deprive any person of life, liberty, or property, without due process of law." One by one, as cases came before them, the justices defined virtually all the provisions of the Bill of Rights as essential liberties and made them applicable to the states through the due process clause. In cases decided in 1940 and 1947, the Supreme Court ruled that the First Amendment's two religion clauses were part of the liberty that the due process clause guaranteed against abridgement by the states.[7] From then on, the two clauses on religious freedom applied as restraints on actions by government at all levels, state and federal. Individuals could now invoke the First Amendment's religion clauses in claims for protection against any action of the government at any level.

Now that the First Amendment's umbrella covered all claims of religious liberty against the government, it remained for the Supreme Court to say exactly what the establishment clause and the free exercise clause actually meant. That wasn't so obvious, and there were difficult problems from the outset. Those who ratified the First Amendment had not passed a detailed statute. They had expressed the two great guarantees of religious liberty in all of sixteen words. They had written a general command whose power derived from a revolutionary idea expressed with simplicity and economy. More than a century and a half later, justices would have to apply this general command to religious exercises held in public schools—institutions of which there were few in the framers' time and, therefore, about which they had nothing to say.

When the Supreme Court began considering the meaning of the two religion clauses, the justices knew to probe deeply into the history that concerned the framers. When the framers wrote the religion clauses into the First Amendment, they were reacting against the excessive religious zeal that had bathed Europe in blood for a millennium (this history is discussed in chapter 5). Each country established one faith as the national church, and citizens had to support that church both spiritually and financially. Dissenters suffered severe limitations on their freedom to worship, as well as disqualifications from public office and other privileges. Divisions between Catholics and Protestants and among Protestants themselves brought continuous war and persecution. Over the centuries, millions of dissenters perished in ugly campaigns to compel worship under an officially established religion. In America, the colonies failed to entirely break from their European past. Nine of the original thirteen colonies elevated one or more faiths to the status of established church, with limitations and disabilities placed on those who dissented.

The two religion clauses adopted in 1791 were a direct reaction to experiences both in Europe and in the colonies and were intended to prevent church and state from forming relationships that would cause strife based on faith. Each clause addressed a different aspect of the union of church and state, one clause focusing on the state and the other on individuals. The clause prohibiting an establishment of religion focused on the state, preventing the European model of the government elevating one denomination above others—or, more broadly, as the Court came to interpret the clause, preventing the state from aiding religion in general. Religion would advance through voluntary support by its adherents, not through government favoritism or limitations.

By contrast, the free exercise clause focused on individuals rather than government. It ensured the liberty of conscience, giving to individuals the right to make their own voluntary choices about religious practice, without rewards or burdens from the state—in other words, without any direct or indirect coercion. As Representative Carroll said at the debate in the House on the religion guarantees on August 15, 1789, "the rights of conscience are, in their nature, of peculiar delicacy, and will little bear the gentlest touch of governmental hand."[8] A finding of coercion would become necessary to find a violation of the free exercise clause, and identifying coercion would eventually become controversial in situations involving devotionals in the public schools. Did an excusal provision in the law, enabling students to opt out of devotional exercises, remove the element of coercion to follow prayer and Bible reading activities? Or did coercion still operate implicitly, because children were required to attend school and because peer pressure made it difficult or even impossible for children to excuse themselves each day from an important school-supported activity? The courts in *Schempp* and other cases would have great difficulty grappling with that issue.

Justices decided the early religion cases—and most since—on the grounds of the establishment clause alone. At the outset, the

Supreme Court firmly committed itself to a broad interpretation of the meaning of establishment of religion, a stance that would become increasingly under attack by religious conservatives in the years ahead. Establishment meant more than simply recognizing a state church or otherwise preferring one denomination to all others. Preventing establishment meant, said the justices, a more complete separation of church and state, a prohibition on government promoting religion in general. The government had to act neutrally in regard to religion, neither advancing nor hindering it.

In 1947, the Court faced some of these issues squarely for the first time. In *Everson v. Board of Education of Ewing Township*, the Court upheld the validity under the First Amendment of a New Jersey school board's decision—pursuant to a state law—to use tax money to reimburse parents for the cost of bus transportation for children attending Catholic schools. Writing for the Court's five-to-four majority, Justice Black adopted the broad interpretation of the establishment clause, an interpretation that he said was consistent "in the light of [the clause's] history and the evils it was designed forever to suppress."[9] Black traced the history of religious persecution in Europe. "These practices of the old world were transplanted to and began to thrive in the soil of the new America." Black wrote.[10]

As did many historians, Black considered the fight for disestablishment of the Anglican Church in Virginia to be the seminal battle for religious liberty in America. There, Madison marshaled enough support to defeat a general tax assessment to support teachers of religion. Madison's great *Memorial and Remonstrance* provided the intellectual framework for religious liberty, arguing that as to civil society, "religion is wholly exempt from its cognizance."[11] Defeating the religious assessment bill, they instead enacted Jefferson's religious liberty statute, forbidding the government from compelling any person to support any religious ministry. Alluding to the developments in Virginia, Black concluded that the establishment clause was meant by the framers to prevent all government aid to religion, not just the preference of one sect over another. Black said, in a passage that has often been quoted since:

The "establishment of religion" clause of the First Amendment means at least this: Neither a state nor the Federal Government can set up a church. Neither can pass laws which aid one religion, aid all religions, or prefer one religion over another. Neither can force nor influence a person to go to or to remain away from church against his will or force him to profess a belief or disbelief in any religion. No person can be punished for entertaining or professing religious beliefs or disbeliefs, for church attendance or non-attendance. No tax in any amount, large or small, can be levied to support any religious activities or institutions, whatever they may be called, or whatever form they may adopt to teach or practice religion. Neither a state nor the Federal Government can openly or secretly, participate in the affairs of any religious organizations or groups and vice versa. In the words of Jefferson, the clause against establishment of religion by law was intended to erect "a wall of separation between Church and State."[12]

Despite his strong words, Black had a surprise still to spring. He went on to say that the practice of reimbursing parents of parochial school students for the cost of bus transportation did not breach the wall of separation. The subsidy did not support religious education specifically, he said; it was a general government service comparable to police and fire protection and thus had a secular, not a religious, purpose.

Interestingly enough, the four dissenters in the *Everson* case agreed with the majority's expansive interpretation of the establishment clause. However, they thought that the majority had not applied it faithfully to the facts of the case and that Ewing Township had breached the wall of separation. Even two of the Court's most conservative members, Justices Robert Jackson and Felix Frankfurter, agreed with the wall metaphor, which would become the target of Christian conservatives and many conservative legal scholars in the years to come. The modern conservatives felt that the separationist position excluded religion from public life and created a culture of secular humanism in American public schools. In the fifties, though, it seemed that the conservatives on the Court had few such qualms. In fact, they, more than almost anyone else, seemed to be guardians of the wall.

Justices Jackson and Frankfurter both dissented from Black's opinion. Jackson, joined by Frankfurter, wrote critically that the Court had created a strict separation principle but then refused to enforce it. He concluded: "[T]he undertones of the opinion, advocating complete and uncompromising separation of Church from State, seem utterly discordant with its conclusion yielding support to their commingling in educational matters. The case which irresistibly comes to mind as the most fitting precedent is that of Julia, who, according to Byron's reports, 'whispering 'I will ne'er consent,'—consented.'"[13] Justices Jackson and Frankfurter opposed any subsidies for religious instruction, as violations of the establishment clause.[14]

Another dissenting opinion—written by Justice Wiley B. Rutledge, joined by three other justices, including Frankfurter and Jackson—showed just how far the two leading conservatives of the time went in supporting complete separation of church and state. Rutledge appended a copy of Madison's *Memorial and Remonstrance* to the end of his opinion and called it "a broadside attack upon all forms of 'establishment' of religion, both general and particular, nondiscriminatory or selective."[15] Rutledge wrote:

> The Amendment's purpose was not to strike merely at the official establishment of a single sect, creed or religion, outlawing only a formal relation such as had prevailed in England and some of the colonies. Necessarily it was to uproot all such relationships. But the object was broader than separating church and state in this narrow sense. It was to create a complete and permanent separation of the spheres of religious activity and civil authority by comprehensively forbidding every form of public aid or support for religion.[16]

The next two important Supreme Court cases related to matters of church and state didn't seem to clarify matters. In *McCollum v. Board of Education* in 1948, the Court struck down a released-time program in which the public schools permitted teachers employed by private religious groups to teach religious matters on school property during time normally reserved for regular secular teaching. The program violated the establishment clause by involving the public schools in direct support of religious groups.[17] Most notable again was the work of the conservative justice Frankfurter, this time in a concurring opinion joined by Jackson. Frankfurter concluded that the released-time program "furthers inculcation of the religious tenets of some faiths" and made clear the religious differences among the schoolchildren. "These are consequences not amenable to statistics," Frankfurter wrote. "But they are precisely the consequences against which the Constitution was directed when it prohibited the government common to all from becoming embroiled, however innocently, in the destructive religious conflicts of which the history of even this country records some dark pages."[18]

Four years later, though, in *Zorach v. Clauson*, the Court approved of a released-time program held off of the public school property. Students who did not participate had to stay in school, but the Court said, "[T]he public schools do no more than accommodate their schedules to a program of outside religious instruction."[19] Once again, one of the liberal justices, William O. Douglas, wrote the opinion for the Court; and the two leading conservatives, Justices Frankfurter and Jackson, wrote that the wall of separation had been breached. Jackson said that the state required students to attend public school and then released a portion of that time back only if the student agreed to attend religious exercises. "No one suggests that the Constitution would permit the State directly to require this 'released' time to be spent 'under the control of a duly constituted religious body,'" wrote Jackson. "This program accomplishes that forbidden result by indirection." Taking the broad view that the establishment clause prohibited government support of religion in general, he added, "The day that this country ceases to be free for irreligion it will cease to be free for religion—except for the sect that can win political power."[20]

Sawyer and Rhoads had to apply whatever principles they could discern from these decisions to the experience of religious exercises in the Pennsylvania schools. Bible reading had been widespread in Pennsylvania through the nineteenth century. No less than the superintendent of public instruction in Pennsylvania was eager to assist teachers and students in their Bible exercises. Nathan C. Schaeffer selected passages from the Bible and published them in a book in 1897. In the preface to *Bible Readings for Schools,* Schaeffer explained that his purpose was to select passages that provided moral lessons for the students. "The Bible is the Book of books," he wrote. "As a means of imparting moral and religious instruction, nothing equal to it is found in all the other books which the ages have produced." He maintained, "Bible reading cannot be omitted from the exercises of the school without the gravest loss and the most serious consequences."[21]

Bible reading in Pennsylvania finally became compulsory with the passage of a state law in 1913.[22] Codified in the public school law of 1949, it specified that ten verses of the Holy Bible be read without comment at the beginning of each school day; this was the statute challenged in the *Schempp* lawsuit. The law required that the local school board discharge teachers who did not comply.[23] Schools were not required to include the Lord's Prayer in the morning exercises, but many, including Abington, did just that.

⁂

All this made for a confusing start to the U.S. Supreme Court's interpretation of the establishment clause. It seemed that the Court, including its brightest conservative lights, agreed with the metaphor of a wall of separation. But the Court's application of that general principle had been so inconsistent as to make it difficult to predict what the Court might say about devotional exercises in the public schools.

Henry Sawyer had this legal history in mind as he arrived at the federal district court on the morning of August 5, 1958, and he knew exactly how he wanted the proceedings to unfold. He had a number of goals to accomplish. First and most generally, he had to establish a trial record that would educate the judges as to what transpired each morning in the Abington schools—the morning devotionals that had driven Ellery Schempp to his protest. For that, he would call on Ellery; his father; and his siblings, Roger and Donna.

Once he had done that, the more difficult challenge would follow. He needed to convince the judges that the Bible-reading and Lord's Prayer exercises amounted to a religious ceremony. Although the religious orientation of the exercises might seem obvious, Sawyer knew that Rhoads would argue that Pennsylvania had not chosen the Bible to promote religious teaching; he expected Rhoads to argue that the state wanted to expose schoolchildren to great moral and ethical teachings and that there was no better book to do that than the Bible. If Sawyer could prove the religious nature of the exercise, this alone might be enough to win the case under the establishment clause, but he couldn't be sure.

Two schools of thought existed on this issue. Some scholars maintained that state endorsement of any religious exercise would amount to a prohibited establishment of religion. Others argued that the First Amendment allowed the government to promote all religion as long as it did so evenhandedly. According to this argument, only promotion of one religion over all others or the injection of sectarian practice into public life would be a violation of the religion clauses. So Sawyer needed to prove to the judges that the morning devotionals were not only a religious practice but also a sectarian one that promoted Protestantism over Catholicism, Judaism, and other faiths. In addition, he wanted to show that the schools had violated the second religious freedom guarantee, the free exercise clause, because Ellery had been forced to participate in religious ceremonies that conflicted with his own beliefs.

Sawyer had prepared carefully for this moment. In June, he had asked the ACLU and Leo Pfeffer to provide him with the trial record for a case Pfeffer had argued successfully in New Jersey.[24] The school board of Rutherford had permitted Gideons International, a nonprofit organization that spreads Christian faith through distribu-

tion of the Bible, to hand out Bibles to children in the local schools.
A Jewish and a Catholic family sued the school board, arguing that
the Gideon Bible, largely based on the King James Version, was "a
sectarian work of peculiar religious value and significance to members of the Protestant faith."[25] The trial record included testimony by
religious experts detailing the differences between various versions of
the Bible. In 1953, the New Jersey Supreme Court unanimously
agreed with Pfeffer that the Gideon Bible was sectarian and that its
distribution in the public schools violated the state and federal constitutions. William J. Brennan, Jr., an associate justice on the U.S.
Supreme Court by the time of the *Schempp* case, had served on the
state supreme court in the case brought against Gideons International.[26]

Rhoads, of course, entertained different ideas entirely. He had to
counter Sawyer's charge that the public schools were sponsoring a
religious ceremony in violation of the establishment clause. He
wanted to convince the judges that Bible reading and recitation of
the Lord's Prayer were not religious ceremonies at all—that, instead,
the morning exercises used the Bible and Lord's Prayer not to teach
religion but, rather, in an effort to instruct students in virtue and
morality. Beyond that, Rhoads prepared to argue that the Bible was
not a sectarian religious text but was acceptable to all faiths.

⟳

The first witness on the stand on August 5 was Ellery Schempp. It
was his birthday. Much had changed for Ellery in the twenty-one
months since his protest in homeroom class. Now eighteen years old,
he had graduated from Abington Senior High School and was a
month away from beginning his college studies at Tufts University.
Ellery says that he later found out that the Abington principal,
W. Eugene Stull, had written negative recommendations for his college applications. Stull had even contacted the admissions officer at
Tufts and urged the school not to admit him.[27]

In the courtroom, Sawyer began with a few easy questions establishing where Ellery had attended school.[28] Rhoads immediately objected. Here was his opportunity to knock the main plaintiff from the case. He said that because Ellery had graduated, the issues raised in the lawsuit were moot as to him, so Ellery should be disqualified from any further testimony. Ellery was a critical witness: it was his protest that had brought this matter before the court. Without him, the case could carry on with Ellery's two siblings, but Rhoads knew that Ellery was the most passionate of the three. Biggs replied that he would reserve any ruling on the motion.

Ellery's testimony resumed, but he had to stop again when Rhoads and then Biggs asked him to slow down. Ellery was nervous about testifying, but already he was feeling a lot more comfortable with Biggs. "It was clear that the other judges and everyone in the courtroom gave him a lot of respect," says Ellery. "The chief judge got that automatically. But somehow he commanded it no matter what his title might have been. When he spoke to me, admonished me to speak slowly, he said it in a very kind way."[29]

Sawyer wanted to show that Abington Senior High School had endorsed a specific religious doctrine by requiring devotional exercises, so he asked Ellery how the King James Bible conflicted with his own beliefs as a Unitarian Protestant. "Mr. Schempp," he began, "do you believe in the divinity of Christ?"

"I do not."

"Were you read in the course of your instruction at Abington High School material from the Bible which asserted the divinity of Christ?"

"Yes, sir."

"Do you believe in the Immaculate Conception?"

"No."

"Were you read material during the course of your time at Abington High School which asserted the truth of the Immaculate Conception?"

"There was."

Rhoads interrupted with a question about whether all of this came from the morning Bible reading. Ellery said yes. Then Sawyer continued, "Do you believe in God?"

"Yes."

"Do you believe in an anthropomorphic God?"

"No."

"Were you read material from the King James version during your time in school which asserted the concept of an anthropomorphic God?"

"Yes."

"Do you believe in the concept of the Trinity?"

"No."

"Were you read material from the King James version during your time at Abington which asserted the truth of the concept of the Trinity?"

"I believe so."[30]

After moving briefly to another point, Sawyer returned to the same line of questions. "Ellery, do you believe in your own conscience in the concept of petitional prayer?"

"I do not."[31]

When Sawyer was finished, Rhoads had his opportunity for cross-examination. His strategy seemed directed at raising doubts about the depth of Ellery's conscience on the issue of Bible reading and the Lord's Prayer. He asked about the months leading up to Ellery's protest. Ellery conceded that his parents had not complained to officials at the high school and had not asked for Ellery to be excused from attending the morning exercises.[32]

With a leading question, Rhoads questioned Ellery about how long he had felt troubled by the morning devotionals: "And up to November of 1956 you had not felt that way; is that correct?"

"No, that's not correct. I had been thinking about it for some time; I had not decided what I could do or should do until that time."[33]

Ellery's testimony soon ended. Now it was his father's turn on the witness stand.[34] Ed Schempp said that his personal faith made him disagree with many of the statements from the Bible that were read to his children: "Well, we have Leviticus where they mention all sorts of blood sacrifices, uncleanness and leprosy. Nobody believes in these things today. . . . And in some parts, some of the lower grades the children are allowed to select verses and they could just as well pick verses from Leviticus. I don't believe that they would be picked by an adult. The Old Testament has Jehovah as a God of vengeance. We have—there is a verse sandwiched right in between the Ten Commandments in which 'God will visit the sins upon the fourth generation.' That has been read in Abington High School. A human father would not visit the sins upon the children of a fourth generation, in my opinion. That makes God less than man and I do not want my children believing that God is a lesser person than a human father. My concept of God is bigger than that. We have parts—another part that says something like, 'The animal that dies of itself—' or 'The meat that dies of itself thou shalt not eat,' but then 'Thou mayest feed it to the stranger within thy gates.' That's nothing—that's quite foreign to my concept of being good and religious and moral. There's many things like that."[35]

When it was his turn, Rhoads only had a few questions for Ed Schempp. He wanted to know if he had ever complained to the Abington school authorities about the morning devotionals. Echoing his son's answer, Schempp said that he had not.

Ellery's siblings were plaintiffs in the suit, so they took their turns testifying as well. Roger, then fifteen years old and about to enter the ninth grade at Huntingdon Junior High School, talked about the morning Bible readings at his school.[36] Because the junior high did not have a public address system to broadcast the exercises, the teachers themselves put on the exercises in each homeroom class. For the first half of the school year just completed, the responsibility for reading the Bible rotated to each of the students, who chose the verses they wanted to read. Then there was a change, and for the balance of the year, the teachers chose verses and read them.

Roger answered questions from Rhoads about his own objections to the morning devotionals. With Ellery having graduated from high school, Rhoads figured that he would eventually be stricken from the suit because the issues were now moot as to him; that is, whether the Bible exercises continued or not would no longer affect his rights in any way. Were Ellery's siblings objecting out of a deeply felt conscience as well? Rhoads asked Roger when he had started feeling strongly about this issue. Roger responded, "It was about the same time Ellery—when he brought it up, I thoroughly agreed with him on the Bible reading; when my brother talked about it with my parents."

"Did that have anything to do with about the time that you realized that Ellery would be graduated before you had a chance to tell the Court about this?"

"I had realized that, yes."

"It was about that time?"

"Yes, it was about that time."[37]

Donna Schempp testified next.[38] Twelve years old and soon to begin eighth grade at Huntingdon Junior High, she described several biblical lessons that she said conflicted with her beliefs. Sawyer asked her if she recalled any of her classmates reacting to the Bible reading exercises. She responded, "Well, I do know a Jewish friend who was listening to a part of the Bible where I think it was when Jesus washed the feet of a man and something happened—I don't exactly recall—and she got almost so fed up with it because she didn't believe in it that she was going to walk out of the room." When Rhoads objected, Judge Biggs struck the testimony because it involved a subjective interpretation of what another person was thinking. Sawyer rephrased his question, and Donna replied, "She said that she was just plain fed up."[39]

Then, as he did with Roger, Rhoads asked questions designed to raise doubts about Donna's actual opposition to the morning devotionals. Donna said that she had never asked either her mother or her father to complain to school authorities about the devotionals. Rhoads asked, "Now, the practice of reading the Bible was, as you said, a voluntary practice in your room, is that correct?"

"Yes."

"And did you ever volunteer to read the Bible?"
"I did."
"And on how many occasions did you volunteer to read it?"
"I don't recall."
"More than once, though, wasn't it, my dear?"
"I think so."[40]

10. Is the Bible Sectarian?

Following the Schempp family's testimony, the trial moved on to a battle of the expert witnesses. While most witnesses at trials testify to convey their firsthand knowledge of the facts, experts appear for a much different purpose. As people of special skill or knowledge, expert witnesses draw inferences and opinions from the facts and thus help judges and juries to better understand the issues before them.

In the *Schempp* case, the judges' analysis of the constitutional issues rested in large part on their understanding the religious significance, if any, of reading the Bible and reciting the Lord's Prayer in public schools. Were these devotional activities? Was the Bible a sectarian book? How did different religious faiths view the King James Bible? Would certain passages offend children who were not raised in the religious traditions of the majority? The answers to such questions would help the judges determine whether these activities in the classroom offended the First Amendment's establishment clause and free exercise clause.

Judge Biggs and his colleagues were not the first jurists to consider whether Bible reading in the classroom constituted a sectarian practice. They could look back to state supreme courts that had faced similar questions beginning about a century earlier. These decisions were not binding on the three judges hearing *Schempp*. Because these cases were brought many years before the First Amendment was made applicable to the states, they relied on provisions of state constitutions that prohibited sectarian teaching in public schools. So state supreme courts had to decide whether Bible reading and prayer were sectarian practices within the meaning of their own state constitutional provisions. The courts divided on the question.

A significant early victory for those who wanted to remove the Bible from the public schools came in Ohio. Dissenting from a superior court ruling that permitted religious activities in the Cincinnati public schools, Judge Alphonso Taft concluded that use of the King James Bible "is Protestant worship" and that "its use is a symbol of Protestant supremacy in the schools, and as such offensive to Catholics and to Jews."[1] On review, the Ohio Supreme Court agreed with Taft and ended Bible reading in the public schools (see discussion in chapter 8).

One of the most distinguished opinions came from the Illinois Supreme Court in 1910. In *People ex rel. Ring v. Board of Education*, brought by Catholic plaintiffs, the judges found that religious practices in the classroom constituted worship. "If these exercises of reading the Bible, joining in prayer and in the singing of hymns were performed in a church there would be no doubt of their religious character, and that character is not changed by the place of their performance," the court said.[2] The state constitution banned sectarian practices, and the court reasoned that reading of the Bible constituted just such an activity, because different versions of the Bible provided the theological foundation for many different denominations.

> Protestants will not accept the Douay Bible as representing the inspired word of God. As to them it is a sectarian book containing errors, and matter which is not entitled to their respect as a part of the Scriptures. It is consistent with the Catholic faith but not the Protestant. Conversely, Catholics will not accept King James' version. As to them it is a sectarian book inconsistent in many particulars with their faith, teaching what they do not believe. The differences may seem to many so slight as to be immaterial, yet Protestants are not found to be more willing to have the Douay Bible read as a regular exercise in the schools to which they are required to send their children, than are

Catholics to have the King James version read in schools which their children must attend. Differences of religious doctrine may seem immaterial to some while to others they seem vitally important. Sectarian aversions, bitter animosities and religious persecutions have had their origin in apparently slender distinctions.[3]

The judges then decided that the Bible readings each day amounted to instruction, and they listed what religious lessons the students were apt to learn: "They cannot hear the Scriptures read without being instructed as to the divinity of Jesus Christ, the Trinity, the resurrection, baptism, predestination, a future state of punishments and rewards, the authority of the priesthood, the obligation and effect of the sacraments, and many other doctrines about which the various sects do not agree."[4] Finally, the judges concluded that the state of Illinois had no right to instruct public school students in religious doctrine. Religion, the judges said, should be taught in churches, at religious parochial schools, and at home.[5]

A clear majority of the state courts that considered the issue upheld readings from the Bible, and they offered a variety of reasons for doing so. To reach that result, though, the judges had to find that the Bible was not a sectarian book. Some courts extolled the Bible's literary quality, or what they called the Scriptures' "universal moral lessons." Other courts regarded the Bible as nonsectarian solely within a Christian or Protestant context, conveniently ignoring the beliefs of all non-Christians.

To many of these judges, the Bible was a kind of generic book that enjoyed an enormously wide following. They refused to look further at the doctrinal differences, even among Christians, that caused one denomination to reject the other's version of the Bible. Though authors of a dissenting opinion in the *Ring* case, Judges Hand and Cartwright expressed the idea of the Bible's universal appeal as well as anyone: "Its plan of salvation is broad enough to include all the world, and the fact that those who believe in the Bible do not agree as to the interpretation of its teachings and have divided into sects, and are therefore sectarian in their beliefs, does not change the Bible or make it a sectarian book."[6]

A Kentucky court regarded the Bible as a Christian document acceptable to all, even though a Catholic parent brought the suit in question. The state's court of appeals, then the highest court in Kentucky, first remarked on the universal respect given to the Bible regardless of edition or version, implying that so revered a book could not be sectarian. "It is not the least of its marvelous attributes that it is so catholic that every seeming phase of belief finds comfort in its comprehensive precepts," the court said.[7] The court wasn't bothered by the fact that different versions of the Bible had been the source of bitter religious conflict for centuries. The Bible, said the Kentucky judges, had to teach dogma in order to be considered sectarian.

> That the Bible, or any particular edition, has been adopted by one or more denominations as authentic, or by them asserted to be inspired, cannot make it a sectarian book. The book itself, to be sectarian, must show that it teaches the peculiar dogmas of a sect as such, and not alone that it is so comprehensive as to include them by the partial interpretation of its adherents. Nor is a book sectarian merely because it was edited or compiled by those of a particular sect. It is not the authorship nor mechanical composition of the book, nor the use of it, but its contents, that give it its character.[8]

Having tagged content as the critical question, though, the court simply let the matter drop and never examined the Bible's content. It considered neither the various biblical passages that offended one denomination or the other nor the fact that it was on theological grounds that Protestants, Catholics, and Jews rejected each other's Bible.

In Pennsylvania, whose law was being challenged in *Schempp*, no case challenging Bible reading had ever reached the state's highest court. But two county courts had upheld the practice. In 1885, a court of common pleas approved use of the King James Version against charges by Roman Catholic parents that Bible reading and the singing of Protestant carols violated their freedom of religion under the state constitution. Noting that the Douay was the only version recognized by the Roman Catholic Church, the plaintiffs argued, "all other English versions of the Sacred Scriptures are incorrect, unauthorized and sectarian in character."[9] The court, though, rejected their argument that the religious devotionals in school gave a preference to Protestantism. It said that the King James Version was not sectarian and that, in any case, students who objected could excuse themselves from the devotionals.[10]

Thirteen years later, in 1898, another of the state's lower courts upheld use of the King James Version in the classroom.[11] The court noted that the state had had an antiblasphemy law on the books since 1700, making it a criminal offense to vilify the Christian religion, and that "the laws and institutions of this State are built on the foundation of reverence for Christianity." It confirmed that a large number of school districts in the state conducted opening exercises with the Bible. "The Bible is not a sectarian book," the judge stated. "On its broad foundation Christianity rests." Were there any substantial differences between the Douay and the King James Version? Overlooking the Philadelphia riots between Catholics and Protestants over Bible reading in his own state, the judge concluded, "The Bible in either version is substantially and essentially the same book."[12]

☙

With state courts split, it was up to the expert witnesses to guide Judge Biggs and his two colleagues in the *Schempp* case. Each side called only one expert witness. Sawyer's witness was Solomon Grayzel, editor of the Jewish Publication Society, a publisher of works on Jewish life and religious matters.[13] Born in Minsk in 1896, Grayzel came to the United States with his family in 1908. Ordained a rabbi in 1921 by the Jewish Theological Seminary, he went on to earn a doctorate in history from Dropsie College and became well known as an expert on Jewish life and religion. He taught at Gratz College and then Dropsie and wrote several books of Jewish history.[14]

Rhoads, meanwhile, called on Luther Allan Weigle, dean emeritus of the Yale Divinity School.[15] Weigle, ordained in 1903 as a Lutheran minister, earned both a PhD from Yale University and an LLD from Gettysburg College. He began teaching at the Yale Divinity School in 1916 and then served as its dean from 1928 to 1949. While dean, he chaired a committee of Protestant scholars that undertook a revision of the American Standard Version of the King James Bible. The committee's revision was published as the Revised Standard Version. His literacy as a scholar extended to both Hebrew and Greek, so he was capable of reading in the original language most of the writings that formed the basis of the Bible.[16]

Grayzel went to the witness stand first. Sawyer's goal was to convince the judges that the morning devotionals were a religious ceremony and that the King James Version was a sectarian book. In calling Grayzel as his expert witness, Sawyer chose to focus on the Judeo-Christian tradition. He wanted to show that the King James Version was acceptable to Protestant denominations but was regarded as sectarian—and therefore unacceptable—to Jewish and Catholic students. That was perhaps easiest to accomplish in regard to Jewish students, whose Bible does not include the New Testament and whose theology does not recognize the divinity of Christ. Sawyer could have punctuated that point by also showing how the use of the Bible excluded students of other faiths (e.g., Muslim, Hindu, and Buddhist), but he chose not to, perhaps because there were few if any such students in Abington in the 1950s.

After establishing Grayzel's credentials, Sawyer focused on Abington's choice of the King James Version as the only Bible purchased with public funds and placed in all the school district's classrooms. The King James Bible was not accepted either by the Jewish or the Catholic faiths. Grayzel pointed out that the Jewish Bible contains the Torah, or the five books of Moses, plus the books of the prophets and the sacred writings. The King James Version adds the New Testament, with its acceptance of Jesus as divinity, a concept that is no part of Jewish theology. Meanwhile, Catholics use their Douay Version and reject the Protestant King James Bible.[17]

Sawyer asked Grayzel about exposing Jewish children to a reading of the New Testament in school. Grayzel answered that Jews do not believe in the divinity of Christ and that "certain portions of [the New Testament] are distinctly offensive to Jewish tradition." He added, "I don't want to step on anybody's toes but the idea of God having a son is, from the viewpoint of Jewish faith, practically blasphemous."[18]

Sawyer probed for specific passages in the King James Version that indicated doctrinal differences between the faiths. Certainly there was no more powerful example than Matthew 27, the trial of Jesus before the Roman governor Pontius Pilate. As the New Testament in the King James Version relates it, a Jewish crowd refused to exchange the prisoner Barabbas for Jesus and instead insisted on Jesus's crucifixion, despite Pilate's question, "Why, what evil hath he done?" The King James Bible says of the Jewish crowd, "But they cried out the more, saying, Let him be crucified." Then Barabbas is released and soldiers lead Jesus away to his crucifixion. "I submit to you," said Grayzel, "that this verse, this exclamation has been the cause of more anti-Jewish riots throughout the ages than anything else in history. And if you subject a Jewish child to listening to this sort of reading, which is not at all unlikely before Christmas or before Easter—rather, before Easter, I think he is being subjected to little short of torture."[19] Grayzel added, "it is a direct accusation and a threat which is very disturbing."[20]

Grayzel discussed a number of instances in which the King James Version and the Jewish Holy Scriptures differed in ways considered significant by the faiths. The differences were evident from the very beginning of the biblical texts, he said, with "the description of the Creation, 'And the Spirit of God hovered—or floated, whatever the word is—on the face of the waters.'" Grayzel explained:

Now, in every Christian translation the word "spirit" would be capitalized because the assumption there is that it's a reference to the

Holy Ghost. Now, the Jews understand it, assuming that it does mean "spirit," it means the actual presence, the essence of God and it would not be capitalized. You will find in our translation that it is with a small "s."

Now, these physical differences sometimes manifest themselves also in differences of translation. Any number of passages in the King James version will have a superscription . . . in the Christian Bible especially you have the various passages, the various Psalms described, summarized by a brief statement which is not essentially in, of the Bible but is a description of the translator or the editor of what the next passage contains. . . . Now, that superscription very frequently will say that this refers to Jesus; it describes Jesus' life.[21]

Grayzel also pointed to another key difference that has been the subject of Christian-Jewish debate for many centuries. In Isaiah 7:14, the dispute concerns the proper translation of the Hebrew word *almah*—whether it means "virgin" or "young woman." In the King James Version, the passage reads: "Therefore the Lord himself shall give you a sign; Behold, a virgin shall conceive, and bear a son, and shall call his name Immanuel." But the Jewish translation says, "Behold, the young woman is with child, and she shall bear a son, and she shall call his name Immanuel." Christians interpret Isaiah 7:14 as predicting the virgin birth of Jesus. Grayzel testified that "there we come up against a distinct difference in religious faith." He added: "Now, the Christian church subsequently took this, as it did any number of other passages, as a prophecy, a prediction of things that were to happen many centuries later and took the words 'young woman,' which could be from the Hebrew viewpoint, could be either a married young woman or an unmarried young woman, took it to be a virgin. And so you have here an example, one of the basic examples of deviations between the two, the differences between the two faiths."[22]

Sawyer moved on to blunt another issue that he felt might become important in the proceedings. Proponents of Bible reading argued, of course, that the Bible was nonsectarian. They also said that the law's

provision that it must be read each morning without comment further ensured that sectarian influence would not enter the classroom.
Reading the Bible without comment had been a brilliant innovation
in the 1840s by Horace Mann, the Massachusetts education commissioner, who pleased various Protestant factions by including the
Bible in the curriculum while avoiding the commentary that had
caused bitter divisions in the past. Sawyer knew, however, that taking biblical passages at face value without discussion brought its own
problems. Without commentary to help them, students might mis-
understand the meaning of some words and passages and might even
take meaning from them that would be prejudicial to other faiths.
Beyond that, sharp differences existed in how various faiths regarded
the unaided reading of biblical text. Protestants alone placed high
value on reading the biblical text itself, without comment. For
Catholics, textual meaning derived from Church doctrine
expounded in Rome. For Jews, reading the Bible itself had little
significance; it was study and discussion of the Bible that provided
meaning.

Grayzel said that he wanted to "indicate how the Bible is misunderstood when it is taken without explanation." He continued: "I
mean this reference to a passage in the Bible in Leviticus, which certainly is rarely read, but if an animal is found dead, killed or died naturally, that a Jew may not eat it but a non-Jew may. Now, if you study
the passage it becomes perfectly clear that it was not an act of contempt for the non-Jew but an act of further sanctification for the Jew.
He was to abide by certain rules. But since the non-Jew in those days,
and presumably now, wouldn't hesitate to eat that kind of animal,
you are not to deprive him of it. But as a Jew you are not supposed to
eat it. Now, that does not come out from a mere reading of the Bible
but it does come out from a study of the Bible, and there are any
number of such instances."[23] Grayzel also pointed to the Genesis
story of Jacob and Esau, sons of Isaac and Rebekah. Esau, the first
born, returned exhausted from hunting one day and, instead of waiting patiently for his food, he sold his birthright to his brother Jacob
for some pottage. "Now, if you read the passage as it is written," said

Grayzel, "without paying too much attention to it, it is possible, as happened, for a child, for a non-Jewish child to come to a Jewish friend and say, 'I see now your ancestor was a cheat. He took advantage of his brother who came in tired and hungry and made him give up something valuable for a mess of pottage.' But the point of the story, which I had to—I remember having to explain to the complaining child—was the last phrase in it. The point was, 'Thus, Esau despised his birthright.' It wasn't the question of whether Jacob took advantage of him or not; the point of the story is that Esau had so little regard for his birthright that he was ready to sell it or give it away for a petty thing."[24]

꒓

On his cross-examination, Rhoads wanted to counter Grayzel's portrayal of the King James Version as a sectarian book. To win the case, he had to convince the judges that, far from being a sectarian work, the Bible conveyed universal moral and literary qualities that made it a good pedagogical tool for use with schoolchildren. In other words, he wanted to make the argument that the public schools used the Bible as a source of moral values, not of religious doctrine.

Rhoads probed Grayzel's opinion of the Bible and got the concession he wanted. Grayzel agreed with him that the King James Version had passages of literary merit and moral value.[25] This was a significant concession, because it reached the heart of Rhoads's case: that the state of Pennsylvania, having decided to convey moral teachings to its students, had made a reasonable choice in selecting the Bible as the book for doing so.

But then Rhoads, perhaps a bit unfamiliar with biblical scholarship, made the mistake of asking a question to which he did not already know the answer. Apparently only superficially familiar with the Good Samaritan story, Rhoads left Grayzel a huge opening to explain how even passages conveying moral lessons can be sectarian and divisive. Rhoads got Grayzel to concede that the Good Samaritan story had moral values, but Grayzel continued.

You have the story—I think we are all familiar with it—of this very sick, dead—a dead person or a sick person lying on the road. There are three people who pass by, a priest, a Levite and a Samaritan. Now, notice . . . the three divisions were priests, descendants of Aaron who were priests officiating in the temple who had to be pure in order to enter the temple—"pure," I mean ritually pure—the Levites, whose purity was not expected to be so great but they were also descendants of Aaron, and Israelites, ordinary Israelites, who were not subject to the laws of purity quite as much.

Now, think of the story as it must have been told in those days. A priest passes by. He sees what he think is a dead body. The laws of purity apply to him. He wouldn't touch it because he would make himself impure and couldn't officiate in the temple. He passes it by. It is a cruel act. He should have let, forgotten the laws of impurity and should have attended to the burial of the person, but he preferred— being a stickler for the law he preferred to take care of his purity.

Then comes the Levite; the same thing. Then, along comes an Israelite to whom the laws of impurity do not apply in the same thing and he attends to the person who is lying on the ground.

Grayzel said that the story told in this way had a good moral effect but that the story had been changed.

In the story as it came to be told the Israelite was obviously removed and the Samaritan put in. Why a Samaritan? Well, the Samaritans and the Israelites in those days, the Samaritans and the Jews were not on good terms. Very likely the Samaritan was deliberately put in as a slap at the Jews of that day who refused to join the Christian Church, because the story on the face of it must have been, must have included priest, Levite, Israelite. That was the division. There was no such division as priest, Levite, Samaritan.

Now you tell this story in a school to a Jewish child or in the pres- ence of a Jewish child and a Christian child and the Christian child has every right to say, "See, you come of a people that is cruel, that doesn't understand the decencies of life." And even if the Jewish child is not told that, it is made to feel that, and I submit to you, sir, that that destroys all the moral value of the story. And I don't think that that kind of story ought to be read in a public school where there are—in any public school—because it makes for division rather than for union.[26]

༃

When Rhoads called Luther Weigle to the witness stand on the afternoon of November 25, he could hardly have hoped for a more respected person to testify on his behalf. The retired dean of the Yale Divinity School had, after all, chaired a committee that had published a new translation of the King James Version. With expectations for Weigle so high, Rhoads looked forward to several hours of testimony that would persuade the three judges that the Bible was a nonsectarian book and the best possible source for the moral lessons that school authorities wanted to convey to the children.

Grayzel had made a strong case that many passages were at odds with the traditions of Judaism and other religions. But it was difficult to gauge how the judges felt at this stage of the proceedings. If Grayzel had pushed them in one direction, Rhoads had the man capable of pulling them back. When Weigle finished his testimony, however, it seemed clear that Rhoads had not gained the traction he needed. In fact, at several junctures, Weigle expressed an opinion that seriously wounded Abington's case.

After he introduced Weigle, Rhoads led him through a lengthy exposition on the various versions of the Bible and how they came about. His purpose was to trace all versions of the Bible back to common sources—the Masoretic Hebrew text as the basis for the Old Testament and the Greek text for the New Testament—and to make the point that this foundation was by its very nature nonsectarian. Translations of the Bible differed because of incomplete source material and the accumulated errors that came from laboriously copying manuscripts by hand. Dissenters had their own ideas about the Bible and the proliferation of versions caused widespread strife, especially during the Reformation. Finally, in England, King James attempted to unite the Anglican Church behind one new translation of the Bible. Weigle explained that King James convened a conference in 1604 in an attempt to resolve differences. King James agreed to a suggestion that he commission a new translation of the Bible that would be less sectarian than the Geneva Bible. As a result, a commission of British scholars drafted and published the King James Version in 1611.[27] Questioning Weigle about the King James Version, Rhoads asked, "Was it intended, so far as the translation was concerned, to be an objective approach to a subject of scholarship?" Weigle responded, "It was so intended, and it succeeded."[28]

After a brief discussion of the Catholic Douay Bible and Jewish Old Testament, Rhoads tried to tie the various strands together. In answer to a question, Weigle said that various versions of the Bible had been based on certain original source material that had been available to scholars for centuries. He said that this source material was not sectarian.[29] A few minutes later, Rhoads asked, "Dean Weigle, from your knowledge of the sources and methods available to early scholars, do you believe that the King James Version, that is the Standard King James Version, is an accurate and scholarly piece of work?" Weigle responded, "It is, yes."[30] Having carefully laid his foundation, Rhoads went directly now to a key issue before the three judges—whether the Bible is a sectarian book in any of its major versions: "Dean Weigle, coming to the issues in this case, there is a statute in Pennsylvania which provides—and I am merely summarizing it—that there shall be read in the public schools of this Commonwealth ten verses of the Holy Bible without comment at the opening of school. May I ask you whether you have any opinion as to whether the reading of ten verses of the King James Version of the Bible without comment is sectarian in character?" Following an objection by Sawyer, Weigle responded: "In my opinion, because the Bible is not a sectarian book, that practice is not sectarian." Rhoads then asked, "Would that answer be the same, Dean Weigle, if there were a reading in the same manner as I have described from the Douay Version of the Bible?"

"The same."

"Would the same apply if the reading were from the Jewish Version of the Bible which you have identified a moment ago?"

"The same."[31]

Although Weigle testified that none of the major versions of the Bible were sectarian, he clouded the matter a moment later when Judge Kirkpatrick asked him a series of questions. He posed a hypothetical: If a teacher eliminated the King James Version from the school and only permitted readings from the Hebrew Scriptures, would the children be reading from the Holy Bible? Weigle responded, "He would certainly be conducting exercises which would involve the reading of the Holy Scriptures, as he understands the Holy Scriptures."

"But the trouble is the law says the Holy Bible is what must be read."

"Yes. His practice would be a sectarian practice."

Rhoads interrupted, "If he permitted nothing else, you mean."

"Yes, if he permitted nothing else."[32]

Judge Kirkpatrick let that line of questioning go without anything more. Weigle's statement, as far as it went, seemed potentially damaging to Abington's case. No version of the Bible, according to Weigle, was sectarian, but a school that permitted only readings from the Jewish Holy Scriptures would be engaging in a sectarian practice. What was left hanging was the situation in the Abington schools. The school district theoretically permitted students and teachers to read any version of the Bible. But it purchased and distributed just one particular version of the Bible to its teachers—the King James Version. Nobody probed that point, but it surely was not lost on anyone.

For his part, Sawyer was thinking about another of Weigle's points. Weigle had testified that, in his opinion, the King James Bible was nonsectarian. But he had also said that the King James Version had been published as a compromise to satisfy various factions within the Protestant Anglican Church at the time. If the King James Version was indeed nonsectarian, for whom was it nonsectarian? Sawyer waited his turn.

Rhoads returned to the other major point in his case, asking Weigle about the value of Bible reading to schoolchildren. Weigle said:

> It possesses a moral educational value because, after all, the Bible is the record of the experience of the people that discovered what God really is like, and has given us the Ten Commandments and other moral precepts which are contained in the Holy Bible. It is of very high literary value because the King James Bible is what one authority has called the noblest monument of English prose. It has contributed to the making of the English language as no other English book has done.
>
> It is of great value, it seems to me, to the perpetuation of those institutions and those practices which we ideally think of as the American way of life, because the Bible has entered vitally into the stream of American life. I won't stop to say anything more than that Lincoln was an assiduous student of the Bible; that much that Lincoln did and much that Lincoln wrote bears the stamp of his understanding of the Bible upon it.[33]

Now it was Sawyer's turn to cross-examine Weigle. Sawyer's strategy aimed at convincing the judges that Bible reading and recitation of the Lord's Prayer were religious exercises and that the King James Version, whatever its moral and literary value, was above all a sectarian book whose message conveyed the core religious beliefs of Protestants. Sawyer varied his pace, sometimes serving up easy questions and other times vigorously pressing the attack. His preparation for trial was so extensive and his cross-examination so skilled that he managed to extract key concessions from Weigle.

Sawyer first tried to establish that even Protestants argued about parts of the King James Bible. Weigle himself had supervised a new translation of the King James Bible, so Sawyer pressed several issues that Weigle knew well. Sawyer asked, "Dean, the New Revised Standard Version . . . was greeted with some controversy in the Protestant world, is that correct?" After Sawyer repeated the question, Weigle responded, "No, it wasn't greeted with any controversy in the Protestant world. It received some controversy from certain fringes, but—"

"What were those fringes?"

"It has been welcomed very heartily in the Protestant world."

"What were the fringes that you speak of that took exception to the New Revised Version?"

"Well, people who thought that there ought be no revision."

After a question by Judge Kirkpatrick, Sawyer continued, asking Weigle if he was familiar with the International Council of Christian Churches, of which Carl McIntyre was the founder and president. Weigle said he had heard of him. Sawyer asked, "Did he take up a crusade, so to speak, against the New Revised Standard Version?"

"Yes, but of course he has taken up a great many crusades, including one against the Presbyterian Church."

"People feel strongly about these matters, don't they, translations of the Bible? Don't they, Doctor?"

"Of course people feel strongly. . . ."[34]

Sawyer then asked Weigle about the controversy surrounding the prophesy of the virgin birth in Isaiah 7:14. As Grayzel had explained earlier in the proceedings, the King James Version had translated the Hebrew word *almah* to mean "virgin" rather than "young woman," thus giving the Isaiah passage the translation "a virgin shall conceive, and bear a son . . ." But when Weigle's committee published the Revised Standard Version, which was intended to update the King James Version, the new version used the translation "young woman" and thus moved away from the more Christological translation that anticipates Christ's birth. Sawyer asked Weigle, "Now, did there come a time, sir, if you know, when there was a burning of the Revised Standard Version a few weeks after it was published in December of 1952, down in North Carolina? Do you remember that incident?"

"Yes."

"Do you recall that one of the things that was attacked was the fact that in I believe it is Isaiah 7:14 the new Revised Standard substitutes the word 'woman' for the word 'virgin' in speaking of the prophesy of Isaiah which the Christian Church has widely acclaimed and heralded in the coming of Christ? Is that an incident which is familiar to you, sir?"

"Yes."

Sawyer continued, "Would you say, sir, that in the translation of Isaiah that there is no sectarian aspect as to whether or not one believes that the word of God there set forth is that a young virgin shall conceive or a young woman shall conceive? Is that a sectarian issue?"

"That is not a sectarian issue. . . . The translation of this word by scholars generally is young woman. It has been so accepted by all of the basic Hebrew dictionaries. It has been accepted by fundamentalist scholars who may have objected to other points of the Revised Standard Version but do not object to this. It has been accepted by churches that, well, you wouldn't expect to accept it."

"Has it been rejected by others?"

"I don't know anyone that has rejected it that understands the Hebrew."

"I am not asking you whether they are wrong or right in their rejections, as your answer was, sir, but do you know that there are bodies of opinion within the Protestant world and outside of it which specifically rejected this translation?"

"Oh, yes."[35]

Sawyer clearly had scored some valuable points. He had been waiting patiently, though, for the right time to take on Weigle on perhaps the most critical point. Earlier, Weigle had said that he believed the King James Version was a nonsectarian book. Sawyer first asked him to define what he meant by the term *sectarian*. Weigle explained, "A movement is sectarian when it is meant to establish the distinctive doctrines of some particular sect as opposed to the doctrines of other sects."

"And when would a Bible be sectarian?"

"When it was so translated as to do just that, that is, . . . to tend to establish the distinctive doctrine of that particular sect as opposed to other sects."[36]

Now Sawyer, using Weigle's definition of sectarian, backed him into a critical concession—that what he really meant was that the Bible is nonsectarian only for Protestants. For Catholics and Jews, the disagreements with the King James Version were profound enough that they had their own versions of the Bible. Sawyer asked, "Doctor, would you say that the Holy Bible—and I am using those particular words—the Holy Bible would be complete without the New Testament?"

"No."

"You defined, I believe, a sectarian Bible as one in which the message of a particular sect were conveyed by that version of the Bible. On that definition, Doctor, would you say that the New Testament was sectarian in that it conveys the message of a particular sect?"

"It conveys the message of Christians."

"Yes, as opposed to non-Christian sects?"

"Yes."

"When you said 'non-sectarian,' did you mean as among the various Protestant sects?"

"I meant among the various Christian bodies."[37]

Next, Sawyer focused on who did and did not participate in the translation that resulted in the King James Version. Weigle conceded that there were no Jews or Roman Catholics on the scholarly committee. Nor were there any Separatists.[38]

Having established the narrow sectarian cast of the group that put together the King James Version, Sawyer moved next to the dedicatory epistle that appeared before the biblical text itself. The epistle expressed a strong anti-Catholic prejudice growing out of the religious upheavals of England in the early seventeenth century. Sawyer clarified his position: "Well, I was referring to a portion, and I will read: '. . . so that if, on the one side, we shall be traduced by Popish Persons at home or abroad, who therefore will malign us, because we are poor instrument to make God's Holy Truth to be yet more and

more known unto the people, whom they desire still to keep in ignorance and darkness; . . .' Would you think that statement had a sectarian aspect to it, sir?"

"It sounds a little that way, but that is not part of the Bible."

"Well, we are speaking now of the aegis under which the Bible
came into being rather than the text."

"Well, of course it did not come under the aegis of the Roman
Church."[39]

In preparation for the trial, Sawyer had read some of Weigle's
writings on the Bible, including *The English New Testament from
Tyndale to the Revised Standard Version,* published in 1949. Weigle
had testified on the witness stand about the outstanding moral and
literary qualities of the Bible, which he said made it appropriate for
reading to schoolchildren. His writings, however, revealed that Weigle viewed the Bible's main value as conveying a religious message—
"the word of God to man," as he put it. Sawyer didn't even have to
ask the most obvious question: If religious doctrine was the primary
lesson, wouldn't schoolchildren absorb that meaning above all else?
Instead, he said: "I will put the question this way, Doctor: In your
opinion as an expert is the King James Version of the Bible to be
regarded primarily as an historic record, as a piece of English literature or as the revelatory word of God?"

Weigle responded: "Again, you are asking me, sir, about my
belief. I have stated that I think that this is a justified practice of educational value from the standpoint of morals, from the standpoint of
literature, from the standpoint of the place that the Bible has occupied and continues to occupy in American life. Now, over and above
that what I believe does not seem to me to be relevant to this
inquiry."

Sawyer regrouped: "Doctor, maybe I can approach it this way. I
would like to read you a paragraph from your book, sir, entitled *The
English New Testament* which was referred to by Mr. Rhoads. The
paragraph says: 'The message of the Bible is the central thing, its
style is but an instrument for conveying the message. The Bible is
not a mere historical document to be preserved. And it is more than

a classic of English literature to be cherished and admired. The Bible contains the Word of God to man. And men need the Word of God in our time and hereafter as never before.' Now, would that fairly express your feeling as to the respective proportion and importance of the three factors, historical, literary and religious, shall I say, embodied in the work that we think of as the Bible?"

Weigle answered: "It does. Yes, I stand on what I said there. The point, however, is this. I stressed the moral value and the literary value and the historical value of the Bible as pertinent to the case that is before us. Now, the actual fact is that the Bible has those values because people have believed it, because they believe that there is something revelatory in it of what true morals are. It is not simply a literary exercise but its literature has arisen out of that faith. Now, I am perfectly willing to grant that. I still would say that the reasons why it may have a place in our educational system are these three reasons that I gave."[40] Weigle, former dean of the Yale Divinity School and Abington's primary witness, had all but endorsed the main points of Sawyer's legal arguments.

11. Why Not Recite the Navajo Invocation to Beauty?

Just as the expert witnesses were grappling with the difficult issues surrounding *Schempp*, another conflict involving school prayer was reaching a courtroom on Long Island. At this point, few people had noticed. It would not stay that way for long.

In New York, the conflict focused on a prayer that the state had composed and designated for use during the morning homeroom period. In the early 1950s, the nation was consumed by the increasing challenge posed by godless communism and its chief patron, the Soviet Union. Congress amended the Pledge of Allegiance to add the words "under God."

In 1951, the New York State Board of Regents made its own contribution to this cold war fight. Eager to bring prayer to children in public school but mindful of the controversy engendered by sectarian offerings, the board composed a twenty-two-word prayer that it felt was universal enough for use by all students. The regents recommended to local school boards that "at the commencement of each school day the act of allegiance to the Flag might well be joined with this act of reverence to God." The Regents' Prayer read, "Almighty God, we acknowledge our dependence upon Thee, and we beg Thy blessings upon us, our parents, our teachers and our Country."[1]

Prayer in the schools had a long history in the state of New York. From 1837 through at least 1909, the state's superintendent of common schools followed a policy that a "teacher might open his school with prayer, provided he did not encroach upon the hours allotted to instruction, and provided that the attendance of the scholars was not exacted as a matter of school discipline."[2] Catholic children were not required to participate in whatever prayer the students recited.

The Board of Regents changed this policy in 1951 with its drafting of the Regents' Prayer, justifying it with a mixture of patriotism and religion. Pointing to "the dangers of these difficult days," the regents adopted a statement saying that "the securing of the peace and safety of our country and our State" required that children must be taught "that Almighty God is their Creator, and that by Him they have been endowed with their inalienable rights of life, liberty, and the pursuit of happiness."[3]

It did not take long before a group of civil liberties lawyers convened to discuss filing a lawsuit to challenge the Regents' Prayer as a violation of the First Amendment. On May 28, 1952, Leo Pfeffer attended a meeting at the New York office of the ACLU. Pfeffer was opposed to a lawsuit, writing afterward that he had "strongly advised against the presenting of such a case because of the probabilities that we would lose it." Pfeffer reported that the ACLU attorney was disappointed that Pfeffer and the three Jewish organizations refused to cooperate in any lawsuit: "During the course of the presentation of my views I emphasized the need for a public relations campaign and the ACLU, seeing litigation go out the window, was quite prepared to take over the public relations campaign."[4]

Pfeffer wielded enough clout that, with his active opposition, the possibility of a lawsuit collapsed. Later in the decade, though, came another opportunity. In 1958, a majority of the Herricks school board backed a motion to adopt the Regents' Prayer, with the proviso that students could be excused from participating.[5] Some parents, however, opposed the new prayer requirement and vowed to fight it.

Lawrence Roth, a parent of two children in the local schools, took the lead. "My immediate reaction was that the state and the school board had no right to impose religion or prayers on the school children," he said. "My basic feeling was that if the state could tell us what to pray and when to pray, and how to pray, that there was no stopping." So Roth sought help from the ACLU, which referred him to William J. Butler, an attorney. Butler thought that the school board's injection of a state-composed prayer into the public schools violated the First Amendment.[6]

Butler wanted to know if other people in the school district felt as strongly as Roth did about the Regents' Prayer. A group of plaintiffs would make it possible for the lawsuit to survive if one or a few plaintiffs dropped out, either on their own or because the court eliminated them. (In an extended case, for example, the children of one plaintiff might graduate, making the case moot as to them.) At his own expense, Roth placed an advertisement in two local newspapers announcing that a lawsuit would soon be started and requesting interested people to call him at home. About fifty people called Roth in response to the ad. Eleven were willing to personally join in a lawsuit challenging the Regents' Prayer under the First Amendment.[7] Butler finally settled on five of them, eliminating those who did not have children in the public schools.

Meanwhile, as Butler pursued the grievance against the Regents' Prayer, the nation's chief strategist on church-state litigation once again wasn't happy with the prospects of a lawsuit coming out of Long Island. After receiving what appeared to him to be a draft of a legal complaint, Pfeffer wrote to Shad Polier on November 24, 1958, the day before the expert witnesses testified in the *Schempp* case in Philadelphia: "I doubt very much that it will succeed and I think it may offer another opportunity for a court to become religious and patriotic." Pfeffer briefly mentioned four alternatives that the American Jewish Congress could consider, including the one he recommended: "Urge the attorneys to drop the suit."[8]

A month later, Pfeffer wrote once again to Polier, this time reminding him that the two of them had agreed that a lawsuit would be "ill advised and that I should seek to induce the Civil Liberties Union to refrain from bringing this suit." But the ACLU refused to go along with him this time. Pfeffer reported that he had failed to convince the ACLU of his views and that it was planning to file the lawsuit without him.[9] In February 1959, Pfeffer set out more clearly why he opposed litigation on the Regents' Prayer: he felt that this twenty-two-word prayer, as weak and watered-down as it was, would make too insubstantial a case to take before the U.S. Supreme Court. Once again, as when he tried to apply the brakes to other litigation involving religious observance in the schools, Pfeffer feared that a relatively thin case would prove an unfavorable basis for the justices' decision on the momentous question of prayer in schools. On February 2, 1959, Pfeffer articulated his objection to a Regents' Prayer lawsuit: "We were consulted about the suit before it was started and we advised against the bringing of the suit. The reason for our advice is that the prayer involved is the 'Regents Prayer' which is as non-sectarian as a prayer can be and would be considered by the courts to be quite innocuous. We believe that the first prayer case to be brought should be based upon better facts."[10]

Engel v. Vitale, though, was under way. Of the five plaintiffs, two were Jewish, one was Unitarian, one was a member of the Society for Ethical Culture, and one was a nonbeliever. First alphabetically among the five plaintiffs, Steven I. Engel became the named plaintiff in the lawsuit; William J. Vitale, Jr., president of the school board, became the lead defendant.

Once filed, the case moved quickly to Nassau County Courthouse on February 24, 1959, before Justice Bernard S. Meyer of the state supreme court. Despite its lofty title, the supreme court happens to be the trial court in New York State—not the highest court, as the name implies. (The highest court of the state is the Court of Appeals.) The trial was held without a jury, because the two sides did not disagree significantly on the facts of the case. The question was one of law for the judge—specifically, whether the recitation of the Regents' Prayer violated Engel's First Amendment rights.

چ

A little more than two weeks after the start of *Engel v. Vitale*, the *Schempp* trial itself resumed. With the main part of the trial over at the end of November and the pertinent evidence entered into the record, the lawyers had retired to their offices to write briefs and prepare for their final oral argument before the three judges. The court scheduled the final arguments for March 12, 1959.

Meanwhile, Pfeffer was stirring in New York. Shortly after the suit was filed on February 14, 1958, Pfeffer had decided that he and the American Jewish Congress should not become actively involved in the suit, although he continued to provide advice to Sawyer and to Theodore Mann.[11] A day after the conclusion of the trial, however, he changed his mind. As he had done in some other church-state cases around the country, Pfeffer decided to enter the case from the position of amicus curiae, providing a brief and a court appearance on the Schempp's behalf.[12]

On March 12, once again at the U.S. district court in Philadelphia, Judge Biggs called the session to order. Sawyer and Wayland Elsbree were there for the Schempps. Rhoads headed up a five-man legal team for the Abington school district; the team included his younger partner, Philip H. Ward III. Pfeffer waited in the wings to speak in support of the Schempps. Judge Biggs had brought his own amicus curiae, Lois Forer, to provide the court with legal assistance. Forer had been Biggs's law clerk for many years and now worked as a deputy attorney general for Pennsylvania. She was in the courtroom to help Biggs and the other two judges, not to represent Pennsylvania. Introduction of evidence was over, and the task for the lawyers now was to argue their legal points directly to the judges.

☙

Sawyer was first up to speak, and he conceded that because Ellery had already graduated from Abington Senior High School, the case was moot for him. He also told the judges that the court would be justified in issuing an injunction to stop the prayers and Bible reading as a violation of the establishment clause if he convinced them of a key point—that both practices constituted religious observances. Beyond that, he wanted to argue that these practices were not only religious but also sectarian in nature and that because children were required to participate in a religious exercise that violated their own beliefs, the state was interfering with the Schempp children's practice of religion under the free exercise clause.

In starting his argument, Sawyer compared the morning exercises to commonplace pedagogical materials and courses found in the schools. In covering history or math, for example, teachers required that specific material be covered. In the case of Bible reading, however, there was no curriculum whatsoever—only the statutory requirement that ten verses of the Bible be read each day. "I contend that that is the kind of provision that is made for a ceremonial observance rather than for a pedagogical one," he said.[13]

Sawyer also attacked Abington's contention that the purpose of Bible reading was to expose children to great literature. In fact, he said, any literary purpose was secondary to the religious significance of the exercises, which was "its essential character."[14] If the purpose of the statute was to ensure that students learn great literature, why, he asked, was only the Bible specified? "And if the statute," said Sawyer, "were only to be designed, and if it were only to insure the exposure of the children to a great work of literature and to a piece of history, we would wonder why no other work in the whole vast expanse of Western thought and literature from Homer and Herodotus to Shakespeare was ever singled out by the legislature for such exaltation and for such a requirement." He concluded: "In fact, there is nowhere in the Public School Code, that I have been able to find, any other instance in which pedagogical material is specifically required to be taught. We grant, of course, that it is a great literature. We wonder whether or not it is indispensably great as literature."[15]

Not only was the Bible the only work required to be read, but the Pennsylvania statute also required it to be read without comment. The provision against commentary had its genesis a century earlier, when Horace Mann, the school commissioner of Massachusetts, attempted to satisfy Protestant sects that wanted the schools to have Bible reading but not biblical commentary with which they might disagree. Sawyer argued that although the provision indeed helped to keep sectarian influences out of the public schools, it represented a clear indication that Bible reading amounted to a religious observance. Sawyer said that reading the Bible without comment defeated Abington's contention that the Bible was primarily used for literary, historical, or moral lessons, "for it is hard to think how anything could be taught, although it might have some inspirational value, without comment, particularly the book which is in today's vernacular portions almost incomprehensible because of the antiquity of the language."[16]

Sawyer also reminded the judges that the Pennsylvania law specified that teachers could be fired for failing to read the Bible to schoolchildren each morning. In no other instance could teachers be so seriously disciplined for not utilizing a particular text. Sawyer observed, "This again is hardly the sort of draconic provision that a legislature would contrive if it were interested in essentially a pedagogical aspect of a work."[17]

Sawyer then compared the Abington situation with the U.S. Supreme Court finding in *McCollum v. Board of Education*.[18] In *McCollum*, the U.S. Supreme Court invalidated the practice of early dismissal of public schoolchildren from their regular instruction in order to attend religious classes held by clergy inside the schools. In both *McCollum* and *Schempp*, Sawyer pointed out, the authorities used school classrooms and other facilities for the purposes of supporting a religious ceremony. He argued that one major difference, though, made the Abington Bible reading a more egregious violation of the First Amendment: the Illinois school district permitted students to participate or not in the released-time program, but Abington provided no way to opt out of its exercises. In fact, the school officials forced Ellery Schempp to participate. The coercion of religious practice denied Ellery and his siblings the right to practice their own religion.[19]

Sawyer had to cover several bases. Most precedent indicated that a violation of the establishment clause occurred with any government endorsement of religious observance, even if it involved religion generally and without any denominational preference. But a minority view held that violation of the establishment clause required that the government prefer one denomination to another. So Sawyer argued

Ellery Schempp was sixteen years old on November 26, 1956, when he read from the Koran as a protest against listening to the mandatory Bible-reading exercise in his public school. After Abington school district administrators disciplined the high school junior, he initiated the lawsuit that would bear the family name all the way to the U.S. Supreme Court. (Courtesy of Ellery Schempp.)

The Schempp family received hundreds of letters—most of them negative—about their lawsuit to end Bible reading and recitation of the Lord's Prayer in the public schools. Ellery's younger brother and sister carried on the lawsuit after Ellery graduated from high school. *From left:* Ellery's brother, Roger; mother, Sidney; sister, Donna; and father, Edward Schempp. Circa 1963. (Photograph from AP/Wide World Photos.)

Madalyn Murray—the outspoken atheist whose lawsuit was combined with the Schempps' at the U.S. Supreme Court—sued to stop Bible reading in the Baltimore schools. She and her sons, William (*left*) and Garth (*right*), suffered extreme mental and physical harassment as well as property damage at the hands of people in their community. On February 28, 1963, they attended the oral arguments at the Supreme Court. (Photograph from AP/Wide World Photos.)

Luther Allan Weigle was the Abington school district's expert witness at the *Schempp* trial, where he argued that Bible reading in the schools conveyed important moral lessons rather than religious teachings. He was a professor and dean of the Yale Divinity School and chaired a committee that completed a revision of the American Standard Version of the King James Bible—published as the Revised Standard Version. Photograph taken in 1952. (Courtesy of Yale Divinity School.)

Rabbi Solomon Grayzel was the expert witness for the Schempp family at the trial in 1958. He analyzed differences between various versions of the Bible to show that many Bible passages were offensive to students whose version of the Scriptures was different. (Courtesy of the Ratner Center for the Study of Conservative Judaism, Jewish Theological Seminary.)

Bernard Wolfman, later a law professor at Harvard, met with Ellery Schempp and his family before the ACLU decided to litigate their case. The first lawyer to work on the case, Wolfman undertook the initial research on Ellery's claim that Bible reading and recitation of the Lord's Prayer in the public schools violated the First Amendment. Wolfman voluntarily withdrew from representing the Schempps, concerned that his Jewish heritage would attract even more critics. Photograph circa 1964. (Courtesy of Bernard Wolfman.)

Theodore Mann (*right*), then a twenty-nine-year-old attorney, was the second ACLU lawyer who worked on the case. He drafted the ACLU's complaint that initiated the *Schempp* case in 1958. Just four years out of law school, he thought he lacked the experience required to litigate the case to the U.S. Supreme Court and turned it over to Henry W. Sawyer III. Senator Arlen Specter, then Philadelphia's district attorney, is pictured on the left. Photograph taken in 1971. (Photograph by Alan D. Hewitt. Courtesy of Theodore Mann.)

Henry W. Sawyer III litigated the Schempp family's case and made the oral argument before the U.S. Supreme Court. A veteran of both World War II and the Korean War, he was one of the most effective civil liberties lawyers of the time and won several other cases he argued before the justices, including the landmark church-state case *Lemon v. Kurtzman*. Photograph taken in 1987. (Courtesy of Drinker Biddle & Reath LLP.)

C. Brewster Rhoads, one of Philadelphia's most prominent attorneys, was the lead litigator for the Abington school district. When the *Schempp* case reached the U.S. Supreme Court, he bowed out for health reasons and turned the oral argument over to his partner, Philip H. Ward III. (Photograph by Fabian Bachrach. Courtesy of Stephen G. Rhoads and Montgomery, McCracken, Walker & Rhoads, LLP.)

Philip H. Ward III argued the case for the Abington school district before the U.S. Supreme Court. After the Court invalidated the Regent's Prayer used in New York's public schools the previous year, Ward knew the odds were against his winning. "We thought nothing good could come out of that Court on something like this," he admitted forty years later. Photograph taken in 1966. (Courtesy of Philip H. Ward III.)

Clark Byse, who later became a Harvard law professor, was president of the Philadelphia chapter of the ACLU in 1957. He cast the deciding vote after the chapter's board split evenly on whether to represent Ellery Schempp and bring a lawsuit against the Abington schools. Without Byse's vote to offer pro bono legal representation, the Schempps would not have been able to sue. Photograph taken in 1977. (Courtesy of Harvard Law School.)

Leo Pfeffer, a lawyer for the American Jewish Congress, was perhaps the most influential strategist of church-state litigation in the fifties and sixties. He opposed the filing of the *Schempp* case and ultimately litigated another case in Florida that competed with *Schempp* for the attention of the U.S. Supreme Court. (Courtesy of the American Jewish Congress.)

Judge John Biggs, Jr., was chief judge of the U.S. Court of Appeals for the Third Circuit in Philadelphia when he headed a three-judge panel that struck down the Pennsylvania law requiring Bible reading in the state's public schools. A close friend of F. Scott Fitzgerald when the two were students at Princeton University and later executor of his estate, Biggs himself was a published novelist before he was appointed to the federal bench by President Franklin Roosevelt in 1937. Photograph of Biggs delivering a speech, circa 1956. (Courtesy of Anna B. Pierce.)

Associate Justice Tom C. Clark (*left*), known for his conservative views, wrote the U.S. Supreme Court's opinion ending Bible reading and recitation of the Lord's Prayer in the nation's public schools. Associate Justice William J. Brennan, Jr. (*right*), wrote a long and influential concurring opinion. Photograph circa early 1960s. (Photograph by Lebanon Zahle, from the Collection of the Supreme Court of the United States.)

that Bible reading was also by nature a sectarian practice, promoting some religions at the expense of others. Reading the King James Version not only preferred Christianity to non-Christian religions but also preferred Protestantism to Catholicism. Even Weigle had agreed with that.[20]

Sawyer argued that the law's requirement that the "Holy Bible" be read excluded the Jewish Holy Scriptures and the Catholic Douay Bible. Weigle himself had testified that it would be a sectarian practice to read the Jewish Holy Scriptures alone. Sawyer had confined virtually all of his argument to the Bible's place within the Judeo-Christian tradition, but he here attempted to broaden his point. Bible reading at Abington discriminated against all non-Christian religions—not only Judaism, but also Buddhism and Islam, for example.[21]

Not only did the Bible favor Christianity, said Sawyer, but parts of the King James Bible offended the Jewish faith. He reminded the judges of Grayzel's testimony about a number of passages, especially the controversial scene in Matthew in which the sealed fate of Jesus is followed by the Jewish crowd saying, "His blood be on us and on our children," a sentence that Sawyer said was "responsible for more anti-Jewish feeling than anything else."[22] Catholics also regard the King James Version as sectarian. "The Popes have called the King James Version the chief arm of the Protestant revolt," said Sawyer. "They say that the encouragement for individuals to read the Bible themselves and interpret it for themselves without note or comment is one of the salient features and errors of the Reformation."[23]

Even within the Protestant world, said Sawyer, there remained sharp disagreement about the King James Version. Such Protestant groups as the Unitarians, Universalists, Quakers, and Mormons disagreed with parts of it. Sawyer recounted the way in which the Bible conflicted with the beliefs of Ellery Schempp and his family. Sawyer said: "The doctrines of the Trinity, of the divinity of Christ, of the ascension, of the miracles, all of these are religious concepts and religious doctrines. If they are couched in beautiful language, fine, but they are religious concepts and no reading of the Bible can fail, even if it is at random, as it appears to be in the schools in most cases, to convey these ideas as being truth. The Book is designed to convey them as being truth."[24]

Sawyer criticized the practice of reciting the Lord's Prayer after the conclusion of Bible reading. There are differences between the Protestant and Catholic wording of the prayer, and Jews believe that the word *Lord* as used in the King James Version implies the divinity of Jesus. Above all, Sawyer argued, recitation of a prayer can have no pedagogical purpose in a public school—it is there solely for the purposes of a religious ceremony. The juxtaposition of the Lord's Prayer and Bible reading, he said, showed that school authorities intended the two to convey religious meaning.[25] Sawyer argued that the violation of the First Amendment in this case was "even stronger because there isn't any other aspect that I can conceive of to a prayer but a religious one." He explained: "This is the meaning of 'prayer.' And prayer in unison, a rising thing, is perhaps a more strikingly religious ceremony than even the reading of the Bible."[26]

꒓

Judge Biggs was troubled. If the three-judge court invalidated Abington's morning devotional exercise under the First and Fourteenth Amendments, how would its ruling affect other situations in which the name of God was invoked in a public place? Judges often look beyond the conflict directly before them and try to understand how their ruling may affect the larger body of law and other situations that share similar characteristics. As they anticipate additional cases coming their way, judges try to figure whether there is a principled way to distinguish among them and thereby resist extending the legal point too far.

Sawyer certainly must have anticipated the question of how a ruling in the *Schempp* case might affect other prayers and references to God in public forums. After all, the U.S. Supreme Court itself opens its public session each day with a marshal intoning, "God save this honorable court"; and many legislative bodies open their sessions with a short prayer. Sawyer had a serious problem if the judges believed that invalidation of morning prayers in the schools would lead logically to throwing out all such religious references in other government venues.

To distinguish the Schempps' situation from the others, Sawyer argued that most intrusions of religion into public life are de minimis—that is, they are of too trifling a nature for the law to notice. Biggs started a colloquy with Sawyer on the question, asking what would happen to a person who claimed that the call of the crier at the beginning of a court session violated the establishment clause. "I think he loses easily," Sawyer said. "It is de minimis, it is noncompulsory, it isn't required by statute, and nobody has to go and participate in it. All of those, an amalgam of reasons. . . . [A]nybody that brought a case like that I think would just be a damn fool, and I think that that is often true in the law and I think the courts have legal ways of expressing that feeling. I think that that is true in every one of the rights under the First Amendment, that there comes a point where you just simply say, 'Well, now, this is just too ridiculous.' . . ."[27]

When Sawyer sat down, his argument over, he could not have felt very good about his last exchange with Judge Biggs. Saying that someone would be "a damn fool" to bring such a case was far from the careful logic and craftsmanship of his oral argument. Had he helped Biggs see his case as one with definable boundaries? He could only hope so.

⌗

Lois Forer rose to her feet next, a fortuitous event that could not have been better for Sawyer had he scripted the trial himself. Forer sensed that Sawyer had not satisfied Judge Biggs in distinguishing the morning prayers at Abington from the use of prayers in courtrooms and legislative chambers. She certainly knew Judge Biggs better than anyone else in the courtroom. A graduate of the Northwestern University School of Law, Forer had clerked for Biggs for four years beginning in 1942. Long before flextime became part of the American work style, Biggs had permitted Forer, who had a baby at the time, to split her work hours between home and the courthouse. Once, when they were working together on a complex case and shipping boxes of documents back and forth to each other, Biggs opened a box from her and found both the trial transcript and diapers inside. When Forer gave birth to her second child, whom she named John in honor of the judge, Biggs went to the hospital and worked on an opinion with her there.[28]

At just ten minutes per day, Forer said, Abington's morning devotionals would consume about thirty hours of classroom time each academic year. This amount of time, she said, was not a de minimis, or trifling, experience for students. Moreover, she argued, a religious exercise done with young impressionable children in a school classroom carried far more importance than a prayer among adults in a legislative meeting.[29]

Next, Forer criticized Rhoads's contention on behalf of the Abington schools that the different versions of the Bible and other holy books are not in themselves sectarian works. If the Koran were read in the schools each morning, said Forer, the reading would, for non-Muslims, "certainly be a sectarian practice within the school." She continued, "One can imagine the effect upon a Christian child, who would say, 'And what of Jesus?' or upon a Jewish child, who would say, 'And what of Moses?'"[30]

Nearing her conclusion, Forer wondered aloud why the Bible and Lord's Prayer had been required above any other available sources. "There are many prayers," she said. "The Egyptian Hymn to the Sun, the Navajo Invocation to Beauty, or the Rig-Vedas, which could all be recited or read for inspirational value and, as a matter of cultural interest, but none of these is required to be read every day, and we are within the stream of our own culture in calling for a reading of the Bible which can be in my opinion for no other purpose than a religious one in this ceremonial way."[31]

꒰

Now it was Leo Pfeffer's turn. The Lord's Prayer had been little discussed up to then, and Pfeffer made it clear that he thought it enjoyed even less justification than Bible reading for use in the public schools. He referred to one of Abington's justifications, literary value, for using the Bible. "There has been no contention," he said, "nor can there be contention that one reads a prayer because of any literary significance in it, although the defendants here contend that the Bible is read because of its literary significance."

Pfeffer continued: "Prayer recitation far antedates written religious documents in the history of religion and the Bible is a comparatively recent document in religious development. Prayer was thousands of years before the Bible." The Lord's Prayer in particular, he said, "is not deemed non-sectarian by those who do not subscribe to the Christian religion." He added that "the whole history of the Jewish religion indicates quite clearly that the Lord's Prayer is not accepted as within the, consistent with the doctrines and principles and mandates of the Jewish faith."[32]

Listening to the proceedings earlier, Pfeffer had been troubled by Sawyer's analysis on the critical point of what differentiated Bible reading and prayers in the public schools from the prayers that open many judicial and legislative sessions. Sawyer had been wrong, Pfeffer said, in arguing that prayer invocations before government bodies were distinguishable because they were of small consequence. Instead, the answer involved history and tradition. Ever the legal scholar, Pfeffer took the three judges on a brief excursion into how prayers came to be associated with legislative sessions. This practice started in the Continental Congress, before the Constitution came along to guarantee religious freedom. The Continental Congress, Pfeffer said, passed numerous resolutions involving religious matters and began starting its sessions with a prayer because there was no First Amendment to prohibit it from doing so. Later, after ratification of the amendments to the U.S. Constitution, the prayer invocation to start a legislative session continued on despite the objections of Madison and Jefferson. Pfeffer said, "[I]t had been so ingrained upon our [legislative] culture that it could not be dis-lodged." The danger, said Pfeffer, is that such very old traditions with minor value as legal precedents could be used to justify some-thing wholly different, such as morning devotionals given to school-children who were a captive audience.[33]

Now Pfeffer moved on to another point. Earlier in the day, Judge Kraft had noted that the Pennsylvania law requiring Bible reading did not specify that the King James Version be used. The Abington school district purchased only the King James Version. But even if teachers could select any Bible for use in their classrooms, Pfeffer said, the abridgement of religious freedom would be the same: "If the teacher is a Protestant and selects the King James Version of the Bible, that constitutes a wrong against the Catholic and Jewish chil-dren in that class. The fact that in the room next door a Catholic teacher is committing a similar wrong against the Protestant and Jewish children in no way mitigates against the wrong committed against the Catholic and Jewish children in this class. I think the test therefore is not the fact that the statute does not prescribe the King James Version of the Bible. I think the test is the fact that any ver-sion of the Bible will be an offense to some children." Pfeffer further explained: "I don't think there is such a thing as nonsectarian version of the Bible. If you accept, as religious persons do, that the Bible is the word of God, then there are no two words of God. . . . But the facts of life are that we have so many religions because each is con-vinced that it alone is a repository of God's one and exclusive will."[34]

જ

Having listened intently for three hours, C. Brewster Rhoads now had his opportunity to speak. Three lawyers had addressed the judges in support of Ellery Schempp, and now it was up to Rhoads to carry the full burden for Abington. Rhoads, however, enjoyed a significant advantage in going last. Like a general who is presented a map of where his enemy has deployed his forces, Rhoads could adjust his presentation to blunt the strongest arguments of his opponents and also take advantage of any openings they presented to him.

Rhoads did have an opening to exploit, and he did so quickly. Leo Pfeffer had said that prayer at legislative sessions had survived the strictures of the First Amendment because of its long tradition, starting with the Continental Congress. Following this lead, Rhoads tried to provide a similar justification—a long history in Pennsylvania—to support the survival of Bible reading and recitation of the Lord's Prayer in the Abington public schools.[35]

This statute, said Rhoads, was carefully crafted to avoid sectarian influences or, indeed, anything that could make the exercise devotional and therefore offensive to anyone's religious conscience. The state of Pennsylvania required that the Bible must be read without comment, a critical safeguard that avoided the possibility of proselytizing and teaching the dogma of any sect. So the Bible readings were just that—nothing more than readings. Readings without comment could not amount to an establishment of religion, because, Rhoads argued, there were no trappings of religious observance in its presentation. For Abington, this was a critical argument, and Rhoads defended it by arguing: "[T]here is no instruction, there is no proselyting, there is no ceremonial, there is no suggestion 'This shall you do,' 'This shall you believe,' 'This is the Word of God,' or otherwise. It is merely a reading of ten simple verses from the Bible without comment."

Judge Kirkpatrick asked: "Don't you think there is instruction involved if the pupils of the school are read, for instance, the account of the Israelites escape from Egypt? Aren't they being instructed in something that we might call Bible History?" Rhoads answered that state legislators had chosen the Bible for its moral truths and literary value: "And to say that the great words of St. Paul, for example, that the Sermon on the Mount, that the parables, and any number of other things to which we could advert, should not be read simply because someone might attach to them a completely sectarian, that is sect relation or connotation, I think—" Kirkpatrick interrupted: "A devotional exercise the person takes part in and addresses himself to the Deity in some fashion, either directly or through an intermediary. But instruction is quite a different thing. He is on the receiving end of that and he can't help learning if he listens to what is read." Rhoads replied, "And if what is read, sir, is read in such a manner, and without comment, as to indicate only that it is a portion from the Holy Bible being read, and that it is not being read with sectarian overtones or for the purpose of convincing, proselyting or for dogma, then I suggest, sir, that there is certainly no impropriety in such reading, and that the whole intent of the legislature, as I have pointed out in my brief, indicates that that was to be the fact."[36]

Rhoads contrasted Bible reading to the kind of religious exercise ruled unconstitutional in the 1948 case *McCollum v. Board of Education*, the released-time case:[37] "But the point was that there was definitely a religious observance; there was the wearing of the clerical garb, the kind of thing that is prevented in our own legislation, to which I have adverted. There is an attempt to prove to the person to whom the religious gentleman or person may be talking the validity of some given faith. That is what I consider to be the concept of a religious observance mandated which would fly in the face of establishment." Judge Biggs then entered the colloquy: "You think then a simple ceremony involving religious observance, unless there was an attempt to prove the truth of the religion or reach the truth of the religion, would not fall within the interdiction of the [First] amendment?" Rhoads answered: "That, sir, may be the one end of the pole. There may be some other. One may be black and one may be white. I am thinking in the gray land of the courts." Judge Biggs explained: "I am trying to see where these poles lie. Here is a class in chemistry; an instructor gets to his feet and reads several paragraphs about the property of certain chemicals. He reads that by way of instruction and the pupil accepts it—I assume he does, he accepts it at least as the furthermost point in that science in which he and the teacher can reach at that given day. There is, we will say, an hour later, at noon a ceremony or a period in which the King James Version or some other version of the Bible is read, and the Lord's Prayer is recited. You say that that is not religious instruction." Rhoads clarified, "I would contend, sir, that it is not religious observance and at that point it did not amount to religious instruction, yes, sir."

Rhoads was asked if proselytization was required for a religious ceremony. He responded, "No, sir, there must not be as such that but it must have in some way that objective, sir, in order to be the establishment of religion, as I view the constitutional interdiction in the First Amendment." Judge Kirkpatrick interjected, "You say the objective, but how about the effect of it, regardless of the objective? I mean the effect is to convince the listeners, the young listeners, that these things are true; isn't that religious instruction?" Rhoads responded: "That, sir, is the issue which Your Honors have to decide here. I think Your Honors should say no from the evidence in this case."[38]

Having finished that point, Rhoads went on to another critical contention on behalf of Abington—that Bible reading and recitation of the Lord's Prayer did not violate the free exercise of the Schempp family's religious beliefs. Rhoads maintained that what was read to Ellery Schempp in homeroom class lacked any compulsion that he believe. The First Amendment guarantees, Rhoads said, were not meant to filter out of the environment all doctrines and beliefs that are unacceptable to people. Rhoads argued that to be in violation of the free exercise of religion, Abington would have had to suggest that the children actually believe the material read to them as the word of God.[39] Rhoads added that the requirement that students show respect and attention during the exercises was not the same thing as compelling them to agree with the readings themselves.[40]

Finally, Rhoads focused on whether the law permitted the rights of a few in the community (in this case, the Schempps) to prevail over the wishes of the majority (who, in this case, wished to pray). The religious freedom guarantees, said Rhoads, "were not conceived to be used as weapons to enable the minority to strike down the spiritual and ethical aspirations of the majority."[41] When Judge Biggs called on Sawyer for a rebuttal, Sawyer didn't want to leave unchallenged Rhoads's final assertion—that the First Amendment did not

empower a minority of people in the community to deny the majority its desire for Bible reading and prayer in the classroom. Earlier,
Forer had explained that the Bill of Rights protected the rights of
individuals against the actions of a majority of people in the community. Now Sawyer added that Rhoads's stance on protecting the
rights of the majority could be used to bring all manner of religious
observance and sectarian teaching into the public schools: "[It]
would justify complete religious or chapel services, which might be
desirable to the majority in the public schools. You could go very far,
in other words, with that argument."[42]

⌇

Sitting in the courtroom throughout the entire day was Ed
Schempp, taking notes of every argument made by the lawyers. That
evening, he sat at his typewriter and wrote out a one-page, single-
spaced memo to himself about what had transpired. "Sawyer's talk
was superb," he wrote. As for Rhoads, Schempp wrote that he "got
up with his flourishes and oratory, and probably did as well as possible considering he knew he was wrong!" Never lacking for confidence, Schempp concluded his memo with a prediction: "The decision of the Judges may be months away according to Sawyer. But as
of now I feel they are leaning our way—definitely."[43]

12. The Race to the Supreme Court

Less than a month after Leo Pfeffer appeared in Judge Biggs's courtroom to assist Henry Sawyer in his oral argument in the *Schempp* case, Pfeffer's patience was finally rewarded. He had never liked the *Schempp* or *Engel* cases and in fact had advised against bringing those cases from the very beginning. Now he heard of a situation that he felt was much more compelling, involving religion in the public schools of Miami.

Students at a Miami Beach public school had gathered in their homerooms early one morning to participate in their usual opening exercises. In accordance with Florida law, the students listened to a few verses from the Bible each day over the public address system, followed by their recitation in unison of the Lord's Prayer. Then came the Pledge of Allegiance and a kind of inspirational message delivered by one of the students. But this particular morning would be different—much different.

On this day, the public address system crackled with a fire-and-brimstone sermon by a fundamentalist clergyman. The students, many of whom were Jewish, had to accept Christ, he said. If they didn't, they would suffer damnation forever in hell. Parents of minority religions had put up with many different kinds of religious observances in the school system over the years, but the threat of eternal damnation aimed at their children was more than some of them could easily ignore.[1] An atheist named Harlow Chamberlin decided to sue the Dade County Board of Public Instruction, which ran the Miami and Miami Beach public schools, arguing that his and his child's rights to religious freedom were being violated.

Pfeffer apparently received his first notice of an impending legal action through a memorandum written to him on April 3, 1959, by Haskell L. Lazere, head of the American Jewish Congress's regional office in Miami.[2] A few weeks later, Chamberlin's attorney, Herbert L. Heiken of Miami, wrote to Pfeffer to say that he was planning to file suit with the backing of the local chapter of the ACLU. He asked for Pfeffer's help. With this letter, Pfeffer understood that—unlike *Schempp* and other cases about which he was so dubious—this case involved a broad array of religious practices. Heiken said that the lawsuit would demand that the school board "stop the following practices: the recitation of prayers in the morning, before lunch, and at every school assembly; the celebration of Christmas, Hanukah and Easter at school assemblies and in the classrooms; sectarian comment by teachers when reading the bible to the class every morning; releasing of school facilities for bible classes; requiring an oath of belief in God from those seeking to teach in the public schools; and by at least tacit approval, granting permission to different religious groups for the distribution of their literature in our public schools." Heiken concluded, "As you can see, this is what may be called the 'shotgun' approach which we will be taking."[3]

Pfeffer saw this as nearly a perfect case. It involved more than the limited Bible reading and Lord's Prayer of *Schempp* and more than a tepid state-composed prayer, as in *Engel.* Here, the extensive nature of the religious practices in the public schools would make the case much more compelling for what Pfeffer feared would be skeptical justices on the U.S. Supreme Court. In his mind, all these religious activities in the public schools certainly amounted to an establishment of religion. The required participation of students in so many sectarian activities was strong evidence as well of a violation of the free exercise clause—if Jewish students and others were required to engage in Christian prayer, Bible readings, and religious holiday celebrations, they were denied the right to freely exercise their own beliefs. The extensive nature of the violation would be hard to ignore, Pfeffer believed. So Pfeffer replied two days later to praise the "shotgun" approach of attacking many religious practices in the schools at once.[4]

In the first week of May, Pfeffer went to Miami for a series of meetings that included intensive discussions of the situation in the schools. He met with Heiken there on May 4 and offered to draft the initial complaint to start the case, which they decided would be filed in a Florida state court. Two days later, Pfeffer met with the Rabbinical Association of Greater Miami and told them of the impending Chamberlin case. According to Haskell Lazere, Pfeffer, anticipating a public backlash from Christians once the case reached the court, "emphasized the need for creating a sympathetic climate of opinion re the Chamberlin action" and "urged the rabbis to begin giving sermons and holding community meetings in regard to religion in the schools."[5]

The Chamberlin matter began moving quickly through the spring and early summer, with Pfeffer considering filing an additional lawsuit on behalf of a group of Jewish parents. Both of the AJ Congress's sister organizations, the American Jewish Committee and the Anti-Defamation League, opposed the filing of the Chamberlin case and a second one involving Jewish plaintiffs. Aside from the problem of relations with the Christian community, the two groups "felt that the nature and composition of the U.S. Supreme Court at this time would make a victory unlikely." Instead, both groups proposed meeting with the school board to negotiate an end to the religious practices. Pfeffer thought that strategy futile but agreed to hold off on the litigation for six weeks while the two sides met.[6]

When the talks went nowhere, the legal struggle commenced. The ACLU filed suit on behalf of Chamberlin. Meanwhile, another group of litigants had emerged. A group of Jewish parents led by Edward Resnick—unconvinced that Chamberlin, an atheist, would adequately represent their interests—agreed to sue the school board on behalf of themselves and their children. Pfeffer and a local attorney, Bernard Mandler, agreed to represent them with the backing of the AJ Congress, and Mandler filed suit in September. Courts often consolidate cases that raise similar issues as a matter of conserving judicial resources, but this was not something that either the ACLU or Pfeffer favored. Lazere wrote on September 8 that they were "against consolidating the cases if we can avoid it," under the argument that "if we don't consolidate we will have a chance for two bites at the apple instead of just one." Nonetheless, the two cases were consolidated into one as they moved into litigation. Lazere also reported that the superintendent of the Dade County schools, Joe Hall, had told a meeting of school principals that losing the case would, as Lazere paraphrased it, "mean the destruction of the whole moral fiber of the school program." He added, "[I]n taking this action Hall has precipitated what may very well be a community-wide campaign against the Chamberlin action and ours."[7]

Indeed, the Miami community began to mobilize. A group of ministers succeeded in adding themselves as defendants in the lawsuits, probably concerned that the schools might capitulate in the face of the legal battle. Meanwhile, the two recalcitrant Jewish organizations closed ranks behind Pfeffer. They supported the lawsuits now because, according to Lazere, "it is a *fait accompli* and every effort must be lent to assure its success."[8]

The battle of Miami was joined. Pfeffer finally had the case he had been waiting for—the chance for a broad assault on a wide range of religious practices in the schools. This, he believed, was the strongest case to take before the justices in Washington, the ultimate audience for the arguments he had made in his major work *Church, State, and Freedom*.

꒐

Meanwhile, on Long Island, Judge Meyer handed down his opinion in *Engel v. Vitale* on August 24, 1959. The school district won nearly a complete victory in its defense of the Regent's Prayer.[9] Meyer ruled that such a practice did not violate either the New York State Constitution or the U.S. Constitution. But he did make clear that the prayer had to be noncompulsory, and he required that the school

board develop a formal procedure for excusing children from participating. With that provision in place, he said, "legislative permission
for the noncompulsory public recital of prayer cannot be said to be
repugnant to the conscience of mankind."[10] William Butler, Steven
Engel's attorney, had lost round one of *Engel*. Regardless of the outcome in the lower court, however, he knew the case was headed
much higher—certainly to New York's highest court, possibly to the
U.S. Supreme Court.

᛭

The lawsuits in Miami, Philadelphia, and Long Island all challenged
devotional exercises in the public schools, and there was still a fourth
lawsuit on this subject to come. All of them would compete to be first
to reach the U.S. Supreme Court. The fourth litigant, Madalyn
Murray O'Hair, moved to Baltimore from Houston early in 1952, and
it's fair to say that neither Murray nor Baltimore were ever quite the
same after.[11] She brought with her a commitment to atheism, a pen-
chant for activism and confrontation, and a young son who was,
along with her, willing to tolerate a severe reaction in the community
in order to challenge Bible reading and prayer in the public schools.
In 1964, *Life* magazine published a profile of Murray in which it
called her, in the headline of the story, "the most hated woman in
America."[12]

Madalyn Mays was born on April 13, 1919, in a suburb of Pittsburgh. Her father was Presbyterian and her mother Lutheran. She
was baptized in a Presbyterian church and attended religious school
there on Sundays. How she came to reject religion is unclear. In his
biography of her, Brian Le Beau recounts the story that Madalyn, at
the age of twelve or thirteen, read the entire Bible in one weekend
and found the content so unrelentingly brutal and repugnant that she
refused after that to go to church services or to Sunday school. But
Madalyn wrote elsewhere that her embrace of atheism took place
more gradually. She maintained that upon graduating high school,
she had stated that her goal was to serve God.[13]

However her turning away from religion took place, Madalyn rejected the conventional values of society early in her life. She dropped out of the University of Pittsburgh and, in 1941, at the age of twenty-two, eloped with a steelworker named John Henry Roths. Their life together lasted only a few months before World War II split them apart. Roths went to the Pacific as a marine, while Madalyn enlisted in the Women's Auxiliary Army Corps and went to North Africa and Europe. She took up a relationship in Italy with William Murray, Jr., an officer, and together they conceived a child. When she returned to the United States, her husband, Roths, offered to remain married and help raise the child, but Madalyn decided to divorce him. Although she never married Murray, she nonetheless named her infant William J. Murray III when he was born, in 1946. Later, she dropped her maiden name in favor of Madalyn Murray.[14]

In 1952, Murray finished a law degree at South Texas College of Law. But apparently she either never took the bar exam or did not pass it. In the crass and exaggerated language that became her hallmark, Murray boasted to *Life* magazine in 1964 about what her education meant: "Everything I learn makes me realize I don't know a thing. But compared to most cud-chewing, small-talking stupid American women, I'm a brain. We might as well admit it, I'm a genius."[15]

What Murray was without question was a person who found trouble with the reliability of a compass pointing north. When Murray moved to Baltimore with her parents and son in 1952, she started what became a long career of activism. She joined the Americans for Democratic Action but quit in favor of much more radical politics, attending Socialist Labor Party meetings in the mid-1950s, even as McCarthyism continued its destructive path through American society. Meanwhile, she met a man from New York City, Michael Fiorillo, and gave birth to their child, Jon Garth Murray, on November 16, 1954. She never married Fiorillo. Although by now an atheist, she baptized Bill Murray a Presbyterian and Jon a Methodist, apparently to appease her parents, in whose house she continued to live.[16]

As her role in radical politics deepened, Murray explained in her diary how she saw her place in society: "I can see my role. I'm pleased with it. So, I'm an outsider. What better is there to be? I'm a dissenter. I'm a critic and there is always a need for them. I think I see the outline of our future here in America and me in a barbed wire enclosure with my ilk as a political renegade. At least I'll have a planned future." Making her affiliations ever more radical, she dropped the Socialist Labor Party and joined the Socialist Workers Party. Involvement with a pro-Castro group came next, along with an application for Soviet citizenship in 1959. When she did not receive a response on her request, she and her son William went to the Soviet Embassy in Washington, D.C., in the summer of 1960, but still no answer to her application for citizenship was forthcoming.[17]

Meanwhile, William had been enrolled in a private school. When the school switched locations and the commute from home to classroom became too difficult, Murray switched William to the local public school, Woodbourne Junior High, early in 1960. William had already been subject to religious observance in the schools, recalling from as early as second grade that a teacher read verses from a Bible in the morning and that he and all his classmates then bowed their head and recited the Lord's Prayer. But he had never talked about the practice with his mother, who apparently remained unaware of it—at least until she took Bill, then thirteen years old, to Woodbourne on his first day of school there.[18]

Woodbourne was a two-story school of red brick and white trim. When mother and son entered through a side door shortly after 9 a.m., they walked down long corridors and past open classroom doors, where the students and teachers were holding their short homeroom. "As we passed one open classroom door after another," Madalyn recalled in *An Atheist Epic,* "we heard the recitation, in unison, of the Lord's Prayer. We were caught up in a moment that transcended time, and we seemed to walk forever hearing only the waves of prayer from medieval ages of man, and the steady, even-paced click of our leather heels on the tiled floors as we walked down another and yet another corridor."[19] Madalyn and Bill's recollection of what happened next differs. What they do agree on is that Madalyn's anger about hearing prayer in the schools led to a confrontation.

Madalyn recalled that she and Bill entered the principal's office to complete the paperwork necessary for transferring Bill from the private school to Woodbourne. According to her account, when that business was done and Madalyn was walking to the door, she turned to the principal and inquired about the Lord's Prayer, saying: "It's quite inappropriate. I want to register my opposition to it." Madalyn remembered that unpleasant words followed and that she then left.[20]

Bill's version, recounted in his book *My Life Without God,* was that the two of them saw the school's counselor, not the principal. He remembered that Madalyn and the counselor engaged in an increasingly heated discussion about the Lord's Prayer, with Madalyn becoming "so furious she had nearly turned purple." Bill recalled that as they were leaving the office, his mother said, "This won't be the last time you hear from me about your g—— prayers in this school." The counselor suggested that Madalyn enroll Bill elsewhere. "It doesn't matter where I put him," Madalyn replied. "You people have to be stopped." Exasperated, the counselor said, "Then why don't you sue us?"[21] It was, as it turned out, an invitation that Madalyn could not refuse.

13. "Colored by Our Own Experiences"

More than six months after the trial concluded, the court filed its decision in the *Schempp* case. On September 16, 1959, all three judges agreed that the Bible-reading law in Pennsylvania, as well as the practice of reciting the Lord's Prayer along with the reading, violated the religion clauses of the First Amendment. The court's opinion, written by Judge Biggs, made frequent reference to the testimony of the Schempp family and the two expert witnesses, Solomon Grayzel and Luther Weigle.

The court's reasoning in support of this result was critically important. Lower courts speak not only to the community but also to the appeals courts that may hear the case later. This case would go directly to the U.S. Supreme Court, skipping the usual review by the federal court of appeals. A federal law required that the three-judge court hear the *Schempp* case and that any appeal go directly to the Supreme Court, which would not enjoy its usual discretion to refuse to hear the case. Sitting as the trial court in the case, Biggs and his colleagues made findings of fact that were binding on any court reviewing the opinion, including the Supreme Court. Review by the justices would be confined to whether the Biggs court had reached the proper legal conclusions from the facts of the case.

The court made a critical finding at the outset. Biggs wrote that Bible reading and recitation of the Lord's Prayer amounted to a religious ceremony and religious instruction in the public schools. Rhoads had argued that the public schools in Pennsylvania engaged in Bible readings for their literary, moral, and historical value, not for any religious lessons. The three judges rejected that position at the outset and referred (in a footnote) to a passage in Weigle's book *The English New Testament,* which Sawyer had inserted in the record during the trial the previous fall: "The Bible contains the Word of God to man." Biggs now wrote, "Inasmuch as the verses of the Bible address themselves to, or are premised upon a recognition of God, the Bible is essentially a religious work. To characterize the Bible as a work of art, of literary or historical significance, and to refuse to admit its essential character as a religious document would seem to us to be unrealistic."[1]

Certainly not all uses of the Bible in school would amount to promotion of religion. The Bible might be used legitimately, for example, in an academic course on comparative religion. But its use in the Abington schools, Biggs reasoned, had little to do with teaching literature, history, or morals and everything to do with imparting religious doctrine.

> The verses of the Bible, though they are of great literary merit, are embodied in books of worship, regardless of the version, devoted primarily to bringing man in touch with God. If study of the Bible as an artistic work, a treasury of moral truths, or historical text can be separated from the espousal of doctrinal matters and religiousness, we should find no objection. But the manner in which the Bible is employed as required by the legislative fiat does not effect this division. The daily reading of the Bible buttressed with the authority of the State and, more importantly to children, backed with the authority of their teachers, can hardly do less than inculcate or promote the inculcation of various religious doctrines in childish minds. Thus, the practice required by the statute amounts to religious instruction, or a promotion of religious education.[2]

Having made the factual finding that the Bible was a religious document utilized for promotion of religious education, Biggs then had to reach the central legal question. Did its use in the public school classrooms violate the First Amendment? Here, he had to analyze a pair of issues raised by the two religion clauses of the amendment. Did the requirement that students read the Bible and then recite the Lord's Prayer amount to an establishment of religion by the state of Pennsylvania? Did this requirement interfere with the Schempps' free exercise of their Unitarian faith?

Biggs referred to the Supreme Court's 1947 decision in *Everson v. Board of Education,* in which the Court said that the establishment clause prohibited the state or federal governments from setting up a church. "Neither can pass laws which aid one religion, aid all religions, or prefer one religion over another," the Court ruled.[3] Biggs said that the Pennsylvania law violated this test. The state law aided all religion, said Biggs, by requiring readings that reminded students daily of man's relationship to God. More particularly, he argued, because "the 'Holy Bible' is a Christian document, the practice aids and prefers the Christian religion."[4]

Biggs alluded also to another of the Supreme Court decisions on religion, *McCollum v. Board of Education,* the released-time case.[5] In that case, local clergy came on campus to teach religious doctrine for forty-five minutes of the school day. In the Abington schools, the schoolteachers themselves—not visiting clergy—delivered the religious message to the students. In Biggs's view, the fact that government employees were doing the instruction put the state even more powerfully behind the promotion of religion.

Biggs then went on to dismiss an argument that Rhoads had hoped would save the statute from invalidation under the First Amendment. Rhoads had argued that the provision requiring that the Bible be read without comment distanced the readings from any attempt by the school district at inculcating religion. Biggs strongly disagreed with this analysis.

> This argument falls for two reasons. First, it either ignores the essentially religious nature of the Bible, or assumes that its religious quality can be disregarded by the listener. This is too much to ignore and too much to assume. The religiousness of the Bible, we believe, needs no demonstration. Children cannot be expected to sift out the religious

from the moral, historical or literary content. Second, the testimony of the Schempps and Dr. Grayzel proves that interpretations of the Bible, dependent upon the inclinations of scholars and students, can result in a spectrum of meanings, beginning at one end of the spectroscopic field with literal acceptances of the words of the Bible, objectionable to Unitarians such as the Schempps, and ending in the vague philosophical generalities condemned by fundamentalists.[6]

Biggs also felt that the combination of Bible reading and recitation of the Lord's Prayer exhibited the characteristics of a religious exercise. He noted, in fact, that students often referred to the exercises as morning devotionals and that even a lawyer for Abington had called them "devotional services." Quite surprisingly (because it is so rarely done), Biggs interjected a note concerning the judges' own personal experience with Bible reading in the schools. "Our backgrounds are colored by our own experiences and many of us have participated in such exercises as those required in the Abington Township schools in our childhood," wrote Biggs. "We deemed them then and we deem them now to be devotional in nature, intended to inculcate religious principles and religious beliefs."[7]

Finally, Biggs moved to the next consideration, whether the Bible-reading statute violated the Schempp's free exercise of religion. A violation of the amendment's free exercise clause normally requires that the state either compel or forbid participation in a religious exercise, and Biggs said that this requirement had been satisfied on a number of levels. Teachers had to conduct the Bible reading and Lord's Prayer exercises on pain of discharge from their jobs. As for Ellery, when he had returned to school for his senior year, the school officials had required him to stay in his homeroom class during Bible reading and to stand for the Lord's Prayer. It was true, Biggs said, that only the Schempps complained of the morning devotionals. But compulsion in respect to children can be quite subtle, Biggs said, since young children typically imitate each other and since peer pressure tends to douse any nonconformity.

Finally, Biggs said that the Bible-reading exercises violated the rights of the parents in this case, Edward and Sidney Schempp, as well. The Schempps disagreed with much of the substantive messages in the King James Version and said it contradicted some of the core religious beliefs that they taught to their children. "The right of the parent to teach his own faith to his child, or to teach him no religion at all is one of the foundations of our way of life and enjoys full constitutional protection," Biggs concluded.[8]

ॐ

The decision brought outcries from almost everywhere. The trial itself had been covered by the press, but not as a major story that dominated the news. At the time (the late 1950s), the nation still had little experience with church-state litigation and had heard relatively little discussion of church-state issues in the media. So, for many in the Philadelphia area, the court's decision to end Bible reading in the public schools came as something of a lightning strike on a cloudless day.

By far, the sentiment of the community weighed heavily against the court's opinion. Local clergy were especially vociferous. Bishop Oliver J. Hart, speaking for the Episcopal Diocese of Pennsylvania, said: "I don't see how the reading of the Bible can be considered imposing any doctrine on the school children. It is simply sound moral teaching."[9] Methodist Bishop Fred Pierce Corson, who would become president of the World Methodist Council in 1961, warned a gathering of Methodists that there were "militant atheists in this country who want to deny Christians their basic rights." The Schempps were Unitarians, not atheists, but bringing atheism to the fore enabled Corson to more easily link the *Schempp* case to the country's fight against godless communism. As the case progressed through the courts, references to communism became a dominant focus for criticism of efforts to end religious observances in the schools.[10]

The Reverend George D. Munro, moderator of the Presbytery of Philadelphia, representing approximately two hundred Presbyterian churches, said that it was "regrettable that a nation which has as its motto, 'In God We Trust,' should find it unconstitutional to read God's word in public schools."[11] The Presbytery of Philadelphia passed a resolution backing Bible reading in the schools and favoring an appeal to the U.S. Supreme Court.[12] The Greater Philadelphia Council of Churches said, "[W]e are gravely concerned by the implications of this decision for religious under girding of governmental activities and our public education in particular."[13] The ruling shocked Pennsylvania schoolteachers, too. At their 107th annual convention in Harrisburg in December, the teachers backed continued readings from the Bible in the public schools.[14]

Voices defending the decision were difficult to find. In a quote in the *Philadelphia Inquirer*, Theodore Mann, who was not there identified as the chief architect of the complaint that initiated the lawsuit, admired *Schempp* as "a case of the first importance which will further strengthen the religious liberty of all Americans."[15] Benjamin B. Levin, president of the Delaware Valley Council of the AJ Congress, said similarly that the court's opinion "demonstrates once again the vital role of our American courts in upholding the civil rights and civil liberties of American citizens."[16] Appeals to civil liberties, however, lacked resonance at a time when few people understood that the Bill of Rights existed in large part to protect the rights of minorities against the will of the majority.

One person did confront the issue of religious observances in the classroom more directly. H. B. Sissel, an Abington Township commissioner, came forward rather bravely, with a long commentary—published in local papers—in which he applauded the decision. Identifying himself as a Protestant, Sissel echoed some of the testimony at the trial, by noting that while more than two hundred Protestant groups in the United States accept the Bible, even they disagree on the interpretation of specific passages. "To assume," he said, "that the Bible, uninterpreted, will convey a common body of truth is to ignore the last 400 years of church history." To buttress his point, Sissel added a compelling reminder. He wrote that the founding fathers "needed only a short memory to recall the chaos and carnage that resulted when instruments of religious coercion were placed in the hands of the state." He continued, "One of my own spiritual ancestors had his tongue drawn out, his nostrils slit, and the letter 'S' (for sedition) branded on his forehead because he refused to obey an edict of parliament to use the prayer book of the Church of England."[17]

ॐ

On Tuesday, September 29, thirteen days after the district court's decision, 250 people packed the cafeteria at Huntingdon Junior High School to discuss the Bible-reading case. Nine school officials, all men and all wearing coats and ties, sat at a long table facing the crowd. Of the nine, six were members of the Abington school board. It was warm inside the room, and the oversized windows behind the officials were all pushed open to allow a breeze to cool it off.

No doubt a good bit of the heat was generated by the anger expressed inside the room. After the court's ruling, the school board had ordered the practice of Bible reading and recitation of the Lord's Prayer stopped throughout the Abington public schools. Then, however, acting on a petition by Rhoads, the court had issued a sixty-day stay of its order ending the morning exercises, pending Abington's appeal of the decision to the U.S. Supreme Court. So the school board temporarily, at least, reinstated the morning exercises in the schools. That much seemed to please the school superintendent, Dr. O. H. English. "It is regrettable," he said, "that we have minority groups who want to eliminate that which makes America great."[18]

The question before the meeting was whether the school board should authorize an appeal of the decision to the U.S. Supreme Court. The discussion focused for a while on the reach of the decision. If Abington failed to appeal the case, thus letting stand the district court's decision, only Abington schools and other public schools in the geographical reach of the district court would have to do without morning exercises; no other schools around the country would be affected. However, a decision by the U.S. Supreme Court would set policy for the entire nation. Albert McCoy, one board member, argued that Abington should look out for its own interests and not worry about anything else. "We are public servants in Abington Township, not fighting, at this moment, for 50,000 other school districts," he said. Charles Smith, the school board president, agreed. "I have faith in the Supreme Court not to outlaw Bible reading," he said. Another member of the school board, Clayton Worster, added, "Let's fight it!"[19]

The large majority of those present favored appealing the case. The school board's solicitor, Percival Rieder, reported that the cost of defending the *Schempp* case to date had been $12,683 and that an appeal to the U.S. Supreme Court would add another $7,000 in costs. So well was he prepared that he even told the crowd that the entire case, through an appeal, would cost one dollar of additional property tax for a homeowner living in a house with the township's average assessment of $4,000.

Before the vote, President Smith noted that there were "two civilizations in the world." Of these, he said: "One has a God. The other doesn't." He added that there could be no meeting "the godless" halfway. Raymond S. Kraft, another board member, added: "I belong to the Lord Jesus Christ, body and soul. I could not personally be against an appeal, although I think taking an appeal now is wrong." Albert McCoy, another board member, noted that most people in Abington favored Bible reading. When Smith finally called for a vote, five of six members of the school board voted to support an appeal to the U.S. Supreme Court. Only James F. Kaehler, who predicted that the school district would lose on appeal, voted against taking the case further. "I feel we should explore other areas and not rush into this facing certain defeat," he said.[20]

◈

Just as Spencer Coxe and the lawyers for the ACLU had predicted, the lawsuit against the Abington school board bought some serious problems for the Schempp family. On several occasions, the family came home to find excrement smeared on the handle of their front door. Ellery had initiated the lawsuit, but he actually suffered least from the hostility surrounding the family.

After his protest, Ellery had sometimes heard pejorative comments as he walked the hallways between classes. But he says that he was never harassed in a serious way. "My circle of friends were all rather supportive," he says. "Allan Glatthorn's class, and the students around him, provided me with a bubble that insulated me a lot. From these people I got very positive feedback. Not that they all agreed. But those who disagreed disagreed in a very genteel way, a polite and respectful way."[21]

Donna and Roger suffered a great deal more, especially after the decision. Donna lost some friends. Ed wrote up an explanation that she could use when kids asked her about the lawsuit. "I remember being given a piece of paper my Dad had written saying why we were doing this," she says. "I was to hand it out. That was embarrassing to me. I was just starting junior high. I was at a point in my life where I just wanted to be invisible. I just wanted to be like everyone else." Donna blamed her parents, not Ellery, for her feelings of isolation. Ellery was by then away at Tufts. Donna says: "Ellery was my big brother. I idolized him. I was never angry with him. I blamed my parents. It was easier to blame them. They were around, he wasn't. They were the ones not understanding me."[22]

Roger suffered harassment from some students in his school. They sometimes shoved him in the hallways. There were no physical attacks, but Roger always had to be on guard. "I was called anti-Christ, communist, and on occasion when I rode the bus and the bus went past the house, [they said] there's the atheist, the communist house," Roger says. "The favorite phrase was communist and anti-Christ."[23]

Beyond the in-your-face harassment, hundreds of letters—almost all negative—poured into the Schempp house. A few of the letters contained excrement, and others suggested vague threats, which the family turned over to the postal authorities for investigation. A large number of the letters were vitriolic. "If you succeed, always remember you have helped sell our country out to the Communists whose main fight is to rid the world of all religion," wrote one person. "It is really a test of are you for God or against God." Another person wrote: "This greater Philadelphia Branch of the American Civil Liberties Union smells like Communists to me, and anyone that agrees with these theories is no better." Some of the letters attacked with religious prejudice. "How much are you getting to front for these grabbing Jews?" read one. Another read: "The Unitarians must be Infidels. Why don't you move to a Heathen country?" Finally, one letter writer suggested, "Why don't you move to Red China."[24]

⤳

With Ellery off studying at Tufts University in Massachusetts, he was far from the intensifying heat scalding his family back in Abington. At Tufts, Ellery became president of the Unitarian student association on campus. He answered a few reporters' questions about the lawsuit but otherwise followed developments through conversations with his family over the telephone and on visits home.

Ellery needed an outlet for his political interests. So while on campus, he became increasingly engaged in the developing presidential campaign of 1960 and the prospects for the young Massachusetts senator John F. Kennedy. Like many people at that time, Ellery and his father viewed John Kennedy with some skepticism in regard to his Catholic faith. Their skepticism was a matter not of anti-Catholicism but, rather, of general concern—shared by many others in the country—that Kennedy would feel bound to bring church doctrine into decisions he would make on public policy issues. Ellery eventually decided that Kennedy would act independent of religious doctrine, but Ed hung on stubbornly to his fears. "I can remember writing home letters saying, 'It's time you gave up this nonsense about the Pope. Kennedy's clearly the better man over Nixon,'" says Ellery. "I added two votes to the Kennedy camp."[25]

Politics had always engaged Ed Schempp, and as time went on, he had become more of a liberal firebrand. Now, he devoted increasing amounts of his time to the case that bore his family's name. The conflict that his son had started in a quiet classroom had become, for Ed, an opportunity to talk on a highly visible stage about his passion—church-state relations. A number of local newspapers carried his letters to the editor. He appeared in many public discussion groups on church-state relations throughout the Philadelphia area. Again and again, he said that he and his children did not believe in the divinity of Christ, in the concept of the Trinity, and in the Immaculate Conception. At a public meeting at the Delaware County Unitarian Church, in a suburb of Philadelphia, Schempp pointed to a number of Bible passages that he felt were violent or that provided an account of events that he did not believe ever took place. The Bible, he complained, was "unfit for children to read" and was, beyond that, an "unclean book." It was no business of the government, he railed, to force prayer and Scripture on his children.[26]

᠅

With public sentiment against the court's decision coming to a boil, Pennsylvania's legislators went back to work in Harrisburg. They thought that perhaps they could craft a new law that would meet the objections of the three judges and allow the morning exercises to continue. So, on October 13, two legislators in the state House of Representatives—Clarence E. Bell, a Republican from Delaware County, and Mary Varallo, a Democrat from Philadelphia—introduced a measure that added an excusal provision to the morning exercises. The new measure would make Bible reading mandatory in the schools except for children whose parents or guardians asked in writing for them to be excused.

Bell picked up on a statement by the Greater Philadelphia Council of Churches that children who object to Bible reading should not have to participate. Bell explained that an excusal provision in the amended law would adequately protect the rights of children who did not want to participate, while at the same time permitting the majority in the community to continue with a longtime practice. For good measure, Bell tossed in another reason he favored continued Bible reading, although he offered nothing to back up his assertion. "It is also the belief of the sponsors that much of today's juvenile crime and adult delinquency would vanish if more people read the Bible," he said.[27]

An excusal provision had been tried before in Pennsylvania in an attempt to save Bible reading. Back in 1844, the Philadelphia school board passed a measure excusing Catholic children from participating in readings from the King James Bible, in an attempt to placate Catholics who objected to the practice. The ruling helped instigate riots that engulfed the city, leading to a dozen deaths and to widespread arson of Catholic churches (see a fuller discussion in chapter 8).

Had the legislators closely read the Biggs opinion, they could have seen that their amendment was still likely to fall short of First Amendment requirements, at least as far as Biggs and his two colleagues saw them. Bell's proposal had not addressed the main part of the *Schempp* rationale—that the morning exercise violated the establishment clause, because it was religious in nature and because the state was promoting religion generally and the Protestant denominations specifically. Compelled participation had nothing to do with an establishment clause violation, so constitutional infirmity would presumably still exist. Compulsion did pertain to violations of the free exercise clause. But even if compelled participation were removed from the law, the court had noted the subtle pressures of conformity that made it difficult for young students to complain about the religious ceremony.

When he heard that legislators were offering an amendment designed to save Bible reading in the public schools, Ed Schempp jumped back into the fight. He wrote a letter to the *Philadelphia Daily News*. The amendment, he charged, was "no more than a dishonest subterfuge of legal quibbling, completely beside the main point that devotional services have no place in the Public Schools."[28]

✌

On November 12, 1959, C. Brewster Rhoads submitted his notice of appeal to the U.S. Supreme Court in Washington, D.C. Although his filing listed twelve questions presented on appeal, the central focus remained the same: whether the morning exercises in the Abington public schools violated the First Amendment rights of the Schempp family; that is, whether they amounted to an establishment of religion or a denial of the free exercise of religion?[29] The justices of the Supreme Court had no discretion to turn down the appeal. Federal law required them to take on the case, unless some procedural matter got in the way.

Just such a potential complication came five weeks later. On December 17, 1959, just three months after the Biggs opinion came down, Pennsylvania governor David L. Lawrence, a Democrat, signed the bill into law permitting students to be excused from Bible reading and recitation of the Lord's Prayer in the state's public schools.[30] With the amendment now in place, the law that Biggs and his colleagues had struck down had changed substantially since their decision. Nobody knew if the justices would hear the case or send it back down to Biggs for reconsideration.

14. Passion Plays for All

It was no mystery why Leo Pfeffer felt drawn to the *Chamberlin* case in Florida's Dade County. He thought it was a nearly perfect test case to attack religious practices in the public schools. Pfeffer had never much liked the *Schempp* case, confined as it was to Bible reading and the Lord's Prayer and involving only a Unitarian family. It would be preferable, Pfeffer reasoned, to litigate a case that would present the Supreme Court justices (and he did expect to go to Washington with the *Chamberlin* case) with a much broader array of religious practices in the schools. He was now effectively in control of the two consolidated cases, *Chamberlin* and *Resnick*, which went forward under the lead name, *Chamberlin*.

Pfeffer was convinced that what went on in the Dade County schools would be difficult for the justices to ignore. The public schools sponsored devotional exercises that Pfeffer thought would surely run afoul of the establishment clause, which prohibited any state endorsement of religion. Pfeffer thought that the broad array of religious practices—prayer, Bible reading, sectarian holiday celebrations, Easter crucifixion plays, and representations of Jesus—surely violated the free exercise clause as well. All those practices, Pfeffer believed, put many children in the position of having to observe the religious beliefs of others, thus encroaching on their constitutional right to freely exercise their own religion.

Pfeffer knew that with other cases also winding their way through courts in other parts of the country, it would be a horse race to reach the Supreme Court first. As much as he wanted to argue the case that would make new law, Pfeffer also felt committed to compiling an exhaustive trial record that would record all the religious practices in the Dade County public schools in detail. He wanted to impress on the court the extent to which the state of Florida had used its public schools to teach and support religious practices that more properly belonged in the home and in houses of worship. He wanted the testimony of students and parents in order to educate judges in how religious observances affected students who practiced a minority religion or no religion at all.

No practice in the schools was more shocking than the crucifixion plays acted in schoolwide assemblies in the Miami junior and senior high schools at Easter. To Pfeffer, the requirement that even Jewish students watch these crucifixion plays was a particularly egregious violation of the free exercise clause. Many Christians, after all, had blamed Jews for the death of Christ, and this charge had been the source of persecution and killing of Jews for ages. Participation of Jewish children in the assembly was as cruelly insensitive to their beliefs as was possible.

As the lights dimmed in the auditorium, a spotlight illuminated a student tied to a cross on an otherwise bare stage. Two students, a boy and a girl, alternated reading passages from the New Testament describing the events surrounding the crucifixion of Christ.[1]

One of the witnesses, Donald Crocker, who testified on July 20, 1960, had graduated earlier that year from Miami Edison High School. He told Judge J. Fritz Gordon that during the Easter assembly, there was a processional by a chorus, and then the program started. A male student was stretched out on a cross, arms extended, his body draped in a sheet. "The lights were focused on the boy," said Crocker, "and then at Christ's death there was heavy breathing from the boy, and then finally collapse, and that was the end of the program, I mean then they told everyone to go back to their rooms."[2] The next day, the judge heard the passion play confirmed in more detail by another student, Marcia Robinson. She had graduated from a different high school, Miami Senior High. Robinson had been impressed by the realism of the play—including the use of makeup showing that the Christ figure was bleeding from where he had been "nailed" to the cross. A student portraying Mary knelt close by.[3]

While Easter provided the backdrop for dramatic renderings of the crucifixion of Christ, the Christmas holiday season boasted the broadest array of religious observances. Rabbis came into some of the schools for Hanukkah programs that included candle lighting and the reading of stories about Hanukkah. The most extensive religious observance in the schools, however, focused on an intensively sectarian observance of Christmas. On the instruction of their teachers, students created scenes to celebrate the holiday and placed them throughout the schools in display cases and on windows. There were crosses, Nativity scenes, depictions of Christ on the cross, and quotations from the Bible.[4]

Throughout the school district, students attended assemblies to commemorate the holiday through plays that depicted the birth of Christ. Students joined in singing Christological carols with such words as "Oh come let us adore him, Christ the Lord" and "Hark the herald angels sing, glory to the newborn King."[5] Nativity scenes and plays were routinely presented, along with Bible readings on the birth of Christ and movies with strong Christmas themes.[6] In one movie, *The Littlest Angel,* students heard what was presented as the voice of God saying that one angel had given him a box that "pleases me most." The voice continues: "Its contents are of the Earth and of men, and My Son is born to be King of both. I accept this gift in the name of the Child, Jesus, born of Mary, this night in Bethlehem."[7] At Miami Senior High School, officials printed a message on the program for the special Christmas assembly attended by all students, including non-Christians. It included this admonition: "Gifts are wonderful things to receive, but you should never forget the greatest gift of all, Jesus. On Christmas morning before opening your presents, say a small prayer to God, thanking him for your many blessings and His son."[8]

Observances on a smaller scale took place daily throughout the year. They centered on what was known as the morning devotionals, typically a five-minute period at the beginning of the day when, as at

Abington, the students participated in prayer and Bible reading. A Florida statute required "once every school day, readings in the presence of the pupils from the Holy Bible, without sectarian comment."[9] In 1953, as an aid to teachers and administrators unsure of what specific readings to choose, the state's Department of Education issued the pamphlet *Suggestions for Bible Readings in the Florida Public Schools.*[10]

The Bible used most often in the schools was the King James Version. Despite the prohibition on sectarian comment, some teachers or outside visitors provided commentary on biblical passages. Lois Milman, who had graduated from North Miami Senior High School, remembered that a Christian religious leader had once come in and delivered a devotional that was sectarian enough to elicit comments from both students and faculty: "[H]e concluded with, 'In Jesus Christ, Our Savior's Name, We Pray.'"[11] The trial record also established that a variety of religious films were shown from time to time, including several produced by a missionary organization to help explain Bible verses.[12] After completion of the Bible reading, students typically recited the Lord's Prayer. Although the school district denied it, the trial evidence showed that teachers sometimes engaged students in other prayers as well, with the prayers often made "in Christ's name" or with a similar offering.[13]

Many of Pfeffer's witnesses, parents and students alike, said that they were offended by the religious practices in the schools and that the observances contradicted their own religious beliefs. Offensiveness to those practicing minority religions or no religion at all was to be expected, but Pfeffer added another significant twist to the testimony. Some students testified that they felt just as offended when their own religious beliefs were observed in the schools and that classrooms were an inappropriate forum for presenting lessons best left to their own home and to their house of worship.[14]

The Florida law did not contain a provision allowing students to excuse themselves. However, throughout the hearings, Dade County school officials maintained that it was their unwritten policy that student participation in the morning devotionals and other religious activities was voluntary. The excusal policy was important in their defense of the school district's religious practices. Officials argued that because no student was compelled to participate, anyone who was offended did not have to be exposed to religious observances and thus had no valid basis on which to complain. On June 29, 1960— only three weeks before the trial started and apparently in anticipation of the issue—the Dade County school board adopted a resolution that put its unwritten policy into a formal public position. After stating that the Bible "be read daily without sectarian comment," the board stated, "Any pupil shall be excused from such Bible reading, or attending such Bible reading, upon the written request of his parent or guardian."[15]

Throughout the years, the school board's excusal policy was at best illusory. The policy was unwritten and also unannounced, which meant that some students and teachers knew about it, but many did not. Some students testified during the trial that they never heard teachers or officials talk about an excusal policy.[16] Some students testified that they had made a request for excusal but were denied, because the teachers either did not understand the policy or simply chose not to follow it. Thomas A. Teasley, who had graduated from North Miami Senior High School, testified that his homeroom teacher had denied his request to be excused from the Christmas assemblies in 1959. On cross-examination by Edward F. Boardman, an attorney for the school board, Teasley recalled that his homeroom teacher "told me that it was not her policy or prerogative to excuse me from any religious, or from any activities, such as was concerned, for purely personal reasons." He continued, "In other words, she told me that I would have to have another reason to be excused, such as going to a doctor or going to a dentist, or something like that."[17] Teasley wouldn't let it go; he appealed next to the school's dean of men, Richard J. Henley, who also refused him. Boardman asked, "Now, Tom, did you tell him particularly that the reason you wanted to get released was because of your religious conscience?" Teasley responded, "I did."[18]

Pfeffer argued that an excusal policy, even if students and parents knew of its existence, was ineffective in protecting a student's rights under the First Amendment. Excusal did not remove the element of compulsion from participation in the devotional activities. A wide range of social and psychological factors deterred students and parents from requesting excusal. Many students found it difficult to confront adult teachers or school officials to ask for what seemed to be a significant exception to rules that everyone else was following. Others felt the inevitable tug of peer pressure and did not want to be regarded as weird or different. Parents, of course, worried about the same thing. Harlow Chamberlin, one of the plaintiffs, said that he had discussed excusal with his son, then fifteen years old, and realized that excusal would not work because "it would be persecution, it would be setting him apart, he would be subject to derision by his schoolmates, he would be subject to persecution, divisiveness, and his life would be miserable."[19] Another plaintiff, Philip Stern, testified that despite his opposition to the morning devotionals, he didn't ask that his seven-year-old daughter be excused because "it would upset the child too much."[20]

At least one student worried that a request of this kind could ruffle teachers who were writing recommendations for college. Whether such a perception was fair or accurate is not the point; the fact is that it was a strong enough fear that it convinced the student not to ask for excusal from the religious activities. Marcia Robinson, a student from Miami Senior High School, said, "It was before I took my examinations, but we didn't lodge the complaint, because we were afraid of what was going to happen from our teachers, and so we waited until the end of the school year."[21]

By their very nature, some of the religious practices were not ones that afforded any possibility of opting out. Pfeffer produced evidence that surveys of religious preference were sometimes taken in classrooms. One student, Michael M. Landis, who was entering his senior year at Palmetto Junior-Senior High School, testified that his teacher read off a list of religions and asked students to respond whether they were adherents. He recounted: "[T]he teacher said, 'Is there any students who do not belong to a church?' And I believe that two students stood." Asked if he was one of the two who stood, Landis answered, "Yes." Later, in answer to a lawyer's question, he said that he did not belong to any religious faith.[22]

To fortify the students' religious faith, Dade County school officials permitted Gideon International to distribute copies of the New Testament to willing children.[23] An administrator at one high school distributed a pamphlet to students that urged their attendance at Sunday religious school.[24] Officials also permitted religious groups to use school facilities to conduct after-school Bible instruction—as long as it was voluntary and nonsectarian—and helped to promote it through announcements in the school and to parents. It wasn't clear how Bible instruction could be nonsectarian, and school officials did not attempt to confirm how the instruction was given. One group, the Child Evangelism Fellowship, taught courses on the divinity of Christ and "the fact of the Resurrection."[25]

Religious faith was important in terms of a teacher's professional advancement in the Miami schools. People seeking a teaching position in the district had to reveal in the employment application whether they believed in God. Religious affiliation also figured into decisions on promotions. Under what was called the "career increment program," teachers earned a rating of zero to four depending on their "cultural attitudes." Under the category of religion, a teacher who "takes part in his own religious organizations and respects other religious beliefs" received the top rating of four. On the other end of the scale, a teacher who simply "conforms to his own religious belief" received a rating of one.[26]

In November, a week after the trial in Miami had concluded, Pfeffer traveled throughout the Midwest and met with educators and journalists. One of his goals was to round off the sharp edges of his attack on religious observances in the schools. A widespread perception then—and one that would continue unabated for many years—was that opponents of religious practices in the public schools wanted all vestiges of religion removed from the classroom. Pfeffer's actual stance was considerably more nuanced. Religious observances had to go, but academic study of religion did not. He argued that school-teachers should receive more extensive training in religion, so that they could better deal with religious differences in the classroom.

In St. Paul, Pfeffer spoke at a luncheon attended by state educa-tion personnel, discussing the difficulties that observation of reli-gious holidays posed for children who did not share the majority reli-gious faith in the community. In the evening, he spoke to parents of high school students.[27] He made it clear that he did not oppose the teaching of religion as an academic subject—how religion affected history, religious influences in music, and the Bible as literature, for example—because "all these things are within the function and scope of any meaningful educational system." He explained, "What we believe violates the Constitution is the use of the public school to promote belief instead of knowledge, and to seek to impose commit-ment rather than understanding." Pfeffer was an implacable foe of any attempt to promote belief and impose commitment, and he promised a fight to the end.[28]

When he returned from his Midwest swing, Pfeffer completed his work on the final briefs in the Miami case. He argued that the reli-gious practices that he had documented so extensively before Judge Gordon violated the Declaration of Rights of the Florida Constitu-tion, which prohibited preferences or financial aid to any church, sect, or sectarian institution.[29] Pfeffer, however, focused most intensely on what he said were violations of federally protected rights. Forcing the trial judge to rule on his First Amendment claims would help provide jurisdiction for a review by the U.S. Supreme Court, which is the final authority on rights guaranteed by the U.S. Constitution. Pfeffer constructed a careful argument to convince the judge that the Dade County schools had violated each of the two religion clauses of the First Amendment.[30] The two clauses are related but different, and a finding that the Florida statute violated either one of them would have been sufficient to have it overturned.

Pfeffer's extensive trial record, he argued, showed that the Dade

County schools violated the establishment clause. The government was participating in and aiding religion by directing the schools to be used for a wide array of religious practices. Pfeffer reminded the judge of the long history of conflicts between Catholics and Protestants throughout the nineteenth century, largely based on each group's refusal to accept the other's version of the Bible. He pointed out the obvious differences between Christians and Jews over the New and Old Testaments.[31] As for the Lord's Prayer, recited by the children after the Bible-reading exercise, Pfeffer noted that it appears twice in the Christian New Testament, both times spoken by Jesus. It is the most important prayer for Christians, wrote Pfeffer, because "it is the only prayer that actually came from Jesus."[32]

Proving a violation of the establishment clause did not depend on the existence of sectarian practices, although Pfeffer believed sectarian practices made his case even stronger. Even if all religious faiths could enthusiastically agree on their children hearing some version of the Bible and reciting some version of a prayer, these practices would still offend the First Amendment. The prior cases, Pfeffer argued, made it clear that the Constitution banned the promotion of religion generally.[33]

Pfeffer believed he had at least as strong a case that Dade County was also violating the free exercise clause of the First Amendment. The cumulative impact of Dade County's practices, he said, was to "force persons to profess a belief or disbelief in religion" and to "punish them for entertaining or professing religious beliefs or disbeliefs."[34] Critical to a violation of the free exercise clause is a finding of compulsion—meaning, in this case, that it had to be evident that the children were forced by the schools to participate in the religious exercises against their will. Pfeffer pointed out that the school district had no formal policy on excusal until almost the eve of the trial and that teachers and administrators routinely denied requests from students that they be excused from participating.

Pointing to Justice Felix Frankfurter's concurring opinion (joined by three other justices) in *McCollum,* Pfeffer argued that even if an excusal policy existed, true voluntariness did not, due to "psychological compulsion."[35] Frankfurter recognized that schoolchildren differ from adults in their ability to withstand the pressure of peers and others. "That a child is offered an alternative may reduce the constraint; it does not eliminate the operation of influence by the school in matters sacred to conscience and outside the school's domain," said Frankfurter. "The law of imitation operates, and non-conformity is not an outstanding characteristic of children. The result is an obvious pressure upon children to attend."[36] If he got to the U.S. Supreme Court, Pfeffer knew that the conservative Frankfurter might in fact cast a key vote. Sensitive as he was to compelled participation that violated the free exercise of religion, Frankfurter might find it hard to swallow that Jewish children were forced, on a matter "sacred to conscience," to attend plays depicting the crucifixion of Christ.

☞

Up the coast in Brooklyn, meanwhile, the case concerning the Regents' Prayer took another step on its own long journey toward the U.S. Supreme Court. Back in August 1959, the trial judge, Bernard S. Meyer, had upheld the short prayer composed by the New York State Board of Regents that had been intended as a nondenominational and nonsectarian devotional to start the school day. But he had required the state to make participation in the prayer noncompulsory, and he had ordered that the schools put into place a procedure that would enable them to excuse students who objected. Now the case, *Engel v. Vitale*, moved to an intermediate state appeals court, which heard oral arguments and then, on October 17, 1960, affirmed the trial judge's order. In an unsigned opinion that was just a few paragraphs long, the court simply stated that it agreed with Meyer's views, adding no comments of its own.[37]

The court's decision didn't discourage William J. Butler, Steven Engel's attorney. Routed in the first two skirmishes in the lower courts, Butler now took the case to the loftier battleground where it had been destined to go from the start. The highest court in New

York, the Court of Appeals, was the next stop, and it was in that court where Butler felt he had to win. He couldn't assume that the U.S. Supreme Court would agree to hear the case, so he needed to make his arguments resonate before the state's top judges.

꩜

While the *Chamberlin, Schempp,* and *Engel* cases proceeded on the East Coast, from Miami to New York, Madalyn Murray had become too radicalized to abide American society any longer. She decided that she and her sons, Bill and Jon, should abandon the United States for Russia. By now a member of the radical Socialist Workers Party, Murray applied for Soviet citizenship in 1959 and went to the Soviet Embassy the next year to help expedite her application. But she received no help from the bureaucrats there. Determined to find a different door that would be easier to open, Madalyn and her sons boarded the *Queen Elizabeth* for France at the end of August 1960. They visited the Soviet Embassy there frequently during the next month but still could not persuade anyone there to grant them Soviet citizenship. Finally, she and the two boys returned to their home in Baltimore late in September.

By then, Murray was a few weeks late in placing her children back in school. When she had focused during the spring and summer on gaining Soviet citizenship, she had left festering the issue of Bible reading and recitation of the Lord's Prayer. Now that she was definitely staying in Baltimore, she steeled herself for a fight. As Bill resumed his studies at Woodbourne Junior High, Murray called Vernon Vavrina, the assistant superintendent for secondary schools, and told him that Bill would no longer participate in the morning religious exercises.

Vavrina stood firm. Bill would not be excused from the morning Bible reading and prayers, Vavrina told her on the phone. Although Bill did not have to say the prayer, he would have to display a respectful attitude and bow his head.[38] The decision incensed Murray. That same day, she and Bill wrote a letter that she sent to Vavrina, Baltimore school superintendent George Brain, and every member of the school board. In the letter, she informed them that she refused to comply with Vavrina's decision because it was a "flagrant violation" of the First Amendment. She announced her intention to henceforth teach William at home herself.[39]

Despite Maryland law that considered truancy a misdemeanor, Murray kept Bill home from school for a month. On October 27, the Baltimore *Morning Sun* ran a front-page story with Bill's picture. The article claimed that Murray's action was the first protest of the Baltimore school board's rule—enacted in 1905—that required Bible reading and recitation of the Lord's Prayer.[40] That local article unleashed a flurry of calls from both local and national media. A local civil rights attorney, Fred Weisgal, who worked for the ACLU, called Murray and said that the ACLU had not yet determined whether to represent her. He advised that Murray had to send Bill back to school, in order to keep the matter focused on religious exercises in the public schools, not on the issue of Bill's truancy.[41]

When Bill returned to school, his mother instructed him to make a statement to his homeroom teacher that he refused to participate in the opening exercises. But Murray maintained that the school authorities, wishing to avoid a confrontation in the classroom, locked him out of his homeroom the first morning. For the next few days, the school posted a teacher in the hallway to intercept him before the morning exercises and escort him directly to Vavrina's office. Finally, on October 31, he eluded the teacher and slipped into his homeroom, where he objected to the Bible reading and Lord's Prayer and then left the room.[42]

Two days later, the state of Maryland itself responded to Murray's challenge. Thomas G. Pullen, Jr., the state superintendent of schools, had asked the state's attorney general for a legal opinion on the Bible-reading controversy in Baltimore. C. Ferdinand Sybert replied with a legal analysis mostly favorable to the school board. The school attendance law, he said, required Bill Murray to attend school regardless of his objection to Bible reading and prayer. Bill's only valid alternative was enrollment in private school. If he did not attend, both Madalyn and Bill should be prosecuted for truancy, he said. Regarding the opening exercises, Sybert concluded that the First Amendment did not require that "the state need be stripped of all religious sentiment." Bible reading and prayer did not violate Bill Murray's religious freedom. However, the opinion did provide an escape for Madalyn and anyone else offended by the devotional exercises. Sybert ruled that devotional exercises in public schools must not involve direct compulsion to participate and that the school board must therefore amend its rule to include an excusal provision. Sybert suggested that such students could either remain silent or be excused from the exercise.[43] Two weeks later, on November 17, the school board accepted Sybert's suggestion and amended the rule on devotional exercises to enable students to be excused on the written request of a parent or guardian.

వు

In December 1960, Madalyn Murray O'Hair and the Schempps apparently made contact for the first time. On December 4, she sent a typed letter to the Schempps inquiring about their case, which she said she hadn't heard about until the past week. Some people, she said, had suggested that she not pursue a lawsuit herself because the *Schempp* case would soon go before the U.S. Supreme Court, raising similar issues. Murray asked for information that would help her decide what to do—although, as it turned out, her attorney filed her lawsuit just three days later.

In one long paragraph, she summarized her own situation in Baltimore and added that Bill, consistent with the Baltimore school board's new excusal policy, had been permitted to sit in an empty room or to stand in the hallway during the morning Bible reading. But for Murray, that concession fell far short. "I refuse to accept this and I am demanding the complete abolition of the entire religious ritual each morning," she said. Then she asked whether the Schempps had "the same piles of opprobrious mail that I have" and "economic pressures, and physical assault and all the other actions that goes [*sic*] with this." She lamented, "I have learned this last month how very unkind many people can be."[44]

The Schempps must have answered her immediately, for Murray wrote once again on December 10 and referred to the Schempps' response. This time, sensing kindred spirits in the Schempps, she wrote much more candidly and personally of her skirmish in Baltimore and her insistence that her attorney push the case through the courts for a decision: "I am so militant my attorney threatens to lock me in his closet to cool off for a few days at a time." She asked how the Schempp children were faring in relation to her own son: "How are you [*sic*] children holding up? Bill just this week found out what an excellent weapon his fellow students have in their rosaries! They are nice sharp instruments and the beads are just long enough for a good swing. Some of his teachers refuse to talk to him. The principal is campaigning for 'psychological testing.' The students ostracize him completely."[45] Murray also revealed to the Schempps that, only a few days earlier, on December 7, she had filed suit in the Baltimore Superior Court. The ACLU had decided not to represent her, probably because it was pursuing the *Schempp* case in Philadelphia.

⌘

In a case that became known as *Murray v. Curlett,* Madalyn Murray sued the entire school board of the city of Baltimore and its president, John N. Curlett. In legal terms, Murray's attorney, Leonard J. Kerpelman, filed a petition for a writ of mandamus (*mandamus* being Latin for "we order"). Such a writ, if the court decided to issue it, is an order from a court directing another inferior court or, in this case, a governmental officer, to perform an act the court or officer has previously refused to perform. In this instance, the school board had refused to comply with Murray's request that it stop Bible reading and recitation of the Lord's Prayer in the Baltimore public schools. So now she asked the court to issue a writ to the school board that would order it to rescind the rule requiring Bible reading.

Murray alleged that the school board had brought sectarian religious exercises into Baltimore's public school classrooms and, in so doing, had violated her family's right to freedom of religion under the First Amendment. Madalyn and her sons were atheists, and they argued that Bible reading and prayer promotes belief in God as the source of important values and "thereby renders sinister, alien and suspect the beliefs and ideals of your Petitioners, promoting doubt and question of their morality, good citizenship and good faith." Murray also dismissed the school board's recent amendment to the rules that permitted students to be excused from the exercises, arguing that such a request would cause her son Bill "to lose caste with his fellows, to be regarded with aversion, and to be subjected to reproach and insult."[46]

Reproach and insult, as it turned out, would have been mild treatment compared to what was actually happening between Bill Murray and the school's resident bullies—and between the family and the community, for that matter. A major reason why the framers of the U.S. Constitution put religion and state in separate spheres was to avoid the sectarian conflict that attended various religious groups vying for the government to lift their beliefs above all others. It was also done to avoid the persecution that often hounded the followers of minority sects that lived outside the mainstream.

Although the sectarian bloodletting of Europe was a distant cousin of the experience on American shores, it was still true that conflicts over control of religious practices in the schools brought exactly the persecution and outcast status that the First Amendment was designed to prevent. That a government-run institution—in this case, the schools, full of impressionable children—had become a battleground of religious belief should have been evidence enough that the feared dangers were real. The torched churches in Philadelphia in 1844 and the severe animosities engendered in such places as New York and Cincinnati in the previous century had not disappeared. The Schempps and the Murray's were simply the latest to suffer.

For the Murrays, the mail and telephone brought angry denunciations. Someone painted the word *Communist* in two-foot red letters near their house. Others repeatedly snapped the antennae on the

Murrays' cars and slashed their tires. Some people shattered a few of the windows on their house.[47] Kids in school ridiculed Bill and called him names, and he absorbed elbows, fists, and shoves in the hallways. According to Madalyn, students spit through the air slots into Bill's locker; he came home many nights with his jacket or sweater spotted by saliva. One day, a student put a knife to his back and threatened, "you're a dead Commie."[48] Outside of school, he faced assailants who sometimes beat him. "It would have been impossible for him to even think of going to a football game, having a date, going to a movie, or even walking down the street," Madalyn wrote in *An Atheist Epic.* "He had a bicycle and he would try to outrace them at times," she wrote. "Everyone knew him."[49]

Another time, Bill went to a local shopping center to pick up some parts for his ham radio. A group of boys accosted him there, taunting him with labels like "commie" and "atheist." He walked away with the group in pursuit, heading toward a bus stop so that he could get back home. Coming up behind him, some of the boys hit him with belts. The scuffle continued as a bus approached, and the boys pushed him in front of it. Bill got out of the way just in time, escaped the pulls and tugs of those trying to pull him back, and scrambled onto the bus. When he got home and took off his shirt, his back had large red welts.[50]

Harassment continued at home against the family as well. Some people got the bright idea that they could drive Madalyn crazy by disguising their identity and ordering all kinds of goods and services to be delivered to her address. As she reported, an undertaker rang her doorbell one day to pick up a dead body he had been told was there. Then, of course, a tombstone salesman followed with a call to sell her a monument. A hundred gallons of ice cream arrived on their doorstep. Subscriptions for magazines, book clubs, and record clubs came in the mail. A truck showed up with a load of lumber. The phone rang repeatedly with callers who inquired about the furniture that was advertised for sale in the newspaper. Tow trucks came for her car, and repairmen came about her television set.[51] Some people in the community decided that if Madalyn and Bill Murray wanted the Bible removed from the Baltimore public schools, the Murrays would pay a high price for the effort.

↢

On January 16, 1961, almost six weeks after Madalyn Murray filed her lawsuit, John Curlett and the Baltimore school board responded. In a three-paragraph filing, Curlett simply demurred to her petition, stating that it did not state a cause of action—any valid legal or factual grounds—on which the court could conceivably grant relief. Judge J. Gilbert Prendergast of the superior court ultimately agreed with the school board.

In an unpublished opinion released on April 27, 1961, Prendergast ruled that the school board had acted within its discretion in issuing the Bible-reading rule and had not violated Bill or Madalyn's constitutional rights of religious freedom. In the first sentence of his opinion, Prendergast referred to them as "avowed atheists," and he made frequent additional references to their atheism throughout his opinion. Responding to Madalyn's claim that Bible reading threatened her family's religious liberty, he wrote, "Just how the religious liberty of a person who has no religion can be endangered is by no means made clear."[52]

That comment would have been unsurprising if made by neighbors talking over the backyard fence. For a judge, though, it showed a serious lack of understanding. In the few religious freedom cases decided by the U.S. Supreme Court up to that time, the justices had made it clear that the First Amendment protected believers and nonbelievers alike. The establishment clause prohibited the government from using its laws to aid any religion or all religions or to promote religious ceremony or belief. Clearly, the judge could cite no authority for his proposition that the rights of nonbelievers could not be legally affected by a religious exercise in the public schools.

Prendergast ruled that the school board had acted consistent with a Maryland statute that empowered it to select textbooks for classroom use as long as the books contained no sectarian influences. This provision, said the judge, showed that the state legislature intended only to forbid sectarian teachings from the public schools, not religious materials in general—a policy, he claimed, that conformed with constitutional requirements. That the Bible would be regarded as a sectarian book was "a rather startling and novel thought," Prendergast concluded.[53] Of course, the idea that the Bible was a sectarian book was by then anything but a novel thought. Many state supreme courts had batted about that very contention for the last hundred years, and the *Schempp* case had brought out testimony on the same issue. (The issue is discussed more fully in chapter 10.)

Prendergast continued on. If religion were removed from the classroom, he said, only atheism would remain. In addition to promoting atheism, the plaintiffs wanted to suppress religion. "The two concepts," he wrote, "are mutually repugnant." Prendergast concluded that one of the nation's principles was that "people should respect the religious view of others, not destroy them."[54]

Finally, Prendergast found reason to differentiate the *Murray* case from the *Schempp* decision handed down by the three-judge federal court in Philadelphia. He pointed out that the Baltimore schools allowed students to be excused from devotional exercises, whereas the Abington schools did not. If Ellery Schempp could have been excused, he said, "a different conclusion would probably have been reached."[55]

Prendergast's wrong claim showed a fundamental lack of understanding of the two religion clauses. Claims under the free exercise clause do require that a person be compelled to act in violation of his belief, so an excusal provision might resolve that claim. Yet a court might find compulsion even with the existence of an excusal provision, because schoolchildren might not be strong enough to resist peer pressure to participate. In any case, the Biggs court had also ruled that Abington had violated the establishment clause by aiding and promoting religion. An excusal provision did not remedy that problem at all.

Prendergast's decision in favor of the Baltimore schools came just nine days after the trial court in Florida ruled in Pfeffer's case, *Chamberlin v. Dade County*. Despite sitting through days of testimony about religious practices in the schools, Judge J. Fritz Gordon, as it turned out, wasn't troubled in the least by the vast majority of them. He did make some gestures in Pfeffer's direction, tossing out a few devotional exercises as violations of Chamberlin's rights.

Judge Gordon's decision, which he handed down on April 18, 1961, contradicted the three-judge federal panel in Philadelphia on key points, upholding the two daily practices that they had struck down. The practice of reading the Bible each morning was fine, said Gordon, as long as it was done without sectarian comment and as long as complaining children were excused. He found that the Lord's Prayer was not sectarian. He also upheld the practices of singing religious hymns and displaying religious symbols. But he declared an end to religious observances of Christmas, Easter, and Hanukkah and to showing films with religious content. He also stopped the use of the public schools for Bible instruction at the end of the school day.[56]

Both sides understood that Judge Gordon's opinion had little real importance. The case would be won or lost before judges in a court of appeals—first at the Florida Supreme Court and perhaps later at the U.S. Supreme Court itself. These courts would be more interested in the trial record than in what Judge Gordon made of it all. That's why Pfeffer had painstakingly created about fourteen hundred pages of testimony about religious practices in the Dade County public schools.[57] That record was complete, and Pfeffer had already vowed to take the case all the way to the top. "We look for an ultimate decision from the U.S. Supreme Court that would be on our side," he said. "We expect it to be one of the important decisions in the history of religious liberty."[58]

15. Back to Judge Biggs

With *Abington School District v. Schempp*, Henry W. Sawyer III had won the race to the U.S. Supreme Court among all the major cases involving religion in the public schools—*Schempp* in Philadelphia, *Murray* in Baltimore, *Engel* on Long Island, and *Chamberlin* in Miami. *Schempp* was the first to land inside the marble courthouse across from the Capitol in Washington, D.C., having reached there with the filing of the Abington school district's notice of appeal on November 12, 1959. Races to the Supreme Court, though, are far different than a sprint of thoroughbreds at Churchill Downs. Lawsuits run on a peculiar set of procedural rules that can snare the fastest horse and require him to run the last lap a second time.

In December, five weeks after Abington appealed its case, Governor David Lawrence signed into law the amendment to the Pennsylvania Bible-reading statute, allowing for the excusal of any student who did not wish to participate in the morning exercises. With the Bible-reading law that the Biggs court had thrown out now amended in a substantial way, the appeal was certainly in doubt. The amendment raised serious issues about whether the justices should hear the case now or send it back down to Biggs for additional hearings that would elicit new testimony on the excusal provision.

Not surprisingly, the attorney for Abington, C. Brewster Rhoads, thought that the amendment changed everything, so he submitted a motion to the three-judge court asking it to vacate its ruling striking down the practice of Bible reading and prayer in the public schools. Three months later, on March 18, 1960, and then again on May 27 (still before the U.S. Supreme Court had scheduled the case for oral argument), Rhoads went before Judges Biggs, Kraft, and Kirkpatrick in Philadelphia for a hearing on his motion. It was to be the first of several such hearings that would ensnarl lawyers and judges alike in complicated procedural issues that seemed to have no clear resolution.

With the excusal provision now part of the law, Rhoads maintained that the court's earlier decision was moot. All the evidence and testimony taken previously, he said, concerned a law now dead. The current law with the excusal provision was substantially different, he said, and no testimony had been taken on it. So Rhoads urged the court to dismiss the case and force Sawyer to file a new lawsuit directly testing the new law.

Any good lawyer would have filed such a motion, and Rhoads was a good lawyer. The potential for a mootness ruling was an obvious possibility that Rhoads could not overlook. It offered tantalizing additional benefits beyond wiping off the books the unfavorable earlier ruling against his client. Starting over with all new testimony and witnesses would probably add a year or more to the litigation. Rhoads knew that the case was vulnerable because the Schempps were the sole plaintiffs; their two younger children could graduate from high school before the litigation was completed, just as Ellery already had. If no Schempp children remained in school, the case could subsequently be dismissed for mootness—this time because no plaintiff who could be legally affected by the outcome would remain in the case.

In another prong of his attack, Rhoads offered a much more ambitious argument to the court. He urged the court to abstain entirely from hearing any case brought under the amended statute and, instead, to allow the controversy to be fought out in Pennsylvania's state courts. Under the doctrine of abstention, a federal court may refuse to entertain a case that might more properly be decided in a state court. Here, Rhoads argued that Pennsylvania state courts were the more appropriate venue for interpreting a Pennsylvania law and that they had never had the opportunity to do so with the amended Bible-reading law.

Beyond the substantial delay that such a ruling would bring, Rhoads couldn't conceivably find himself in a less favorable position by forcing the case into a state court. Biggs and his colleagues had already issued a strong opinion that had rejected Rhoads's defense of the Bible-reading statute. Rhoads had to know that the new excusal provision still would not win the case for him if it were argued again before the Biggs court. An excusal provision might cure the violation of the free exercise clause, which required a finding of government coercion on an individual—forcing him to follow or not follow a religious practice, for example. Regardless of how that argument turned out, the Biggs court also had overturned the statute on the separate grounds of violation of the establishment clause. This conclusion would be unaffected by an excusal provision, because the establishment clause focused solely on the government's action in supporting religious exercises (which remained unchanged), not on the coercion of individuals to participate. Given all of that, the Biggs court would surely affirm its earlier decision. So Rhoads had nothing to lose by starting over with a state court judge.

Sawyer vigorously attacked the idea that the court's decision should be thrown out. He argued that the complaint initiating the case never mentioned anything about students being compelled to take part in the morning exercises. He asserted that if the judges forced him to file a new complaint and start the case over, nothing about the Schempp's complaint would change.[1]

Before any of these questions could be resolved, the justices in Washington finally acted. On October 24, 1960, the Supreme Court vacated the judgment of the district court and remanded the case back to Biggs for additional proceedings consistent with the amended Bible-reading law.[2] In other words, the judgment of the three-judge court declaring the morning devotionals to be a violation of the Schempps' First Amendment rights had been set aside. Thirteen months had elapsed since Biggs handed down his opinion, and now Sawyer and Rhoads were back to where they had been in 1958. Sawyer's horse, as it were, had an extra lap to run.

With the Supreme Court taking a pass on the case for now, C. Brewster Rhoads and Henry W. Sawyer III were back in front of Judge Biggs and his two colleagues in Philadelphia two months later. On December 20, 1960, Rhoads asked that the judges dismiss the case and force Sawyer to file a new lawsuit against Abington. He argued that the judges were now entertaining questions about the validity of a new law and that they should eliminate all previous testimony from the record, because it pertained to a law no longer in force. Rhoads maintained again that the judges should abstain from hearing the case at all. "Your honors," he said, "will be dealing with an Act which has not been seasoned by forty years of experience, and so forth, as was the old Act under which the original proceeding was brought." The Pennsylvania courts, he said, had not dealt with the procedures through which the excusal provision would be administered, evidence that could weigh on whether the statute measured up to First Amendment requirements.[3]

In the end, what seemed to carry the day was Sawyer's focus on the wording of the Supreme Court's order. He pointed out that Rhoads had explicitly asked the Supreme Court justices to send the case back to the three-judge court with direction "that the final decree should be vacated and the case remanded with a direction to dismiss." As Sawyer pointed out, the justices had remanded the case and vacated the lower court's opinion but had said nothing of dismissal. "That [dismissal] was [Rhoads's] argument," said Sawyer, "and that is what they didn't do."[4]

Sawyer won the skirmish. Six months later, on June 22, 1961, the three-judge court ruled for Sawyer on this important procedural ground. Instead of dismissing the case and starting over, the court retained jurisdiction of the original case and permitted Sawyer to file amendments to his complaint.[5] So Sawyer added the excusal provision to the amended complaint and deleted Ellery Schempp, who was off at Tufts University and could no longer be affected by the outcome of the lawsuit he had started. Now the case could proceed once again. In additional hearings to follow before the three judges, Sawyer could continue to rely on the testimony taken earlier. He only had to address the excusal provision.

⁂

While the *Schempp* case bounced from Washington, D.C., back to Philadelphia, *Engel v. Vitale* gathered speed in New York. The state's highest tribunal, the Court of Appeals, handed down its opinion on July 7, 1961, affirming by a five-to-two plurality vote that recitation of the Regents' Prayer was permissible in the public schools.[6] Writing for himself and one other judge, Chief Judge Charles S. Desmond first brushed aside any possible violation of the free exercise clause, because the schools permitted students to excuse themselves from the prayer exercises. Emphasizing that compulsion was required for any free exercise violation, he observed that the excusal provision took away the possibility that students were being compelled to pray. Desmond didn't consider whether, even with an excusal provision, a kind of psychological compulsion still existed because of the peer pressure exerted on children.

Desmond also ruled that recitation of the Regents' Prayer did not violate the establishment clause. Here, the chief judge adopted the narrowest interpretation of the clause—that it meant nothing more than a prohibition against the government favoring one religious sect above all others. That plainly contradicted the U.S. Supreme Court's ruling in *Everson v. Board of Education of Ewing Township,* that the government could not "pass laws which aid one religion, aid all religions, or prefer one religion over another."[7]

Two judges dissented. Religious inscriptions on coins and reference to God in official oaths and benedictions may very well be permissible, wrote Judge Marvin R. Dye, but they are of far different character than a prayer in the classroom that is considered part of the school's teaching function. The state, he said, had entered into an area that the First Amendment required be left to the home and the church; thus, the state had overstepped its bounds.[8]

Steven Engel's attorney, William J. Butler, now absorbed his third straight loss (losing at the trial court, at the intermediate appeals court, and now at the Court of Appeals), with eleven judges in all casting their vote against his position. But he must have been heartened by Dye's dissenting opinion. If the Supreme Court would accept the case, he had something to build on.[9]

ᴏᴏ

Part 2 of the *Schempp* trial resumed in Judge Biggs's courtroom in Philadelphia on Tuesday morning, October 17, 1961. A few days earlier, Henry Sawyer had written to Ed Schempp, suggesting that they meet at 10 a.m. that morning at his office at Broad and Chestnut Streets and then walk together to the courthouse for the 10:30 start of the proceedings. Sawyer let him know that the testimony would focus on the excusal provision of the Pennsylvania Bible-reading law and went over in some detail his understanding of what Schempp would say in response to the expected questions.[10]

In the courtroom, as Sidney and Roger Schempp looked on, Henry Sawyer wasted no time in putting the excusal question directly to Ed Schempp. Sawyer asked if he had ever invoked his right to excuse Roger and Donna, his two children presently at Abington Senior High School, from the morning exercise. Schempp said that he had not. When Sawyer asked him why he had not, Schempp replied that he had worried about the psychological pressure his children would face in school.

> We originally objected to our children being exposed to the reading of the King James version of the Bible, which we felt was against our particular family religious beliefs and under those conditions we would have theoretically liked to have had the children excused. But we felt that the penalty of having our children labeled as "odd balls" before their teachers and classmates every day in the year was even less satisfactory than the other problem.
>
> There were a number of things that we considered at the time. The

children, the classmates of Roger and Donna are very liable to label and lump all particular religious difference or religious objections as atheism, particularly, today the word "atheism" is so often tied to atheistic communism, and atheism has very bad connotations in the minds of children and many adults today. They consider Johnny as an atheist, therefore, he is un-American, . . . he is immoral and other things.[11]

Schempp added that excusal from the devotional exercises "would be very detrimental to the psychological well-being of our children."[12] Moreover, he explained that from a practical point of view, moving the children in and out of the classroom would be disruptive and would likely mean that they would miss the morning announcements that followed immediately after the exercises. Roger Schempp testified for only a few minutes, confirming what his father had said earlier.

After the proceeding, Schempp scribbled some notes about his impressions of what went on. He gave a sober assessment of the eventual chances of success before the U. S. Supreme Court. "Sawyer thinks we have a fair chance of getting our case to Supreme Court," he wrote, "but not so good a chance of winning the Supreme Court decision." Schempp continued of Sawyer's estimation, "He believes the complexion of the court is not leaning toward liberal side with civil rights at present—except in race cases."[13]

๛

With all the evidence now on the table, part 2 of the *Schempp* proceedings had ended except for the final arguments. The lawyers returned to court two months later, on December 18, 1961, to summarize and argue their legal points to the three judges. Sawyer quickly reminded the judges that they had declared the original Bible-reading statute invalid on two separate rationales under the First Amendment.

The new excusal provision, Sawyer said, had no legal bearing on the judges' earlier finding that Abington violated the establishment clause by promoting a daily religious ceremony in its public schools. Such a violation occurred even if the law provided that individual students could be excused on the written request of their parents. Sawyer recalled that Abington's own expert witness, Luther Weigle, had himself conceded that the King James Version read to the students was a sectarian work; Sawyer argued that from that concession, it was clear that the Bible-reading law preferred Christianity over other religious traditions. Sawyer also said that the statute preferred all religion to no religion, also a violation of the First Amendment.[14] As for the excusal provision, Sawyer argued that it did not cure the free exercise violation that the judges had found in their earlier opinion. The fact that students had to get a note from their parents required a profession of belief or disbelief in the religious ceremony in the classroom, and the state was forbidden from requiring any statement from an individual about religious belief.[15]

Rhoads's main point focused on his claim that the Schempps could not suffer any legal injury. Because the amended law permitted anyone to be excused from participation in the morning devotionals, it fully protected the Schempps in their beliefs and enabled them to sidestep any exposure to religion that they deemed offensive. But Rhoads went too far with an analogy, saying that there was little merit in Edward Schempp's concern that his children would be labeled "oddballs" if they were excused from Bible reading. After all, children had to make many choices. If a student declined to go out for the football team, he said, another student might belittle him for that, calling him an oddball and a chicken for making that choice.[16] Sawyer couldn't let that opening go without having a little pointed fun, arguing to the judges that "the essence of it is not the question of the excuse but really the fact that football is not protected by the First Amendment."[17]

Another tough moment for Abington came a short time later, with the testimony of the deputy attorney general of Pennsylvania, John D. Killian III. The Commonwealth of Pennsylvania had entered the case to defend the law, but Killian seemed surprisingly unprepared to address one of the most basic questions in the litigation. In an extraordinary exchange that completely caught him off guard, Killian practically surrendered to one of the central claims of Sawyer's case. This electric moment in the courtroom started with Judge Kirkpatrick asking Killian if reading the Bible and reciting the Lord's Prayer "constitutes an act of worship." Killian first tried to evade: "I think that is for another case to decide, and I think that is for another time, for arguments to be made and testimony to be taken." Of course, this question was a major element of the *Schempp* case, and much testimony had been taken from expert witnesses at the first trial. Judge Kirkpatrick persisted with his question, and twice Killian deferred.

Finally, Judge Biggs entered the fray, obviously frustrated: "I would just like to get your view straight on this. Do you think the recital of the Lord's Prayer is not an act of worship?" Killian responded, "Your Honor, I am not a theologian." Judge Biggs countered: "No, but you are a human being and a member of the Bar. What is your view on that?" Killian finally answered, "Well, I do feel that you are recognizing the existence of God, and you are making an appeal to him, and you are asking God to bestow blessings upon you and these things, and you are asking forgiveness, and so forth, and in a broad outlook I would suppose this could be considered an act of worship."[18] Killian's response, laying out succinctly the many purposes of prayer, made recitation of the Lord's Prayer sound exactly like what takes place every Sunday in churches across America. The trouble was that he was describing what was taking place in the Abington public schools.

જી

The young man who had initiated this conflict, Ellery Schempp, watched from afar as the hearings went on. Now a senior at Tufts University, he kept up with the lawsuit through letters and phone calls home. That fall, he became news editor of the campus weekly newspaper. He also got involved in the civil rights movement that was growing around the country.

Less than two years earlier, four black college students had sat down on stools at a lunch counter in the F. W. Woolworth store in Greensboro, North Carolina. They wanted coffee and doughnuts, a simple enough request—except for the fact that they were blacks asking to be served at a counter reserved for whites only. Refused in their request, they continued sitting there until closing time. Thirty students came the next day and sat in. Soon, sit-ins spread throughout the South and throughout the country.

In Medford, Massachusetts, not far from the Tufts campus, Ellery and others marched on and off for several months in front of an F. W. Woolworth store. They carried signs opposing segregation. Ellery also participated in antisegregation marches downtown on the Boston Commons.[19] Ellery's protest at Abington had been quite lonely. But now the 1960s, a decade of noisy marches and sometimes angry confrontation, had definitely arrived.

જ

Meanwhile, in Baltimore, Madalyn Murray regularly picked up her son Bill from school, trying to reduce the chances of his being attacked by classmates after he left the building. One day, though, he got into the car with bruises on his face and blood on his chin and his shirt. He told his mother he had been attacked on the playground after lunch by a group of as many as twenty kids. He said that the vice principal had seen the attack and had done nothing.

Madalyn rushed into the school and past the vice principal's secretary into his office. "I went over to the desk," she wrote in *An Atheist Epic*, "and I hit him across the face with my open hand so hard that he staggered back at least three feet." She recounted: "I used all the force I could. 'How do you like it? You son-of-a-bitch?' Suddenly I had it in my mind to kill him." Madalyn then drove to the police station, where she demanded an investigation. Her lawyer arrived and eventually got her to leave, telling her that she could be arrested for assault.[20]

_↗_

On February 1, 1962, the three-judge court handed down its second decision in the _Schempp_ case. Once again, Judge Biggs delivered a unanimous decision for himself and Judges Kraft and Kirkpatrick, striking down Pennsylvania's amended Bible-reading law. The excusal provision made the morning exercises noncompulsory for students, said Biggs, but in the end it made no practical difference.

In their first decision, the judges had declared that the morning exercises violated both the free exercise clause and the establishment clause of the First Amendment. Theoretically, at least, permitting students to be excused from the morning exercises would remove compulsion and thereby might cure the free exercise problem. Biggs, though, sidestepped the issue of compulsion by basing the decision solely on a violation of the establishment clause. In this regard, his opinion differed little from the legal conclusion that he and his two colleagues had reached in the earlier decision—that the state of Pennsylvania and the Abington schools had impermissibly promoted a religious observance. Even the new statute, Biggs said, "unequivocally requires the exercises to be held every school day in every school in the Commonwealth." He continued:

> The exercises are held in the school buildings and perforce are conducted by and under the authority of the local school authorities and during school sessions. Since the statute requires the reading of the "Holy Bible," a Christian document, the practice, as we said in our first opinion, prefers the Christian religion. The record demonstrates that it was the intention of the General Assembly of the Commonwealth of Pennsylvania to introduce a religious ceremony into the public schools of the Commonwealth.[21]

Once again, the three judges of the district court declared that the Bible-reading statute, as well as the practice of reading the Bible and reciting the Lord's Prayer in Abington's public schools, violated the First Amendment.

On the day after the decision, W. Eugene Stull, the principal of Abington Senior High School, made an announcement over the same public address system used to broadcast the Bible-reading exercise the previous morning. "Reading of the Holy Bible and recitation of the Lord's Prayer," he said, "will be omitted today in compliance with an order of the U.S. court."[22]

⌁

As it had almost a year and a half earlier, the court's decision lit firecrackers around the Philadelphia area. Area newspapers filled with letters critical of the decision.

Soon after handing down its decision, the Biggs court issued an order staying the injunction and permitting the morning exercises to continue pending an appeal by Abington to the U.S. Supreme Court. Once again, the Abington school board held a public meeting to decide whether to file such an appeal. On Monday evening, March 12, about five hundred people gathered in the cafeteria at Huntingdon Junior High School, the scene of a similar meeting following the first district court decision in 1959. At the front of the room, with an American flag before them, sat all but one of the school board members.

The school board president, Stanley S. Paist, Jr., said that the question before the gathering was whether there was support for continuing to spend tax money to finance continued litigation. He added that everyone who wanted to would have their say and that he would tolerate "no demonstrations, applause or derision." The school district's business manager reported that legal fees had reached $15,726.34 and that an appeal and argument to the Supreme Court would add about $5,000 to the legal costs for taxpayers. Percival Rieder, the school district's solicitor, then summarized the progress of the lawsuit and praised the efforts of C. Brewster Rhoads and his law firm. Apart from representing Abington, Rieder said, the lawyers "want to see America stay the way it is, and they don't want to see it made over into another image." He let everyone know that Abington's case could affect similar practices throughout the country: twelve states currently required Bible readings, he said; another twelve permitted it, and eleven prohibited it.[23]

Thirty-one residents got up on their feet and addressed the crowd, and only one counseled against an appeal. "It's time to fight these agitating groups," said Stan Mogel. Furman Mayhew added, "It's an outrage that God, Who made the heaven and earth, cannot be present in our public schools." Mrs. Frank White had another thought. "If we deny God," she said, "we no longer have God's blessing." She argued: "Christianity has tolerated other sects in this country. Now it is time they tolerated Christianity." The only resident who spoke against an appeal, Robert H. Brown, did so with a defeatist thought: "[T]he recent trend of the Supreme Court is to guarantee the rights of individuals, so I see no hope for success."[24]

After two hours of comment, the school board members present at the meeting voted unanimously to appeal the *Schempp* case to the U.S. Supreme Court. Two months later, the appeal reached the Supreme Court. Pennsylvania's attorney general, David Stahl, and the state superintendent of public instruction, Charles H. Boehm, joined with Abington in its defense of the religious exercises.[25]

ॐ

Ed Schempp looked forward to Abington's appeal of the case. It was his intention all along to work for a definitive ruling on the morning devotionals, and bringing the case to the justices made such a ruling a strong possibility. At the same time, though, the second decision of the Biggs court unleashed another round of letters to his house, excoriating the Schempp family.

When a reporter from the *Evening Bulletin*, Philadelphia's afternoon paper, called on him, Schempp was eager to state his case and to diffuse accusations that his family was atheist and bent on undermining belief in God. That wasn't true, Schempp said. He was in favor of Bible reading, just not in the schools. He said that his family read the Bible frequently in their home. Reading the Bible in public school without comment, though, could "plant the seeds of bigotry, hate and intolerance," Schempp explained. "Unitarians do not believe in a literal, infallible Bible as the 'Word of God.' We have seen men over the centuries burning and persecuting each other under the authority of the words of their bibles."[26]

Abington school district and the Commonwealth of Pennsylvania filed their notice of appeal to the U.S. Supreme Court on March 28, 1962. C. Brewster Rhoads and the deputy attorney general, John D. Killian III, asked the Court to decide whether reading the Holy Bible in the public school classroom violated the First Amendment's establishment and free exercise clauses.[27] For the second time, the *Schempp* case went to Washington, D.C. This time, there appeared to be no obvious procedural grounds on which the Court could avoid taking the case.

16. New York's "Clay-Footed Pigeon"

In 1962, the four cases testing whether religious exercises in the public schools violated the First Amendment were moving quickly through the courts. The *Schempp* case had reached Washington, D.C., at the end of 1959. Its chances of being the first of the four cases to be reviewed by the U.S. Supreme Court had evaporated when Pennsylvania's legislators amended the Bible-reading law to allow students to excuse themselves. But now, after the second Biggs decision, the case headed back to Washington.

Already before the justices was *Engel v. Vitale,* testing the Regents' Prayer composed by the New York State Board of Regents. It was scheduled for oral argument for April 3. Meanwhile, in Baltimore, *Murray v. Curlett* was awaiting a decision by the Maryland Court of Appeals, the highest court in that state. In Miami, *Chamberlin v. Dade County*—Leo Pfeffer's case—was before the Florida Supreme Court.

That *Engel* had won the race to the Supreme Court did not automatically relegate *Schempp* and the others to a spot in the deep shade. *Engel* involved a short and innocuous state-composed prayer—quite possibly a unique situation in the country. If the Court struck down the prayer, it could be because the state education board had composed it, a situation not duplicated in the other cases. If the Court upheld the prayer, lawyers representing the plaintiffs in the other cases could point out that their situations involved religious practices that were far more extensive and carried deeper Christological significance.

The dominoes were about to fall.

꒦

The Supreme Court that awaited all these cases was in the throes of major changes that would affect the lives of all Americans. When President Dwight D. Eisenhower appointed Earl Warren, a former Republican governor of California, to be chief justice in 1953, men of conservative judicial philosophy controlled the Court, exercising a restraint that saw them typically defer to the decisions of legislative majorities. At the time, the only two reliably liberal votes on the Court came from Hugo Black and William O. Douglas. Arrayed against them were the Court's two leading conservatives, Felix Frankfurter and Robert Jackson, with the other four justices typically falling in line with them.[1]

At the time that Frankfurter and Black ascended to the Court, a reasonable expectation would have placed each man in a philosophical role completely opposite to what he assumed as a justice. Frankfurter had been an eminent professor at Harvard Law School and a leading progressive; on the Court, he became the intellectual leader of the conservative bloc. Black had been a senator from Alabama and, early in his life, a member of the Ku Klux Klan. Yet as a member of the Court, he felt, along with Douglas, that he had a deep responsibility to protect individual rights and liberties against encroachment by the government.[2]

As Black and Douglas faced off against Jackson and Frankfurter, the personal relationships between these two blocs disintegrated into acrimonious feuding on a level rarely seen on the Court. When Jackson died in 1954, Eisenhower replaced him with John Marshall Harlan, a Princeton graduate, Rhodes scholar, and grandson of another justice of the same name. Harlan would become an erudite and respected conservative and leader of that bloc after Frankfurter's retirement in 1962.

The swing toward a Court more activist in protecting and recognizing constitutional rights and liberties—the so-called Warren Court—began with the school desegregation cases of 1954, but it took a few years and some significant changes in personnel before the votes became more reliable in that direction. In his first few years on the Court, Warren himself often voted with the conservative bloc. By 1956, though, he had finally found his voice within the more liberal wing of the Court.[3] That same year, Eisenhower appointed William J. Brennan, Jr., a judge on New Jersey's highest court, to a seat on the Supreme Court. Although Brennan was a Democrat, Eisenhower expected him to live on the conservative side of most issues. In reality, though, Brennan immediately provided a fourth vote with Black, Douglas, and Warren. In time, Brennan became one of the most influential justices of the twentieth century, combining a fierce defense of First Amendment and other freedoms along with a keen political ability to build a consensus for his point of view on the issues most important to him. Conservatives, though, continued to hold a five-to-four advantage until 1962, when Frankfurter retired and the appointment of Arthur Goldberg swung the fifth vote to the Warren faction. Goldberg had been President John F. Kennedy's secretary of labor.

As the school prayer cases began to reach the Court in the early 1960s, their outcome was by no means certain, even with Goldberg on board. Representing *Schempp*, Henry Sawyer could have probably counted on three votes: Brennan, Warren, and Black—the latter a strong believer in the separation of church and state and author of several of the Court's earlier rulings on religion in the schools, including *Everson v. Board of Education*, in which he had invoked Jefferson's metaphor of a "wall of separation" to describe the meaning of the establishment clause. Douglas looked like a possible fourth vote, although his stance on separating religion and the schools seemed somewhat wobbly. Douglas had written for the Court majority in upholding the off-campus released-time program of religious education in *Zorach v. Clauson* and had even said, in explaining why the justices held no antagonism toward religion, "We are a religious people whose institutions presuppose a Supreme Being."[4] That didn't necessarily sound like a justice who would definitely ban prayer and Bible reading in public schools. It was unclear how the other members of the Court—Harlan, Tom C. Clark, Potter

Stewart, and Byron R. White—would come out on devotional exercises in the schools. All four were judicial conservatives, although that is a broad designation. White, appointed by Kennedy in 1962, was perhaps the most moderate of the group.

The Court's leading conservative of the previous two decades, Felix Frankfurter, would hear the *Engel* case but leave the Court and not participate in the decision. Ironically, he might have been the best candidate to supply a fifth vote to ban religious exercises in the schools, because he had agreed strongly with the "wall of separation" in the fifties cases. He might well have found Jewish students compelled to attend crucifixion plays in *Chamberlin* too much to bear under the free exercise clause. But that did not mean that those who generally followed him would see it the same way.

ॐ

By April 3, 1962. *Engel v. Vitale* had finally completed its long journey to the U.S. Supreme Court. It wasn't clear, though, why the justices had voted to hear the *Engel* case. The Court had the discretion to accept the case or not, and *Engel* did not pose the most compelling case for the justices to decide. It was true that the Board of Regents had composed the prayer for children to use in the public schools, but it would have been hard to find a prayer that was more innocuous. As Yale law professor Louis H. Pollak wrote at the time, the possibility that the Court might turn down review of the case "might have been strengthened by a feeling that New York's attempt to write a prayer had produced such a pathetically vacuous assertion of piety as hardly to rise to the dignity of a religious exercise." Pollak observed, "The court might very reasonably have decided to save its scarce ammunition for a prayer that soared, rather than squander it on New York's clay-footed pigeon."[5]

Perhaps the justices felt they had no choice. The *Schempp* case was certainly headed back to the Court, and because it would be on appeal from a three-judge court, the justices would have no discretion to turn it away. So they may have felt that they had no way to avoid the issue. Or, as Pollak speculated, the justices may have seen *Schempp* as potentially a far more explosive case, involving as it did both Bible reading and the Lord's Prayer, both emotional hot buttons for many Christians. If the justices knew that a majority of them might conceivably strike down Bible reading and the Lord's Prayer in the schools, they may have thought it better to prepare the country for what was soon to come by first striking down a purely contrived prayer to which few, if any, people had an emotional attachment.[6]

William Butler, Engel's lawyer, was first up before the justices on April 3. He had prepared for an hour-long argument. To be safe, he had to be ready to speak without interruption, although such monologues never take place in practice. Justices interrupt anytime they want and as frequently as they want. Attorneys must answer their questions while still being sure that they circle back to make the critical points for their case. That's the challenge Butler faced from the beginning.

Butler had barely started speaking when the first question came from the justices, and for the next hour, he rarely got back to his prepared argument. When he did, he tried to bring *Engel* within the ruling of *McCollum v. Board of Education,* the released-time case in which clergy came into the schools in Champaign, Illinois, to teach religion to students.[7] Butler argued that his case, like *McCollum,* involved religious activities during school hours, cooperation of state officials in presenting the religious activity, use of tax-supported buildings to aid in teaching religious doctrine, and the potential of students not to participate.[8]

Butler struggled, though, to make his points amid tough questioning by the justices. They weren't so much antagonistic as they were trying to understand Butler's rationale for outlawing the short, bland Regents' Prayer as a violation of the Constitution. After all, the prayer—"Almighty God, we acknowledge our dependence upon Thee, and we beg Thy blessings upon us, our parents, our teachers and our Country"—seemed nonsectarian and not terribly different from the many reverential statements made in governmental meetings. Butler made a mistake when he agreed, in response to a question early on, that the whole premise of his argument was that the prayer amounted to the teaching of religion in a public institution.[9] That led to a number of confusing exchanges, with Butler trying again and again to move the justices toward his more powerful argument: that by composing a prayer and asking youngsters to recite it specifically in a public school, the state was impermissibly sponsoring a religious devotional observance that is typically performed in a house of worship.

Two of the justices helped Butler out toward the end of his argument. Justice Frankfurter, who seemed to be losing patience, compared objections to the Regents' Prayer to the problem posed, in other contexts, by reading the King James Version of the Bible in the classroom. Catholics use the Douay Version, not King James, "however beautiful that may be," he observed, deducing, "therefore you make Catholic children listen to formulations that they reject." Butler picked up on that cue, arguing that the Regents' Prayer assumes belief in God. Two of the plaintiffs in *Engel*, he said, were of nontheistic religions: "[T]his is an attempt to force down the throats of believers in nondeistic religions a theistic prayer, and in that sense the content of the prayer is objectionable."[10]

Minutes later, just before the close of Butler's argument, Justice Brennan himself articulated the potential establishment clause violation: while the state could not promote any religious sect's ritual or holy books, neither could it promote religion in general—even if the group of students believed in the religious concepts being promoted. Brennan observed: "And what you're saying, Mr. Butler, if I understand your argument: If there were schools in which concededly every member of the school was a communicant of the Episcopal Protestant Church, and the Lord's Prayer as sanctioned by that church were required to be uttered at a morning assembly, a devout Episcopalian parent could object to having that prayer said. You would have legal standing to object to it, although it's precisely the prayer that is uttered in the petitioner's—in that petitioner's church every Sunday morning." Butler responded, "Yes, Your Honor, because it violates the establishment side of the First Amendment." Justice Brennan replied, "All right, now you get down to a real legal point."[11]

The justices continually probed Butler with what-ifs. What, they asked, if someone challenged the invocation—"God save this honorable Court"—that was recited at the beginning of each public session of the Supreme Court? Butler answered that the state requires each student to attend school; that is not the case with sessions of the Court. In addition, students recite the Regents' Prayer in a teaching environment with the assistance of teachers, who are state officials; the circumstances surrounding the Court's opening invocation are completely different.[12] What, the justices asked, if someone challenged the "under God" phrase in the Pledge of Allegiance? Butler said that the pledge is at its heart a political affirmation. By comparison, the Regents' Prayer "is solely religious."[13]

When his turn came, Bertram B. Daiker, attorney for the school board, remembered standing before the justices and feeling like "perhaps the most lonesome person in the world." He wondered if he had prepared adequately, knowing "that if they ask you a question, and you don't know the answer, there's no one in that courtroom to help you."[14] Daiker went directly to the heart of his case. In composing a prayer that acknowledged the students' reliance on a Supreme Being, he said, the state was "proceeding fully in accord with the tradition and heritage which has been handed down to us." Daiker reminded the justices that the Declaration of Independence has four references to the Creator and that forty-nine of the fifty states in 1962 had references to God in either the preamble to their state constitution or in their state constitution itself.[15]

Under questioning, Daiker conceded that the Regents' Prayer was an avowal of religious faith. But he argued that the New York State Board of Regents did not intend it to serve as a religious ceremony or as the teaching of religious faith. Instead, reminiscent of Brewster Rhoads's argument defending Bible reading in the Abington public schools, Daiker argued that the state "was interested in promoting the belief in traditions, the belief in the moral and spiritual values which make up part of our national heritage."[16]

Some of the justices couldn't accept Daiker's assurance about the regents' intention in authoring a prayer for students to recite in school, and it led to several tough exchanges, including the following:

"Why do you say ethical purposes and things of that kind, but shy away from religion, when the entire wording of the prayer is in the words of religion?"

"Well, I don't want to have the Court understand my words as saying that the board of education was trying to teach religion in the schools."

"Well, I know you want to keep away from that. (General laughter) But what I'm trying to find out is, how you analyze the language of the Board of Regents, the action of the Board of Regents, the action of your school board, and the delivering of this prayer every morning, without getting to the question of religion."

"I don't think you can stay away from religion. So long as you have a prayer, there is a religious facet to it."[17]

A few minutes later, Daiker had to come back to the same point when he was asked if the Regents' Prayer was a religious practice. He argued: "Is it a religious practice? No more so than the saying of any prayer on any public occasion is a religious practice. Any group of men who gather together for dinner commence with a prayer. This, to that extent, is a religious practice." One of the justices responded, "Well, Mr. Daiker, as I understand Mr. Butler, neither he or his clients object to any such prayers anyplace except in the public schools, where the children are compelled to come, and where they will be indoctrinated with the prayer as a matter of training, and where they will be held up to contempt or ridicule if they or their parents should want them to be excused, and pointed out as being different from the others."[18]

Neither of the lawyers had performed brilliantly. The justices had quickly seized control of both arguments and sent both Butler and Daiker on the defensive, where they often had trouble answering the questions. As the session came to an end, both sides had reason to worry. The justices seemed concerned that if they outlawed recitation of the Regents' Prayer in the schools, they might soon face challenges concerning prayers and invocations in other places—including those in their own courtroom. Yet some of the justices clearly didn't accept the assertion that recitation of the Regents' Prayer honored a long tradition and the teaching of moral values.

⁒

Just three days after the oral argument in *Engel v. Vitale*, the Maryland Court of Appeals handed down its decision in Madalyn Murray's case, *Murray v. Curlett*. In a case similar to the *Schempp* case, Murray had complained about Bible reading and recitation of the Lord's Prayer in the public school attended by her son Bill. With four judges voting to uphold the practice of Bible reading and three judges dissenting, it was the closest decision in any of the four cases.[19]

Like the other cases, *Murray* presented difficult questions of law, but Maryland's highest court showed little interest in exploring them. In what was a lazy intellectual effort, Judge William R. Horney said that the dedication of public funds and school time to the morning devotionals was negligible. Bible reading in the schools, he wrote, differed little from other public displays of religion—the prayers used to open sessions of state and federal legislatures and the references to God at the beginning of many public meetings and court sessions. He didn't attempt to explain why those other displays of religiosity met First Amendment standards or how the practices differed from or were similar to each other.

Horney thought that the provision allowing excusal of students from the devotionals was a controlling factor in the case, although he didn't explain why—except to say that the Supreme Court had vacated the *Schempp* decision and remanded the case to the Biggs court after the Pennsylvania law had been amended. "It seems to us," Horney speculated, "that the remand of this case at least indicated that the use of coercion or the lack of it may be the controlling factor in deciding whether or not a constitutional right has been denied."[20] Horney noted that the three-judge federal court in Philadelphia had reheard the case and decided once again that the Bible-reading practice violated the First Amendment. Without attempting to explain why, Horney said that he and his three colleagues "do not find the decision on remand persuasive and decline to follow it."[21]

Madalyn Murray's lawyer, Leonard J. Kerpelman, submitted his petition for a writ of certiorari in *Murray v. Curlett* to the U.S. Supreme Court on May 15, almost six weeks after losing in Maryland's highest court. After recovering from a hysterectomy, Madalyn Murray had gotten a job at the Department of Public Welfare in Baltimore, supervising social workers. The day after Kerpelman filed his petition with the U.S. Supreme Court, however, she said that her boss fired her for "incompetence." She got two weeks notice and vacation pay, but no unemployment compensation. Out of money, she sold her fur coat, her piano, and her dinette set. Her legal bills, including the printing cost associated with filing the case, consumed the last of her checks from her lost job.[22]

Within a few months of the filing, the Murrays were out of money. "The food supply in the basement was about gone," she wrote in *An Atheist Epic.* "The big freezer was empty. I had made a job application anywhere job applications were being taken in Maryland." She applied for jobs as a sales clerk, a secretary, a waitress, and a dishwasher, to name a few, but claimed later that she was turned down because of the case.[23] Madalyn had received some supportive mail over the last few years, much of it from atheists like herself. Now she decided, on Bill's suggestion, to put out a newsletter and ask her ideological supporters to financially support her appeal to the U.S. Supreme Court. She bought a small mimeograph machine, stencils, paper, and other supplies, and proceeded to write what she called the *Newsletter on the Murray Case.* Out it went to about 750 people. Back, she reported, came 325 letters, bearing a total of $134 for the legal fund and $709 for other expenses. Some people pledged to send money every month. Over the next few years, it was largely the newsletter and donations that supported Madalyn Murray and her family.[24]

Madalyn and her son continued to be the target of abuse, and all of that came on top of the myriad plagues she brought on herself. Her neighbors constantly complained of the loud barking of Marx and Engels, her self-proclaimed "atheist dogs," and since she did nothing about it, they eventually filed a formal complaint. When Madalyn received a summons to come to court and refused to show up, the judge ordered her arrested and jailed. She managed to post $500 bail to get out of jail. Fearing the dogs would be taken from her and destroyed, she began searching for a place to keep them. One farmer who had agreed to take them changed his mind, she said, "because he was a Christian and could not have the Atheist dogs on his farm."[25] Meanwhile, some prankster was tampering with her mail, crossing off the last four letters of her first name—"alyn"—when they appeared in her address. The mail reached her box addressed to "Mad Murray."[26]

ॐ

On June 6, just two months after the *Engel* case was argued before the justices in Washington, D.C., the Florida Supreme Court handed down its decision in *Chamberlin v. Dade County*. It was a complete victory for the school district. All seven judges agreed to affirm the trial court's decision upholding most of the religious practices in the Dade County schools, including Bible reading and prayer recitation.[27]

Certainly, Leo Pfeffer wasn't surprised by the result. He had been creating a deep and detailed trial record all along for the purposes of a showdown in Washington, D.C. The Florida court's reasoning, however, must have shocked him at first. In the annals of American jurisprudence, few decisions have been more openly rebellious than what Florida's highest court announced that day, in effect telling the

justices in Washington that their interpretation of the U.S. Constitution was worthless. When the U.S. Supreme Court interprets constitutional law, all federal and state tribunals—including the highest
courts of each state—must follow the Court. Other courts may not
reject the justices' rulings or, in cases involving the Bill of Rights,
constrict individual rights and liberties that the Court has recognized
and defined. In the 1960s, though, several Southern courts tested the
Court's supremacy in cases involving the civil rights of black citizens;
here, the challenge came on conceptions of religious freedom. In the
Chamberlin case, the Florida court refused to follow the Supreme
Court's interpretation of the First Amendment's establishment
clause and was only too happy to say so. Its *Chamberlin* decision in
1962 would turn out to be the start of a battle between the two courts
that would grow in two years to even more aggressive defiance by the
Florida judges.

Justice Millard Fillmore Caldwell delivered the unanimous decision. Caldwell was a man of unusual dexterity, having served in high
office in all three branches of Florida government. After serving in
the Florida state legislature and then in the U.S. House of Representatives, Caldwell won the race for governor in 1944 and held the
office for four years. He joined the Florida Supreme Court in 1962,
not long before the *Chamberlin* decision, and became that court's
chief justice.[28]

Caldwell quoted from the Supreme Court's opinion in *Everson v.
Board of Education*. Justice Black had written that the establishment
clause prohibited the government from more than only setting up an
official church or promoting one particular sect; it could not promote
religion generally. It was not the Florida court's prerogative to reject
the justices' interpretation—yet that is precisely what it did.

> We are not impressed with the language quoted as being definitive of
> the "establishment" clause. It goes far beyond the purpose and intent
> of the authors and beyond any reasonable application to the practical
> facts of every day life in this country. We feel that the broad language

quoted must, in the course of time, be further receded from if weight is to be accorded the true purpose of the First Amendment.[29]

If not the U.S. Supreme Court, whose interpretation of the establishment clause would the Florida tribunal follow? Caldwell cited Thomas M. Cooley, a preeminent constitutional scholar of the previous century, whose views, according to Caldwell, "more appropriately and accurately states the proposition" of what the establishment clause means.[30] Cooley had looked at the establishment clause narrowly, believing that it prohibited only the recognition of an official state church, such as in England, or special advantages conferred on one or a few sects apart from all others. In his treatise *General Principles of Constitutional Law in the United States of America*, Cooley said that the government could recognize religion "where it might be done without drawing any invidious distinctions between different religious beliefs, organizations or sects."[31] To further buttress his views, Caldwell went on to quote from other sources that he surely knew carried no weight at all in his rejection of the Supreme Court's interpretation of the establishment clause—the dissenting opinions in several state court decisions.[32]

For good measure, again referring to the U.S. Supreme Court, Caldwell added that the First Amendment religion clauses had "been tortured beyond the intent of the Authors."[33] He rejected Pfeffer's contention that the Dade County schools violated his clients' rights under the free exercise clause; the excusal provision removed any possibility that the students had been compelled to participate. It was "the tender sensibilities of certain minorities" that Pfeffer was trying to protect, said Caldwell, and he and his colleagues would not permit "disrupting the lives of others because of some hyper-sensitivity or fractious temperament" or because "a minority might suffer some imagined and nebulous confusion."[34] The Florida court, he said, did not "feel impelled to indulge in flights of fanciful philosophy."[35] Caldwell couldn't resist bringing into his discussion the clash between civilizations that marked the showdown of America against communism. As to the Supreme Court's interpretation of the First Amendment, he said, the Florida judges would "preserve those clauses and the rights of the States and the people thereunder against weasel-worded constructions and distinctions designed to impute to them either more or less than was originally intended."[36]

Leo Pfeffer could not have been happier with the Florida Supreme Court's opinion. Sure, Caldwell and his colleagues had forcefully rejected his position. The opinion was so extreme, though, that it undoubtedly increased the probability that the justices in Washington would agree to hear the case. After all, unlike the *Schempp* case, which the Court would be required to hear on appeal, the *Chamberlin* case would have to go to the Court by the more usual, but uncertain, route of a petition for certiorari, which the Court could deny. "Moreover," Pfeffer wrote in a letter to Tobias Simon, who was a member of the team of lawyers representing Chamberlin, "if we had to lose in the Supreme Court of Florida, we could not ask for a better opinion, from our point of view, than the one written by that court—an opinion which is a bald defiance of the U.S. Supreme Court."[37]

Pfeffer saved his anger—and it must have flashed white hot, given some of his correspondence—for his colleague Simon. After the Florida Supreme Court's decision came down, Simon filed a petition with the judges for a rehearing. If granted, such a hearing would permit Simon to address the court and ask it to reconsider its decision. How Simon thought he could convince the judges to make a 180-degree turn on such a rebellious and disrespectful opinion is unfathomable.

Pfeffer had not been consulted, and when he found out about the petition, he seethed at Simon. He wanted *Chamberlin* to be the primary case for the Supreme Court to consider on devotional exercises in the public schools, because he was sure he had the most compelling of all the cases—easily stronger than *Schempp* and *Murray*. Now, instead of immediately asking the U.S. Supreme Court to hear the case, he was stuck waiting for the Florida judges to answer the petition for a rehearing. The additional wasted time that would be involved if the Florida judges actually agreed to a rehearing was doubtlessly more than Pfeffer could even contemplate. In a letter to Simon on June 25, 1962, Pfeffer said that he was "a little puzzled" by the rehearing petition and that they needed to get the *Chamberlin* case to Washington "as quickly as possible so that it could be argued together with the Pennsylvania and Maryland cases, rather than be disposed of on the basis of the decisions in those cases."[38]

Three days later, Simon replied a bit sheepishly that the petition "had no value at all except some therapeutic value for me."[39] Given Pfeffer's intensity about getting the *Chamberlin* case to the justices, that response was akin to teasing a hungry Bengal tiger. Pfeffer wrote back on July 5, more upset than ever. He scolded Simon that "it is not the principal purpose of petitions for rehearing to provide therapeutic services to attorneys." He chastised that the petition was "a serious error," because the case was now out of their hands, leaving them forced to wait on the schedule of the Florida judges. Pfeffer was convinced that his case offered the best chance for success before the Supreme Court.

> For all we know, they can hold it until after the Pennsylvania and Maryland Bible reading cases are decided by the United States Supreme Court. This to me would be highly unfortunate. Of the three cases, ours presents by far the best record and certainly should be before the Supreme Court at the same time as the other two cases. . . . This would have been possible had there been no petition for rehearing but in all likelihood will not prove possible if the petition for rehearing is permitted to stand.[40]

Pfeffer asked Simon to formally withdraw the petition and threatened, should Simon refuse to do so, to go to the Florida Supreme Court himself and explain that all the lawyers in the case had not authorized the petition. Such a radical step proved unnecessary, however. Less than four weeks later, the Florida Supreme Court denied the petition for a rehearing. Now Pfeffer was free to ask the justices in Washington to hear his case. But he feared that he was too late to overtake *Schempp* and *Murray*.

∽

The 1961 term of the Supreme Court was drawing to a close. June 25, 1962, was decision day for *Engel v. Vitale*. Justice Black delivered the opinion of the Court, as the justices split six to one in striking down the Regents' Prayer as a violation of the First Amendment. Two justices, Felix Frankfurter and Byron White, did not participate in the decision, and Justice Potter Stewart was the lone dissenter.

Justice Black had already put his fingerprints on the Court's emerging stance on religious freedom. He had written the *Everson* opinion in 1947,[41] approving taxpayer subsidies of bus fares for parochial school students. A year later, he had written for the Court in the *McCollum* opinion,[42] which had struck down a released-time program of religious instruction in the public schools. Now, Black got right to the point, with a forceful statement that the Regents' Prayer violated the establishment clause. Black said that "the constitutional prohibition against laws respecting an establishment of religion must at least mean that in this country it is no part of the business of government to compose official prayers for any group of the American people to recite as a part of a religious program carried on by government."[43]

When the justices announce a decision that sets the ground trembling underfoot, they usually try to build credibility for their stance by reasoning from prior cases. But Black chose not to revisit the judicial past. Instead, his quest for historical underpinnings sent him back as long as four centuries earlier, to the ugly skirmishes over the attempt to legislate uniformity in English religious practices. The Book of Common Prayer, approved by Parliament in 1549 as the single accepted form of prayer for the Church of England, became the catapult that launched thousands of religious nonconformists to American shores, where they started a new country. Those who wrote and adopted the Constitution knew those struggles well, said Black, and they guaranteed the right to be free from established churches and the right to practice religion freely in order to avoid divisive conflicts. "These people knew, some of them from bitter personal experience, that one of the greatest dangers to the freedom of the individual to worship in his own way lay in the Government's placing its official stamp of approval upon one particular kind of prayer or one particular form of religious services," Black wrote.[44] So they adopted the First Amendment to "guarantee that neither the power nor the prestige of the Federal Government would be used to control, support or influence the kinds of prayer the American people can say."[45] Black wrote:

> These men knew that the First Amendment, which tried to put an end to governmental control of religion and prayer, was not written to destroy either. They knew rather that it was written to quiet well-justified fears which nearly all of them felt arising out of an awareness that governments of the past had shackled men's tongues to make them speak only the religious thoughts that government wanted them to speak and to pray only to the God that government wanted them to pray to. It is neither sacrilegious nor antireligious to say that each separate government in this country should stay out of the business of writing or sanctioning official prayers and leave that purely religious function to the people themselves and to those the people choose to look to for religious guidance.[46]

New York had argued that the Regents' Prayer met constitutional standards in large part because, after the trial court's decision, students did not have to participate in the recitation. Black swept away that contention easily enough. A violation of the establishment clause, after all, does not depend on the government's compulsion on individuals to participate. Even with an excusal provision, he said, a psychological compulsion may still operate to compel an individual to participate. "When the power, prestige, and financial support of government is placed behind a particular religious belief," he wrote, "the indirect coercive pressure upon religious minorities to conform to the prevailing officially approved religion is plain."[47]

Black likewise dismissed New York's argument that the Regents' Prayer should be upheld because it was nondenominational. The First Amendment, said Black, prohibited the government from adopting any kind of official prayer or religious observance, whether it advanced one sect or all sects. Black acknowledged that the brief and bland Regents' Prayer paled compared to the abridgements of liberty in centuries past. To that, Black responded with the words of James Madison, author of the First Amendment, in his *Memorial and Remonstrance against Religious Assessments:* "[I]t is proper to take alarm at the first experiment on our liberties."[48]

If the Regents' Prayer amounted to such an experiment, how serious and dangerous an experiment was it? Black did not say. Nor did Black deal squarely with the fact—pursued vigorously at the oral argument just three months earlier—that invocations and references to God pervaded patriotic and ceremonial observances. These included invocations at the start of sessions of the Supreme Court, the Senate, and the House of Representatives and the "under God" phrase in the Pledge of Allegiance. Black said only, in a footnote, that these observances "bear no true resemblance to the unquestioned religious exercise that the State of New York has sponsored in this instance."[49] He did not explain what test would delineate the acceptable from the unacceptable observance under the First Amendment. Perhaps the Court could not agree on any such formulation. It was true that these references to God were not before the Court in the *Engel* case, but the Court's banishment of the issue to a brief footnote was probably responsible for some of the anger and misunderstanding that followed on the decision.

Justice Douglas concurred in the decision but was clearly troubled by what he saw as an unclear demarcation between acceptable and unacceptable religious practices. While Black was drafting the Court's opinion, Douglas had written to him articulating his trouble. "If, however, we would strike down a New York requirement that public school teachers open each day with prayer, I think we could not consistently open each of our sessions with prayer," he wrote. "That's the kernel of my problem."[50] In the end, Douglas went along with the Court, although for reasons that were ambiguous. For him, the major point was that the government could not, consistent with the First Amendment, finance a religious exercise. The Regents' Prayer had not established a religion, at least not in the historic understanding of establishment, but "once government finances a religious exercise," argued Douglas, "it inserts a divisive influence into our communities."[51]

Justice Potter Stewart was the lone dissenter, arguing that the Court had "misapplied a great constitutional principle." He disagreed with the Court's historical analysis, arguing that the established Anglican Church in England and the early established churches in the American colonies had little to do with the state of New York allowing schoolchildren to recite a short prayer. Stewart thought that the Regents' Prayer differed little from many other religious references in public life. "What is relevant to the issue here," he said, "is not the history of an established church in sixteenth century England or in eighteenth century America, but the history of the religious traditions of our people, reflected in countless practices of the institutions and officials of our government."[52]

ॐ

A fierce storm of protest followed the *Engel* decision. For the justices, it must have felt like a category 5 hurricane coming ashore. The political reaction was intense and immediate. Politicians attacked the decision and the justices themselves. Representative Mendel Rivers (D-SC) rolled a dozen thunderbolts into one sentence when he criticized "this bold, malicious, atheistic and sacrilegious twist of this unpredictable group of uncontrolled despots." Representative Thomas Abernathy (D-MS) wanted Congress to take action "to calm the power grab of these power-drunken men." Representative Arthur Winstead (D-MS) charged that the justices were "trying to drive God and religion out of our schools and even out of our heritage." Referring to the Court's decision eight years earlier, Representative George W. Andrews (D-AL) said of the justices, "They put the Negroes in to the schools and now they have driven God out of them." Even the litigants who had brought the case suffered scurrilous attacks. W. R. Raleigh Hull, Jr. (D-MO), said that the justices had protected "some fancied rights of a minority of citizens, in some instances communists, murderers, rapists and similar scum."[53]

Even two former presidents joined in the attack. "I have always thought that this nation was essentially a religious one," said Dwight Eisenhower. Herbert Hoover said that *Engel* pointed to "a disintegration of one of the most sacred of American heritages." President Kennedy, a Catholic and the sitting president, was one of the few who tried to calm the situation. Kennedy urged support of the Court even when it issued controversial decisions. He said, "[W]e can pray more at home, we can attend our churches with a good deal more fidelity, and we can make the true meaning of prayer much more important in the lives of all our children."[54]

It took only twenty-four hours for Representative Frank Becker (R-NY) to introduce a constitutional amendment—the first of what would become many over the years—to overturn the *Engel* decision. His amendment said: "Prayers may be offered in the course of any program in any public school or other public place in the United States." The Senate Judiciary Committee then held hearings that turned out to be inconsequential except for offering another platform for vituperative attacks on the Court.[55] In all, the heat from *Engel* generated proposals for constitutional amendments from twenty-two senators and fifty-three representatives during the second session of the Eighty-seventh Congress. One congressman offered legislation, which was defeated, to purchase a copy of the Holy Bible for each justice. On a unanimous vote, the House decided to place behind the Speaker's desk the motto "In God We Trust."[56]

Religious leaders split on the *Engel* decision. Catholics had strenuously opposed Bible reading in the public schools in the nineteenth century, when they were a weak minority to the Protestants, who controlled the schools. Now, Catholics were overwhelmingly critical of the Court. Francis Cardinal Spellman of New York said, "[The decision] strikes at the heart of the Godly tradition in which America's children have for so long been raised." Jewish leaders generally favored *Engel*. Protestant leaders split. The Reverend Billy Graham opposed the decision. "God pity our country when we can no longer appeal to God for help," he said.[57] In 1962, the justices received more than five thousand letters on the case,[58] the vast majority of them negative. Justice Black, the author of the opinion, got enough letters to fill forty-six file folders.[59] Some people scrawled a dozen words on postcards, while others sent long and thoughtful responses.

Engel was certainly controversial in its own right, but the media's reporting of the decision instigated some of the public backlash. In a speech before the American Bar Association convention two months later, Justice Tom C. Clark said that reporters caused misunderstanding with stories written so quickly under time pressure that they were "not complete." He emphasized the limited nature of the ruling—that the Regents' Prayer was a state-written prayer distributed to the public schools with instructions that teachers should read it. "As soon as people learned that this was all the court decided—not that there could be no official recognition of a Divine Being or recognition on silver or currency of 'In God We Trust,' or public acknowledgement that we are a religious nation—they understood the basis on which the court acted," Clark said.[60]

A study of press coverage of *Engel* found many shortcomings. About the stories put on the wire service after the decision, William A. Hachten, an assistant professor at the University of Wisconsin, wrote in the *Columbia Journalism Review* that they met professional expectations for objectivity and accuracy but that "their terseness, especially after pruning by news desks and copy desks, probably contributed to misunderstanding." Some headlines, such as "Court Rules Out Prayers in Schools" in the *Los Angeles Times*, were simply inaccurate—the Court had not banned students from saying prayers under all circumstances. Within a week, more balanced articles came out, according to Hachten.[61] By then, though, much of the misunderstanding had probably hardened into the perception of fact.

17. Fifty-one Buddhist Children

The petition for certiorari in the *Murray* case—the formal request that the justices hear the case—arrived at the U.S. Supreme Court on May 15, 1962. The clerk assigned it the number 119, designating the order in which it arrived at the Court for the 1962 term. Just thirteen days later, Abington's appeal of the *Schempp* case arrived in the clerk's office and, in sequential order, got the number 142.

Once petitions and appeals arrive at the Court, the process begins for deciding which cases the justices will hear. They had little discretion on cases that came on appeal from a three-judge federal court, as *Schempp* did. But the Court retained discretion to grant or deny review of cases that arrived through the much more common process of petitions for certiorari.

Once the opposing party responded with a brief of its own, the clerk's office circulated the documents to the nine justices. In 2000, more than nine thousand petitions competed to gain a place on the Court's docket of only one hundred or so cases scheduled for oral argument each year. In terms of paperwork, the Court estimates that the petitions in one year amount to about 375,000 pages of filings—the equivalent of more than one volume of *War and Peace* each working day. Back in the early 1960s, when *Schempp* and *Murray* reached the Court, the number of petitions amounted to slightly more than two thousand per year, many fewer, but still too many for the justices to handle alone. That's why the task of reading the petitions falls to the law clerks working for each justice.[1]

When the *Schempp* and *Murray* petitions circulated, a law clerk for each of the justices read them and prepared a memo on each case, summarizing the issues and the prior history and recommending either to grant a review or not. Then, at the beginning of October, the justices gathered to consider the *Schempp* and *Murray* petitions, among many others. They met around a long rectangular table in their oak-paneled conference room. A portrait of the fourth chief justice, John Marshall, hung above the fireplace, and the volumes of *United States Reports*, the official publication of Supreme Court decisions, lined the walls.[2]

What transpired that day inside the conference room—indeed, almost everything aside from the courtroom argument itself—was shrouded in secrecy, as are proceedings in all cases. The Court is the most secretive branch of government. The oral arguments are open to the public, and the Court makes audio recordings. But it allows no cameras and no televising of oral arguments. The deliberations, including memos and drafts of opinions, are never released to the public—never, that is, unless a justice chooses to turn his or her papers over to a research library upon retirement or death.

When the justices met early in October to decide which petitions to grant, they followed what is known as the "rule of four," meaning that a positive vote of four of the nine justices was required for a case to be scheduled for oral argument. Earl Warren, who, as chief justice, sat at the head of the table and ran the meeting, brought with him two memos written by one of his three clerks, Timothy B. Dyk, who would later become a judge on the U.S. Court of Appeals for the Federal Circuit. Dyk recommended that the Court hear the *Schempp* case and hold *Murray* for consideration later, after *Schempp* was decided. After the intensely negative public reaction to *Engel,* Dyk was sensitive to how the cases might best play to the public. "My reason for this choice," he wrote, "is that the result of holding that the Bible reading is unconstitutional in this case would result in an affirmance [of the Biggs court's decision] rather than a reversal [of the Maryland court's decision in Murray]—which possibly would be less controversial."[3]

Warren knew where he stood on the *Schempp* case. On the first page of Dyk's *Schempp* memo, he wrote in longhand, "Affirm," with the word underlined, meaning that he felt that the Court should summarily affirm the lower court's decision invalidating Bible reading without even hearing an oral argument. Given the Court's decision in *Engel v. Vitale* less than four months earlier, the chief justice didn't see how the result in *Schempp* could be any different. "The issue is the same although it is a stronger case than *Vitale,*" Warren wrote. "The 3 Judge Court wrote a good opinion on our remand for consideration under the amended statute."[4] Dyk's memo on the *Murray* case got a similarly strong response. On the first page, Warren wrote that the Court should either grant certiorari and hear the case or summarily reverse the Maryland court's decision on the basis of *Engel v. Vitale.* "I find no distinction between this and *Vitale* on the issue of establishment," he wrote. "This is even broader—Chapter of Bible and/or Lord's Prayer."[5]

As the discussion developed, Justices Brennan and Douglas agreed with Warren that the *Schempp* decision of the three-judge court—prohibiting Bible reading and the Lord's Prayer—should be affirmed without oral argument.[6] The three justices agreed that the Court should deal summarily with *Murray* for the same reason, that they should simply reverse the decision of Maryland's highest court to prohibit Bible reading there as well.[7] That left them two votes short of summary treatment. The other justices didn't agree with summary treatment, possibly because they felt that the two cases presented different issues that deserved briefing and argument: the Lord's Prayer had not been composed by the state, as had the Regents' Prayer in *Engel,* nor had that case involved the reading of the Bible.

John Marshall Harlan had a different idea. He argued—as had C. Brewster Rhoads to the Biggs court—that they should remand the case back to the three-judge court, this time on grounds of abstention. Under that doctrine, federal courts should not rule on the constitutional validity of a state law until the courts of that state have had an opportunity to interpret it. Here, the Pennsylvania courts had not yet construed the new Bible-reading statute with the excusal provision. A few months earlier, his clerk, Richard J. Hiegel, had submitted, for the justice's eyes, a draft opinion that the amended statute was unclear on several important points; consequently, he wrote, "we do not think it proper to determine now the applicability of *Engel v. Vitale* to this case."[8] Harlan got no support at all for his view.

Another justice, Potter Stewart, the lone dissenter in *Engel*, once again looked like the only one who at that moment would approve of the religious practices.[9] At the end of the discussion, when the vote was taken, all eight justices who voted were in favor of hearing oral arguments in the two cases. The ninth justice, Arthur J. Goldberg, did not participate.[10] The U.S. Senate had confirmed him as an associate justice only recently. Oral argument was set for the following February 27 and 28, with the *Murray* case, the earlier filer, to go first.

৵৵

Finally, Leo Pfeffer knocked on the door of the U.S. Supreme Court. The Florida Supreme Court had decided *Chamberlin* on June 6. At that point, fast work by Pfeffer would most likely have gotten his certiorari petition before the justices for the early October meeting in which they considered *Schempp* and *Murray* and scheduled them together for oral argument.

But Pfeffer's cocounsel had filed for a rehearing, delaying the case. The Florida court didn't deny the rehearing until July 31. With summer vacations interfering, it appears that Pfeffer did not hear of the denial until a letter of August 20 from Bernard Mandler so informed him.[11] With the delay, Pfeffer did not docket the *Chamberlin* case at the U.S. Supreme Court until October 15.[12]

Chamberlin looked like the strongest case of the three. It had everything that the other two offered—Bible reading and the Lord's Prayer—and many other religious practices as well. But Pfeffer had lost the race to the U.S. Supreme Court.

Not long after the justices set oral argument in the *Schempp* case, a major change took place on Abington's legal team. C. Brewster Rhoads, who had argued twice before Judge Biggs and had guided the case for Abington for four years, decided to withdraw from the argument before the U.S. Supreme Court. Giving up an opportunity to appear before the justices, the highest achievement in the lives of many attorneys, would be akin to a star quarterback voluntarily taking the bench rather than playing in the Super Bowl. But Rhoads, now seventy years old, complained to his partner Philip Ward that he was suffering memory lapses from time to time. "I think he was really worried," says Ward. "I think he was afraid he would sometimes lose his place. He said, 'I know I'm not going to be able to argue it. I live in fear of maybe not being able to carry it out.'"[13] For this proud member of the Philadelphia bar, the possibility of suffering mental confusion while under intense questioning by the justices was too great a risk to bear.

Ward had worked in lockstep with Rhoads throughout the litigation, but that didn't necessarily make him the logical choice to argue the case at the Supreme Court. Ward's primary expertise was corporate law. In fact, he was not even a litigator. His firm did boast a litigation department, and once Rhoads stepped aside, many lawyers there expected that a rich opportunity would naturally fall their way. Much to their surprise, though, the assignment went to Ward. He was then serving as chairman of the Committee of Seventy, a good government watchdog group in Philadelphia, and was interviewed frequently on television. Percival Rieder, the Abington school solicitor, had seen him on television and liked his demeanor. "He said, 'I want you to argue the case,'" Ward remembers.[14]

For the next three months, Ward stopped all his other work in order to concentrate on preparing for his *Schempp* argument. He spent most of that time at home reading and taking notes. "To prepare for one of these cases, you have to know absolutely every case, every law review article, everything, on that particular thing," he says.

"You live in fear. I could see them saying, 'Mr. Ward, are you famil-iar with the case of such and such, as written in the unpublished edi-tion of a Bombay law review from 1912?' I sat at home and thought up every single question that they could ask."[15]

At the Supreme Court, Ward would butt heads with Henry Sawyer, whom he had known from the time they were teenagers growing up in the wealthy suburbs of Philadelphia. They had gone to rival private schools and had seen each other often at social gather-ings and during summers at Cape May. Sawyer ended up marrying a mutual friend of theirs, and Ward had hired Sawyer's former secre-tary and employed her for twenty years. They weren't close friends, but the prospect of their facing each other before the nation's high-est court added a bit of intrigue and personal rivalry to a situation that, for a lawyer, is already as charged as it can get.[16]

The case posed a significant challenge for Ward. With the Court striking down the Regents' Prayer in *Engel* by a six-to-one margin, the justices had started down a path that could easily lead them to invalidate Bible reading and recitation of the Lord's Prayer in *Schempp* and *Murray* as well. After all, the King James Bible and Lord's Prayer carried deep religious significance, and Sawyer had shown persuasively through his expert witness, Solomon Grayzel, that both were sectarian in nature. The same could not be said for the Regents' Prayer, which the New York State Board of Regents had concocted in 1951 specifically for schoolchildren. Ward, though, did have a few arrows in his quiver. The fact that an arm of the state of New York had created the Regents' Prayer represented a level of gov-ernment involvement that was not present in *Schempp*. Also, Ward could argue that the Bible's moral lessons were critical for children.

Ward, however, felt pessimistic as he prepared—during the holi-day season of 1962—for his oral argument scheduled for the end of February. He felt that the justices' decision in *Engel* had shown their cards on the application of the First Amendment to religious exer-cises in the public schools. "We thought nothing good could come out of that Court on something like this," he said forty years later. Looking at the lineup of justices, he felt reasonably confident that he would get the vote of Potter Stewart, who had been the lone dissenter in *Engel*. Ward also thought he had a reasonable chance to get the votes of three other conservatives: John Harlan, Tom Clark, and Byron White. If he did corral those four votes, which justice would provide the critical fifth vote was unclear.[17]

᠅

With the argument before the justices only twenty-four hours away, the litigants and lawyers converged on Washington, D.C., on February 26. Ward took the train from Philadelphia with his wife and son, accompanied by his colleague Rhoads and his wife. Sawyer also took the train from Philadelphia. Ellery Schempp, now a graduate student in physics at Brown University, drove from Providence with his fiancée, Josephine Hallett, and picked up his sister, Donna, in New York. Their snowy trip down the New Jersey Turnpike almost ended tragically, when Ellery's car spun on an icy patch and nearly hit a truck before straightening out. They stayed overnight in Washington with a friend, sleeping on the living room floor.[18]

The next day, February 27, Ellery met his parents outside the Supreme Court building, across the street from the Capitol. Before the building opened in 1935, the justices had met in the Capitol and did some of their work in home offices. But now the Court had its own imposing building of Vermont marble with Greek Corinthian columns, formally symbolizing the Court's status as one of the three coequal branches of government. Inside, American white oak and marble from three continents continued the theme of a judicial temple[19]—one where supplicants came to plead their cases to nine life-tenured gods from whose rulings there was no further appeal.

Inside the courtroom, Chief Justice Earl Warren announced the next case that the Court would hear: "Number, 119, *William J. Murray III, et al. versus John Curlett, et al.*" The *Schempp* case would follow right after *Murray*. Finally, the two conflicts that directly challenged Bible reading and recitation of the Lord's Prayer in the public schools were before the Court for oral argument. Did those two practices violate the religion clauses of the First Amendment as applied to the states by the Fourteenth Amendment? That was a question never considered by the Court in the 172 years since ratification of the Bill of Rights. It was February 27, 1963, and the nation would likely get an answer before the Court's term was over that June.

Over the next few hours and extending into the following morning, the justices would hear from seven attorneys. Normally, no more than two advocates argue a case, one for each side; but on this matter, the justices heard from a flock of lawyers representing the litigants from both cases, plus two high-ranking state officials—the attorney general of Maryland and the deputy attorney general of Pennsylvania, both present to defend their state statutes. Of the seven speakers, only Henry Sawyer truly distinguished himself. The others emerged from their experience with an assortment of bruises inflicted by justices who were sometimes impatient with their arguments and at other times biting and adversarial. In several instances, surprisingly, lawyers offered arguments seemingly without thinking them through to their logical conclusion—something the justices were only too happy to do for them. Sawyer got much different treatment. Professorial at times, without being condescending (a difficult balance to make when arguing to the justices), Sawyer delivered lengthy and often uninterrupted excursions into fields as disparate as First Amendment history and biblical interpretation. Advocates rarely come off looking like scholars, but Sawyer had the sound of a man who could leave for Harvard on the next plane.

First up, though, was Leonard J. Kerpelman, Madalyn Murray's lawyer. Kerpelman had a red light at the podium that would tell him when his time was up. When it went on, he could count on finishing his sentence but nothing more. Kerpelman told the justices of his own unusual circumstances—that he himself had taught in the Baltimore public schools for six years while he was in law school and remembered well how he had read the Bible to his students each morning.[20]

Kerpelman spent much of his time defending himself from assertions by a justice (the transcripts often don't make clear which justice was speaking) regarding the free exercise clause. The justice argued that the majority of citizens in the community, those who wanted prayer and Bible reading in the public schools, enjoyed rights under the First Amendment, too. If they were prevented from holding their morning exercises, he asked, would that not deny them their First Amendment right to the free exercise of their religion? Kerpelman struggled several times to answer, replying that prayers in the public schools would nonetheless amount to a state establishment of religion. Finally, Justice Black rescued Kerpelman by asserting that the free exercise clause did not necessarily permit the majority to engage in prayer wherever and whenever they wanted—certainly not, for example, if they started praying right at that moment in front of the justices. "And would that," Black wondered aloud, "deprive them of their free exercise of religion, to say that they could pray on the outside, or somewhere else?" Kerpelman replied, "Thank you, Mr. Justice."[21]

Chief Justice Warren called a recess for lunch. All the *Murray* and *Schempp* lawyers and litigants went to the cafeteria in the lower level of the building so that they could eat and get back in time. Philip Ward sat at the same table as Madalyn Murray and remembered the experience forty years later. "She was the most profane woman I ever heard in my life," he says. "Every third word was, 'oh that's a lot of shit, fuck you.' She was at our table. I'm no blue stocking, but that was a little much for me."[22]

Back in the courtroom, Francis B. Burch, a lawyer for the Baltimore school board, told the justices that Bible reading in the schools had long been a tradition in Maryland, dating back to 1836 or earlier. Burch argued that the Baltimore schools used the Bible and Lord's Prayer solely for the secular purpose of teaching moral and ethical values and establishing discipline and respect for authority. School officials enjoy the right to reasonably select whatever materials would best serve those goals, he said.[23]

At least one justice was troubled that Burch's use of moral and ethical values as justification provided no obvious limits to the use of religious exercises in the public schools. If school officials were free to choose any materials to teach values, as Burch had argued, then what would constrain them from adding more religious material or even replicating an entire religious service? Burch had no ready answer. "Again I say that I think it goes again to a matter of degree," he said. "As this Court has said, what the wall separates is a matter of degree."[24]

Later, when Burch's colleague George W. Baker, Jr., addressed the Court, Justice Black brought up the problem again. "Is there any reason why if you can have three minutes [for prayer and Bible reading] you couldn't have forty?" asked Black. "Or any reason if you could have forty, why you couldn't have six hours?" He continued: "Well, if you can have it in the opening exercises, why can't you continue to have it during the whole day? Why can't you pick out all of your religious sacred documents from one particular religion or one particular sect of one religion?" Baker replied weakly that such a longer exercise "would be an abuse." But he clearly hadn't anticipated this obvious and troubling point and so had nothing more to offer the justices on how to limit devotional exercises in the classroom.[25]

When Baker was finished, the next advocate was Thomas B. Finan, the attorney general of Maryland. Finan didn't waste any time digging himself into an impressively deep hole. A minute into his argument, he asked the Court to "reevaluate"—in other words, over-turn—its decision in *Engel v. Vitale*. Asking the justices to overturn a prior decision is not usually a winning strategy, especially when the decision had come down within a year and was agreed to with near unanimity. What troubled Finan so much was his view that the Court had rejected theism—the belief in one God who created earth and humankind—and, in its place, had elevated what he called "non-theism" in the classroom. Apparently, by "nontheism," Finan was referring to Madalyn Murray's atheism.[26]

Finan's argument was a misreading of *Engel*. The Court had not chosen nontheism or atheism for the nation's schoolrooms. The justices had simply said that the government could not compose prayers for use in the public schools. Beyond that, Finan had ignored the fact

that in the four relevant cases that had come before the Court—
Engel, Schempp, Murray, and *Chamberlin*—most of the plaintiffs
challenging prayers and Bible reading were Christians and Jews
whose religions were theistic. One justice observed: "Aren't there
people who are opposed to this who are just as fervently, fervent in
their belief in God as those who prescribe this oath, and who yet
oppose it? Why do we have to make an issue between atheism and
Christianity?"27

For Attorney General Finan, perhaps the most damaging
exchange for his case came near the end of his argument. Finan, as
well as his colleagues, had argued that use of the King James Version
and the Lord's Prayer could not violate any child's freedom to practice his or her religion as long as the child had the right to be excused
from the exercise. If this were true, one justice noted, it would set up
a kind of "local option" in which different school districts could
adopt religious practices according to which religious group had the
majority of votes, then simply allow children from minority religions
to walk out. "Then the big contest," he said, "would be which church
could get control of the school board, I suppose."28

The justice was troubled that children of minority religions all
over the country would face the difficult choice of walking out during the devotionals. He challenged Finan, "Now why can't you do
that with reference to the Mormons, if they want to, where they are
in the majority, or any others, where those people are in the majority?"

"Well, I will concur with the Court —"

"That's a local option in determining which particular religion will
be taught in each particular community."

"Now, if it is a sincere representation of that area —"

"Well, gentlemen, let's take a very practical situation, again in
Hawaii where there are a great many Buddhists. Let us say there is a
school where there are 51 Buddhist children and 49 Christian children. And because of the majority of Buddhists it's determined by
the school to have a Buddhist ceremony comparable to this Christian
ceremony that we have here. Would you think because they are in

the majority that the 49 percent of them that are Christians in that school would have to walk out?"

"They would have the right to, and I would —"

"And you think they would have the right to have such a ceremony as a matter of school law?"

"Yes, Mr. Justice, because I feel that it is essential that we keep away from a complete secularism in our outlook to this thing. And if the Christians who were there wanted to have the right . . . not to be subjected to it, they have that right. I see no reason why you cannot reconcile, why it is not compatible to, under our Constitution, to permit such a practice."[29]

The prospect of local conflicts over the control of school boards and which religious traditions would be adopted for use in opening exercises surely reminded the justices of the religious conflict that the First Amendment was supposed to prevent. In his concurring opinion in *McCollum v. Board of Education*, Justice Frankfurter had written that "the Constitution . . . prohibited the Government common to all from becoming embroiled, however innocently, in the destructive religious conflicts of which the history of even this country records some dark pages."[30] Even if the 1844 riots over Bible reading in Philadelphia might never recur, the justices surely knew that the ostracism suffered by the Schempps and Murrays in their own communities spoke loudly of the sectarian divisions still boiling below the surface.

～

Philip Ward finally got his opportunity to argue on behalf of Abington late in the day on February 27. On his way to the podium to address the justices, he thought about the stakes involved in the case. He remembered that something like twenty-three million children participated in Bible-reading exercises around the United States. "I remember saying to myself, Phil, you'd better go to the whip on this one because 46 million little ears are riding on what you do today," he said later in a *CBS News* report.[31] Ward had not progressed far into his argument when Chief Justice Warren adjourned the session for the day. So Ward began anew the next morning.

Ward started right in on his most critical argument, the familiar theme that the legislature had chosen Bible reading for the morning exercises not because of its religious message but, rather, because of its lessons in morality. "We're teaching morality without religion, cut adrift from theology," said Ward. "And that is proper for the people of Pennsylvania."[32] Ward had trouble, though, explaining a question flowing from that assertion. If the purpose of Bible reading was to teach morality, one justice wanted to know, why did Pennsylvania permit students to excuse themselves? Students could not excuse themselves from lessons in mathematics or history. Didn't this mean that Bible reading involved something more than simply a lesson in morality? Ward could only say that the schools also excused children from dental and physical examinations if they had a religious objection—although he never made clear what that had to do with Bible reading. "But my point is this," Ward said. "Pennsylvania has decided this is the way it wants to teach morality."[33] That response didn't answer the question, but Ward had a bigger problem to solve.

The *Engel* decision eight months earlier, striking down the Regents' Prayer, presented a high hurdle for Ward to leap over. That the state itself had composed the Regents' Prayer seemed too flimsy a difference on which to argue that the Court should treat the Lord's Prayer differently under the First Amendment. So Ward had decided to give up on any defense of the Lord's Prayer. Ward determined that if he conceded the obvious religious nature of prayer, he could potentially buttress his argument in favor of the Bible. The only conceivable use of a prayer would be for religious purposes, but the Bible, by contrast, presented a far richer and more complex text. In fact, Ward could continue to argue, as Rhoads had in Philadelphia, that the Bible contained many lessons in virtue and morality and that the people of Pennsylvania had a right to use it for that purpose.

But the difference between a suggestion of the State that children say a prayer, a solemn avowal of faith, and the suggestion that children listen to ten verses of the Bible, is a complete difference in kind. Suggesting the children say a prayer is suggesting they engage in a purely religious act. A prayer has no secular value. A prayer assumes that the child believes in an almighty, that the almighty can hear him and may help him. That is when you suggest to a child to say a prayer. What are we suggesting? We are suggesting the children listen to ten verses of a monumental work which, as Mr. Justice Goldberg says, is a great religious work, but in addition it is a source of moral values.[34]

Ward agreed that any requirement that children repeat the Lord's Prayer would be unconstitutional under *Engel*. This would be true even if there were an excusal provision, he said, "because of the nature of the prayer." He explained: "I think the prayer in *Engel* and *Vitale* and any prayer, to me, has no secular meaning; it's a purely religious act. And I think it certainly can't be required and I think even suggesting the children do it, there may be a compulsion on the child, he may feel he should do it."[35] Summarizing his position on the Bible, Ward argued that the Court should not prohibit use of a book that teaches morality just because it is a religious work. Great religious books can teach children valuable lessons apart from religion, he said, and schools should be free to use them as long as excusal is available: "Must the government, any time any tradition in any way reflects the fact we are a religious people, must they rip out any tradition even, even if that tradition nobody has to abide by?"[36]

Ward had argued well, making his points despite numerous interruptions and avoiding any egregious mistakes that could have seriously hurt his case. His central argument, though—that the Bible imparted moral lessons that transcended the religious—was a dam built with thin concrete. Henry Sawyer knew where the weaknesses were and moved quickly to exploit them.

༄

Ellery Schempp was watching Sawyer anxiously. By then a twenty-two-year-old graduate student at Brown, he had a view of Sawyer from the first row of seats as the latter prepared to address the justices. "He was a tall, lanky fellow," Ellery remembers. "The suit he was wearing when he gave his Supreme Court presentation, the pants were too short. He had quite a bit of ankle showing. He was a distinguished guy, but it was really quite noticeable. I mentioned this to my father. He said, 'I think he did this deliberately. He likes to have this Abe Lincolnesque appearance.'"[37]

Sawyer spoke for a long time almost without interruption, a luxury that enabled him to articulate a large part of his case. In the hour he spent before the justices, he said that the Schempps objected to many doctrinal teachings of the King James Version that conflicted with their own religious beliefs. He conceded that the Bible contained moral lessons, but he argued: "[Y]ou cannot separate the moral leaven from the religious leaven in the Bible. I think the two go absolutely together." He cited specific moral lessons that were difficult for children to comprehend without comment from the teacher (which was prohibited) or that were highly controversial, such as "an eye for an eye and a tooth for a tooth."[38]

The intention of the legislature, Sawyer charged, was not just to teach morality to schoolchildren. He noted, "They didn't single out another single work in the range of the world's literature, and there are other sources of morality; not one other book in all of the range of the world's religious and secular literature is singled out by the Legislature of Pennsylvania to be read."[39] Moreover, he argued, the version of the Bible read in the Abington schools, the King James, was sectarian. He reminded the justices that even Abington's own expert witness, Luther Weigle, had admitted that the King James Version was nonsectarian only for Protestant denominations.[40]

Despite what Abington argued about morality lessons, Sawyer said, the primary purpose of the morning exercise was to engage the children in a religious practice normally carried out in church.

> It is a religious exercise, it seems to me; it was intended to be a religious exercise. I think it's ingenuous to suggest that the legislature had anything else in mind but that. I don't think that you can use the

word "morality" to encompass all that is purveyed to the minds of children by this book. There will be many, many things read out of the King James version which will exclusively—if you can separate them, Gentlemen—but will exclusively concern religious concepts and ideas, without any distinguishable moral truth. Certainly citations could be multiplied endlessly in terms of ritual, in terms of many kinds of beliefs that are religious in nature and have if any but a most minor degree of morality. And if you are teaching morality, again, you would hardly provide for excuse, as has been pointed out. And secondly, why would you have no comment? Every other subject, secular subject that's taught is taught with comment. Why not this one?[41]

Sawyer was asked to respond to Ward's argument that even if the Bible-reading exercise was religious, it constituted a long tradition of practice in Pennsylvania's schools. Sawyer replied acerbically that Ward's contention amounted to saying that "if the Legislature of Pennsylvania has traditionally had an act that violates the First Amendment, then it's entitled to continue." He observed:

I think that tradition is not to be scoffed at, but let me say this very candidly: I think it is the final arrogance to talk constantly about the religious tradition in this country and equate it with this Bible. Sure, religious tradition. Whose religious tradition? It isn't any part of the religious tradition of a substantial number of Americans, of a great many, a great many things and, really, some of the salient features of the King James version or the Douay version, for that matter. And it's just, to me, a little bit easy and I say arrogant to keep talking about our religious tradition. It suggests that the public schools, at least of Pennsylvania, are a kind of Protestant institution to which others are cordially invited.[42]

᠅

After the arguments concluded, the Murrays and Schempps met on the steps outside the Supreme Court building for photographs and then ate lunch together. Ellery was in a serious mood. As he had listened to the proceedings of the last two days, he had realized just how significant it was to ask the highest court of the land to throw out a law supported by so many Pennsylvanians and other Americans. "I realized that we would have to overturn a law," Ellery says. "I felt a little more nervous about that. By now the full consciousness of what it means to have a law declared unconstitutional had sunk in in a pretty deep way. I knew that was going to be a big step. But I did feel quite confident that we would win."[43]

Some of the arguments made by Abington and Maryland—that other religious references in public life would also fall if the Court prohibited Bible reading in the public schools—had given Ellery pause. "I had that little twinge of doubt whether we might be going on the right path because I didn't want to see everything that might possibly be related to our national Christian culture dismissed," says Ellery. "These issues about what was the role of chaplains, what about 'In God We Trust' on coins, all these things I recognized as being wrinkles in the arguments," he explains. "But I was also very clear that what the Founding Fathers intended, a strict separation between church and state, was extremely valid."[44]

〜

Henry Sawyer and Philip Ward talked after the oral argument was over that morning. They compared their impressions of their experience in front of the justices, and then Sawyer asked Ward for a favor. As meticulously prepared as Sawyer had been for the oral argument, he had overlooked one important detail—he didn't have enough money to buy a train ticket back to Philadelphia. Ward lent him ten dollars to get home. "I shouldn't have given it to him," Ward says ruefully.[45]

18. In Chambers

Justice Brennan came to his chambers at the U.S. Supreme Court looking troubled one Monday morning in the fall of 1962. Brennan, the only Roman Catholic on the Court, had intimate experience with religion in the schools. His family had sent him to Catholic schools as a youth, where he had regularly prayed with his classmates. As an adult, he went to Mass on most Sundays.[1]

Brennan felt particularly distressed by what had happened in Mass the previous day. Church members were asked to stand and recite the Pledge of the Legion of Decency, in which they condemned indecent and immoral motion pictures. Brennan felt that taking such a pledge would be inappropriate for a sitting justice, so he had—conspicuously, it turned out—decided to stay seated and quiet. "He [Brennan] came in one Monday morning and he looked gray and shook his head and we said, 'Hey, tough weekend?'" says Robert M. O'Neil, one of his two law clerks at the time. "He said, 'You have no idea what it's like to be in a Catholic mass when a priest asks the entire congregation to rise to recite the Pledge of Decency and you are the only person in that congregation who cannot or will not join. Everybody looks at you and says, hey, the judge isn't standing.' That is a harrowing experience and that had just happened the day before. So he was more conscious [of the line between his roles as a Catholic and a justice] than I think most people today would acknowledge."[2]

Brennan once said in an interview that decisions concerning school prayer were the most difficult decisions he made as a justice.

"In the face of my whole lifelong experience as a Roman Catholic, to say that prayer was not an appropriate thing in public schools, that gave me quite a hard time," Brennan said. "I struggled."[3]

Other justices as well may have been tugged by their own faith. Seven of the justices were Protestant, Arthur Goldberg was Jewish, and Brennan was Roman Catholic. Black, who had written the *Engel* opinion for the Court, had taught Sunday school in Alabama. Chief Justice Warren wrote in his memoirs in 1977, "[A] majority of us on the Court were religious people."[4]

On Friday, March 1, the day after the oral arguments concluded, the justices met in their conference room to discuss the *Murray* and *Schempp* cases. As they went around the room, starting with Chief Justice Warren, each man voted to affirm or reverse the lower court's decision and explained the reasons why. All votes taken at the conference are considered tentative, and sometimes votes change as an opinion is written and circulated.

That day, William O. Douglas took some cryptic notes for himself on what was said, indicating each justice by initials and most likely paraphrasing their remarks rather than taking direct quotes. The justices began with *Murray*. The chief justice stated his views first, and his position was no surprise. He urged reversal of the Maryland high court's ruling that upheld Bible reading in the public schools. "Unless we reverse *Vitale*," Douglas recorded Warren saying, "we must reverse here—case is stronger than it—this is a violation of Establishment Clause." Next was Hugo Black, who also voted to reverse, as did Douglas himself. So did Tom Clark. John Marshall Harlan voted "tentatively" to reverse but urged the justices to consider the whole issue of prayer anew. Potter Stewart, the only dissenter in *Engel*, continued his attack on the results in that case. He wanted to remand the case to the Maryland courts for reconsideration, arguing that the prior case had misinterpreted the historical meaning of the establishment clause. In Stewart's view, the establishment clause prevented the state from setting up an official church, and Bible reading was nothing like that. Douglas's notes reveal Stewart's focus: "Establishment Cl[ause] is obsolete today like the right to bear arms—Free Exercise is the important one—the 18th century fear of Establishment is no longer relevant." Finally, Byron White and Arthur Goldberg voted to reverse, making the final tally eight to one.[5]

Earl Warren's notes from the conference confirm what Douglas recorded. Of Harlan, he scribbled in his notes, "agrees that unless *Vitale* and other cases are reversed, but concerned." As for Stewart's position, Warren wrote, "*Vitale* does not govern either this or 142 [*Schempp*]. That was only concerning a state prepared prayer." Stewart, he wrote, felt that the establishment clause was "obsolete" and "would remand both cases."[6]

Now *Schempp* came up for discussion, and the vote down the line was an identical eight to one, this time for affirming the Biggs court decision against devotional exercises. In the discussion, Goldberg rejected Stewart's contention that the establishment clause was now obsolete because it pertained only to setting up official churches. He raised the possibility, discussed just the day before at oral argument, that approval of Bible reading and prayer would set religious groups vying for control of local school boards so that they could bring their own observances into the classrooms. According to the notes scribbled by Douglas, Goldberg said: "Affirmance here is necessary from *Vitale* because this is a much more religious prayer than the one in *Vitale*—this issue is a heated one—people however should be reassured—he thinks Establishment Clause is not obsolete—schools can't be opened to every sect—how about Black Muslims? How about screwball groups! You can't draw a line that's a usable one—it would mean drawing lines that would interfere with Free Exercise. No better way to respect religion than to follow *Vitale*."[7]

ॐ

When the conference was over, Brennan returned to his chambers and greeted his two law clerks. He had chosen a pair of extraordinary young men during the October 1962 term, both graduates of Harvard Law School and both destined to become among the leading legal scholars of their generation. Robert M. O'Neil became president of the University of Wisconsin and then the University of Virginia before settling in as a law professor at Virginia. He is a constitutional scholar and director of the Thomas Jefferson Center for the Protection of Free Expression. The second clerk, Richard A. Posner, became chief judge of the U.S. Court of Appeals for the Seventh Circuit and senior lecturer at the University of Chicago Law School. He is a prolific author of books and articles on law and economics.

O'Neil remembers that Brennan, when he returned from the conference, told them that the Court planned a short per curiam decision that would simply affirm *Schempp* and reverse *Murray* on the basis of the *Engel* precedent, without delving into the issues any more deeply. "He smiled and said, 'What do you think?'" O'Neil recalls. "We all said, 'That's a terrible idea. It's much too important.' Then he said, 'I'm just kidding.'" Brennan then told them of his plans to write his own concurring opinion because *Engel* had been badly misunderstood and that a scholarly analysis of the issue would surely help in that regard. Brennan asked O'Neil to help him research and draft his concurring opinion.[8]

On Monday, the chief justice, who assigns majority opinions when he himself is voting with the majority, officially gave the assignment to Tom Clark. A former governor of California, Warren understood political ramifications of Court decisions as well as anyone. *Schempp* and *Murray* would be yet another controversial decision on religion in the public schools, and the political reaction could be extreme. After all, *Engel* had generated an earthquake even though it involved no more than a vague, tepid prayer invented by a group of state education officials. The *Schempp* and *Murray* cases, though, involved banning from devotional use in the public schools religious materials at the other end of the scale—the holiest book of Christianity and one of its most well-known and revered prayers. Warren was surely aware that trouble lay ahead.

Hugo Black, who had authored *Engel* and a few other key church-state decisions, would have been the logical choice to write the majority opinion in these cases as well. But Black was already regarded as a strong proponent of church-state separation, and his authorship of yet another decision on religion in the schools would certainly not bring any more weight to the Court's position. In comparison, Clark was a cautious, conservative Texan. A former attorney general under President Truman, he had conducted prosecutions of American Communist Party leaders. It would be impossible to pin a liberal label on Clark, and his hard-line anticommunist reputation would make it difficult to say, as some critics did after *Engel,* that the Court was aiding atheists and communists. With those credentials, Clark would bring additional credibility to the Court's decision.

Clark also seemed likely to produce the kind of centrist opinion that would keep the Court from splintering. When the Court issues a decision whose impact on society registers on the Richter scale, a unanimous or near unanimous decision enhances its authority. Warren had worked assiduously to produce a unanimous decision just nine years earlier in *Brown v. Board of Education,* prohibiting racial segregation in the public schools. With Stewart already certain to dissent in the two cases involving the Bible and Lord's Prayer, Warren couldn't afford to lose any more justices from the majority and still have the Court speak with the weight that he thought was necessary. Clark was bright but not brilliant, a man who produced workmanlike opinions largely without doctrinaire positions. He was certainly capable of crafting a centrist opinion with sufficient gravity to keep other justices from flying off into separate orbits.

᠊᠊᠊᠊᠊᠊ ᠊᠊ ᠊᠊ ᠊᠊᠊᠊ ᠊᠊

For both Clark and Brennan, work started immediately on the opinions. Although the Supreme Court justices meet to discuss and decide cases, they operate for the most part as nine small, independent law firms. Those people who work in each justice's chambers—at the time of *Schempp,* there were two law clerks (now typically four), a few secretaries, and a messenger—support the individual work of their justice. Interaction among chambers on cases is typically done through memos and correspondence. The clerks perform a variety of important legal tasks for their justice. In addition to reading petitions for certiorari that arrive at the Court and writing memos that prepare the justices for oral argument, the clerks help to produce the opinions. The practice varies from justice to justice and even from case to case. Some justices write their own opinions from scratch, but most ask their clerks to prepare first drafts. That doesn't mean clerks decide cases. The justices give their clerks directions in how to draft a specific opinion, telling them generally or in detail what they want to say. Then the justices edit or rewrite the drafts given to them.[9]

Clark went through a number of drafts in writing the majority opinion for the Court, and figuring out their significance and chronological order requires some detective work. Nine drafts are on file in the Tom Clark Papers at the University of Texas School of Law in Austin and have been made available online,[10] but they may not be all the drafts he wrote. In general, justices or their clerks might compose in longhand or on a typewriter; some had their early drafts printed by the Court's own press inside the Supreme Court building, even though the drafts were not yet ready for circulation. One draft, which Clark composed in longhand and which is probably his first, is twenty pages long and is undated, although it most likely was produced in late March or in April.[11] Another draft is typed with handwritten insertions and almost certainly was a later developmental draft that never left Clark's chambers.[12] A third draft in the Tom Clark Papers was printed by the Court's own press inside the Supreme Court building and simply carries the imprint "May," without any specified day.[13] It probably represents either Clark's first circulation of the opinion to his colleagues—recorded in his records as May 20—or a recirculation on May 27. Only three of the nine available drafts carry the imprint "June"; two are undated, and another is dated June 10, a week before the Court announced its decision. Clark's written record of circulation shows drafts going out to colleagues on June 10 and June 12.[14]

Because most colleagues joined his draft of the opinion within a week of its original circulation in May, the major themes of the decision would most likely have been established by then. Could any drafts be missing? Justices save or dispose of records according to their own wishes. Moreover, manuscripts of any one draft—and comments written in the margins and between lines—may not contain any identification of authorship. Even so, any draft is the product typically of only the justice and the clerk working with him on it. Comments by other justices come back in memos or scribbled in the margins of copies of a circulated draft, not the original, which is kept in the authoring justice's chambers.

From the very beginning of his drafting right through to the finished opinion, Clark appeared unusually sensitive to the impact the decision would likely have on the public. In 1989, Thomas M. Mengler, then a law professor at the University of Illinois, wrote in the law journal *Constitutional Commentary* that Clark was "strongly motivated in *Schempp* to engage in public relations." Mengler argued that the decision tried to soothe public fears that the justices in *Engel* had campaigned against religion. "Reading the *Schempp* decision as an ordinary example of Court reasoning, therefore, misses the point," Mengler wrote. "Clark's opinion primarily functions as a defensive attempt to temper the expected unfriendly response."[15]

When he received the assignment to write the opinion, Clark began working with one of his clerks, Martin J. Flynn, who had graduated Phi Beta Kappa from Indiana University. He earned his law degree in 1962 from the same school, where he was editor of the *Indiana Law Journal*. In the future, he would go on to a corporate practice at a prominent firm in Washington, D.C. (Shea and Gardner, now Goodwin Procter), and to part-time teaching of commercial law at the Catholic University of America.

Clark began the long process of producing an opinion by writing in longhand on lined paper. It's likely that this first draft was Clark's original composition. Clark's draft quickly moved into a detailed recitation of the facts of the *Schempp* case, with various details added or dropped as the work proceeded through several versions.

In the Court's published opinion, Clark's presentation of the facts was extraordinarily effective. Clark made the point that the Schempps regularly attended a Unitarian church. He wrote, "At the first trial Edward Schempp and the children testified as to specific religious doctrines purveyed by a literal reading of the Bible 'which were contrary to the religious beliefs which they held and to their familial teaching.'"[16] Clark thus made several points: the Schempps worshiped within a Protestant denomination, attended church, held deep religious beliefs, and taught religious lessons at home. These points carried critical weight. The assumption had always been that people who did not believe in God, people who did not revere the Bible as a sacred text, or those whose religions were nontheistic—Buddhists, for example—would be the most likely people to object to Bible reading and recitation of the Lord's Prayer in public schools. Clark made clear that even some to whom the Bible was a sacred text and the Lord's Prayer was a sacred prayer objected as a matter of conscience to their use in the classroom as part of a religious ceremony.

Quoting from the Biggs opinion, Clark then made use of the expert testimony that Sawyer adduced at the trial. If Christian parents could object to Christian ceremonies in the classroom, so could Jewish parents, whose Bible was not the King James Version and whose supplication was not the Lord's Prayer. Clark reviewed Solomon Grayzel's testimony that many passages of the King James Version brought Jews into ridicule and that other passages contradicted Jewish teachings. He highlighted the testimony of Luther Weigle, Abington's expert witness, that the King James Version was nonsectarian only within the Protestant faiths.[17]

In his first draft of the opinion, though, as Clark finished discussing the facts of the cases, something significant was oddly missing—one of the two cases. Clark said nothing of the *Murray* case itself and made not the slightest mention of its colorful litigant. That was quite an oversight. Ignoring Madalyn Murray was like overlooking a town fireworks display taking place on your front lawn, but Clark managed to do exactly that. He discussed the facts of the *Schempp* case in some detail, but he made no mention at all of the

Murray facts, as if the case did not exist. Clark did not mention *Murray* at all until page 12, where he referred to it only as the "companion case" to *Schempp*.[18]

Murray made an appearance in the two subsequent drafts, but only in a cameo role. Clark's second internal draft, mostly typewritten, contained his handwritten insert that mentioned Madalyn Murray and William Murray once by name and included sparse details of the case. But he made no mention of the fact that Murray was an atheist, even while pointing out that the Schempps were members of the Unitarian church in the Germantown section of Philadelphia.[19] In what appears to be the third draft, which was circulated to his brethren on May 20, Clark backpedaled even more. He omitted the Murrays by name and substituted "the petitioners" instead, and he cut one reference to Madalyn asking that her child, William, be excused from the morning exercises.[20] But the two later drafts in June finally did mention Madalyn and William by name and disclosed that they were "professed atheists."[21]

In the final published opinion, Clark continued to include the Murrays and their atheism. There is nothing in the Clark Papers that explains why he changed his mind and became more forthcoming about them, but it could have come at the suggestion of another justice. He included the names of Madalyn and William and the disclosure that they were "professed atheists." He also quoted a line from their petition to the Court. But the short mention of their case consumed only one page, compared to a detailed retelling of the *Schempp* proceedings over more than six pages.[22]

In addition to almost dropping out of sight in the opinion, the *Murray* case lost its expected marquee billing in the naming of the case. Normally, when cases are consolidated for decision (as *Murray* and *Schempp* had been), the case with the lowest number—signifying that it had been docketed earlier with the Court—would be listed as the title case. For his law review article, Thomas Mengler surveyed the Court's opinions during the 1961–63 terms and found that thirty-three out of thirty-five consolidated cases decided during this period had been named for the case docketed earlier.[23] Had it followed its custom, the Court would have made *Murray* the lead case, since it had been docketed as number 119 and *Schempp* as number 142. The first draft, though, mentioned *Murray* as the companion case to *Schempp,* and when Clark's third draft circulated, it showed *Schempp* listed first, as the title case. Thus, *Schempp* became the name by which the Court's opinion would forever be known in the legal and religious history of the nation. The *Murray* case was then and continued to be listed second, as a historical afterthought.

Did the Court title the decision after *Schempp* to distance itself from Madalyn Murray, the avowed atheist, whose larger billing in the decision might have further infuriated the Court's critics? Mengler thought so, although the Clark Papers contain no memo explicitly addressing the issue. Justice Clark had shown reluctance in the earliest drafts of the opinion to even mention Murray and her case or, once he did so, to describe her as an atheist. It was not unheard of for the Court to elevate one particular case over all others for a strategic reason. In the decision on *Brown v. Board of Education* nine years earlier, the Court had purposely chosen *Brown* as the title case out of a number of similar cases that had been consolidated, some of them from the South. *Brown* had originated in Topeka, Kansas. The justices wanted to make a point by choosing *Brown,* as Justice Clark admitted later. "We felt it was much better," he is quoted in Richard Kluger's *Simple Justice,* "to have representative cases from different parts of the country, and so we consolidated them and made *Brown* the first so that the whole question would not smack of being a purely Southern one."[24]

In the case of *Murray* and *Schempp,* however, concern for any potential furor may have been of secondary importance to the justices. The *Schempp* case presented the more compelling factual situation on which the Court could build its opinion: though Protestants themselves, the Schempps objected to the use of Protestant sacred writings in public schools. The Court may also have focused on *Schempp* simply because there had been a trial with expert witnesses and was a stronger factual record from which Clark could draw for his opinion. The *Murray* case, by contrast, lacked a factual record, because the city of Baltimore had proceeded by a demurrer, in effect admitting the facts in Murray's complaint and thereby obviating the need for witnesses and testimony. "In an opinion, when you state the facts, you have to state them based on the record," says Martin Flynn, Clark's law clerk. "There was nothing in *Murray*. You didn't have any record."[25]

Having finished his discussion of the facts of the cases, Clark dedicated the next few parts of his opinion to a spare discussion of the historical context of the decision. Part 2 changed little from Clark's draft to his final opinion, and it seemed to speak directly to the American people.[26] It assured them that despite declaring Bible reading and recitation of the Lord's Prayer impermissible in the public schools, the justices deeply respected religion and its important place in the life of the country. "It is true," Clark wrote, "that religion has been closely identified with our history and government." Clark mentioned a number of ways that this religious orientation continued on in public life (e.g., oaths of office, opening prayers for each house of Congress). Then he made his pivot, pointing out that the connection between religion and government must have a limit if individual freedom is to survive. He mentioned the religious persecution "suffered by our forebears" in Europe and the guarantees in the Constitution. He observed that the nation's increasing diversity made freedom of religion even more important. "This freedom to worship was indispensable in a country whose people came from the four quarters of the earth and brought with them a diversity of religious opinion," Clark wrote. "Today authorities list 83 separate religious bodies, each with membership exceeding 50,000, existing among our people, as well as innumerable smaller groups."[27]

In part 3, which also moved from first draft to final opinion without many changes, Clark began a legal analysis that he would carry forward in the two concluding sections.[28] Clark here addressed the two most fundamental legal principles on which the Court relied for its decision. First, he dealt with the fact that two states, Pennsylvania and Maryland, had allegedly violated the plaintiffs' legal rights. Clark said that the Court had "decisively settled" that the First

Amendment guarantees of religious freedom applied not only to actions of the federal government but also, through the Fourteenth Amendment, to actions by the states. Over the years, the Court had "repeatedly reaffirmed" this principle.[29] Second, Clark aimed directly at Stewart's contention that the establishment clause prohibited only the setting up of official churches. Clark declared that the justices had "rejected unequivocally" that the First Amendment's establishment clause barred the government only from favoring one religion over another or establishing a church. Instead, the clause meant more broadly that the government could not provide public aid or support for one religion or for religion in general. This stance, said Clark, had been "firmly maintained" through a number of cases. In summary, Clark wrote that both principles "have been long established, recognized and consistently reaffirmed . . ."[30]

Clark then moved on to the opinion's fourth part, in which he reviewed prior religion cases. Although the number of cases that the Court had decided up to that time was limited, explaining them cogently was a challenge. The Court had zigzagged through half a dozen cases and reached results in a few that were difficult to reconcile. Yet it was important for Clark to extract precedents that would apply to the cases at hand. In his first, handwritten draft, he discussed a number of cases at some length, including *Everson v. Board of Education,* the case in which the Court had upheld the reimbursement of parents of parochial school students for the cost of bus transportation.[31] He also explored *Zorach v. Clauson,* which upheld the practice of releasing children early from public schools for religious programs off the school grounds and included the dissenting opinions of three justices.[32] But he crossed out much of this material on *Everson* and *Zorach* in the second draft.[33] On *Zorach,* for example, what circulated to the justices in the third draft was just a short quotation from Justice Douglas's majority opinion.[34]

A kindly law professor probably would have given a student an average grade for such work. Clark's part 4 amounted to little more than quotations from prior cases, without any explanation of the facts of each case, how the cases differed from one another, or how the uneven results could be reconciled—all of which Clark could have marshaled, albeit with some difficulty, in support of the inevitability of the decision in *Schempp*. Why would a justice actually delete material that contributes to his legal analysis? The answer is not in his files, but perhaps Clark realized that an adequate explanation would require much more analysis than he already had included in his first draft and that a legalistic approach was not what was most needed. As Mengler surmised, "Any extended discussion of the prior Establishment Clause cases would have detracted from Clark's mission: to create for the public the illusion of 'unequivocal' and 'unanimous' support on religion issues."[35] In the long run, though, a more thorough legal analysis might have served the Court better as the years brought critics who challenged the legal underpinnings of the decision.

Finally, in part 5, the concluding section of his opinion, Clark made an important advance in the analysis of cases involving the establishment clause. He enunciated a two-part test that the Court could use as a standard—in this and future cases—to judge whether some tie between government and religion violated the clause. Martin Flynn, Clark's clerk, says he helped Clark frame the test. "To me the most difficult aspect of the opinion was trying to come up with a test that would have some lasting effect so that every single case wouldn't simply come up on its own facts and have to be decided without some measurable standard," says Flynn.[36] As Clark and Flynn conceived it, the Court would examine "what are the purpose and the primary effect of the enactment? If either is the advancement or inhibition of religion then the enactment exceeds the scope of legislative power as circumscribed by the Constitution."[37] In other words, the Bible-reading statute would violate the establishment clause if legislators had intended that it aid religion or if the actual readings in school primarily had that effect.

Clark applied this purpose-and-effect test to the *Schempp* case. As had the Biggs court, Clark concluded that Bible reading and recitation of the Lord's Prayer were intended by Pennsylvania to be—and clearly did amount to—a religious ceremony. He made the same finding in the *Murray* case. Clark didn't buy the state's contention in either case that the purpose was primarily related to moral teachings. "Surely the place of the Bible as an instrument of religion cannot be gainsaid," wrote Clark, "and the State's recognition of the pervading religious character of the ceremony is evident from the rule's specific permission of the alternative use of the Catholic Douay version as well as the recent amendment permitting nonattendance at the exercises."[38] That students could excuse themselves from the exercise was irrelevant to the case, Clark said. Under First Amendment precedents, excusal provisions only cure potential violations of the free exercise clause.[39]

Clark's final thought in the opinion was an important one: he emphasized the Court's assurance that religion was not being evicted from the public schools. Only religious ceremonies were prohibited. Students could study the Bible in academic courses on comparative religion or religious history. "Nothing we have said here," Clark wrote, "indicates that such study of the Bible or of religion, when presented objectively as part of a secular program of education, may not be effected consistently with the First Amendment."[40] Six months after the *Schempp* decision was announced, Irving R. Kaufman, a judge on the U.S. Circuit Court of Appeals for the Second Circuit, wrote that the Court had given important assurances to the public: "Written much more with an eye toward public perusal and in anticipation of public criticism, the opinions drew with greater clarity the line between the proscribed and the permitted."[41]

⁂

Clark circulated his draft of the opinion on May 20. That same day, Douglas became the first to sign on, writing, "I join your fine opinion."[42] The next afternoon, Brennan circulated the draft of his concurring opinion, noting that he joined Clark's opinion but wanted to express his own thoughts separately. As Robert O'Neil, Brennan's clerk, wrote at the time of his justice's concurrence, "He had already made clear to the other Justices and now reemphasized, that he wished this to be in every sense his own opinion, expressing solely his own views of the case, and for that reason would join with him no other member of the Court."[43] The chief justice noted on May 22, the next day, that he would join Clark, becoming the fourth to sign on.[44]

At that point, Flynn wrote to Clark, updating him on where he stood on getting a "Court," or a five-justice majority for his opinion. "We now need either Justice Black, Justice Goldberg or Justice White for a Court," wrote Flynn. "I am assuming that Justice Harlan is unlikely to join."[45] Douglas's notes from the conference indicated that Harlan had voted "tentatively" to join the majority, but his final position was still at that point unknown. On May 23, Stewart sent around a note that was no surprise, considering his vote at conference: "In due course I shall circulate a dissenting opinion in these cases."[46] On May 24, the next day, Byron White sent Clark a terse memo: "Dear Tom: I join."[47] With that, Clark had the five votes he needed for the majority opinion.

In coming days, Black, Goldberg, and Harlan would agree to join Clark, for an eight-vote majority. Significantly, three of the four most conservative members of the Court—Harlan, White, and Clark—were voting to strike down religious observances in the public schools. As in *Engel,* only Stewart stood apart in dissent.

Clark's opinion was well received in Brennan's chambers when the draft landed there on May 20. When Brennan circulated his own concurring opinion the next day,[48] he noted that he joined Clark's opinion but that the "deep conviction with which views on both sides are held" had convinced him to explore the issues in more depth.[49] O'Neil had been working on the Brennan concurrence for more than a month. He had done the research and writing of the draft by himself, under instructions from Brennan to explore three major points. First, Brennan wanted to mine the rich history behind the First Amendment's religion clauses, as well as the experience with religion in the public schools. Second, he wanted to explain why prohibiting religious ceremonies in the schools did not mean banning religion from public life or even from the schools. Third, like Clark, he wanted to devise a test that could guide the Court in adjudicating future conflicts of this kind.[50] In all, the goal was to remedy the opportunity missed in *Engel* a year earlier to fully explain the rationale for removing religious ceremonies from the public schools. Brennan hoped to therefore calm the anticipated public storm. "I think there was a sense that they [the justices] had not really spoken to moderates about the limited consequences of these decisions," says O'Neil.[51]

O'Neil ran into problems when he began his research in March. Although the Court has an extensive law library, he had to leave the building several times to find specific materials that were not available at the Court. When he prepared for one of those forays, he discovered just how secretive the Court can be; O'Neil had to keep his fingerprints off anything that could be traced back to the Court and thereby provide clues as to how the decision might turn out. He recalls:

> I combed the Supreme Court library. This was long before any Internet or electronic databases. Once I had to get stuff from the Agriculture Department library. They all had to go through the Supreme Court librarian—trying to get people off the trail because if it became known that a particular justice was looking for historical works about school prayer this would not be good. They actually sent me one day to the Department of Agriculture library because that was the only way to find this stuff, but we were nervous. The Supreme Court librarian said, don't let anybody see you. Park some blocks away or take—there wasn't a Metro yet—take a bus or something. Don't let anybody see you. We don't want it known that you or anybody else from the Court is actually looking for something. So just wander in like you're a farmer or something.[52]

O'Neil, who had earned three degrees from Harvard by then, didn't drive a tractor to the Department of Agriculture, but he successfully kept his secret nonetheless. As he gathered his research material, he spread it out on a long table and on shelves in a room on an upper floor of the Supreme Court building. The opinion went through at least three drafts, with O'Neil doing the primary writing and Brennan making substantive additions either in longhand directly on the manuscripts or in dictation to his secretary, Mary Fowler (whom he later married in 1983 after the death of his first wife). Fowler then typed up his comments as inserts to the drafts. Richard Posner, Brennan's other clerk, also made some comments on the manuscript.[53] In the end, O'Neil and Brennan produced a scholarly opinion that, at more than seventy pages, was more than three times the length of Clark's and provided the depth of analysis that Clark often did not provide.

The drafts and final concurrence tackled some of the difficult historical questions surrounding the First Amendment and religion in the schools. Brennan conceded that the primary concern of the framers of the First Amendment in ratifying the two religion clauses was to prohibit the federal government from setting up an official church, such as had existed in England and in some of the American colonies. "But," wrote Brennan, "nothing in the text of the Establishment Clause supports the view that the prevention of the setting up of an official church was meant to be the full extent of the prohibitions against official involvements in religion."[54] Brennan quoted Justice Frankfurter's concurring opinion in *McGowan v. Maryland* in 1961. Frankfurter said that the framers tried to end "the extension of civil government's support to religion in a manner which made the two in some degree interdependent, and thus threatened the freedom of each." Frankfurter further observed, "The purpose of the Establishment Clause was to assure that the national legislature would not exert its power in the service of any purely religious end; that it would not, as Virginia and virtually all of the Colonies had done, make of religion, as religion, an object of legislation."[55]

Now turning his attention to the question of how the establishment clause affected devotional exercises in the public schools, Brennan said that it was "futile and misdirected" to search for specific advice from the framers.[56] He offered three cautions. First, the historical record was unclear, and the framers "were concerned with far more flagrant intrusions of government into the realm of religion

than any that our century has witnessed."⁵⁷ Second, in a key thought
he had inserted (in his own script) into O'Neil's first draft,⁵⁸ Brennan
added that the framers never knew the issue now before the justices.
"While it is clear to me," he said, "that the Framers meant the Establishment Clause to prohibit more than the creation of an established
federal church such as existed in England, I have no doubt that, in
their preoccupation with the imminent question of established
churches, they gave no distinct consideration to the particular question whether the clause also forbade devotional exercises in public
institutions."⁵⁹ Brennan noted that American education had under-
gone vast changes since the late eighteenth century. In the framers'
time, private schools under church auspices typically educated the
young, so there was no reason for the framers to question the appro-
priateness of religious exercises in what were essentially church-run
schools. It was not until well into the next century that public education took root. "It would, therefore, hardly be significant," he wrote,
"if the fact was that the nearly universal devotional exercises in the
schools of the young Republic did not provoke criticism; even today
religious ceremonies in church-supported private schools are constitutionally unobjectionable."⁶⁰ Third, said Brennan, the diversity of
religious groups in the America of the 1960s had created a situation
unknown to the framers. In their time, diversity was almost entirely
among Protestant denominations. "In the face of such profound
changes," Brennan wrote, "practices which may have been objectionable to no one in the time of Jefferson and Madison may today be
highly offensive to many persons, the deeply devout and the nonbelievers alike."⁶¹

Then Brennan reached his conclusion:

> Whatever Jefferson or Madison would have thought of Bible reading
> or the recital of the Lord's Prayer in what few public schools existed
> in their day, our use of the history of their time must limit itself to
> broad purposes, not specific practices. By such a standard, I am per-
> suaded, as is the Court, that the devotional exercises carried on in the
> Baltimore and Abington schools offend the First Amendment

because they sufficiently threaten in our day those substantive evils the fear of which called forth the Establishment Clause of the First Amendment.[62]

Brennan argued that religious diversity in the American population had been instrumental in shaping the development of public education supported by public funds. The public schools trained young people "in an atmosphere free of parochial, divisive, or separatist influences of any sort—an atmosphere in which children may assimilate a heritage common to all American groups and religions." Brennan wrote, "This is a heritage neither theistic nor atheistic, but simply civic and patriotic."[63] Brennan concluded that the morning devotionals in the Abington and Maryland public schools were religious in character. He wrote: "Thus the panorama of history permits no other conclusion than that daily prayers and Bible readings in the public schools have always been designed to be, and have been regarded as, essentially religious exercises. Unlike the Sunday closing laws, these exercises appear neither to have been divorced from their religious origins nor deprived of their centrally religious character by the passage of time."[64]

Brennan's jet was at full throttle, and he wasn't about to let go without taking on specific claims made by Abington in its argument before the Court. Abington had argued that Bible reading had served the nonreligious ends of promoting moral values and discipline in the schools. If that were the purpose, Brennan answered, there were other readings and exercises—for example, great speeches and writings or the nation's historical documents—that could accomplish the same ends without infringing the religious liberty of schoolchildren.[65] The schools had also argued that Bible reading and recitation of the Lord's Prayer had not elevated any religious denomination over another. Brennan recalled here that more than a century of controversy had swirled around religious practices in the schools precisely because the Bible was a sectarian book. Many devout people found offense in Bible reading because some passages conflicted with their beliefs or because they felt strongly that the Bible was meant for private study.[66] Lastly, Abington and Maryland had argued that their excusal provisions saved the morning devotionals from violations of the First Amendment. But Brennan answered that it was settled law that an excusal provision did not cure a violation of the establishment clause and that, in any case, excusal of young schoolchildren was at best illusory. He said "even devout children may well avoid claiming their right and simply continue to participate in exercises distasteful to them because of an understandable reluctance to be stigmatized as atheists or nonconformists on the basis of their request."[67]

In the last section of his concurring opinion, Brennan discussed where the *Schempp* decision might lead the Court in the future. Would banning devotional exercises involving the Bible and the Lord's Prayer in the public schools lead inevitably to the removal of religion in other areas of public life—acting as the first hard fall in a line of dominoes? This had been the question on everyone's mind after *Engel,* which had not touched on the matter. It probably was the source of some misunderstanding of that decision, which brought an angry response directed at the justices. The Court, including Brennan, had no obligation to take on the question of the ruling's limits. In fact, there were grave risks in doing so. It could in effect decide cases not then before the justices, controversies more appropriately left to careful consideration when and if the time came for it. In his majority opinion, Clark had said that the decision did not affect study of the Bible for its literary and historical value in a secular education program. This was vague and safe enough. He didn't provide an example, but surely a course on comparative religion would bring no objection.

"For Brennan," says O'Neil, his former clerk, "that was only one illustration among many of a much larger point, which is not only that we're not throwing God out of the public schools but we're not throwing God out of public life in a much broader sense."[68] Brennan saw no problem in the government providing chaplains for prisons and military establishments, because this practice enabled citizens under the government's control to exercise their right to worship under the free exercise clause. He also found no challenge to the establishment clause in reciting invocational prayers at meetings of legislative bodies, because they involved mature adults who could excuse themselves without penalty. Brennan said that the imprint of the motto "In God We Trust" on coins might not violate the First Amendment either: "The truth is that we have simply interwoven the motto so deeply into the fabric of our civil polity that its present use may well not present that type of involvement which the First Amendment prohibits."[69]

Then Brennan parachuted into a controversy that would land at the Supreme Court forty-one years later—a challenge to the words "under God" in the Pledge of Allegiance. The Court didn't reach the merits of the issue in the 2004 case *Elk Grove Unified School District v. Newdow*,[70] but a similar challenge to the pledge is likely to recur. Brennan said that the words "under God" might no longer convey a religious meaning and thus might survive a First Amendment challenge.[71] O'Neil regrets not having sufficiently cautioned Brennan about prejudging a likely future legal controversy. "We discussed each of these at the time," O'Neil says. "What I didn't do, I think, particularly with respect to legislative chaplains, tax exemptions, and the Pledge, was sufficiently to caution against pre-judging issues that might well later come before the Court without benefit of any record, without argument from either side." O'Neil adds: "I think the only clear explanation is that he was very anxious to go as far as he possibly could in assuring people that the Supreme Court was not taking religion out of public life."[72] In fact, Brennan later changed his views on legislative chaplains, dissenting in a case in 1983 in which the Court found no violation of the establishment clause in the Nebraska legislature's practice of starting each session with a prayer read by a minister paid with public funds.[73]

Although he surely could not have anticipated it, Brennan received an endorsement from John Marshall Harlan, the intellectual leader of the Court's conservatives. When Harlan read the first circulated draft of Brennan's concurring opinion in May, he wrote in longhand in the left-hand margin of the first page: "This is a massive, and in many respects very impressive piece of work. Although I have some troubles, there is much that I think is unusually well said."[74] Arthur Goldberg, the only justice of the Jewish faith, also filed a concurring opinion, joined, significantly, by none other than Harlan. Both men seemed motivated to answer Potter Stewart's argument, contained in his dissent, that the First Amendment required the government to show neutrality toward religion and thus must accommodate those who wished to read the Bible. Goldberg wrote that the government had involved itself in sectarian practices that "give rise to those very divisive influences and inhibitions of freedom which both religion clauses of the First Amendment preclude." He continued, "The pervasive religiosity and direct governmental involvement inhering in the prescription of prayer and Bible reading in the public schools, during and as part of the curricular day, involving young impressionable children whose school attendance is statutorily compelled, and utilizing the prestige, power, and influence of school administration, staff, and authority, cannot realistically be termed simply accommodation, and must fall within the interdiction of the First Amendment."[75]

For the credibility of the decision in the eyes of the public, it was critical that the conservative wing of the Court hold firm with the majority. Three of the four conservatives had joined Clark. Harlan had signed on to the majority opinion and had even joined the liberal Goldberg in his concurrence. White was on board. Only Stewart, as he had in *Engel* the previous year, remained in dissent.

For a while, Stewart's position on *Schempp* and *Murray* was enigmatic. Stewart had been the lone dissenter in the conference vote early in March. Then he seemed to move closer to the majority for a while. In his notes on the decision, O'Neil wrote, Stewart "seemed on the verge of joining the Court and expressed views nearly in accord with those advanced in Justice Brennan's concurrence."[76] On April 10, however, Stewart circulated a memorandum to the justices outlining his views. To him, the important legal issue was the free exercise clause, not the establishment clause.

To Stewart, the establishment clause did not apply, because he thought it referred only to the recognition of a national church. That left the free exercise clause, which protected the right of individuals to practice their religion free of coercion by the state. Here, Stewart focused on the rights of those in the majority. Students who wanted to read the King James Version in public school should be protected in their desire to do so—as long as other kids were not coerced into participating as well. Was there coercion against the Schempp and Murray boys? Stewart wrote in his April 10 memo to his brethren, "The ultimate issue in these cases . . . is whether there exist coercive factors in these cases of a nature to deny any person the free exercise of religion." His most likely ally, it would seem, would have been Harlan. But the eminent conservative saw it quite the other way from his colleague. In the margin of his copy of Stewart's memo, Harlan scribbled, "I think this is the crucial issue, and that it must be resolved against the state."[77]

Stewart repeated his assertion that the establishment clause prevented the recognition of a national church and not much more. What was relevant instead to these two cases was the free exercise clause, he said, which prevented the government from interfering with the desire of parents who wanted their children to read Bible passages each morning in the public schools. The government's duty of neutrality toward religion involved "the extension of evenhanded treatment to all who believe, doubt, or disbelieve," said Stewart. In Abington and Baltimore, he argued, the government's inclusion of Bible reading in the schools was simply an attempt "to accommodate those differences which the existence in our society of a variety of religious beliefs makes inevitable." Stewart considered such accommodation permissible unless evidence existed that individual students were coerced to participate or that the state favored one or more set of beliefs.[78]

Coercion would exist, Stewart said, where the law did not allow for students to be excused from Bible-reading exercises if they requested it. If the religious exercises took place during the school day, he added, school officials would have to provide students with an "equally desirable alternative." Otherwise, he conceded, "the likelihood that children might be under at least some psychological compulsion to participate would be great."[79] Stewart said that the trial records in the *Schempp* and *Murray* cases did not provide adequate answers to the coercion question. He wanted both cases sent back to the trial courts for additional hearings.

Though only a single voice in dissent, Stewart's analysis of the free exercise clause would bring aftershocks many years later. He had tried to shift the Court's focus from the actions of the government under the establishment clause to the right of individuals to practice their religion under the free exercise clause. His position was fundamentally different from that of the Court and a light-year from that of Leo Pfeffer, who had become excited by the *Chamberlin* case because he believed that the wide-ranging religious practices in the Dade County schools were a coercive act that burdened the ability of non-Christians to freely practice *their* religion. Both Pfeffer and Stewart saw the primacy of the free exercise clause, but they disagreed on its meaning. Stewart regarded the clause as protecting the rights of the religious majority to practice their religion. Decades later, Stewart's approach would become the backbone of attempts by Christian conservatives to return religious practices to the public schools.

‿

On June 17, 1963, Justice Clark announced the Court's decision in the two cases. By identical votes of eight to one, the justices affirmed the decision of the Biggs court in *Schempp* and reversed the decision of the Maryland Court of Appeals in *Murray*. The justices unequivocally ordered the end of Bible reading and recitation of the Lord's Prayer in the public school classrooms of Pennsylvania and Maryland—and in the public schools of every other state in the nation.

At 3:18 p.m. that day, a Western Union telegram reached Philip Ward, the attorney who had argued for Abington, at his office in Philadelphia. It was from John F. Davis, clerk of the U.S. Supreme Court, and had been sent forty-five minutes earlier. It read simply:

"JUDGMENT SCHOOL DISTRICT ABINGTON TOWN-SHIP AGAINST SCHEMPP AFFIRMED TODAY."[80]

჻

That same day, the U.S. Supreme Court decided another case with far less fanfare. There had been no oral argument and no extended debate among the justices, and now there was no opinion with detailed analysis of the First Amendment. The *Chamberlin* case that Leo Pfeffer thought would be the one best suited to change religious practices in the public schools—and for which he had helped to create a rich trial record detailing religious practices in the public schools—was decided in a dry one-line opinion by the Court: "The judgment is vacated and the case is remanded to the Supreme Court of Florida for further consideration in light of *Murray v. Curlett* and *School District of Abington Township v. Schempp*, ante, p. 203, both decided this day."[81] The *Chamberlin* case was over, or so Pfeffer thought.

჻

Ellery Schempp was driving on a two-lane road near the Badlands of South Dakota when the news of the decision on his case came on the radio. Exactly a week earlier, he had married his college sweetheart, Josephine Hallett.[82] They had set out on an extended honeymoon driving across the country, hiking and camping in national parks. "We were driving along just listening to the news," says Ellery. "Suddenly it was announced that the Supreme Court had a historic decision about Bible reading and prayer in the public schools." Ellery remembers that the report was "relatively brief": "They interviewed a couple people and that was the end of it." He further recalls:

> We wanted to get more information and see the evening television news, which was not available in our tent. So we stopped at a motel. We were poor students so we weren't too inclined to spend the night

there and rent a room. So we came to the motel and said, "Can we have a room for an hour? We just want to watch television." They didn't believe a word of it. Here's a young man and woman, and God knows whether they've had the benefit of clergy or not. The idea of renting a room for an hour! Then I tried to explain it to them and they weren't having any part of this. They said, "You must be kidding."

We were ushered out of that one. So we went to another one down the road. They happened to have a television in their lobby. So we sat and watched the television without renting a room.[83]

For Madalyn Murray the decision brought no peace. Or so she told a wire service. "Well, it's been a continual harassment," she said. "I can't tell you how often our windows have been broken. Just since the decision we've had police patrolling the area almost every fifteen minutes. The tires on Bill's car have been slashed, oil's been drained from the tank. Absolutely no one will hire me."[84]

19. Days of Defiance

Earl Warren may have been chief justice of the United States, but he commanded neither an army nor an air force to enforce the decisions of the Supreme Court. That was left to the goodwill of officials who controlled the public schools and to the political apparatus of each state, including its judges and elected officials. Without their cooperation in assuring compliance with the law as set forth in *Schempp*, plaintiffs would have to file lawsuits to force local compliance through court orders.

Unfortunately, goodwill was lacking. Just thirty miles south of Abington, in the state of Delaware, Attorney General David Buckson was planning some serious mischief. The highest-ranking legal officer of the state, Buckson saw that Delaware's law on classroom devotionals was essentially the same as the Pennsylvania statute struck down in *Schempp*. Failure of teachers to comply brought the draconian consequences of revocation of teaching credentials for the second offense. Moreover, participation in the morning devotionals was compulsory, giving the law even a greater constitutional infirmity than the Pennsylvania law, which had been amended with an excusal provision. After *Schempp*, all such laws in the United States on prayer and Bible reading were unconstitutional. So Delaware's law seemed to have no brighter future than a brown leaf fluttering to the ground in November.

Nonetheless, Buckson defied the nation's highest court. On August 12, just eight weeks after the Supreme Court ruled in *Schempp*, he issued an opinion letter saying that the Delaware law was nonetheless valid. With that, George R. Miller, secretary of the state board of education, ordered the state's public schools to continue with their morning devotionals when sessions resumed the following month.[1]

Soon the state proceeded in its hopeless defense of a lawsuit filed by a husband and wife, both Protestants, whose children attended a Dover elementary school. Buckson would sooner flap his arms and fly than win before any competent judge, but perhaps he thought that defying the U.S. Supreme Court on the issue of Bible reading would bring him some political advantage. He probably wasn't counting on trying the case before a three-judge federal court headed by no less than Judge John Biggs himself. After a trial that established a set of facts not unlike the situation in Abington, the Biggs court ruled against the state and issued a permanent injunction preventing the morning devotionals from continuing.[2]

Cooperation among public officials in Florida was no better. In its decision in *Chamberlin v. Dade County* on June 6, 1962, the Florida Supreme Court had placed itself in outright defiance of the U.S. Supreme Court's interpretation of the two religion clauses, saying they "have been tortured beyond the intent of the Authors."[3] The U.S. Supreme Court swatted aside that attack on June 17, 1963—the same day it decided *Schempp* and *Murray*—by issuing its one-sentence opinion vacating the decision and sending the *Chamberlin* case back to the Florida Supreme Court, to be reconsidered there in light of *Schempp* and *Murray*.[4]

The U.S. Supreme Court had spoken clearly, forcefully, and with near unanimity in *Schempp*. But when the Florida judges followed through with another opinion on January 29, 1964, they admitted feeling "in doubt as to the manner and the extent to which our judgment should, by reason thereof, be modified."[5] Additional briefs and arguments from counsel, including Leo Pfeffer, had not seemed to bring the judges any additional clarity. Despite *Schempp*, Florida's highest court once again unanimously declared that Bible reading and recitation of the Lord's Prayer in the state's public schools did not violate the First Amendment. For good measure (and just in case the justices in Washington had put their defiance of nineteen months earlier out of mind), Judge Caldwell wrote that the establishment clause "was never designed to prohibit the practices complained of."[6] So the Florida judges reaffirmed their earlier opinion.

Four months later, in a one-paragraph opinion, the U.S. Supreme Court once again reversed the Florida court's decision on prayer and Bible reading.[7] On February 10, 1965, the Florida court finally backed down, but Judge Caldwell wouldn't let go easily. He complained, "[W]e would have been grateful for the assistance a considered opinion rationalizing the dissimilar facts would have afforded . . ."[8]

Finally, the Florida matter was over, but resistance to the *Schempp* decision was not. Defiance of Supreme Court rulings was not unknown, the most dramatic recent example also having involved the public schools. The Court's desegregation order in *Brown v. Board of Education* was routinely ignored in the South. In the eleven states that had the largest proportion of African Americans, less than 2 percent of black students were studying with white students a full ten years after the case.[9]

Defiance of *Schempp* was also widespread, and it took on vastly different forms. In Washington, congressmen put in an endless stream of proposals to amend the Constitution to allow devotional exercises in the public schools. In fact, if amendment proposals were raindrops, the Capitol building would have floated down Pennsylvania Avenue in a biblical flood. Congressmen also tried to strip the federal courts of any authority to hear cases on public school devotionals. In many states, local and state officials refused to enforce *Schempp* or actively defied it. As it turned out, respect for the Court's decision was nonexistent in many parts of the country. Although devotional exercises declined rapidly in the East and the West, defiance of the Supreme Court's directive was widespread throughout the South and, to a lesser extent, in the Midwest.

༈

Perhaps the place where dismantling of public school devotionals went most smoothly was in Abington. Bible reading and recitation

of the Lord's Prayer ended immediately. To his credit, the superintendent of Abington's schools, Matthew W. Gaffney, used the decision to make a larger point. "The Constitution has been interpreted
by the Supreme Court," he said. "It is therefore our professional
responsibility to act in a accordance with that decision." He added
that the decision highlighted "the importance of law in the protection of our American and World civilization." He advised, "Each
teacher should find the opportunity to bring this lesson to the attention of the students."[10] Richard C. J. Kitto, an attorney whose office
was near Abington, wrote to Justice Goldberg on June 20 (three days
after the *Schempp* decision) to report that his wife, a substitute
kindergarten teacher in Abington, had seen compliance with the law.
"In the morning the principal of the local school had the Bibles col-
lected and removed from the classrooms to avoid any possible acci-
dental violation of the decision," Kitto reported.[11]

A few weeks later, Gaffney elaborated on his plans for dealing
with religion in the Abington schools. Holiday observances would
continue, he recommended, but with "good judgment" and with
understanding of the religious differences among students. Invocations and benedictions could continue as long as representatives of all
faiths in the community could participate.[12] Pennsylvania officials
announced an alternative plan on the same day that the *Schempp*
decision came down. Charles H. Boehm, the state superintendent of
public instruction, said that students would start the day with silent
meditation, followed by inspirational music and literature.[13]

Like Abington, all public schools throughout the country should
have rid themselves of devotional exercises immediately after
Schempp. But many did not. One study, by H. Frank Way, found
that compliance was best in the East, where schools conducting
prayers declined from 83 percent to 11 percent, and in the West,
where the number declined from 14 to 5 percent. But in the South, 87
percent of elementary school teachers led their students in morning
prayers before 1962, and 64 percent still did so in 1964–65. In the
Midwest, 21 percent of elementary school teachers conducted
prayers, not a significant change from the 38 percent in 1962.[14]

Results of other surveys were even more dismal. In a 1960 survey, R. B. Dierenfield found that 42 percent of school districts in the United States conducted Bible readings; by 1966, three years after *Schempp*, this percentage still stood at 19.5 percent, or about one district in five. Dierenfield found that 50 percent of school districts conducted some kind of devotional exercises in 1960 and that 14 percent still had prayer recitation in 1966.[15]

A third survey, conducted by Kenneth M. Dolbeare and Phillip E. Hammond, showed roughly the same rate of compliance. Building on Dierenfield's 1960 survey, Dolbeare and Hammond sent questionnaires to the school districts that had responded to Dierenfield that they conducted devotional exercises. They examined whether the *Schempp* decision had caused these districts to end their religious practices. About one-third of the school districts retained their practices despite the Supreme Court rulings. Regional variations were extensive. Defiance was common in the South, where only about one school district in five complied with the Court's prayer and Bible-reading edicts. A little more than half of the districts in the Midwest and almost two-thirds of those in the West complied. School districts in the East fell in line behind *Schempp*, with 93 percent in compliance.[16]

The authors' most interesting finding related to the reasons why compliance varied so widely. Public officials influenced compliance by their public comments on the *Schempp* decision and on religious ceremonies in the public schools. "Clearly, public statements by state officials are strongly related to the likelihood of compliance," the authors concluded, adding, "Thus, strong public affirmation by state officials seems to promote a high rate of compliance, and public negation seems to inhibit it." The six states with a preponderance of negative actions by state officials were all in the South, where compliance by school districts was rare. Officials in many states made no public pronouncements at all on religious exercises after *Schempp*, and in that group of states, compliance fell below 50 percent. The authors found that in the absence of leadership by state officials, compliance depended on the actions of local officials.[17]

To understand the local dynamics that produced defiance of the *Schempp* decision, the authors went to an unidentified state in the Midwest and studied five small communities ranging in population from about five thousand to forty-five thousand. Four of the five towns were county seats. In those communities, the authors found "flagrant noncompliance."[18] The authors said, "Those [community members] who might have wanted to follow the law of the land were discouraged, isolated, or rendered impotent."[19]

Dolbeare and Hammond found four reasons for the widespread defiance of the *Schempp* decision. First, officials simply did not see compliance with *Schempp* as important enough an issue on which to expend political capital. Second, after many officials decided to disregard *Schempp*, they conveniently ignored information that might force the issue to the table: some officials regarded their schools as being in compliance even when they clearly were not; some overlooked information about religious practices, enabling them to claim ignorance of what was going on; some misinterpreted the Court's ruling, thinking it perfectly acceptable under *Schempp* for each teacher to exercise the discretion to hold devotionals or not. Third, some local leaders wanted to maintain religious exercises in the classroom simply to avoid conflict in the community. Fourth, no easy process existed for raising the question of compliance, so the practices continued absent someone willing to challenge them (typically in court) and absorb the ostracism likely to follow.[20]

Dolbeare and Hammond interviewed extensively within the five school districts. Some superintendents said that they believed *Schempp* banned only sectarian practices, and most said that any religious practice was acceptable as long as students did not feel coerced to participate—a complete misreading of the decision. Among the school principals, few communicated with their teachers about the legal restriction on devotionals in the classroom. Few if any of the principals understood the decision anyway. They held the idea that devotionals were inappropriate only if the majority didn't want it or only if the devotionals included comments by the teacher.[21]

How did the *Schempp* decision affect teachers? Dolbeare and

Hammond found that few teachers had received any guidance from superiors. Left to their own devices, many teachers did not change anything they had done previously. One teacher continued to have students say prayers in class (in the morning and afternoon and before meals) and sing religious songs learned in Sunday school. She claimed never to have heard a directive on *Schempp* from anyone. "I consider it my professional responsibility to teach children religion," she told an interviewer.[22]

Of course, in many instances, local officials understood *Schempp* and simply defied the ruling. Like Delaware, Idaho simply ignored the ruling. The state superintendent of schools and the state board of education continued to require that schools follow a state law that required the daily reading of Bible passages taken from a list compiled by the state board. In July 1964, thirteen months after *Schempp*, a three-judge federal court in Idaho unanimously struck down the Bible-reading law, citing *Schempp*, despite the unusual admission that "members of the court may have personal reservations."[23]

In Tennessee, meanwhile, state law required reading of the Bible in public schools across the state. Two months after the *Schempp* decision came down, the state commissioner of education said that Bible reading in the public schools was still legal and that local school commissioners could make a decision on their own to follow either the state law or *Schempp*.[24] It is little surprise that under those official instructions, only one school district in the entire state banned Bible-reading and devotional exercises. In a survey of 121 school districts conducted in 1964 and 1965, Robert H. Birkby, an associate professor of political science at Vanderbilt University, found that seventy districts had made no changes whatsoever in their practices and were still following state law. The other fifty districts had changed their policy only to the extent of making Bible reading voluntary.[25]

Some school districts tried various dodges instead of outright defiance. In ingenuity, perhaps no school district could top the district of Netcong, New Jersey. In September 1969, just as the new school year was starting, the Netcong school board enacted a resolution requiring a five-minute period at the beginning of school for

students and teachers who wanted to participate voluntarily in religious exercises. Trying mightily to sidestep *Schempp*, school officials
convened a daily assembly at 7:55 a.m. in the gymnasium. A student
read the verbatim proceedings of the U.S. Congress from the *Congressional Record*—specifically, what the school called the "remarks"
of the chaplain who opened the proceedings each day. The chaplain's
"remarks" consisted of passages from the Bible and then offers of
prayer. This invocation always began with the words "Oh God" or
something similar and ended with "Amen." As the court found,
every exercise by the chaplain amounted to "a solemn avowal of
divine faith."[26]

Who could object to the students immersing themselves in the
daily business of the U.S. Congress? New Jersey's state board of education saw through the ruse and sued the Netcong school district in
state court. "To call some beautiful prayers in the *Congressional
Record* 'remarks' for a deceptive purpose is to peddle religion in a very
cheap manner under an assumed name," said the court. "This type of
subterfuge is degrading to all religions."[27] The New Jersey Supreme
Court affirmed the trial court's judgment, saying there was no meaningful difference between Netcong's program and the exercises ruled
unconstitutional in *Schempp* and *Engel*.[28]

As the years passed by, many of the school districts in the South
and Midwest that initially defied the *Engel* and *Schempp* rulings came
slowly into compliance. Although state officials or local school
boards eventually stopped the practices of organized prayer and Bible
reading, some pockets of resistance remained. If the vast majority of
people in a school district agreed with carrying on the devotionals
and if nobody had the courage to bring legal action and absorb a
fierce reaction by the community, the practice might continue.

In 2001, Louisiana still had a law on its books permitting the
devotional exercises outlawed by the U.S. Supreme Court. A parent
in the West Monroe school district sued the school board and the
state over the Christian prayers read over the public address system
in the local high school. After the plaintiff's son declined to participate in the devotionals, some other students had called him a devil

worshiper. The plaintiff felt she had to sue as "Jane Doe on behalf of David Doe" to avoid additional harassment.[29] Writing for a unanimous federal court of appeals on December 11, 2001, Judge John M. Duhe, Jr., ruled that the Louisiana law violated the First Amendment.[30] Nearly four decades after *Engel* and *Schempp,* the federal courts were still trying to enforce the law of the land on devotionals in the public schools.

✦

Once the justices say what the Constitution means, the icy reality for opponents is that there is no further appeal. Opponents can hope for one of two developments, both unlikely. The Court could eventually reconsider the issue and reverse itself, something the justices do only with great reluctance, because of the value placed in the law on respecting precedent. Or opponents can use the process set out by the Constitution itself to pass an amendment that would override the decision, a difficult task because of the supermajorities required to get the job done: two-thirds of each house of Congress and then three-quarters of the states must vote in favor of an amendment.

With only Potter Stewart dissenting in the *Engel* and *Schempp* cases, everyone saw clearly that the justices would not change direction anytime soon. So *Schempp*'s critics in Congress began submitting proposals for constitutional amendments to overrule the decision. During the Eighty-eighth Congress, the one in session at the time of *Schempp,* congressmen introduced 146 resolutions proposing amendments to overturn the decision.[31] The resolutions made their way to the House Judiciary Committee, chaired by Representative Emanuel Cellar, a New York Democrat and staunch foe of amending the Constitution to bring back devotionals in the public schools. Cellar's opposition seemed to doom all of the proposals. But then Frank Becker, a New York Republican congressman, emerged from the crowd and made the overturning of *Engel* and *Schempp* into a personal crusade.

Following the *Engel* decision, Becker had submitted an amendment resolution that would have restored prayer to the public schools: "Prayers may be offered in the course of any program in any public school or other public place in the United States."[32] A year later, however, he recognized that the variety of proposals on prayer and Bible reading made it virtually impossible for advocates to get any one of them passed. Everything seemed to fall apart on the details. Should the amendment cover prayer or Bible reading—or both? What prayer and whose Bible should it cover? Who would choose? The possibilities were endless, but patience was not. To bring the pro-devotional forces into alignment, Becker convened a bipartisan group of congressmen to draft a new amendment, which he then introduced. This one went well beyond his first attempt the year before, allowing prayers and Bible reading on a voluntary basis in public schools and institutions.[33] Cellar reluctantly agreed to hold hearings. The hearings, though, did not give Becker the lift he needed.

Two hundred and twenty-three constitutional lawyers and professors submitted a petition opposing passage of an amendment.[34] The strongest advocates in Becker's corner were a group of his colleagues in the House of Representatives, but some of them made hyperbolic statements not much different from those made by Southern segregationists after the *Brown* decision a decade earlier. No doubt, such exaggeration and extremism repelled many moderates and thus diminished the push for a constitutional amendment. Next to the calm and thoughtful testimony of many religious leaders were the declamations of Mendel Rivers of South Carolina, who charged that "the religious faith of the nation has been subjected to judicial interpretations that deny our heritage, defy our traditions, undermine our beliefs, ridicule our religious resolve, and make a mockery of the faith of our Founding Fathers."[35] The Becker amendment failed, as have dozens of others offered since then. Some of the proposed amendments gained a legislative majority but not the supermajority needed for passage.

Never giving up, opponents of *Engel* and *Schempp* have tried to dismantle the decisions in any way possible. The adoption of some of their efforts would have inflicted major damage on the fundamental processes of American government. Senator Jesse Helms, a Republican from North Carolina, tried repeatedly, as part of various appropriations bills, to pass provisions that prohibited federal funds from being used to enforce bans on school prayer—an effort to prevent the federal government from assuring compliance with U.S. constitutional law. But even when they passed, these provisions were pointless and probably just for show, because public education is funded by local and state taxes, not by the federal appropriations the provisions were supposed to restrict.[36]

Activists also attacked the very federal courts that were making the prayer decisions. They repeatedly tried to amend spending bills that provided money to run the federal courts, inserting language that would prevent the courts from using their funds to stop programs of voluntary prayer in the public schools. These attempts were unsuccessful and might well have been unconstitutional if enacted.[37] Another attack on the courts was far more threatening. Called "court stripping," it attempted to remove entirely the jurisdiction of the Supreme Court and the lower federal courts to even hear cases involving religious exercises in the public schools.

An extreme example of the ends justifying the means, court stripping attacked the fundamental basis of American government itself. With all the federal courts excluded from hearing school prayer cases, the entire matter would fall to state court judges who, over time, had shown considerably more sympathy for devotionals in the public schools than had the federal courts. If the state courts did not follow *Schempp*, their decisions would stand in the absence of Supreme Court review.

Court-strippers only felt emboldened as time went on. One court-stripping bill introduced in 2003 sought to remove from federal jurisdiction all matters concerning display of the Ten Commandments, placement of the word "God" in the Pledge of Allegiance, and the motto "In God We Trust."[38] Early in 2004, some congressional conservatives found yet another weapon to attack *Schempp*. They submitted a bill that declared that federal courts could not review any government or government official's "acknowledgement of God as the sovereign source of law, liberty, or government."[39] Passage of this bill would have made any prior decision on these matters no longer binding in state courts—essentially ripping *Engel* and *Schempp* from the pages of American constitutional history.

༄

Most of the firepower behind efforts to return religion to the public schools has come from a politically powerful base of Christian conservatives, including fundamentalist Christians in the South and Midwest.[40] The culture wars that started in the 1960s with the judicial decisions on school prayer and Bible reading and with the shattering of norms on drugs, sex, and lifestyles gained momentum in the following decade, with the battle over the Equal Rights Amendment and the abortion ruling in *Roe v. Wade*. These and other threats to traditional moral values brought many conservative Christians together under the Reverend Jerry Falwell's banner of the Moral Majority in 1979. They believed that America had strayed far from what they regarded as the Christian biblical morality on which the nation had been founded and that they had lost their ability to define the nation's prevailing culture. Most of the blame, they said, belonged to liberals and to an activist Supreme Court.

As the Moral Majority faded a decade later, the Reverend Pat Robertson started the Christian Coalition and hired Ralph Reed to help build its membership and political activities. Intent on combating the secularization of American society, they allied themselves with conservative Republican politicians to start winning back the ground they had lost over the past few decades. Beyond their opposition to abortion, pornography, and same-sex marriage, they defined a far-reaching agenda of religious causes that included prayer and Bible reading in the schools, the teaching of creationism and intelligent design as an alternative to evolution, and religious displays on public property. They employed their own lawyers and law firms to litigate their conservative agenda, much as the ACLU had done so effectively for many years.

Opposition to *Engel* and *Schempp* has also come from the Roman Catholic Church, in a reversal of the position it held for a century. Catholics had opposed Protestant devotionals in the public schools from the time of their first massive immigration to American shores in the early nineteenth century. They especially opposed their children listening to recitations from the Protestant King James Bible, a stance that helped instigate the Philadelphia riots of 1844 as well as political and religious conflict in New York, Cincinnati, and other places. With the Pan-Protestantism of the public schools inhospitable to Catholic children, Catholics began opening their own parochial schools in the mid-nineteenth century and lobbying for public funds to help support them. Millions of Catholic children, though, continued attending the public schools. Taxpayer funding of parochial schools was not forthcoming, and many families couldn't afford the extra cost of their own schools, even with a church subsidy. Whatever their route to public schooling, many Catholic families saw the value of a civic education in helping their children prepare for jobs in an increasingly competitive society and were content to provide their children with religious training in after-school released-time and Sunday programs. From some parents, there was grudging acceptance of the Protestantism that remained in some of the public schools—typically the five-minute exercise of Bible reading and recitation of the Lord's Prayer—and a feeling that it would at least provide the daily dose of Christianity that students might not otherwise receive.

By the time of *Engel* and *Schempp,* the church hierarchy favored prayer and Bible reading in the schools as something inherently Christian rather than specifically Protestant. Roman Catholic leaders criticized the Supreme Court's decision in *Schempp.* All five American cardinals had traveled to Rome at the time to help find a successor to Pope John XXIII, and three of them denounced the decision from there. "No one who believes in God can approve such a decision," said Cardinal Spellman of New York.[41] A year later, at congressional hearings on the school prayer amendments, Bishop Fulton J. Sheen, auxiliary bishop of New York, gave tepid support to efforts to amend the Constitution. He wanted prayer and Bible reading returned to the public schools but was sensitive to the conflict sure to arise over whose prayer would be said. He favored adopting the prayer "In God We Trust," already used by congressmen. "Inasmuch as every Congressman has been carrying that prayer with him from the earliest days, I would suggest that it be a very fitting prayer for schools," he said. Sheen seemed concerned that Bible reading would cause sectarian disagreements, but he nonetheless favored its inclusion in any amendment that went forward.

> I would be satisfied with this [prayer alone]. First of all, because of the pluralistic views that we have. When it comes to Scripture reading, someone might say we should have the St. James version, others the Douay-Rheims, others Phillips, others the authorized version. All of these are legitimate versions. I would not be opposed to any of them, but I think that this prayer is sufficient and the answer to the problem of pluralism. "In God We Trust" is already on the seal of the United States, it is already in our tradition and it is a perfect prayer.

Sheen seemed almost apologetic about asking for some religion in the public schools. "I am presenting my answer on the basis of the pluralistic views of the United States and the tradition of the United States and I do not believe that we should ask too much," he said. "I am only asking for a recognition."[42]

Catholics were not the only ones to change positions on public school prayer and Bible reading. Ironically, a large segment of the Protestant community itself—allied with the majority of the Jewish community—blunted the attack on *Schempp* and *Engel.* However unusual the role reversal may seem, it was perhaps the inevitable result of long years of slowly pulling back from defending devotional practices in the public schools.

Whereas the schools started out in the colonies as places where children learned Anglican and Congregationalist dogma, that was no longer possible by the 1840s. The growing diversity among Protestant sects made it impossible to continue teaching the dogma of one sect or another. Horace Mann's development of a common Protestantism for the schools—centered on a short ceremony of prayer and Bible reading without comment—enabled Protestants to agree on a religious experience acceptable to all of them. As the religious landscape broadened to include a large number of Roman Catholics and non-Christians, many liberal Protestant leaders agreed to take even those exercises out of the public schools, in the interest of interfaith relations. By the time that the New York Board of Regents released the Regents' Prayer for use in the state's public schools, some elements of the Protestant community had already moved to a position of opposition to prayer in the public schools. The *Christian Century*, one of the most prominent Protestant publications, editorialized in 1952 that the Regents' Prayer did not violate the First Amendment but that prayer by rote in the public schools was unwise anyway because it was "likely to deteriorate quickly into an empty formality with little, if any, spiritual significance."[43]

Twelve years later, at hearings for the constitutional amendments to overturn *Schempp*, the position of mainstream Protestantism had largely hardened into opposition to devotional exercises in the public schools. If the pro-amendment forces assumed the support of all religious people, their arrow disintegrated in midflight. Horace Mann's "common religion" was dead, at least as far as most mainstream Protestants denominations were concerned.

After the *Schempp* decision, the National Council of Churches, representing thirty-one denominations with a membership of forty million American Christians, said that the teaching of religion belonged in the home and in houses of worship. "Neither the church nor the state should use the public school to compel acceptance of any creed or conformity to any specific religious practice," the group said in a statement on the day of the *Schempp* ruling. The council had warned a few days earlier that reliance on the government to help churches inculcate religious beliefs "endangers both true religion and civil liberties."[44] The United Presbyterian Church, also arguing that religion properly belonged with the family and the church, rejected the notion that Bible reading was justified for its moral lessons. "Prayer is cheapened when it is used as a device to quiet unruly children and the Bible loses its true meaning when it is looked upon as a moral handbook for minors," it said in a statement.[45] At congressional hearings on the prayer amendments in 1964, the executive council of the Lutheran Church went even further.

> If the Lord's Prayer were to be recited in schoolrooms only for the sake of the moral and ethical atmosphere it creates, it would be worth nothing to the practicing Christian. The Lord's Prayer is the supreme act of adoration and petition or it is debased. Reading the Bible in the public schools without comment, too, has been of dubious value as either an educational or religious experience. The more we attempt as Christians or Americans to insist on common denominator religious exercise or instruction in the public schools, the greater risk we run of diluting our faith and contributing to a vague religiosity which identifies religion with patriotism and becomes a national folk religion.[46]

The National Council of Churches followed through on its earlier statements opposing prayers and Bible reading. Edwin H. Tuller, general secretary of the American Baptist Convention, spoke for the council in 1964 as he presented reasons why church leaders opposed prayer and Bible reading in the public schools. First, he said, the public schools belong to everyone and "it is not right for the majority to impose religious beliefs or practices on the minority in public institutions." Second, the nation's religious diversity made the public schools a melting pot of children with a variety of traditions or no traditions at all and thus "particularly inappropriate places for corporate religious exercises." Tuller answered Justice Stewart's contention, discussed in his *Schempp* dissent, that the majority should be free to practice their religious exercises in the classroom as long as children from minority faiths could excuse themselves. So-called voluntary participation, said Tuller, was never truly voluntary in a pub-

lic school. "In such a setting," he argued, "children are almost always
not given a genuinely free choice by glib use of the words 'voluntary
participation,' when the whole atmosphere of the classroom is one of
compliance and conformity to group activities."[47]

Tuller also argued that different religious faiths would surely battle over the critical details of religious observance in the classroom.
The Bible and prayers came in multiple forms, and many of the differences had generated centuries of religious conflict in both Europe
and the United States. "Who is to compose the prayers, and who is
to select the Scriptures?" Tuller asked.

> What form of the Lord's Prayer will be used, and which version of the
> Bible? In those who take their faith seriously, these things are impor-
> tant. They do not consider all prayers or Scriptures interchangeable.
>
> Many devout Christians do not want their children to conclude
> that their transactions with the Most High are something routine,
> casual, and indiscriminate, in the same category with algebra and
> spelling.[48]

For the largest part of the Protestant movement, a journey of
more than three centuries seemed to have come to conclusion. They
no longer commanded a homogeneous religious community as they
had in colonial days, enabling them to require a strict religious curriculum in the schools. In this new day of religious pluralism, children from hundreds of Christian and non-Christian denominations
crowded the schools and the public square. The new age required
new understandings.

20. Does *Schempp* Have a Future?

Beyond defiance, beyond those who tried to punish the courts for rulings they didn't like, the law resulting from the *Schempp* case has continued its inevitable march through new circumstances. The ban on devotional readings from the Bible and recitations of the Lord's Prayer did not end the questions involving religion in the public schools. The law announced by the U.S. Supreme Court established principles to guide future decisions, but applying these principles to different circumstances has often presented a considerable challenge.

The very principles behind the *Schempp* ruling have been under siege. A coalition of the religious Right and conservative politicians, most of them from the Republican Party, have litigated cases under various legal strategies designed to return devotional exercises to the public schools. At the same time, the Court itself has become far more conservative, through the inevitable turnover of justices. By 1993, every justice who had participated in *Schempp* was gone from the Court.

The new conservative wing of the Court is far different from the conservatives of the past who decided the *Engel* and *Schempp* cases. The bloc of William Rehnquist, Antonin Scalia, and Clarence Thomas brought far different views of the religion clauses of the First Amendment than were held by most of the conservatives who came before them. To Scalia, the Court's work on religion in public life since the 1940s amounted to "our embarrassing Establishment Clause jurisprudence."[1] He and others didn't just disagree with the results of some of the past cases; they even disagreed with the fundamental historical analysis that provided the foundation for the Court's decisions in this area. The most recent additions to the Court—Chief Justice John G. Roberts, Jr., in 2005 and Associate Justice Samuel A. Alito, Jr., in 2006—will certainly have a major hand in deciding whether the *Schempp* principles hold up in the future.

Cases will continue to bubble up through the system, presenting various challenges to *Schempp*. They tend to fall into several categories, representing different strategies. Many states now require moments of silence or quiet reflection at the beginning of the school day. During this time, students can pray, meditate, or think about anything at all. As long as teachers don't require or encourage students to pray, these moments of silence could get the legal blessing of the Court. Another strategy challenges *Schempp* by presenting cases in which students themselves—not school authorities, using the power of the state—have initiated prayers and other religious exercises. These situations raise issues of free exercise of religion and freedom of religious speech for the students who request such observances. Still other cases may challenge once again whether religious exercises should be permitted in public schools as long as students have the option of not participating. Questions of religion in the public schools will engage lawyers and judges well into the twenty-first century.

⭒

Even before vocal prayer in the public schools was ruled unconstitutional, rule makers began to question how the Court would view a moment of silence. Pennsylvania school officials understood the likelihood that they would lose the *Schempp* case. On the same day that the decision was announced, the state superintendent of public education unveiled a plan to replace Bible reading and recitation of the Lord's Prayer with silent meditation.[2] The move proved to be prophetic of a strategy that would gain popularity throughout the country and a provisional green light under the First Amendment.

By 1985, a little more than two decades after the *Schempp* ruling, twenty-five states either required or permitted their public schools to involve students in a moment of silence.³ Many of the state laws required that the students use this time to pray, meditate, or think about the upcoming day. Tested in federal courts, some of the statutes requiring silent prayer as opposed to meditation were invalidated because, said the courts, the purpose and effect of these laws were to involve the public schools in promoting prayer.

That year, the U.S. Supreme Court heard *Wallace v. Jaffree,* a case involving silent prayer at a school in Alabama. In 1978, Alabama enacted a law requiring a one-minute moment of silence in all classrooms for the purposes of "meditation." That law was relatively uncontroversial, but the state's legislators didn't let it go at that. Three years later, the state enacted a law authorizing a moment of silence "for meditation or voluntary prayer." One year after that, it enacted a law that authorized teachers to lead a vocal prayer. The primary sponsor of the last law conceded that his main purpose was to engage willing students in prayer.

According to the Court's majority, this legislative intent violated the first part of the establishment clause test enunciated fourteen years earlier in *Lemon v. Kurtzman.* Henry W. Sawyer III had argued that case on behalf of plaintiffs challenging the validity of a salary supplement for nonpublic schoolteachers. The "*Lemon* test," as it came to be known, asked whether a law had a secular purpose, whether its primary effect was to advance or inhibit religion, and whether the law fostered excessive entanglement with religion.⁴ The first two prongs of the test had been set in Justice Clark's opinion in *Schempp;* the third, "entanglement" prong was added in *Lemon.* In the Alabama case, said the justices, legislators had enacted the second law "for the sole purpose of expressing the State's endorsement of prayer activities for one minute at the beginning of each school day." This endorsement "is not consistent with the established principle that the government must pursue a course of complete neutrality toward religion."⁵

The Court didn't consider the validity of state laws that required a moment of silence but did not mention prayer at all. In her concurring opinion, however, Justice Sandra Day O'Connor indicated that, at least for her, a moment-of-silence law would not violate the First Amendment. In the *Schempp* case, officials led what was clearly a devotional exercise that was part of the day's curricular activities, and these official exercises were inherently coercive of students to participate. Moments of silent meditation were different. O'Connor said that they typically would have a secular—not a religious—purpose and would not involve any coercive elements, such as the Court had found in vocal classroom prayers. She wrote: "[A] moment of silence is not inherently religious. Silence, unlike prayer or Bible reading, need not be associated with a religious exercise. . . . [A] pupil who participates in a moment of silence need not compromise his or her beliefs. During a moment of silence, a student who objects to prayer is left to his or her own thoughts, and is not compelled to listen to the prayers or thoughts of others."[6]

Justice Brennan, in his concurring opinion in *Schempp*, had made the same distinction. Discussing activities that he thought would remain unaffected by the Court's decision, Brennan had mentioned moments of silent meditation. To Brennan, who strongly believed vocal prayer violated the establishment clause, a moment of silence served "the solely secular purposes of the devotional activities without jeopardizing either the religious liberties of any members of the community or the proper degree of separation between the spheres of religion and government."[7]

In 2001, a moment-of-silence law was upheld in Virginia on a two-to-one vote by the U.S. Court of Appeals for the Fourth Circuit. Although the law was similar in some respects to the one ruled unconstitutional in *Wallace v. Jaffree*, the two judges in the majority found enough difference to conclude that it passed all three prongs of the *Lemon* test. The statute, they said, did not have a religious purpose. It offered students a minute to use for prayer or any other nondistracting purpose. "On its face, therefore, the statute provides a neutral medium—silence—during which the student may, without the knowledge of other students, engage in religious or nonreligious activity," the judges said.[8] The U.S. Supreme Court declined to hear the case.

There has been no definitive ruling on the constitutionality of state laws requiring a moment of silence for meditation alone, without mention of prayer. As O'Connor and Brennan suggested, there seems no constitutional harm in requiring students to reflect for a short time at the beginning of the day. They could engage in silent prayer or think about anything they wish without affecting their classmates. As long as the school or the teacher did not encourage students to use the time to engage in prayer, no endorsement of religious activities would have taken place, and no student would feel overt or subtle coercion to participate.

⌇

No wallflower when writing in dissent, Justice Scalia had harsh words for his colleagues on a school prayer case in 1992. The question was whether students felt coercive pressure to participate in a benediction offered at a high school graduation ceremony. The five-justice majority in *Lee v. Weisman* found that such pressure did exist. Scalia disagreed. To him, the so-called pressure of conformity on students amounted to "ersatz, 'peer-pressure' psycho-coercion."[9]

At least nobody had to puzzle over where Scalia stood on the question. The issue of coercion has followed the debate over public school prayer and Bible reading for a century and a half. When Protestants set the religious agenda for the public schools, Catholics protested use of the King James Bible and, failing to get it removed from the schools, asked that their children be excused from participation. Bridget Donahoe was suspended from her school in Maine for refusing to participate in 1854, and Thomas Wall was whipped with a rattan stick five years later. Each child simply wanted to be excused from the devotionals. (See discussion of both cases in chapter 8.) The government's application of coercion in those instances surely amounted to a violation of the First Amendment's free exercise clause, which prevents government from rewarding or punishing individuals for their religious practices. Unfortunately for the two children, it would be nearly a century before the First Amendment's two religion clauses were applied to the states. In their time, they had no recourse under the federal Constitution.

The strategy of denying excusal worked for a time, but Protestant hegemony was soon eroded by the increasing waves of immigrants to American shores. Catholics and non-Christians held different ideas about religion than did the Protestants, and by the mid-twentieth century, the only way for Protestants to retain their control over religion in the schools in many locales was to offer excusal to those who did not wish to participate. During litigation of both the *Schempp* and *Murray* cases, public officials added excusal provisions to the law in eleventh-hour attempts to escape possible constitutional problems.

Critics of the Supreme Court's rulings on devotionals in public schools have argued that coercion is critical to finding any constitutional violation. Coercion has always been an element of a free exercise violation—as when the government pressures people to follow or not to follow a religious belief. But a finding of coercion was not required in order to find a violation of the establishment clause, which prohibited government support of religion. Thus, the two clauses were designed to safeguard against different violations of religious liberty. Requiring a finding of coercion for both clauses of the First Amendment would essentially make one clause redundant of the other in many ways, not something that logically follows from the constitutional framers' articulation of two distinct clauses protecting religious freedom.

Defenders of school prayer and Bible reading argue that coercion is absent as long as students of minority faiths can excuse themselves, opting out of the religious exercises, and that this allows the majority who do want to participate in the devotional exercises to go ahead and enjoy their own free exercise of religious beliefs. The problem is that all of this happens in the context of a school, where direct coercion is not the only kind of coercion that exists. Coercion can also occur indirectly, through peer pressure. But that is not something that the four dissenters in *Weisman*—Scalia, Rehnquist, White, and Thomas—accepted.

Benedictions have long been common at graduation ceremonies, and at one middle school in Providence, Rhode Island, a local rabbi delivered a prayer. As was the usual practice, the school advised him that the prayer should be nonsectarian and gave him a pamphlet, published by the National Conference of Christians and Jews, advising that public prayers show "inclusiveness and sensitivity." When *Weisman*—the legal case resulting from the rabbi's prayer—reached the Supreme Court, the justices ruled by a five-to-four majority that the practice of having clergy offer prayers at public school graduations violated the establishment clause. That conservative Justice Anthony Kennedy not only voted with the majority but also wrote the Court's opinion was a bitter disappointment to religious conservatives, who could well have anticipated a five-to-four vote in the other direction.

Kennedy and four other justices found that the state's participation in the religious exercise was too extensive to ignore under the establishment clause. The school had decided that prayers would be included in the ceremony, invited the rabbi, and supplied him with advice on the contents of the prayer. "The government involvement with religious activity in this case is pervasive, to the point of creating a state-sponsored and state-directed religious exercise in a public school," Kennedy wrote.[10] Kennedy's four colleagues would have banned the prayer on grounds of government sponsorship alone, but they agreed with Kennedy that the students had been coerced into participating in the prayer.

In dissent, though, Scalia brought up the matter of coercion and instigated a debate, still continuing today, about what coercion actually means in regard to students in school. Scalia argued that there was no coercion forcing students to participate. He seemed to concede that prayer within a classroom setting (as in *Schempp*) contained elements of coercion that made the practice illegal. Prayer in the classroom, he said, is not a public ceremony as is a benediction at graduation, and students are compelled by law to attend school. By contrast, he argued, prayers at public events enjoy a long history in America. The Court's invalidation of the graduation prayer, he said, "lays waste a tradition that is as old as public school graduation ceremonies themselves, and that is a component of an even more long-standing American tradition of nonsectarian prayer to God at public celebrations generally."[11]

Scalia attacked the majority's finding that indirect government coercion forced students to attend graduation ceremonies. He argued that there is no legal compulsion for students to attend graduation exercises and no requirement to recite any prayers when they do attend. If students stand with other people during a prayer, he contended, that does not imply actual participation in the prayer—only respect. For Scalia, coercion should be limited to "acts backed by threat of penalty," and in the *Weisman* case, there was no penalty to any graduating student who chose not to participate either in the prayer or in the graduation ceremony itself.[12] Scalia maintained that dissenting students could skip graduation or, if they attend, choose not to participate in the prayer, entirely without negative consequences imposed by the school.

Scalia's concept of coercion is narrow and legalistic, showing little appreciation for the gravitational force exerted by peer pressure on children too immature to resist. It shows how a narrow coercion test can tilt heavily toward the government and inject majoritarian religious beliefs and symbols into public schools. If coercion can be found only where threats and actual penalties are involved, many religious practices in the schools would not violate the First Amendment. Coercion, of course, can involve something less than threats and penalties, especially where children are concerned. The state can place more subtle and indirect burdens on people, such as the real psychological pressure on children that Scalia denigrates as "psycho-coercion."

Responding to Scalia's argument that no student was forced to attend the event and thus that there was no coercion of beliefs, Kennedy and his four colleagues argued that students were not really free to avoid the ceremony. To do so, he said, would require them to

forfeit many benefits that students and their families found meaningful. Even standing and remaining silent during the prayer "was an
expression of participation in the rabbi's prayer," wrote Justice
Kennedy, who explained: "That was the very point of the religious
exercise. It is of little comfort to a dissenter, then, to be told that, for
her, the act of standing or remaining in silence signifies mere respect,
rather than participation. What matters is that, given our social con-
ventions, a reasonable dissenter in this milieu could believe that the
group exercise signified her own participation or approval of it."
Kennedy added: "Research in psychology supports the common
assumption that adolescents are often susceptible to pressure from
their peers towards conformity, and that the influence is strongest in
matters of social convention. To recognize that the choice imposed
by the State constitutes an unacceptable constraint only acknowl-
edges that the government may no more use social pressure to
enforce orthodoxy than it may use more direct means."[13]

The public school devotional cases of the 1960s demonstrate just
how subtle coercion can be when it involves children. Even after
Pennsylvania added an excusal provision to its Bible-reading law in
1959, Ed Schempp refused to ask that his children be excused,
because he was afraid that other children would regard them as "oddballs" and that they would be subject to rejection by their peers. Likewise, in the testimony taken by Leo Pfeffer in the *Chamberlin* case,
children and parents expressed similar fears about asking to be
excused. One high school senior said she didn't want to do anything
that might jeopardize college recommendations by her teachers. It's
hard to understand how these pressures would not similarly apply to
a graduation ceremony. Scalia's attempt at legally distinguishing
between prayers in the classroom and prayers at graduation seems
not at all responsive to the peer pressure that students actually feel
when faced with devotional exercises that are not their own.

While Scalia and three other justices defined coercion narrowly,
some of the leading conservative justices and scholars haven't seen it
the same way. In his concurring opinion in *McCollum* in 1948, Justice
Frankfurter understood that the pressures on children went beyond

Scalia's narrow idea of threats of penalty. Frankfurter wrote in the context of released-time programs, but his concerns about coercion of children are broad. "The law of imitation operates, and non-conformity is not an outstanding characteristic of children," he wrote. "The result is an obvious pressure upon children to attend."[14]

Michael W. McConnell, a judge on the U.S. Court of Appeals for the Tenth Circuit, has been one of the leading conservative critics of the Supreme Court's approach to the religion clauses. McConnell, though, who believes coercion is a key element in finding an establishment of religion, wrote that it "is vital to understand the concept of coercion broadly and realistically." He added: "I would have thought that gathering a captive audience is a classic example of coercion; participation is hardly voluntary if the cost of avoiding the prayer is to miss one's graduation. Equally seriously, it appears that the content of the prayer was subject to indirect governmental control, which is a species of coercion. For the Court to embrace the coercion test in this form would be a small step back toward permitting the government to indoctrinate children in the favored civil religion of nondenominational theism."[15] McConnell has also written that he opposes prayer in the classroom, on the ground of government coercion. He believes that the government's support of specific religious beliefs in the classroom creates indirect coercive pressure on students to conform.[16]

꒳

The applications of the free exercise clause and the free speech clause of the First Amendment have come rather late into consideration of public school devotionals. For Leo Pfeffer, one of the main attractions of the *Chamberlin* case was the challenge it raised under the free exercise clause. All the religious exercises and pageantry of the Miami schools—the King James Bible, the Lord's Prayer, the passion plays and religious hymns, and more—provided strong evidence that the schools placed children of minority religions in the position of having to participate in extensive religious practices that were not their own. Had *Chamberlin* reached the Supreme Court first, it's possible that the justices would not have banned Bible reading and recitation of the Lord's Prayer based solely on the establishment clause, as they did in *Schempp*. They might have placed equal analytical weight on a free exercise violation, making the decision even stronger and possibly adding another layer of immunity to some of the attacks that are taking place today.

Like Pfeffer, Justice Stewart also saw devotional activities in the public schools as a free exercise problem. But his differences with Pfeffer were profound. While Pfeffer focused on the rights of children in the religious minority to be free of majoritarian devotionals, Stewart argued for the right of the majority of Abington schoolchildren to freely exercise their desire to participate in prayer and Bible reading. The government had to respect this right, said Stewart, as long as children who objected to the devotionals had the opportunity to excuse themselves.[17]

In addition, some critics have argued that the free speech clause should protect religious activities in the public schools. Religious expression, of course, has long been an important part of America's marketplace of ideas. It played a critical role in major historical events of this country, such as abolition and the civil rights movement. Now, though, some observers assert that religious expression in the schools deserves the protection of the free speech clause over claims that they violate the establishment clause.

For Christian conservatives eager to return devotional exercises to the public schools, placing religious speech under the wings of the free exercise clause and the free speech clause has provided plenty of airlift. Prayers required by the government—as in the *Engel* and *Schempp* cases—violate the establishment clause. But encouraging students to initiate prayer and other religious activities on their own, so the argument goes, does not involve the government but, rather, supports the free choice of children practicing their religion and should be protected by both the free exercise clause and the free speech clause of the First Amendment.

These ideas received favorable treatment by the Court in 1981, immediately giving great hope to Christian conservatives that they had found a wedge to bring devotional exercises back to the public schools. The University of Missouri at Kansas City adopted a regulation that banned anyone from using university buildings "for purposes of religious worship or religious teaching." Acting pursuant to the regulation, the university refused permission for a group of evangelical Christian students to meet in university buildings. The group sued, arguing that the university had violated their free exercise rights and freedom of speech. In *Widmar v. Vincent*, the Supreme Court ruled in favor of the students, applying traditional First Amendment speech doctrine. By opening its property for student groups to use for their own activities, the university had created a "public forum" and could not exclude any particular group based on the content of its speech—in this instance religious. Only by showing a compelling state interest could the university refuse the evangelical group on the basis of the content of its speech. The University of Missouri had argued that the compelling interest was to avoid violation of the establishment clause, but the Court didn't agree.

An equal access policy permitting the evangelical group to use university facilities would not, the Court said, advance religion. It would not identify the university with the evangelicals any more than it would with the goals of any other groups.[18] Writing in dissent, Justice White emphasized the danger lurking in using the free speech clause. "I believe that this proposition is plainly wrong," he said. "Were it right, the Religion Clauses would be emptied of any independent meaning in circumstances in which religious practice took the form of speech."[19]

Nine years later, in 1990, the Court applied the *Widmar* principle to secondary schools. Congress had enacted the Equal Access Act,[20] prohibiting public secondary schools that created a limited public forum for speech from closing the forum to students based on the content of their speech. When a high school in Omaha did exactly that in regard to a Christian club, the students sued. In *Westside Community Board of Education v. Mergens*, the Court backed the students by saying that the law did not violate the establishment clause.

It had a secular, not a religious, purpose, because it granted access to all speech. In addition, said the Court, the state had not endorsed religion. The speech in question clearly was private speech delivered by students, and both the free exercise clause and the free speech clause protected it. The Court said: "[T]here is a crucial difference between government speech endorsing religion, which the Establishment Clause forbids, and private speech endorsing religion, which the Free Speech and Free Exercise Clauses protect. We think that secondary school students are mature enough and are likely to understand that a school does not endorse or support student speech that it merely permits on a nondiscriminatory basis."[21] Then, in 1995, in *Rosenberger v. Rector of the University of Virginia,* the Court said that religious publications could not be excluded from the group of student publications eligible for financial assistance.[22]

In these equal access cases, the Court arguably enhanced religious liberty by recognizing that schools do not endorse religion merely by allowing religious groups to meet or publish on a nondiscriminatory basis. But what about devotional exercises carried out as part of a school activity in the presence of those who do not agree with those beliefs? Such cases look more like *Schempp,* even if the praying students are ostensibly acting on their own. In 2000, in *Santa Fe Independent School District v. Doe,* the Court struck down the practice of students voluntarily delivering prayers at high school football games.[23] The high school authorized a vote to determine whether students wanted a prayer at games and then an election to choose a student to deliver it. The U.S. district court ordered that any prayers be nonsectarian and nonproselytizing. All this maneuvering, though, did not save the practice. Contrary to the assertion that the case involved private student speech and was not sponsored by the school, the Court said that the school's involvement was nonetheless pervasive, amounting to a violation of the establishment clause. In his dissenting opinion, Justice Rehnquist, joined by Justices Scalia and Thomas, emphasized that the students had engaged in private speech protected by the free exercise and free speech clauses.[24]

Efforts to categorize prayer as free speech had earlier made some progress in the lower federal courts, though *Santa Fe v. Doe* may have effectively overruled them. In 1992, the U.S. Court of Appeals for the Fifth Circuit upheld one school district's policy of graduation prayers.[25] The Supreme Court refused to hear the case. The Clear Creek schools in Texas had the practice of allowing the senior class to vote on whether to use a prayer at graduation. After an affirmative vote of the senior class, a student volunteer would deliver the prayer, which was supposed to be nonsectarian and nonproselytizing. In *Jones v. Clear Creek Independent School District,* the federal court of appeals ruled that the practice did not have the purpose or effect of advancing religion. "We think that Clear Creek does not unconstitutionally endorse religion if it submits the decision of graduation invocation content, if any, to the majority vote of the senior class," the court said.[26] The judges said that students would not perceive that the government was endorsing religion. The judges also maintained that psychological pressure to participate would be minimal "because all students, *after having participated in the decision of whether prayers will be given,* are aware that any prayers represent the will of their peers, who are less able to coerce participation than the authority figure from the state or clergy." The court added, "The practical result of our decision . . . is that a majority of students can do what the State acting on its own cannot do to incorporate prayer in public high school graduation ceremonies."[27]

In 1996, the Fifth Circuit again upheld nonsectarian, nonproselytizing voluntary prayer initiated by students at graduation ceremonies, this time in the Jackson Public School District in Mississippi.[28] Once again, the Supreme Court refused to hear the case, letting the lower court's ruling stand. Another case reached a different result. A federal court in Mississippi struck down student-initiated prayer and Bible reading over a school's intercom system—a situation that looked much like the Schempp case, except that a student Christian club acted on its own wishes rather than on the direction of school authorities.[29] The judge didn't buy the school's argument that it was simply providing an open forum, under the federal Equal Access Act, for any student group to say anything it wanted over the public address system.

Use of the student choice model enables a school district to do exactly what it cannot do under *Lee v. Weisman*—hold a prayer at graduation. Stopped by the Supreme Court from directing a graduation prayer in *Weisman*, the school in *Clear Creek* had merely passed a rule delegating that responsibility to the students themselves, knowing full well what the students would do. In the end, the student choice model of *Clear Creek* undermines the principle that parents in a community cannot impose their majoritarian religious prayers in the schools through law or school regulations. Their children represent exactly the same majoritarian religious practices, but they could accomplish what their parents could not by initiating prayer supposedly on their own.

Whether a school or students initiate prayer in a school context, the fact remains that a majority of students is imposing prayer on a minority. The government provides support for religious beliefs by accommodating student requests to pray before classmates who do not share their religious practices. Individual students should not have to either brave peer pressure to ask for excusal or go along and participate in the prayer. This remains the essence of a First Amendment violation. Part of the reason the *Schempp* decision barred prayer and Bible reading was because the Abington school district had imposed the dominant Protestantism on students, such as Ellery Schempp, who objected to many of its teachings. Delegation of that decision to the students themselves produces exactly the same majoritarian imposition. The Bill of Rights protects all of us, but as it often has been observed, it most particularly protects the minority against any overreaching by the majority.

ঝ

Yet another way in which *Schempp* and *Engel* stand on shifting sands involves a sharply different view of the establishment clause by some conservative justices. When the two cases were announced in the early 1960s, only Justice Stewart dissented from the two decisions. *Engel* and *Schempp* had the full support even of Justice Harlan, the conservative standard-bearer of the time. The two leading conservative justices before him, Frankfurter and Jackson, both supported the concept of "a wall of separation" between church and state. However, the more recent conservatives on the Court—Chief Justice Rehnquist and Justices Scalia and Thomas—have offered different ideas about the interpretation of the religion clauses.

The broadest and most fundamental attack on *Engel* and *Schempp* has come from Rehnquist, who argued that the Court's constitutional analysis for more than forty years has been fundamentally wrong, based on a faulty understanding of the intent of those who drafted the First Amendment. The chief justice, who died in 2005, argued for a narrow interpretation of the establishment clause. Everyone agrees that the establishment clause prohibits the government from recognizing a national religion—that is, from creating the equivalent of the Church of England in the United States—or from promoting one religious sect over another. But Rehnquist believed that's all the establishment clause prohibits. The Court and most legal scholars go further, however. The justices have consistently said that the First Amendment also prohibits government from promoting religion in general, not just one religion over another, and that it must take a neutral stance between religion and no religion.

The difference in the two positions is no scholarly dispute carried out in a windowless back room of a law library. In fact, it makes all the difference in the adjudication of real-life disputes over the government and religion. As a practical matter, Rehnquist's interpretation would reverse many First Amendment religion cases, including some on religion in the public schools. Under his interpretation, there might be no constitutional bar against the state promoting religious exercises in the schools, so long as the justices were satisfied that it did not favor one denomination's doctrine over another's.

Rehnquist set out his thoughts most fully in his dissenting opinion in *Wallace v. Jaffree,* the case that struck down the Alabama law authorizing one minute of silence for meditation or prayer in schools. Rehnquist attacked the Court's acceptance of Thomas Jefferson's "wall of separation" as a metaphor to describe its approach to analysis of the guarantees of religious freedom. Despite Jefferson's considerable contributions during the founding period—he was the author of the Virginia Statute for Religious Freedom and a key thinker on the right of conscience—Rehnquist dismisses him because he was "of course in France" when the constitutional amendments were ratified and thus "a less than ideal source of contemporary history" on the First Amendment.[30]

Rehnquist's argument centered on James Madison's initial proposed language for the religion clauses. His proposal said: "The civil rights of none shall be abridged on account of religious belief or worship, nor shall any national religion be established, nor shall the full and equal rights of conscience be in any manner, or on any pretext, infringed."[31] For Rehnquist, the key word was *national*. Based on that language and some exceedingly sparse notes from the debate, which Rehnquist admitted did "not seem particularly illuminating," he went on to draw conclusions that evidenced no uncertainty whatsoever.[32]

Rehnquist concluded that Madison meant the clause to apply to the establishment of a single national religion, not to government promotion of religion in general. He argued that even if Madison and Jefferson had favored a much broader interpretation of establishment of religion when they pushed enactment of the Virginia Act for Establishing Religious Freedom in the battle over tax support of clergy in Virginia, the Court had been "totally incorrect in suggesting that Madison carried these views onto the floor of the United States House of Representatives when he proposed the language which would ultimately become the Bill of Rights." Rehnquist went on:

> None of the other Members of Congress who spoke during the August 15 debate expressed the slightest indication that they thought the language before them from the Select Committee, or the evil to be aimed at, would require that the Government be absolutely neutral as

between religion and irreligion. The evil to be aimed at, so far as those who spoke were concerned, appears to have been the establishment of a national church, and perhaps the preference of one religious sect over another; but it was definitely not concerned about whether the Government might aid all religions evenhandedly.[33]

As further evidence of what the framers of the Constitution intended, Rehnquist cited the various Thanksgiving proclamations and prayers offered by early presidents, including George Washington after Congress adopted the constitutional amendments. Rehnquist pointed out that Congress had numerous times appropriated money for churches and clergy to provide religious education for Native American Indians. Applying his analysis to the *Jaffree* moment-of-silence case then before the Court, Rehnquist thought that Alabama was constitutionally justified in endorsing prayer in the public schools, because the law promoted religion generally and not any denomination in particular. "It would come as much of a shock to those who drafted the Bill of Rights as it will to a large number of thoughtful Americans today to learn that the Constitution, as construed by the majority, prohibits the Alabama Legislature from 'endorsing' prayer," he wrote.[34]

Rehnquist's position on the establishment clause has some scholarly support, dating back to the nineteenth century and continuing to this day. But his position has been repeatedly rejected by the Court itself and by most First Amendment scholars for the past half century. The reality is that nobody knows for sure what the framers meant by their wording of the religion clauses—a problem that applies to those on both sides of the establishment clause divide. Neither is it entirely clear what the state legislators who ratified the Bill of Rights thought the religion provisions meant. Tape recorders, twenty-four-hour cable news, and careful transcription of debate would be the fruits of another day. Records from that time are sparse and unreliable, and no source is clear enough to be definitive. The historical evidence of the period—what took place at the First Congress and what Madison and Jefferson are known to have believed—does seem to point in the direction of a broader reading of the religion clauses than Rehnquist supported.

Given the importance of his dissenting opinion in *Jaffree*, Rehnquist's analysis was surprisingly sparse. He based his analysis most heavily on Madison's draft of the First Amendment that said no "national religion be established." Rehnquist's position would be much stronger if Congress had actually enacted such a limitation, but it did exactly the opposite. Congress rejected this draft and entirely dropped "national" as the descriptive term for religion. In fact, four separate drafts of the religion clauses came before the First Congress proposing the national religion position, and all were rejected—evidence that Congress did not want the religion clauses limited to banning only a national church and favored a broader meaning. Rehnquist left out this compelling piece of history. Douglas Laycock, a University of Michigan law professor and one of the preeminent scholars on ratification of the First Amendment, explains:

> The establishment clause actually adopted is one of the broadest versions considered by either House. It forbids not only establishments, but also any law respecting or relating to an establishment. Most important, it forbids any law respecting an establishment of "religion." It does not say "a religion," "a national religion," "one sect or society," or "any particular denomination of religion." It is religion generically that may not be established. . . . An approach to interpretation that disregards the ratified amendment and derives meaning exclusively from rejected proposals is strange indeed.[35]

Rehnquist and others who argue for a narrow reading of the religion clauses also make much of the fact that the framers accepted or at least tolerated certain practices involving public support of religion generally. Congress appointed chaplains who offered prayers before sessions. Most presidents, starting with Washington, issued Thanksgiving proclamations invoking prayer, and Congress funded missionaries to help educate Indians. Proponents of a narrow reading argue that nothing analogous today can therefore be a violation of the First Amendment. But Laycock answers that these earlier practices did not constitute a general support of religion but rather the support of specific denominations that all agree today is impermissible. Missionaries came from specific denominations, and Congress did not hire a chaplain from every faith or even many faiths.

The framers' behavior after ratification of the Bill of Rights cannot be an unerring guide to how they interpreted it. They were politicians, after all, and were subject to the same flames of partisanship as any legislators today. The young nation had a strong Protestant orientation, and in legislating various prayers, the politicians may have been trying to please their constituents in ways that are familiar to Americans in the twenty-first century. The way politicians of the founding period acted in complete violation of the First Amendment's free speech and free press clauses serves as an apt example. Just seven years after ratification of the First Amendment, Congress enacted the infamous Sedition Act of 1798, perhaps the most flagrant violation of the freedom of political expression in the nation's history. In passing the Sedition Act, the Federalist Party was trying anything politically possible to gain the upper hand over their Republican opponents, even if it contravened the Bill of Rights that had been added to the Constitution earlier in that very decade. Jefferson pardoned all those convicted under the law when he became president. Laycock writes:

> The argument cannot be merely that anything the Framers did is constitutional. The unstated premise of *that* argument is that the Framers fully thought through everything they did and had every constitutional principle constantly in mind, so that all their acts fit together in a great mosaic that is absolutely consistent, even if modern observers cannot understand the organizing principle. That is not a plausible premise. Of course the state and federal establishment clauses did not abruptly end all customs in tension with their implications. No innovation ever does.[36]

As for Madison, the most important single figure behind the religion clauses, his extensive public record shows that he firmly opposed all types of governmental support of religion. He and Jefferson led the seminal battle in Virginia against general tax assessments to support all religions, and opposition to government support of religion was the central theme of his incomparable *Memorial and Remonstrance against Religious Assessments.* Madison did not approve of Congress appointing chaplains paid through taxes. In retirement, in 1822, he lamented that development in a letter to Edward Livingston. "As the precedent is not likely to be rescinded," he wrote, "the best that can now be done, may be to apply to the Constn. [Constitution] the maxim of the law, de minimis non curat [the law does not concern itself with trifling things]." In the same letter, Madison wrote that proclamations of fasts and festivals involving prayer were "another deviation from the strict principle." In terms of the "perfect separation" of church and state, Madison wrote to Livingston: "Every new & successful example therefore of a perfect separation between ecclesiastical and civil matters, is of importance. And I have no doubt that every new example, will succeed, as every past one has done, in shewing that religion & Govt. will both exist in greater purity, the less they are mixed together."[37]

Properly applied, the outcome reached in *Schempp* and *Engel* shouldn't change no matter how one views the framers' intentions. Rehnquist's conclusion that the establishment clause permits the government to endorse religion generally but not an individual church or set of beliefs should not enable prayer and Bible reading to return to the public schools. The testimony in *Schempp* demonstrated that all prayer and Bible reading is a sectarian practice that promoted some sects and discriminated against others.

The Bible has different versions that have been the basis of persecution and violence between sects for many hundreds of years, even in the United States. Solomon Grayzel, the expert witness for the Schempps, identified some of the many passages in the King James Version that conflict with Jewish teachings. Even Luther Weigle, Abington's expert witness, admitted that the King James Bible is specifically the Protestant Bible to which Catholics and Jews do not subscribe. He said that the King James Bible is nonsectarian only for Protestants. But it's not clear that the King James is even nonsectarian for all Protestants. Ellery Schempp, although a Unitarian Protestant himself, believed that the devotional use of the Lord's Prayer and the Protestant King James Bible violated his own religious faith. In fact, he designed his protest—reading silently from the Koran during the Bible exercise—to demonstrate the existence of alternative religious traditions.

Prayer is inherently sectarian and has no other purpose than for worship. Even Philip H. Ward III, Abington's attorney, conceded, in his oral argument before the Supreme Court, that the Lord's Prayer violated the establishment clause. The Lord's Prayer is one of the most sacred in all of Christianity and is most certainly not a prayer of non-Christians. Even a prayer written to be "nondenominational"—the Regent's Prayer in *Engel,* for example—discriminates against children who belong to nontheistic religions. Christian conservatives often complain that catering to nontheism amounts to surrender to the atheism, agnosticism, and humanism that they oppose. But Buddhism and Confucianism do not have a theology that includes a god, so "nondenominational" prayers would be sectarian for them. Buddhism was a faith unknown in the colonies, but by 1985, a group of Buddhists in San Francisco objected to school prayer because their faith did not subscribe to the concept of God known in Judeo-Christian religions. Prayer in the classroom, they said, "would be an assault on the religious freedom of Buddhists."[38]

༄

The controversy will no doubt continue for many years to come. The religious freedom bestowed by the Bill of Rights in 1791 created a free market that enabled religion to thrive in America. Madison and the founding generation clipped the ties that had long bound civil and ecclesiastical authority. Bound to the state, religion had long sought adherents with fire, sword, and legislative fiat. Unbound, it renewed itself through free competition based on its ability to connect with the human soul, one soul at a time.

The tens of millions of connections made have brought enormous success to America's great experiment in religious freedom. Free to pray and free to proselytize, people of faith came to America and there planted hundreds of denominations to grow. In 1776, the beginning of the Revolutionary period, only 17 percent of the population was affiliated with any denomination.[39] By the time of the *Schempp* case, more than 63 percent of the American population were adherents to some faith. In 1962, a total of 252 religious denominations reported membership for a survey on faiths in the United States, with tremendous diversity even within major churches. There were twenty-eight Baptist and twenty-two Methodist denominations alone, among 222 Protestant bodies.[40]

In 1822, Madison had occasion to look back at his and his fellow constitutional framers' two greatest achievements, the dual blessings of democratic government and the separation of government and religion into separate spheres. "I cannot speak particularly of any of the cases excepting that of Virga. [Virginia] where it is impossible to deny that Religion prevails with more zeal, and a more exemplary priesthood than it ever did when established and patronised by Public authority," he wrote. "We are teaching the world the great truth that Govts. do better without Kings & Nobles than with them. The merit will be doubled by the other lesson that Religion flourishes in greater purity, without than with the aid of Govt."[41] As freedom produced a proliferation of faiths as well as adherents, so, too, it made prayer and Bible reading in the public schools an idea that no longer worked in a pluralistic society. By the middle of the twentieth century, Americans could no more have devised a nonsectarian devotional exercise for their schoolchildren than Madison could have imagined a new land that welcomed the excessive religious zeal of the Old World.

Epilogue

William Murray, in whose name the *Murray* case was brought, faced a string of difficult personal problems in the years after the litigation. Finally, he renounced atheism and embraced God, writing a letter published in the *Baltimore Sun* in 1980 in which he sought "to apologize to the people of the City of Baltimore for whatever part I played in the removal of Bible reading and praying from the public schools of that city." He publicly forgave "those who assaulted me and destroyed my property during those years that *Murray v. Curlett* moved through the courts."[1] Murray organized a faith ministry and even picketed some of his mother's atheist meetings.[2]

⌇

Madalyn Murray married Richard O'Hair in 1965 and adopted his last name. Throughout her life, she remained the nation's most prominent spokesperson for atheism, headed several atheist organizations, and wrote books about her beliefs on atheism and the separation of church and state. In 1995, Madalyn, her son Jon Garth Murray, and her granddaughter Robin Murray-O'Hair mysteriously disappeared from their home in Texas. Extensive searches failed to turn up their whereabouts. In January of 2001, Madalyn's former office manager, David Waters, led police to a spot in Camp Wood, Texas, where they found the charred bones of the three Murrays. Positive identification of Madalyn came from a metal hip whose serial number was identical to one given to her.[3]

꒰

Ellery Schempp earned his doctorate in physics from Brown University. He taught physics at the University of Pittsburgh and the University of Geneva. Later, at Lawrence Berkeley National Laboratory, a U.S. Department of Energy facility in Berkeley, California, he worked on a research team trying to better understand salt domes and other geological formations important in nuclear waste disposal. He went on from there to General Electric, where he helped develop magnetic imaging technology for biomedical research. He is now semiretired and lives in the Boston area.[4]

At the age of sixteen, Ellery's challenge to Bible reading and recitation of the Lord's Prayer at Abington Senior High School caused great upheaval and bitter feelings in his own community. Ellery says that his own principal wrote to a college admissions officer recommending that the school turn down his application for admission. But the bitterness would not last forever.

In 2002, Ellery Frank Schempp, PhD, class of 1958, received Abington Senior High School's highest honor bestowed on its alumni. He was inducted into the school's hall of fame for his achievements in science. Among Ellery's major accomplishments, the school noted the following: "Initiated school prayer suit against Abington which was eventually decided by U.S. Supreme Court in 1963."[5] Although the controversy over religion in the public schools continues to roil national politics, in Abington at least, people have made their peace with Ellery's protest.

Notes

CHAPTER 1

1. Ellery Schempp spelled his name "Ellory" at the time of the lawsuit and changed it to "Ellery" as an adult. For the sake of consistency, the author uses "Ellery" throughout this book.

2. This section's description of the events of November 26, 1956, is based on Ellery Schempp's discussions with the author at Princeton Junction, NJ, on June 6, 1999; Abington, PA, on December 3, 2003; and Winchester, MA, on November 27, 2004.

3. *School District of Abington Township v. Schempp*, 374 U.S. 203 (1963).

4. *McCollum v. Board of Education*, 333 U.S. 203, 228 (Justice Frankfurter, concurring, 1948).

CHAPTER 2

1. Sloan Wilson, *The Man in the Gray Flannel Suit* (New York: Simon and Schuster, 1955).

2. Ibid., 5.

3. William Manchester, *The Glory and the Dream: A Narrative History of America, 1932–1972* (Boston: Little, Brown, 1973), 578.

4. Ibid., 729.

5. David Halberstam, *The Fifties* (New York: Villard Books, 1993), 592–98.

6. Ellery Schempp, discussion, June 6, 1999.

7. Halberstam, *The Fifties,* 474.

8. Ellery Schempp, discussion, June 6, 1999.

9. Ibid.

10. Ellery Schempp, discussion with the author, Medford, MA, April 17, 2003.

11. Ellery Schempp, discussion, June 6, 1999.

12. Ellery Schempp, discussion, April 17, 2003.

13. Ellery Schempp, discussion, June 6, 1999.

14. Ibid.

15. Ibid.

16. Ellery Schempp, discussion, April 17, 2003.

17. Ibid.

18. Ellery Schempp, discussion, June 6, 1999.

19. *Abington Township Senior High School* (Abington, PA: Abington School District, n.d.), brochure filed at the Abington High School Library.

20. Testimony of Orlando H. English, U.S. District Court for the Eastern District of Pennsylvania, November 25, 1958, *Abington v. Schempp*, Transcript of Record, *Records and Briefs of the U.S. Supreme Court*, 374:125, Law Library of Congress.

21. Testimony of W. Eugene Stull, U.S. District Court for the Eastern District of Pennsylvania, November 25, 1958, *Abington v. Schempp*, Transcript of Record, *Records and Briefs of the U.S. Supreme Court*, 374:104, Law Library of Congress.

22. Ellery Schempp, discussion, June 6, 1999.

23. Ellery Schempp, discussion, December 3, 2003.

24. Ellery Schempp, discussion, November 27, 2004.

25. Ellery Schempp, discussion, April 17, 2003.

26. Allan Glatthorn, discussion with the author by telephone, May 20, 2003.

27. Ibid.

28. Royal Brown, discussion with the author, New York, June 23, 2003.

29. Ellery Schempp, discussion, June 6, 1999.

30. Testimony of Milton E. Northam, U.S. District Court for the Eastern District of Pennsylvania, November 25, 1958, *Abington v. Schempp*, Transcript of Record, *Records and Briefs of the U.S. Supreme Court*, 374:98–99, Law Library of Congress.

31. Testimony of English, at 127.

32. Testimony of Stull, at 106–7; testimony of William W. Young, U.S. District Court for the Eastern District of Pennsylvania, November 25, 1958, *Abington v. Schempp*, Transcript of Record, *Records and Briefs of the U.S. Supreme Court*, 374:108–20, Law Library of Congress.

33. Testimonies of Roger Schempp and Donna Schempp, U.S. District Court for the Eastern District of Pennsylvania, August 6, 1958, *Abington v. Schempp*, Transcript of Record, *Records and Briefs of the U.S. Supreme Court*, 374:75–80, Law Library of Congress; testimony of Northam, at 97–98.

34. *Bible Reading in Public Schools: The Schempp and Murray Cases, 1963*, DVD (Princeton, NJ: Films for the Humanities and Sciences, 2003). This is a repackaging of a one-hour *CBS News* broadcast, "Storm over the Supreme Court," which aired on June 19, 1963.

35. Ellery Schempp, discussion, June 6, 1999.

36. Brown, discussion.

37. Ellery Schempp, discussion, June 6, 1999.

38. Brown, discussion.

39. Ellery Schempp, discussion, June 6, 1999.

40. Edward Schempp, memorandum, July 29, 1958, Schempp Family Papers, 27, in the personal possession of Ellery Schempp (hereafter cited as Schempp Family Papers).

41. Ellery Schempp, discussion, June 6, 1999.

42. Ibid.

43. Ellery Schempp, discussion, April 17, 2003.

44. Ellery Schempp, discussion, June 6, 1999.

45. Glatthorn, discussion.

46. Ellery Schempp, discussion, June 6, 1999.

47. Ibid.

48. Ibid.

49. Edward Schempp, discussion with the author, Barington, NJ, April 29, 1999.

50. Ellery Schempp, discussion, June 6, 1999.

51. Ibid.

52. Ibid.

53. Ibid.

54. Ibid.

55. Ellery F. Schempp to the American Civil Liberties Union, November 26, 1956, Court Docket and Case Files, case no. 24119, *Abington School District v. Schempp,* U.S. National Archives and Records Administration, Mid-Atlantic Region, Philadelphia (hereafter cited as National Archives, Philadelphia).

56. Ellery Schempp, discussion, June 6, 1999.

CHAPTER 3

1. Spencer Coxe, discussion with the author, Philadelphia, PA, September 17, 2003.

2. Board of Directors and Officers, memorandum, Philadelphia chapter of the American Civil Liberties Union, November 13, 1956, ACLU of Pennsylvania, URB 7, Urban Archives, Temple University, Philadelphia, PA (hereafter cited as Urban Archives).

3. Spencer Coxe to Jacob S. Richman, July 5, 1956, URB 7, Urban Archives.

4. Spencer Coxe to Clark Byse, October 25, 1956, URB 7, Urban Archives.

5. Spencer Coxe to Jeffrey Fuller, December 6, 1956, URB 7, Urban Archives.

6. Spencer Coxe to Ellery Schempp, December 6, 1956, National Archives, Philadelphia.

7. Spencer Coxe to Ellery Schempp, February 8, 1957, National Archives, Philadelphia.

8. *Bible Reading in Public Schools.*

9. Spencer Coxe to Ellery Schempp, March 4, 1957, National Archives, Philadelphia.

10. Spencer Coxe, office memorandum, March 11, 1957, box 1669, folder: 1957–60, American Civil Liberties Union Collection, Public Policy Papers, Department of Rare Books and Special Collections, Princeton University Library (hereafter cited as ACLU Collection, Princeton).

11. Bernard Wolfman, discussion with the author, Cambridge, MA, August 7, 2003.

12. Ibid.

13. Ellery Schempp, discussion, June 6, 1999.

14. Wolfman, discussion.

15. Ibid.

16. Ibid.

17. Ibid.

18. Donna Schempp, discussion with the author by telephone, September 19, 2003.

19. Ellery Schempp, discussion, June 6, 1999.

20. Roger Schempp, discussion with the author, Cherry Hill, NJ, December 7, 2003.

21. Wolfman, discussion.

22. Ibid.

23. Samuel Eliot Morison, *The Oxford History of the American People* (New York: Oxford University Press, 1965), 1084.

24. Ibid., 1075.

25. Wolfman, discussion.

26. "Law professor Clark Byse honored for 60 years of service," *Harvard University Gazette,* June 8, 2000, http://www.news.harvard.edu/gazette/2000/06.08/byse.html (accessed October 28, 2006).

27. Wolfman, discussion.

28. Clark Byse, discussion with the author by telephone, July 21, 2003.

29. Wolfman, discussion.

30. Ibid.

31. Ibid.

32. Theodore R. Mann, discussion with the author, Philadelphia, PA, November 5, 2003.

33. Ibid.

34. John A. Garraty and Mark C. Carnes, eds., *American National Biography,* vol. 17 (New York: Oxford University Press, 1999), 419–20.

35. *Cantwell v. Connecticut,* 310 U.S. 296 (1940); *Everson v. Board of Education of Ewing Township,* 330 U.S. 1 (1947).

36. Leo Pfeffer, *Church, State, and Freedom,* rev. ed. (Boston: Beacon, 1967), 728.

37. Mann, discussion, November 5, 2003.

38. Gregg Ivers, *To Build a Wall: American Jews and the Separation of*

Church and State (Charlottesville: University Press of Virginia, 1995), 21. Ivers provides a detailed account of the litigation strategy that the major Jewish organizations followed on church-state relations.

39. *McCollum*, 333 U.S. 203.

40. Ivers, *To Build a Wall*, 71–80.

41. Leo Pfeffer to David A. Sawyer, March 21, 1952, box 15, folder: Correspondence—1952 I, Leo Pfeffer Papers, Special Collections Research Center, Syracuse University Library (hereafter cited as Leo Pfeffer Papers).

42. *Zorach v. Clauson*, 343 U.S. 306 (1952).

43. Leo Pfeffer to Sidney Z. Vincent, August 21, 1956, box 15, folder: Correspondence 1954–1956, Leo Pfeffer Papers.

44. Leo Pfeffer to Shad Polier, memorandum, December 13, 1950, box 13, folder: Bible Reading in Schools—Doremus Case 1952, Leo Pfeffer Papers.

45. *Doremus v. Board of Education of the Borough of Hawthorne*, 5 N.J. 435, 453 (1950).

46. Leo Pfeffer to Shad Polier, memorandum, December 13, 1950.

47. Leo Pfeffer to Shad Polier, memorandum, March 14, 1951, box 20, folder: Bible Reading in Schools—Doremus Case 1952, Leo Pfeffer Papers.

48. Leo Pfeffer to Will Maslow, memorandum, June 7, 1951, box 20, folder: Bible Reading in Schools—Doremus Case 1952, Leo Pfeffer Papers.

49. Leo Pfeffer to Will Maslow, memorandum, July 17, 1951, box 20, folder: Bible Reading in Schools—Doremus Case 1952, Leo Pfeffer Papers.

50. Leo Pfeffer to Jerome Eisenberg, March 13, 1951, box 20, folder: Bible Reading in Schools—Doremus Case 1952, Leo Pfeffer Papers.

51. *Doremus v. Board of Education of the Borough of Hawthorne*, 342 U.S. 429 (1952).

52. Leo Pfeffer to Will Maslow, memorandum, February 16, 1956, box 13, folder: American Jewish Congress, 1954–1957, Leo Pfeffer Papers.

53. *Carden v. Bland*, 199 Tenn. 665 (1956).

54. Leo Pfeffer to Lou H. Silverman, March 23, 1956, box 23, folder: Prayer in School, Leo Pfeffer Papers.

55. Leo Pfeffer to C. Vernon Hines, April 5, 1956, box 23, folder: Prayer in School, Leo Pfeffer Papers.

56. Mann, discussion, November 5, 2003.

57. Ibid.

CHAPTER 4

1. Mann, discussion, November 5, 2003.

2. Leo Pfeffer to Aaron L. Fish, memorandum, February 14, 1956, box 23, folder: Prayer in School—Schempp I, Leo Pfeffer Papers.

3. Theodore Mann to Shad Polier, August 1, 1957, box 23, folder: Prayer in Schools—Schempp, Leo Pfeffer Papers.

4. Shad Polier to Theodore Mann, February 24, 1958, box 23, folder: Prayer in School—Schempp I, Leo Pfeffer Papers.

5. Leo Pfeffer to Shad Polier, memorandum, April 15, 1958, box 23, folder: Prayer in Schools—Schempp, Leo Pfeffer Papers.

6. Theodore R. Mann, discussion with the author, Philadelphia, PA, July 23, 2004.

7. 28 U.S.C. 2281 (repealed 1976).

8. Spencer Coxe to Rowland Watts, May 16, 1957, box 1669, folder: 1957–60, ACLU Collection, Princeton.

9. Mann, discussion, November 5, 2003.

10. Mann, discussion, July 23, 2004.

11. Theodore Mann to Shad Polier, August 1, 1957.

12. Mann, discussion, November 5, 2003.

13. Mann, discussion, July 23, 2004

14. Mann, discussion, November 5, 2003.

15. Mann, discussion, July 23, 2004.

16. Ellery Schempp, undated memorandum, September 1957, Schempp Family Papers, 43.

17. Ibid.

18. Ellery Schempp, discussion, June 6, 1999.

19. Theodore Mann to Leo Pfeffer, November 21, 1957, box 23, folder: Prayer in Schools—Schempp, Leo Pfeffer Papers.

20. Theodore Mann to Henry W. Sawyer III, November 21, 1957, box 23, folder: Prayer in Schools—Schempp, Leo Pfeffer Papers.

21. Spencer Coxe, discussion, September 17, 2003.

22. Mann, discussion, November 5, 2003.

23. Nick Ravo, "Henry Sawyer 3d Dies at 80; Lawyer in Landmark Cases," *New York Times*, August 5, 1999, A21.

24. *Deutch v. U.S.*, 367 U.S. 456 (1961).

25. *Lemon v. Kurtzman*, 403 U.S. 602 (1971).

26. Arlin M. Adams, "In Memoriam: Henry W. Sawyer, III," *University of Pennsylvania Law Review* 148 (1999): 3–4.

27. Theodore Mann to Shad Polier, August 1, 1957.

28. Theodore Mann to Leo Pfeffer, November 21, 1957.

29. Theodore Mann to Leo Pfeffer, December 27, 1957, box 23, folder: Prayer in School—Schempp I, Leo Pfeffer Papers.

30. Leo Pfeffer to Sam Gaber, memorandum, March 27, 1958, box 23, folder: Prayer in Schools—Pfeffer, Leo Pfeffer Papers.

31. Leo Pfeffer to Shad Polier, memorandum, April 15, 1958.

32. Complaint, U.S. District Court for the Eastern District of Pennsylvania, February 14, 1958, *Abington v. Schempp*, Transcript of Record, *Records and Briefs of the U.S. Supreme Court*, 374:1, Law Library of Congress.

33. Ibid.

34. Answer, U.S. District Court for the Eastern District of Pennsylva-

nia, April 25, 1958, *Abington v. Schempp*, Transcript of Record, *Records and Briefs of the U.S. Supreme Court*, 374:6, Law Library of Congress.

CHAPTER 5

1. Eusebius, *The History of the Church from Christ to Constantine*, trans. G. A. Williamson (New York: New York University Press, 1966), 8:337–44.

2. Tacitus, *Annals*, ed. C. D. Fisher (Oxford, 1906), 15:44, quoted in Brian Moynahan, *The Faith: A History of Christianity* (New York: Doubleday, 2002), 73.

3. Moynahan, *Faith*, 89–93.

4. John T. Noonan, Jr., and Edward McGlynn Gaffney, Jr., *Religious Freedom: History, Cases, and Other Materials on the Interaction of Religion and Government* (New York: Foundation Press, 2001), 40–41.

5. Pfeffer, *Church, State, and Freedom*, 14.

6. Noonan and Gaffney, *Religious Freedom*, 40–41.

7. Moynahan, *Faith*, 278.

8. Ibid., 354–55.

9. John A. Garraty and Peter Gay, eds., *The Columbia History of the World* (New York: Harper and Row, 1972), 536.

10. Moynahan, *Faith*, 473–78.

11. Sidney E. Mead, *The Lively Experiment: The Shaping of Christianity in America* (New York: Harper and Row, 1963), 2.

12. English Bill of Rights of 1689, the Avalon Project at Yale Law School, http://www.yale.edu/lawweb/avalon/england.htm (accessed October 20, 2006).

13. Edwin S. Gaustad and Leigh E. Schmidt, *The Religious History of America: The Heart of the American Story from Colonial Times to Today* (San Francisco: Harper San Francisco, 2002), 52—-54; Sydney E. Ahlstrom, *A Religious History of the American People* (New Haven: Yale University Press, 1972), 124–34.

14. Moynahan, *Faith*, 572–73.

15. Leonard W. Levy, *The Establishment Clause: Religion and the First Amendment* (New York: Macmillan, 1986), 1–9.

16. Ibid., 15–20.

17. Ibid., 20–24.

18. Ibid., 10–14.

19. Ibid., 9–10.

20. Noonan and Gaffney, *Religious Freedom*, 124–29.

21. Gaustad and Schmidt, *Religious History of America*, 84–85.

22. Ibid., 86–94.

CHAPTER 6

1. Gaustad and Schmidt, *Religious History of America*, 43–44.

2. Ibid., 95–101.

3. Ibid., 103–10.

4. Ibid., 111–14.

5. Ibid., 58–61.

6. Ahlstrom, *Religious History of the American People,* 263.

7. Mead, *Lively Experiment,* 35.

8. John Locke, *A Letter concerning Toleration* (1688), in Noonan and Gaffney, *Religious Freedom,* 139–55.

9. Pfeffer, *Church, State, and Freedom,* 107–8.

10. Noonan and Gaffney, *Religious Freedom,* 171–73.

11. Levy, *Establishment Clause,* 54–55.

12. James Madison, *Memorial and Remonstrance against Religious Assessments* (1785), in Noonan and Gaffney, *Religious Freedom,* 173–78.

13. Thomas Jefferson, Bill for Establishing Religious Freedom (1779), in Noonan and Gaffney, *Religious Freedom,* 169–70.

14. Levy, *Establishment Clause,* 26.

15. Ibid., 38.

16. Anson Phelps Stokes, *Church and State in the United States* (New York: Harper and Brothers, 1950), 1:525–27.

17. Noonan and Gaffney, *Religious Freedom,* 188–91.

18. Joseph Story, *Commentaries on the Constitution of the United States* (Boston: Hilliard, Gray, 1833), 3:705.

19. Stokes, *Church and State in the United States,* 1:524–26.

20. Levy, *Establishment Clause,* 65–67.

21. Roger Finke and Rodney Stark, *The Churching of America, 1776–1990: Winners and Losers in Our Religious Economy* (New Brunswick, NJ: Rutgers University Press, 1992), 15.

22. Adam Smith, *An Inquiry into the Nature and Causes of the Wealth of Nations,* ed. R. H. Campbell, A. S. Skinner, and W. B. Todd (Indianapolis: Liberty Fund, 1981), 2:789–97.

23. James Madison, Federalist Paper No. 51, February 6, 1788, in *James Madison: Writings* (New York: Literary Classics of the United States, 1999), 297.

24. Gaustad and Schmidt, *Religious History of America,* 146.

25. Mark A. Noll, *Protestants in America* (New York: Oxford University Press, 2000), 60.

26. Gaustad and Schmidt, *Religious History of America,* 152–59, 177–79.

27. Leonard Dinnerstein and David M. Reimers, *Ethnic Americans: A History of Immigration,* 4th ed. (New York: Columbia University Press, 1999), 20.

28. Roger Daniels, *Coming to America: A History of Immigration and Ethnicity in American Life* (New York: Harper Perennial, 1991), 126–35.

29. Ibid., 130, 137–38.

30. Ibid., 188–89.

31. Ibid., 145–53.

32. Ibid., 223.
33. Gaustad and Schmidt, *Religious History of America*, 149–50.
34. Daniels, *Coming to America*, 211.
35. Ibid., 202.
36. Mead, *Lively Experiment*, 107.
37. Gaustad and Schmidt, *Religious History of America*, 277–79.
38. Ibid., 279–80.

CHAPTER 7

1. Carl F. Kaestle, *Pillars of the Republic: Common Schools and American Society, 1780–1860* (New York: Hill and Wang, 1983), 3–4; William Kailer Dunn, *What Happened to Religious Education? The Decline of Religious Teaching in the Public Elementary School, 1776–1861* (Baltimore: Johns Hopkins University Press, 1958), 13–17.
2. Clifton Johnson, *Old-Time Schools and School-Books* (New York: Dover, 1963), 2.
3. Kaestle, *Pillars of the Republic*, 13–19.
4. Ibid., 13, 30–31.
5. Dunn, *What Happened to Religious Education?* 16.
6. R. R. Robinson, *Two Centuries of Change in the Content of School Readers* (Nashville: George Peabody College for Teachers, 1930), 10.
7. Ellwood P. Cubberley, *Readings in Public Education in the United States: A Collection of Sources and Readings to Illustrate the History of Educational Practice and Progress in the United States* (Boston: Houghton Mifflin, 1934), 30–31.
8. Robinson, *Two Centuries of Change*, 9.
9. Dunn, *What Happened to Religious Education?* 18.
10. Johnson, *Old-Time Schools and School-Books*, 101.
11. Ibid., 11–12.
12. Minutes of the Orphan Masters of New Amsterdam, trans. B. Fernow (New York, 1907), 2:115, in Cubberley, *Readings in Public Education*, 66.
13. Julius Gay, *Schools and Schoolmasters in Farmington in the Oldern Time, Connecticut School Document* 13 (1892), in Cubberley, *Readings in Public Education*, 54–55.
14. Thomas J. Wertenbaker, *Fiftieth Anniversary Volume, N.E.A.* (1906), 455–56, in Cubberley, *Readings in Public Education*, 78–80.
15. Advertisement in the *Western Carolinian* (Centre, Iredell County, NC), November 8, 1822, in Cubberley, *Readings in Public Education*, 138.
16. Jean Barth Toll and Michael J. Schwager, ed., *Montgomery County: The Second Hundred Years* (Montgomery County Federation of Historical Societies, 1983), 5.
17. Theodore W. Bean, ed., *History of Montgomery County Pennsylvania* (Philadelphia: Everts and Peck, 1884), 684.
18. Ibid., 678.

19. Frances M. Briggs, "The Abington Presbyterian Church," *Old York Road Historical Society Bulletin* 25 (July 1964): 4–6. See also Roland Bruce Lutz, "Old Abington Church and Her Children," *Old York Road Historical Society Bulletin* 2 (October 1938); Guy S. Klett, "Presbyterian Beginnings along the Neshaminy," *Old York Road Historical Society Bulletin* 4 (1940): 40–49.

20. Horace Mather Lippincott, "The Old York Road," *Old York Road Historical Society Bulletin* 1 (October 1937): 5.

21. Toll and Schwager, *Montgomery County*, 11.

22. Bean, *History of Montgomery County*, 393.

23. Ibid., 394.

24. Ibid., 395.

25. John A. Nietz, "Some Findings from Analyses of Old Textbooks," *History of Education Journal* 3 (spring 1952): 79–87, in Dunn, *What Happened to Religious Education?* 76–77.

26. Charles Kenneth Shannon, "The Religious Content of Secondary School American History Textbooks, 1865 to 1935: An Historical Analysis" (PhD diss., Pennsylvania State University, 1995), 6.

27. Robinson, *Two Centuries of Change*, 11.

28. Noah Webster, letter, in Barnard's *American Journal of Education* 26:195–96, in Cubberley, *Readings in Public Education*, 266.

29. Johnson, *Old-Time Schools and School-Books*, 26–28.

30. John A. Nietz, *Old Textbooks* (Pittsburgh: University of Pittsburgh Press, 1961), 26–27, 45–47.

31. Lawrence A. Cremin, *The American Common School: An Historic Conception* (New York: Columbia University, 1951), 182–83.

32. Johnson, *Old-Time Schools and School-Books*, 69–99.

33. Charles Carpenter, *History of American Schoolbooks* (Philadelphia: University of Pennsylvania Press, 1963), 79–85.

34. Raymond Grove Hughes, "An Analysis of the Fourth, Fifth, and Sixth McGuffey Readers" (PhD diss., University of Pittsburgh, 1943), 63–68.

35. Ibid., 80–81.

36. Preface to *The English School Master* (1635), quoted in Robinson, *Two Centuries of Change*, 7.

37. Robinson, *Two Centuries of Change*, 11–14.

38. Ibid., 26.

39. Shannon, "Religious Content of Secondary School American History Textbooks," 155, 189.

40. A. B. Berard, *School History of the United States*, rev. ed. (Philadelphia: H. Cowperthwaite, 1863), 85, quoted in Shannon, "Religious Content of Secondary School American History Textbooks," 159.

41. Johnson, *Old-Time Schools and School-Books*, 374–79.

42. Ruth Miller Elson, *Guardians of Tradition: American Schoolbooks of the Nineteenth Century* (Lincoln: University of Nebraska Press, 1964), 62, 194–96, 204–6.

43. Ibid., 17.

44. Quoted in Karl Kenneth Wilson, "Historical Survey of the Religious Content of American Geography Textbooks from 1784 to 1895" (PhD diss., University of Pittsburgh, 1951), 17–18, 35–36.

45. Nietz, *Old Textbooks*, 212–13.

46. Hermann Mann, *The Material Creation: Being a Compendious System of Universal Geography and Popular Astronomy* (Dedham, MA: W. H. Mann, 1818), 293, in Elson, *Guardians of Tradition*, 50.

47. Mead, *Lively Experiment*, 66.

48. Laws of Massachusetts, March 1, 1827, chap. 143, sec. 3, quoted in Robert Michaelsen, *Piety in the Public School* (London: MacMillan, 1970), 72.

49. Horace Mann, *Common School Journal*, vol. 8 (1846), in Horace Mann, *Life and Works of Horace Mann*, vol. 5 (Boston: Lee and Shepard, 1891), 162.

50. Horace Mann, *Twelfth Annual Report* (1848), in Lawrence A. Cremin, ed., *The Republic and the School: Horace Mann on the Education of Free Men* (New York: Teachers College Press, 1957), 102.

51. Horace Mann, *Sequel to the So Called Correspondence between the Rev. M. H. Smith and Horace Mann* (Boston: William B. Fowle, 1847), 41.

52. Bean, *History of Montgomery County*, 396.

53. Ibid., 397.

54. Ibid.

55. Daniel Richard Unger, "The Use of the Bible in Pennsylvania Public Schools: 1834–1963" (PhD diss., University of Pittsburgh, 1969), 113.

56. Ulysses S. Grant, Address to the Army of the Tennessee at Des Moines, Iowa, September 29, 1875, in Stokes, *Church and State in the United States*, 2:68.

57. Stokes, *Church and State in the United States*, 2:68–69.

58. Michaelsen, *Piety in the Public School*, 68–69.

CHAPTER 8

1. The account of Philadelphia's Bible conflict is taken from Michael Feldberg, *The Philadelphia Riots of 1844: A Study of Ethnic Conflict* (Westport, CT: Greenwood, 1975).

2. Michaelsen, *Piety in the Public School*, 89.

3. Feldberg, *Philadelphia Riots*, 20, 48, 90.

4. Ibid., 91–95.

5. Ibid., 109–11.

6. Ibid., 111–15.

7. Ibid., 138–59, 172.

8. Pfeffer, *Church, State, and Freedom*, 438.

9. *Donahoe v. Richards*, 38 Me. 379 (Maine Supreme Judicial Court, Eastern District, County of Hancock, 1854).

10. Ibid., at 401, 403–4.

11. Pfeffer, *Church, State, and Freedom*, 438.

12. *Commonwealth v. Cooke*, 7 Am. L. Reg. 417–19, 421 (1859).

13. Ibid., at 423.

14. Ibid., at 425–26.

15. Pfeffer, *Church, State, and Freedom*, 437.

16. James W. Fraser, *Between Church and State: Religion and Public Education in a Multicultural America* (New York: St. Martin's, 1999), 51, 54.

17. Ibid., 54–55.

18. Ibid., 56–57.

19. Francis Michael Perko, "A Time to Favor Zion: A Case Study of Religion as a Force in American Educational Development, 1830–1870" (PhD diss., Stanford University, 1981), 76–81.

20. Michaelsen, *Piety in the Public School*, 89–98.

21. Perko, "A Time to Favor Zion," 101.

22. Ibid., 126–27.

23. Michaelsen, *Piety in the Public School*, 92–93.

24. Ibid., 94–95.

25. *Minor v. Board of Education of Cincinnati*, unpublished opinion, Cincinnati Superior Court, 1870, quoted in *Bible in the Public Schools* (Cincinnati: Robert Clarke, 1870), 414.

26. Ibid., 408.

27. *Board of Education of Cincinnati v. Minor*, 23 Ohio St. 211, 240 (S.C. Ohio 1872).

28. Ibid., at 253.

29. Ibid.

30. Michaelsen, *Piety in the Public School*, 116–17.

31. Kaestle, *Pillars of the Republic*, 170.

32. *Fifteenth Annual Report of the Common Schools of New Hampshire* (Concord: Henry McFarland, 1861), 65–66, in Dunn, *What Happened to Religious Education?* 289–93.

33. "School Committees' Reports," in *Twenty-fifth Annual Report of the Massachusetts Board of Education* (Boston: William White, 1860), 81, in Dunn, *What Happened to Religious Education?* 292.

34. Michaelsen, *Piety in the Public School*, 150.

35. Robinson, *Two Centuries of Change*, 11, 18.

36. Ibid., 26.

37. Ibid., 37–39.

38. Ibid., 47.

39. Ibid., 63.

40. Hughes, "Analysis of the Fourth, Fifth, and Sixth McGuffey Readers," 64–66.

41. Ibid., 80–81.

42. Dunn, *What Happened to Religious Education?* 289.

43. Ibid., 307.

44. Dinnerstein and Reimers, *Ethnic Americans,* 49–53.

45. Daniels, *Coming to America,* 291–92.

46. Ibid., 288, 308.

47. U.S. Bureau of the Census, *We the People: Hispanics in the United States,* Census 2000 Special Reports (Washington, DC, 2004).

48. Daniels, *Coming to America,* 334.

49. U.S. Bureau of the Census, *We the People: Asians in the United States,* Census 2000 Special Reports (Washington, DC, December 2004).

50. Diana L. Eck, *A New Religious America: How a "Christian Country" Has Become the World's Most Religiously Diverse Nation* (New York: Harper-Collins, 2001), 3–4.

51. Ibid.

52. Plaintiffs' Memorandum on the Law, Leo Pfeffer of Counsel, December 1960, *Chamberlin v. Dade County Board of Public Instruction, Resnick v. Dade County Board of Public Instruction,* Circuit Court of the Eleventh Judicial Circuit, 23, brief on file, box 2, folder: Friend of the Court Briefs, Leo Pfeffer Papers (hereafter cited as Plaintiffs' Memorandum on the Law, *Chamberlin*).

53. Daniel Richard Unger, "The Use of the Bible in Pennsylvania Public Schools: 1834–1963," 113, 156–57, 183–84.

54. Commonwealth of Pennsylvania, Department of Public Instruction, *Forty-Second Annual Report of the Superintendent of Public Instruction* (Harrisburg: B. F. Meyers, 1875), quoted in John William Lowe, Jr., "The Holy Experiment and Education: The Public School Bible Reading Legislation of 1913 in Pennsylvania" (PhD diss., Columbia University Teachers College, 1987), 185.

55. Lowe, "The Holy Experiment and Education," 149.

56. Ibid., 158.

57. Pennsylvania General Assembly, *Legislative Journal,* May 15, 1911, 2495, quoted in Lowe, "The Holy Experiment and Education," 83.

58. Ibid., 81–82.

59. Lowe, "The Holy Experiment and Education," 112, 152.

60. Richard B. Dierenfield, *Religion in American Public Schools* (Washington, DC: Public Affairs Press, 1962), 21.

61. "Bible Reading and Religious Exercises in the Public Schools," *Report of the Commissioner of Education* (Washington, DC: U.S. Office of Education, 1903), 2:2445, quoted in Michaelsen, *Piety in the Public School,* 168.

62. Dierenfield, *Religion in American Public Schools,* 50–51.

63. Ibid., 53–56.

CHAPTER 9

1. Seymour I. Toll, *A Judge Uncommon: A Life of John Biggs, Jr.* (Philadelphia: Legal Communications, 1993), 9–17. Biographical information about Biggs comes from Toll's book, unless otherwise noted.

2. Toll, *A Judge Uncommon,* 26.

3. Arthur Mizener, *The Far Side of Paradise: A Biography of F. Scott Fitzgerald* (Boston: Houghton Mifflin, 1951), 34.

4. Ibid., 66.

5. Joan Cook, "John Biggs Jr. Dies; On 3d Circuit Court," *New York Times,* April 17, 1979, B17.

6. Toll, *A Judge Uncommon,* 251.

7. The case on the free exercise clause is *Cantwell v. Connecticut,* 310 U.S. 296. The case on the establishment clause is *Everson v. Board of Education of Ewing Township,* 330 U.S. 1.

8. *Annals of the Congress of the United States,* 1:757–59, cited in Noonan and Gaffney, *Religious Freedom,* 198.

9. *Everson,* 330 U.S. at 14–15.

10. Ibid., at 9.

11. Madison, *Memorial and Remonstrance,* in Noonan and Gaffney, *Religious Freedom,* 173–78.

12. *Everson,* 330 U.S. at 15–16.

13. Ibid., at 19 (Justice Jackson dissenting).

14. Ibid., at 24.

15. Ibid., at 37 (Justice Rutledge dissenting).

16. Ibid., at 31–32.

17. *McCollum,* 333 U.S. at 210.

18. Ibid., at 228 (Justice Frankfurter concurring).

19. *Zorach,* 343 U.S. at 315.

20. Ibid., at 324–25 (Justice Jackson dissenting).

21. Nathan C. Schaeffer, ed., *Bible Readings for Schools* (New York: American Book Company, 1897), 3.

22. *Act of May 20, 1913,* Public Law 226.

23. *Act of March 10, 1949,* Public Law 30, *Public School Code of March 10, 1949,* sec. 1516, as amended May 9, 1949, by Public Law 939, 24 *Purdon's Pa. Stats. Ann.,* sec. 15–1516.

24. Spencer Coxe to Rowland Watts, June 5, 1958, box 1669, folder: 1957–60, ACLU Collection, Princeton.

25. *Tudor v. Board of Education of Rutherford,* 14 N.J. 31, 35 (1953).

26. Ibid., at 48.

27. Ellery Schempp, e-mail message to author, December 16, 2004.

28. Testimony of Ellery Schempp, U.S. District Court for the Eastern

District of Pennsylvania, August 5, 1958, *Abington v. Schempp,* Transcript of Record, *Records and Briefs of the U.S. Supreme Court,* 374:9–30, Law Library of Congress.

29. Ellery Schempp, discussion, April 17, 2003.

30. Testimony of Ellery Schempp, at 17–18.

31. Ibid., at 19–20.

32. Ibid., at 24.

33. Ibid.

34. Testimony of Edward Schempp, U.S. District Court for the Eastern District of Pennsylvania, August 5, 1958, *Abington v. Schempp,* Transcript of Record, *Records and Briefs of the U.S. Supreme Court,* 374:30–34, Law Library of Congress.

35. Ibid., at 30–32.

36. Testimony of Roger Schempp, at 75–79.

37. Ibid., at 78–79.

38. Testimony of Donna Schempp, at 79–86.

39. Ibid., at 82–83.

40. Ibid., at 85.

CHAPTER 10

1. *Minor v. Board of Education of Cincinnati,* quoted in *Bible in the Public Schools,* 408.

2. *People ex rel. Ring v. Board of Education of District 24,* 245 Ill. 334, 339 (1910).

3. Ibid., at 345.

4. Ibid., at 346.

5. Ibid., at 349–50.

6. Ibid., at 360–61 (Justices Hand and Cartwright dissenting).

7. *Hackett v. Brooksville Graded School District,* 120 Ky. 608, 616 (1905).

8. Ibid., at 617.

9. *Hart v. School District of the Borough of Sharpsville,* 2 Chester County (Pa.) Reports 521, 522 (1885).

10. Ibid., at 528.

11. *Stevenson v. Hanyon,* 7 Pa. District Reports (Pa.) 585 (1898).

12. Ibid., at 590.

13. Testimony of Solomon Grayzel, U.S. District Court for the Eastern District of Pennsylvania, August 5 and 6, 1958, *Abington v. Schempp,* Transcript of Record, *Records and Briefs of the U.S. Supreme Court,* 374:34–75, Law Library of Congress.

14. Jewish Theological Seminary, Archives, Papers of Conservative Rabbis and Synagogues, Solomon Grayzel, Biographical Note, http://www.jtsa.edu/research/ratner/conrec/pp_grayzelsolomon.shtml (accessed October 28, 2006).

15. Testimony of Luther Allan Weigle, U.S. District Court for the Eastern District of Pennsylvania, November 25, 1958, *Abington v. Schempp,* Transcript of Record, *Records and Briefs of the U.S. Supreme Court,* 374:134–72, Law Library of Congress.

16. Ibid., at 134–40, 155.

17. Testimony of Grayzel, August 5, at 42–43.

18. Ibid., at 43–44.

19. Ibid., at 52–53.

20. Testimony of Grayzel, August 6, at 60.

21. Testimony of Grayzel, August 5, at 45–46.

22. Ibid., at 48–49.

23. Ibid., at 50.

24. Ibid., at 50–51.

25. Testimony of Grayzel, August 6, at 65–66.

26. Ibid., at 67–68.

27. Testimony of Weigle, at 144.

28. Ibid., at 144–45.

29. Ibid., at 146–47.

30. Ibid., at 149.

31. Ibid., at 149–50.

32. Ibid., at 152–53.

33. Ibid., at 154.

34. Ibid., at 156–57.

35. Ibid., at 157–60.

36. Ibid., at 158–59.

37. Ibid., at 161.

38. Ibid., at 161–62.

39. Ibid., at 162–63.

40. Ibid., at 164–66.

CHAPTER 11

1. *Engel v. Vitale,* 10 N.Y. 2d 174, 179 (1961).

2. *Engel v. Vitale,* 191 N.Y.S. 2d 453, 459–60 (Supreme Court of N.Y., Nassau County, 1959).

3. Brief of Respondents before the Supreme Court of the United States, *Engel v. Vitale,* 9, contained in Philip B. Kurland and Gerhard Caspar, eds., *Landmark Briefs and Arguments of the Supreme Court of the United States: Constitutional Law* (Arlington, VA: University Publications of America, 1975), 56:812.

4. Leo Pfeffer to Will Maslow, memorandum, June 3, 1952, box 23, folder: Prayer in Schools, 1961, Leo Pfeffer Papers.

5. Transcript of "Storm over the Supreme Court," *CBS News,* March 13, 1963, 45, Tarleton Law Library, University of Texas at Austin.

6. Ibid., 46–47.

7. Ibid., 48.

8. Leo Pfeffer to Shad Polier, memorandum, November 24, 1958, box 23, folder: Prayer in Public School, Leo Pfeffer Papers.

9. Leo Pfeffer to Shad Polier, memorandum, December 18, 1958, box 23, folder: Prayer in Schools 1961, Leo Pfeffer Papers.

10. Leo Pfeffer to Sam Gaber, memorandum, February 2, 1959, box 23, folder: Prayer in Public Schools 1961, Leo Pfeffer Papers.

11. Leo Pfeffer to Sam Gaber, memorandum, March 27, 1958, box 23, folder: Prayer in Schools—Pfeffer, Leo Pfeffer Papers.

12. Leo Pfeffer to Will Maslow, memorandum, November 26, 1958, box 23, folder: Prayer in Schools—Schempp I, Leo Pfeffer Papers.

13. Hearings, U.S. District Court for the Eastern District of Pennsylvania, March 12, 1959, 302, *Schempp v. School District of Abington,* National Archives, Philadelphia.

14. Ibid., 301.

15. Ibid., 302–3.

16. Ibid., 304–5.

17. Ibid., 304.

18. *McCollum,* 333 U.S. 203.

19. Hearings, March 12, 1959, 315.

20. Ibid., 323.

21. Ibid., 324.

22. Ibid., 327.

23. Ibid., 329.

24. Ibid., 336.

25. Ibid., 331.

26. Ibid., 356.

27. Ibid., 367–71.

28. Toll, *A Judge Uncommon,* 322–23.

29. Hearings, March 12, 1959, 373–74.

30. Ibid., 380.

31. Ibid., 387.

32. Ibid., 394–95.

33. Ibid., 397–400.

34. Ibid., 402–3.

35. Ibid., 409–10.

36. Ibid., 411–13.

37. *McCollum,* 333 U.S. 203.

38. Hearings, March 12, 1959, 414–16.

39. Ibid., 423–25.

40. Ibid., 425–26.

41. Ibid., 428–30.

42. Ibid., 434.

43. Edward Schempp, memorandum, March 12, 1959, Schempp Family Papers, 40.

CHAPTER 12

1. Pfeffer, *Church, State, and Freedom,* 487.

2. Haskell L. Lazere to Leo Pfeffer, memorandum, April 3, 1959, box 22, folder: Prayer in School, Leo Pfeffer Papers.

3. Herbert L. Heiken to Leo Pfeffer, April 18, 1959, box 22, folder: Prayer in School, Leo Pfeffer Papers.

4. Leo Pfeffer to Herbert L. Heiken, April 20, 1959, box 22, folder: Prayer in School, Leo Pfeffer Papers.

5. Haskell L. Lazere to Isaac Toubin, High Salpeter, Leo Pfeffer, and Will Maslow, memorandum, May 11, 1959, box 22, folder: Separation of Church and State, Leo Pfeffer Papers.

6. Haskell L. Lazere to Seymour Samet, July 3, 1959, box 12, folder: Chamberlin, Leo Pfeffer Papers.

7. Haskell L. Lazere to Leo Pfeffer, memorandum, September 8, 1959, box 12, folder: Chamberlin, Leo Pfeffer Papers.

8. Haskell L. Lazere to Leo Pfeffer, memorandum, May 17, 1960, box 12, folder: Chamberlin, Leo Pfeffer Papers.

9. *Engel v. Vitale,* 191 N.Y.S. 2d 453.

10. Ibid., at 479.

11. Throughout this book, the author refers to this litigant as Madalyn Murray, for consistency with the name of the legal case she brought and the names of her children.

12. Jane Howard, "Madalyn Murray: The Most Hated Woman in America," *Life,* June 19, 1964.

13. Brian F. Le Beau, *The Atheist: Madalyn Murray O'Hair* (New York: New York University Press, 2003), 19–21.

14. Ibid., 25–28.

15. Howard, "Madalyn Murray."

16. Le Beau, *The Atheist,* 29–34.

17. Ibid., 35–39.

18. William J. Murray, *My Life without God* (Nashville: Thomas Nelson, 1982), 17–18.

19. Madalyn Murray O'Hair, *An Atheist Epic,* 2nd ed. (Austin: American Atheist Press, 1989), 5.

20. Ibid., 8–9.

21. Murray, *My Life without God,* 46–48.

CHAPTER 13

1. *Schempp v. School District of Abington Township, Pennsylvania,* 177 F. Supp. 398, 404 (E.D. Pa. 1959).

2. Ibid.

3. *Everson,* 330 U.S. at 15.

4. *Schempp v. School District,* 177 F. Supp. at 405.

5. *McCollum,* 333 U.S. 203.

6. *Schempp v. School District,* 177 F. Supp. at 405.

7. Ibid., at 406–7.

8. Ibid., at 407.

9. John F. Morrison, "School Bible Reading Ban Appeal Likely," *Evening Bulletin,* September 17, 1959, Schempp Family Papers, 16.

10. "Militant Atheists Called Threat to Christian Rights," unidentified newspaper article, Schempp Family Papers, 77.

11. Morrison, "School Bible Reading Ban Appeal Likely."

12. George Riley, "Presbytery Backs School Bible Reading," *Evening Bulletin,* October 14, 1959, Schempp Family Papers, 71.

13. "Bell Co-Sponsors Bill to Preserve Bible in Schools," *County Leader,* October 22, 1959, Schempp Family Papers, 96.

14. Associated Press, *Philadelphia Inquirer,* December 29, 1959, Schempp Family Papers, 103.

15. "Bible Reading, Prayer Barred by U.S. Court," *Philadelphia Inquirer,* September 17, 1959, Schempp Family Papers, 15.

16. Morrison, "School Bible Reading Ban Appeal Likely."

17. H. B. Sissel, *Abington Life,* September 1959, Schempp Family Papers, 21.

18. "Abington Plans to Appeal Case to Supreme Court," *Willow Grove Guide,* October 1, 1959, 1 Schempp Family Papers, 22.

19. Ibid.

20. Various newspaper accounts, October 1959, Schempp Family Papers, 18, 19.

21. Ellery Schempp, discussion, April 17, 2003.

22. Donna Schempp, discussion, September 19, 2003.

23. Roger Schempp, discussion, December 7, 2003.

24. Various letters, Schempp Family Papers.

25. Ellery Schempp, discussion, June 6, 1999.

26. "Bible 'Unclean,' 'Unfit for Children,' Meeting Is Told," *County Leader,* October 22, 1959, Schempp Family Papers, 95.

27. "Bell Co-Sponsors Bill to Preserve Bible in Schools," *County Leader,* October 22, 1959, Schempp Family Papers, 96.

28. Edward L. Schempp to *Philadelphia Daily News,* September 23, 1959, Schempp Family Papers, 85.

29. Notice of Appeal to the Supreme Court of the United States, U.S. District Court for the Eastern District of Pennsylvania, November 12, 1959, *Schempp v. School District of Abington,* National Archives, Philadelphia.

30. "Bible Reading Law Modified," *Evening Bulletin,* December 18, 1959, Schempp Family Papers, 170; *School District of Abington v. Schempp,* 364 U.S. 298 (1960).

CHAPTER 14

1. Pfeffer, *Church, State, and Freedom,* 488–90.

2. Testimony of Donald Crocker, Circuit Court of the Eleventh Judicial Circuit in Dade County, Florida, July 20, 1960, 226–28, box 5, folder: Court Transcripts VI, *Chamberlin v. Dade County Board of Public Instruction, Resnick v. Dade County Board of Public Instruction,* transcript of testimony, Leo Pfeffer Papers (hereafter cited as *Chamberlin* transcript).

3. Testimony of Marcia Robinson, Circuit Court of the Eleventh Judicial Circuit in Dade County, Florida, July 21, 1960, 341, box 5, folder: Court Transcripts V, *Chamberlin* transcript.

4. Plaintiffs' Memorandum on the Facts, Leo Pfeffer of Counsel, December 1960, *Chamberlin v. Dade County Board of Public Instruction, Resnick v. Dade County Board of Public Instruction,* Circuit Court of the Eleventh Judicial Circuit, 8–12, brief on file, box 2, folder: Friend of the Court Briefs, Leo Pfeffer Papers (hereafter cited as Plaintiffs' Memorandum on the Facts, *Chamberlin*). See also testimony of Thomas A. Teasley, Circuit Court of the Eleventh Judicial Circuit in Dade County, Florida, July 21, 1960, 371, box 5, folder: Court Transcripts V, *Chamberlin* transcript.

5. Plaintiffs' Memorandum on the Facts, *Chamberlin,* 7–8. See also testimony of Robinson, 341; testimony of Elsie Thorner, Circuit Court of the Eleventh Judicial Circuit in Dade County, Florida, July 18, 1960, 18–19, box 6, folder: Court Transcripts, *Chamberlin* transcript.

6. Plaintiffs' Memorandum on the Facts, *Chamberlin,* 8–10. See also testimony of Michael M. Landis, Circuit Court of the Eleventh Judicial Circuit in Dade County, Florida, July 18, 1960, 37, and testimony of Katherine Moore, Circuit Court of the Eleventh Judicial Circuit in Dade County, Florida, July 18, 1960, 77, box 6, folder: Court Transcripts, *Chamberlin* transcript.

7. Plaintiffs' Memorandum on the Facts, *Chamberlin,* 9–10.

8. Ibid., 9.

9. *Florida Statutes* 231.09, cited in Plaintiffs' Memorandum on the Facts, *Chamberlin,* 2.

10. Testimony of Joe Hall, Circuit Court of the Eleventh Judicial Circuit in Dade County, Florida, July 19, 1960, 180, box 5, folder: Court Transcripts V, *Chamberlin* transcript.

11. Testimony of Lois Milman, Circuit Court of the Eleventh Judicial Circuit in Dade County, Florida, July 19, 1960, 110, box 5, folder: Court Transcripts V, *Chamberlin* transcript.

12. Testimony of Hall, 150.

13. Plaintiffs' Memorandum on the Facts, *Chamberlin,* 6. See also testimony of Milman, 110–11; testimony of Carol Robin, Circuit Court of the Eleventh Judicial Circuit in Dade County, Florida, July 19, 1960, 129–30, box 5, folder: Court Transcripts V, *Chamberlin* transcript.

14. Testimony of Thalia Stern, Circuit Court of the Eleventh Judicial Circuit in Dade County, Florida, July 18, 1960, 58, box 6, folder: Court Transcripts, *Chamberlin* transcript; testimony of Milman, 123.

15. Plaintiffs' Memorandum on the Facts, *Chamberlin*, 15. See also testimony of Hall, 178–79.

16. Testimony of Landis, 35.

17. Testimony of Teasley, 366.

18. Testimony of Teasley, 367.

19. Plaintiffs' Memorandum on the Facts, *Chamberlin*, 16.

20. Ibid.

21. Testimony of Robinson, 354–55.

22. Testimony of Landis, 36.

23. Plaintiffs' Memorandum on the Facts, *Chamberlin*, 4.

24. Ibid.

25. Ibid., 4–5.

26. Ibid., 14.

27. "Dr. Pfeffer Tells of Miami Case," *St. Paul Jewish News*, November 18, 1960, box 22, folder: Prayer in the Schools—Miami 1962, Leo Pfeffer Papers.

28. Dolores McCahill, "Attorney Sees High Court Ruling on Religion-In-Schools Lawsuit," *Chicago Sun-Times*, November 19, 1960.

29. Declaration of Rights of the Florida Constitution, sec. 6, quoted in Plaintiffs' Memorandum on the Law, *Chamberlin*, 1.

30. Plaintiffs' Memorandum on the Law, *Chamberlin*, 2–3.

31. Ibid., 20–60.

32. Ibid., 32–38.

33. Ibid., 5–7.

34. Ibid., 3.

35. Ibid., 11.

36. *McCollum*, 333 U.S. at 227 (Justice Frankfurter concurring).

37. *Engel*, 206 N.Y.S. 2d 183 (N.Y. App. Div. 1960).

38. O'Hair, *An Atheist Epic*, 30.

39. Ibid., 31–32.

40. Le Beau, *The Atheist*, 44–45.

41. Ibid., 46.

42. Ibid., 47–48.

43. "Public School Opening Exercise, Opinion of Attorney General of Maryland," November 2, 1960, Appellants' Appendix, August 5, 1961, 18–25, Court of Appeals of Maryland, *Murray v. Curlett*, Transcript of Record, *Records and Briefs of the U.S. Supreme Court*, 374, Law Library of Congress.

44. Madalyn Murray to Edward and Sidney Schempp, December 4, 1960, Schempp Family Papers, 200.

45. Madalyn Murray to Edward and Sidney Schempp, December 10, 1960, Schempp Family Papers, 195.

46. Petition for Writ of Mandamus, Baltimore City Superior Court, December 7, 1960, Appellants' Appendix, August 5, 1961, 3–7, *Murray v. Curlett*, Transcript of Record, *Records and Briefs of the U.S. Supreme Court*, 374, Law Library of Congress.

47. Le Beau, *The Atheist*, 49.

48. O'Hair, *An Atheist Epic*, 108–9.

49. Ibid., 155.

50. Ibid., 227–29.

51. Ibid., 196.

52. Memorandum opinion, Superior Court of Baltimore City, April 27, 1961, Appellants' Appendix, August 5, 1961, 8–17, Court of Appeals of Maryland, *Murray v. Curlett*, Transcript of Record, *Records and Briefs of the U.S. Supreme Court*, 374, Law Library of Congress.

53. Ibid.

54. Ibid.

55. Ibid.

56. *Chamberlin v. Dade County Board of Public Instruction*, 17 Fla. Supp. 183 (1961).

57. *Chamberlin v. Dade County Board of Public Instruction*, 143 So. 2d 21, 23 (1962).

58. McCahill, "Attorney Sees High Court Ruling."

CHAPTER 15

1. Argument of Henry W. Sawyer III, Hearing on Defendant's Motion for Relief from Judgment, U.S. District Court for the Eastern District of Pennsylvania, March 18, 1960, 28, *Schempp v. School District of Abington*, National Archives, Philadelphia.

2. *School District of Abington v. Schempp*, 364 U.S. 298 (1960).

3. Argument of C. Brewster Rhoads, Pretrial Conference, U.S. District Court for the Eastern District of Pennsylvania, December 20, 1960, 21, *Schempp v. School District of Abington*, National Archives, Philadelphia.

4. Argument of Henry W. Sawyer III, Pretrial Conference, U.S. District Court for the Eastern District of Pennsylvania, December 20, 1960, 43, *Schempp v. School District of Abington*, National Archives, Philadelphia.

5. *Schempp v. School District of Abington*, 195 F. Supp. 518, 519 (E.D. Pa. 1961).

6. *Engel v. Vitale*, 10 N.Y. 2d 174.

7. *Everson*, 330 U.S. at 15.

8. *Engel*, 10 N.Y. 2d at 191.

9. Transcript of "Storm over the Supreme Court," 58–59.

10. Henry W. Sawyer III to Edward L. Schempp, October 13, 1961, Schempp Family Papers, 207.

11. Testimony of Edward Schempp, U.S. District Court for the Eastern

District of Pennsylvania, October 17, 1961, *Abington v. Schempp,* Transcript of Record, *Records and Briefs of the U.S. Supreme Court,* 374:214, Law Library of Congress.

12. Ibid., at 217.

13. Edward L. Schempp, undated memorandum, Schempp Family Papers, 206.

14. Argument of Henry W. Sawyer III, U.S. District Court for the Eastern District of Pennsylvania, December 18, 1961, 7–10, *Schempp v. School District of Abington,* National Archives, Philadelphia.

15. Ibid., 15–18.

16. Argument of C. Brewster Rhoads, U.S. District Court for the Eastern District of Pennsylvania, December 18, 1961, 52, *Schempp v. School District of Abington,* National Archives, Philadelphia.

17. Argument of Henry W. Sawyer III, U.S. District Court for the Eastern District of Pennsylvania, December 18, 1961, 79–80, *Schempp v. School District of Abington,* National Archives, Philadelphia.

18. Testimony of John D. Killian III, U.S. District Court for the Eastern District of Pennsylvania, December 18, 1961, 69–70, *Schempp v. School District of Abington,* National Archives, Philadelphia.

19. Ellery Schempp, discussion, November 27, 2004.

20. O'Hair, *An Atheist Epic,* 181–83.

21. *Schempp v. School District of Abington,* 201 F. Supp. 815, 819 (E.D. Pa. 1962).

22. "School Drops Bible-Reading in Abington," *Evening Bulletin,* February 1, 1962, Schempp Family Papers, 218.

23. "Abington to Appeal Bible Reading Case to Supreme Court," *Times Chronicle,* March 15, 1962, Schempp Family Papers, 241.

24. Ibid.

25. Anthony Day, "Bible Ruling Taken to U.S.," *Evening Bulletin,* May 25, 1962, Schempp Family Papers, 245.

26. "Bible Is Read in His Home, Schempp Says," *Evening Bulletin,* February 4, 1962, Schempp Family Papers, 218.

27. Notice of Appeal to the Supreme Court of the United States, March 28, 1962, *Schempp v. School District of Abington Township,* Transcript of Record, *Records and Briefs of the U.S. Supreme Court,* 374:237, Law Library of Congress.

CHAPTER 16

1. Bernard Schwartz with Stephan Lesher, *Inside the Warren Court* (Garden City, NY: Doubleday, 1983), 49.

2. Ibid., 55.

3. Bernard Schwartz, *Super Chief: Earl Warren and His Supreme Court; A Judicial Biography* (New York: New York University Press, 1983), 177, 206.

4. *Zorach,* 343 U.S. at 313.

5. Louis H. Pollak, "The Supreme Court 1962 Term; Foreword: Public Prayers in Public Schools," *Harvard Law Review* 77 (1963-64): 62, 63.

6. Ibid.

7. *McCollum,* 333 U.S. 203.

8. Argument of William J. Butler, Supreme Court of the United States, April 3, 1962, *Engel v. Vitale,* in Kurland and Caspar, *Landmark Briefs,* 56:1036-37.

9. Ibid., 56:1037.

10. Ibid., 56:1050-51.

11. Ibid., 56:1052.

12. Ibid., 56:1042.

13. Ibid., 56:1047.

14. Transcript of "Storm over the Supreme Court," 61-62.

15. Argument of Bertram B. Daiker, Supreme Court of the United States, April 3, 1962, *Engel V. Vitale,* in Kurland and Caspar, *Landmark Briefs,* 56:1055.

16. Ibid., 56:1062.

17. Ibid.

18. Ibid., 56:1066.

19. *Murray v. Curlett,* 228 Md. 239 (1961).

20. Ibid., at 248.

21. Ibid.

22. O'Hair, *An Atheist Epic,* 197-98.

23. Ibid., 203.

24. Ibid., 203-11.

25. Ibid., 230-35.

26. Ibid., 235.

27. *Chamberlin v. Dade County Board of Public Instruction,* 143 So. 2d 21.

28. State of Florida Office of Cultural and Historical Programs, "Florida Governors' Portraits: Millard Fillmore Caldwell," http://dhr.dos.state.fl.us/museum/collections/governors/about.cfm?id=36 (accessed November 5, 2006).

29. *Chamberlin,* 143 So. 2d at 24-25.

30. Ibid., at 25.

31. Thomas M. Cooley, *General Principles of Constitutional Law in the United States of America,* 2nd ed. (Boston: Little, Brown, 1891), 213-14, cited in *Chamberlin,* 143 So. 2d at 25.

32. For example, Judge Caldwell cited state court decisions in *Carden v. Bland* (199 Tenn. 665 [1956]) and *Doremus v. Board of Education* (5 N.J. 435), among other cases.

33. *Chamberlin,* 143 So. 2d at 28.

34. Ibid., at 31-33.

35. Ibid., at 33.

36. Ibid.

37. Leo Pfeffer to Tobias Simon, July 5, 1962, box 12, folder: Chamberlin III, Leo Pfeffer Papers.

38. Leo Pfeffer to Tobias Simon, June 25, 1962, box 12, folder: Chamberlin III, Leo Pfeffer Papers.

39. Tobias Simon to Leo Pfeffer, June 28, 1962, box 12, folder: Chamberlin III, Leo Pfeffer Papers.

40. Pfeffer to Simon, July 5, 1962.

41. *Everson*, 330 U.S. 1.

42. *McCollum*, 333 U.S. 203.

43. *Engel v. Vitale*, 370 U.S. 421, 425 (1962).

44. Ibid., at 429.

45. Ibid.

46. Ibid., at 435.

47. Ibid., at 431.

48. Ibid., at 436.

49. Ibid., at 435.

50. Howard Ball and Phillip J. Cooper, *Of Power and Right: Hugo Black, William O. Douglas, and America's Constitutional Revolution* (New York: Oxford University Press, 1992), 248–49.

51. *Engel*, 370 U.S. at 442 (Justice Douglas concurring).

52. Ibid., at 445–46 (Justice Stewart dissenting).

53. Louis Fisher, *Religious Liberty in America: Political Safeguards* (Lawrence: University Press of Kansas, 2002), 126.

54. Leo Katcher, *Earl Warren: A Political Biography* (New York: McGraw-Hill, 1967), 423.

55. Fisher, *Religious Liberty in America*, 127–28.

56. William M. Beaney and Edward N. Beiser, "Prayer and Politics: The Impact of Engel and Schempp on the Political Process," in *The Impact of Supreme Court Decisions: Empirical Studies*, ed. Theodore L. Becker and Malcolm M. Feeley, 2nd ed. (New York: Oxford University Press, 1973), 22–36.

57. Lucas A. Powe, Jr., *The Warren Court and American Politics* (Cambridge: Harvard University Press, 2000), 188.

58. Kenneth M. Dolbeare and Phillip E. Hammond, *The School Prayer Decisions: From Court Policy to Local Practice* (Chicago: University of Chicago Press, 1971), 28.

59. Ball and Cooper, *Of Power and Right*, 250.

60. William A. Hachten, "Journalism and the Prayer Decision," *Columbia Journalism Review*, fall 1962, 4.

61. Ibid., 5–8.

CHAPTER 17

1. David M. O'Brien, *Storm Center: The Supreme Court in American Politics* (New York: W. W. Norton, 2003), 191–93.

2. Ibid., 198.

3. Timothy B. Dyk to Earl Warren, memorandum, July 27, 1962, box 235, folder: October Term 1962, Appellate Nos. 133–40, *School District of Abington v. Schempp*, Papers of Earl Warren, Manuscript Division, Library of Congress.

4. Ibid.

5. Timothy B. Dyk to Earl Warren, memorandum, July 27, 1962, box 234, folder: October Term 1962, Appellate #113–32, *Murray v. Curlett*, Papers of Earl Warren, Manuscript Division, Library of Congress.

6. Earl Warren, docket entries, box 376, folder: October Term 1962, Appellate #1–250, *School District of Abington v. Schempp*, Papers of Earl Warren, Manuscript Division, Library of Congress. See also Jared C. Carter to William O. Douglas, memorandum, July 18, 1962, *School District of Abington v. Schempp*, Papers of William O. Douglas, box 1295, folder: No. 142, 119 (c) *Abington v. Schempp* 1962, Manuscript Division, Library of Congress.

7. William J. Brennan, docket entries, box I:76, folder 2, *Murray v. Curlett*, Papers of William J. Brennan, Jr., Manuscript Division, Library of Congress.

8. Richard J. Hiegel to John Marshall Harlan, supplemental memorandum, September 24, 1962, box 174, folder 142, *School District of Abington v. Schempp*, John Marshall Harlan Papers, Department of Rare Books and Special Collections, Princeton University Library.

9. Earl Warren, docket entries, box 376, folder: October Term 1962, Appellate #1–250, *Murray v. Curlett*, Papers of Earl Warren, Manuscript Division, Library of Congress.

10. Ibid. See also Earl Warren, docket entries, *School District of Abington v. Schempp*.

11. Bernard S. Mandler to Leo Pfeffer, August 20, 1962, box 12, folder: Chamberlin III, Leo Pfeffer Papers.

12. E. C. Schade, Office of the Clerk, Supreme Court of the United States, to Leo Pfeffer, October 16, 1962, box 12, folder: Chamberlin III, Leo Pfeffer Papers.

13. Philip H. Ward III, discussion with the author, Philadelphia, PA, January 20, 2004.

14. Ibid.

15. Ibid.

16. Ibid.

17. Ibid.

18. Ellery Schempp, discussion, April 17, 2003.

19. O'Brien, *Storm Center*, 115–19.

20. Argument of Leonard J. Kerpelman, Supreme Court of the United States, February 27, 1963, *Murray v. Curlett*, in Kurland and Caspar, *Landmark Briefs*, 57:1003–4.

21. Ibid., 57:959.

22. Ward, discussion.

23. Argument of Francis B. Burch, Supreme Court of the United States, February 27, 1963, *Murray v. Curlett*, in Kurland and Caspar, *Landmark Briefs*, 57:970–71.

24. Ibid., 57:979.

25. Argument of George W. Baker, Jr., Supreme Court of the United States, February 27, 1963, *Murray v. Curlett*, in Kurland and Caspar, *Landmark Briefs*, 57:989–90.

26. Argument of Thomas B. Finan, Supreme Court of the United States, February 27, 1963, *Murray v. Curlett*, in Kurland and Caspar, *Landmark Briefs*, 57:990–91.

27. Ibid., 991.

28. Ibid., 997.

29. Ibid., 998–99.

30. *McCollum,* 333 U.S. at 228 (Justice Frankfurter concurring).

31. *Bible Reading in Public Schools: The Schempp and Murray Cases, 1963,* DVD.

32. Argument of Philip H. Ward III, Supreme Court of the United States, February 28, 1963, *School District of Abington v. Schempp*, in Kurland and Caspar, *Landmark Briefs*, 57:1019.

33. Ibid., 57:1020–21.

34. Ibid., 57:1021–22.

35. Ibid., 57:1026–27.

36. Ibid., 57:1032.

37. Ellery Schempp, discussion, April 17, 2003.

38. Argument of Henry W. Sawyer III, Supreme Court of the United States, February 28, 1963, *School District of Abington v. Schempp*, in Kurland and Caspar, *Landmark Briefs*, 57:1036–37.

39. Ibid., 57:1037.

40. Ibid., 57:1043.

41. Ibid., 57:1054.

42. Ibid., 57:1054–55.

43. Ellery Schempp, discussion, April 17, 2003.

44. Ibid.

45. Philip Ward, discussion.

CHAPTER 18

1. Kim Isaac Eisler, *A Justice for All: William J. Brennan, Jr., and the Decisions That Transformed America* (New York: Simon and Schuster, 1993), 182.

2. Robert M. O'Neil, discussion with the author, April 21, 2004, New York.

3. Roger Goldman with David Gallen, *Justice William J. Brennan, Jr.: Freedom First* (New York: Carroll and Graf, 1994), 16.

4. Earl Warren, *The Memoirs of Earl Warren* (Garden City, NY: Doubleday, 1977), 316.

5. William O. Douglas, conference notes, March 1, 1963, box 1281, folder: October Term 1962, 100–125, argued memo, *Murray v. Curlett*, Papers of William O. Douglas, Manuscript Division, Library of Congress.

6. Earl Warren, docket entries, box 376, folder: October Term 1962, Appellate #1–250, *Murray v. Curlett*, Papers of Earl Warren, Manuscript Division, Library of Congress.

7. William O. Douglas, conference notes, March 1, 1963, box 1295, folder: No. 142, 119 (c) *Abington v. Schempp* 1962, *School District of Abington v. Schempp*, Papers of William O. Douglas, Manuscript Division, Library of Congress.

8. O'Neil, discussion, April 21, 2004.

9. O'Brien, *Storm Center*, 131–43.

10. Papers of Justice Tom C. Clark, Tarleton Law Library, University of Texas at Austin, http://utopia.utexas.edu/explore/clark/index.html (accessed November 7, 2006).

11. Tom C. Clark, Draft Opinion 1, undated, box A144, folder 1, Papers of Justice Tom C. Clark, Rare Books and Special Collections, Tarleton Law Library, University of Texas Law School (hereafter cited as Clark Draft No. 1).

12. Tom C. Clark, Draft Opinion 2, undated, box A144, folder 1, Papers of Justice Tom C. Clark, Rare Books and Special Collections, Tarleton Law Library, University of Texas Law School (hereafter cited as Clark Draft No. 2).

13. Tom C. Clark, Draft Opinion 3, undated, box A143, folder 10, Papers of Justice Tom C. Clark, Rare Books and Special Collections, Tarleton Law Library, University of Texas Law School (hereafter cited as Clark Draft No. 3).

14. Tom C. Clark, Record of Circulation, March 5, 1963, box A211, folder 2, Papers of Justice Tom C. Clark, Rare Books and Special Collections, Tarleton Law Library, University of Texas Law School.

15. Thomas M. Mengler, "Public Relations in the Supreme Court: Justice Tom Clark's Opinion in the School Prayer Case," *Constitutional Commentary* 6 (1989): 331–32, 345.

16. *Schempp*, 374 U.S. at 206–8.

17. Ibid., at 209–10.

18. Clark Draft No. 1, at 12.

19. Clark Draft No. 2, insert at 2.

20. Clark Draft No. 3, at 3.

21. See, for example, Clark draft of June 10, 1963, 8, Papers of Justice

Tom C. Clark, Tarleton Law Library, University of Texas at Austin, http://utopia.utexas.edu/explore/clark/index.html (accessed November 7, 2006).

22. *Schempp*, 374 U.S. at 205–12.

23. Mengler, "Public Relations," 339–40.

24. Richard Kluger, *Simple Justice* (New York: Alfred A. Knopf, 2004), 542.

25. Martin J. Flynn, discussion with the author, August 5, 2004, Washington, DC.

26. Clark Draft No. 1, at 7–8.

27. *Schempp*, 374 U.S. at 212–14.

28. Clark Draft No. 1, at 9–12.

29. *Schempp*, 374 U.S. at 215–16.

30. Ibid., at 216–17.

31. Clark Draft No. 1, at 13–14.

32. Ibid., at 16–17.

33. Clark Draft No. 2, at 15, 19.

34. Clark Draft No. 3, at 21–22.

35. Mengler, "Public Relations," 343.

36. Flynn, discussion.

37. *Schempp*, 374 U.S. at 222.

38. Ibid., at 224.

39. Ibid., at 224–25.

40. Ibid., at 225.

41. Irving R. Kaufman, "The Supreme Court and Its Critics," *Atlantic Monthly*, December 1963, 50.

42. William O. Douglas to Tom C. Clark, memorandum, May 20, 1963, box A143, folder 10, Papers of Justice Tom C. Clark, Tarleton Law Library, University of Texas Law School.

43. Notes, October Term 1962, 1–3, Opinions of William J. Brennan, Jr., box II: 6–8, Papers of William J. Brennan, Jr., Manuscript Division, Library of Congress.

44. Clark, Record of Circulation.

45. Martin J. Flynn to Tom C. Clark, undated memorandum, probably May 22 or 23, 1963, box A143, folder 10, Papers of Justice Tom C. Clark, Tarleton Law Library, University of Texas Law School.

46. Potter Stewart, memorandum to the conference, May 23, 1963, box A143, folder 10, Papers of Justice Tom C. Clark, Tarleton Law Library, University of Texas Law School.

47. Byron R. White to Tom C. Clark, memorandum, May 24, 1963, box A143, folder 10, Paper of Justice Tom C. Clark, Tarleton Law Library, University of Texas Law School.

48. Clark, Record of Circulation.

49. William J. Brennan, Jr., Draft Opinion 1, at 3, May 1963, box I:88, folder 10, William J. Brennan Papers, Manuscript Division, Library of Congress (hereafter cited as Brennan Draft No. 1).

50. O'Neil, discussion, April 21, 2004.

51. Robert M. O'Neil, discussion with the author, May 13, 2004, Washington, DC.

52. O'Neil, discussion, April 21, 2004.

53. Richard Posner, email correspondence with the author, October 25, 2004.

54. *Schempp*, 374 U.S. at 233 (Justice Brennan concurring).

55. *McGowan v. Maryland*, 366 U.S. 420, 465 (1961; Justice Frankfurter concurring).

56. *Schempp*, 374 U.S. at 237 (Justice Brennan concurring).

57. Ibid.

58. Brennan Draft No. 1, at 7.

59. *Schempp*, 374 U.S. at 237–38 (Justice Brennan concurring).

60. Ibid., at 238–39.

61. Ibid., at 241.

62. Ibid.

63. Ibid., at 242.

64. Ibid., at 277–78.

65. Ibid., at 280–81.

66. Ibid., at 282–85.

67. Ibid., at 287–90.

68. O'Neil, discussion, May 13, 2004.

69. *Schempp*, 374 U.S. at 294–304 (Justice Brennan concurring).

70. *Elk Grove United School District v. Newdow*, 542 U.S. 1 (2004).

71. *Schempp*, 374 U.S. at 303–4 (Justice Brennan concurring).

72. O'Neil, discussion, May 13, 2004.

73. *Marsh v. Chambers*, 463 U.S. 783 (1983; Justice Brennan dissenting).

74. Brennan Draft No. 1, box 174, folder 142, John Marshall Harlan Papers, Public Policy Papers, Department of Rare Books and Special Collections, Princeton University Library.

75. *Schempp*, 374 U.S. at 307 (Justice Goldberg concurring).

76. Notes, October Term 1962, at 1–3.

77. Potter Stewart, memorandum to the conference, April 10, 1963, 19, box 174, folder 142, John Marshall Harlan Papers, Public Policy Papers, Department of Rare Books and Special Collections, Princeton University Library.

78. *Schempp*, 374 U.S. at 317–18 (Justice Stewart dissenting).

79. Ibid., at 318.

80. John F. Davis to Philip H. Ward III, Western Union telegram, June 17, 1963, in the author's possession.

81. *Chamberlin v. Dade County Board of Public Instruction*, 374 U.S. 487 (1963).

82. "Rockland Girl Bride of Ellory Schempp," *Brockton Enterprise*, June 18, 1963, Schempp Family Papers, 437.

83. Ellery Schempp, discussion, April 17, 2003.

84. Kathleen McDevitt, "Woman Atheist Backed by Bible Ruling Says Now 'I Can Say Just What I Think,'" *Evening Bulletin*, July 2, 1963, Schempp Family Papers, 484.

CHAPTER 19

1. *Johns v. Allen*, 231 F. Supp. 852 (D. Del. 1964).

2. Ibid., at 857–60.

3. *Chamberlin v. Dade County Board of Public Instruction*, 143 So. 2d at 28.

4. *Chamberlin v. Dade County Board of Public Instruction*, 374 U.S. 487.

5. *Chamberlin v. Dade County Board of Public Instruction*, 160 So. 2d 97, 98 (1964).

6. Ibid., at 99

7. *Chamberlin v. Dade County Board of Public Instruction*, 377 U.S. 402 (1964).

8. *Chamberlin v. Dade County Board of Public Instruction*, 171 So. 2d 535 (1965).

9. Kluger, *Simple Justice*, 755.

10. "Dr. Gaffney Directs Faculty to Comply with Bible Decision," *Willow Grove Guide*, June 20, 1963, 1, Schempp Family Papers, 443.

11. Richard C. J. Kitto to Arthur J. Goldberg, June 20, 1963, box II:26, folder 3, Papers of Arthur J. Goldberg, Manuscript Division, Library of Congress, Washington, DC.

12. "Policy on Religion Aired by Abington School Board," *Willow Grove Guide*, July 11, 1963, Schempp Family Papers, 500.

13. "Meditation Will Replace Prayer in Penna. Schools," *Philadelphia Inquirer*, June 18, 1963, Schempp Family Papers, 436.

14. H. Frank Way, "Survey Research on Judicial Decisions: The Prayer and Bible Reading Cases," *Western Political Quarterly* 21 (June 1968), quoted in Kenneth M. Dolbeare and Phillip E. Hammond, *The School Prayer Decisions: From Court Policy to Local Practice* (Chicago: University of Chicago Press, 1971), 30–33.

15. Dolbeare and Hammond, *School Prayer Decisions*, 29, 31.

16. Ibid., 33.

17. Ibid., 34–35.

18. Ibid., 6.

19. Ibid., 5.

20. Ibid., 6–8.

21. Ibid., 78–89.

22. Ibid., 75–78.

23. *Adams v. Engelking,* 232 F. Supp. 666 (D. Idaho 1964).

24. *Nashville Tennessean,* August 23, 1963, 1, quoted in Robert H. Birkby, "The Supreme Court and the Bible Belt: Tennessee Reaction to the 'Schempp' Decision," in Becker and Feeley, *Impact of Supreme Court Decisions,* 110.

25. Birkby, "The Supreme Court and the Bible Belt," 111, 114.

26. *State Board of Education v. Board of Education of Netcong,* 262 A.2d 21, 31 (N.J. Superior Court 1970).

27. Ibid.

28. *State Board of Education v. Board of Education of Netcong,* 270 A.2d 412 (1970).

29. David Firestone, "Court Voids Law Covering School Prayer in Louisiana," *New York Times,* December 12, 2001, 20.

30. *Doe v. School Board of Quachita Parish,* 274 F.3d 289 (2001).

31. House Committee on the Judiciary, *Proposed Amendments to the Constitution Relating to School Prayers, Bible Reading, Etc.,* 90th Cong., 2d sess., 1968.

32. Fisher, *Religious Liberty in America,* 127.

33. Joan DelFattore, *The Fourth R: Conflicts over Religion in America's Public Schools* (New Haven: Yale University Press, 2004), 111.

34. Leo Pfeffer, *God, Caesar, and the Constitution; The Court as Referee of Church-State Confrontation* (Boston: Beacon Press, 1975), 213–15.

35. *Proposed Amendments to the Constitution Relating to Prayers and Bible Reading in the Public Schools, Hearings before the House Committee on the Judiciary,* 88th Cong., 2d sess., 1964, 638 (statement of Rep. Mendel Rivers).

36. DelFattore, *The Fourth R,* 145.

37. Ibid.

38. *Safeguarding Our Religious Liberties Act,* HR 3190, 108th Cong., 1st sess., 2003.

39. *Constitution Restoration Act of 2004,* HR 3799, 108th Cong., 2d sess., 2004.

40. For a general history of the Christian conservative movement, see Ruth Murray Brown, *For A Christian America: A History of the Religious Right* (New York: Prometheus Books, 2002).

41. Pfeffer, *God, Caesar, and the Constitution,* 209–10.

42. *Proposed Amendments to the Constitution Relating to Prayers and Bible Reading in the Public Schools,* 1964, 825–29 (statement of Bishop Fulton J. Sheen).

43. "Prayers in Public Schools Opposed," *Christian Century,* January 9, 1952, 35.

44. George Dugan, "Churches Divided, With Most in Favor," *New York Times,* June 18, 1963, 1, Schempp Family Papers, 428–29.

45. Ibid.

46. *Proposed Amendments to the Constitution Relating to Prayers and Bible Reading in the Public Schools,* 1964, 443 (statement of the Executive Council of the Lutheran Church in America).

47. Ibid., 656–57 (statement of Edwin H. Tuller).

48. Ibid., 657.

CHAPTER 20

1. *Edwards v. Aguillard,* 482 U.S. 578, 639 (1987, Justice Scalia dissenting).

2. "Meditation Will Replace Prayer in Penna. Schools."

3. *Wallace v. Jaffree,* 472 U.S. 38, 70–71 (1985; Justice O'Connor concurring).

4. *Lemon v. Kurtzman,* 403 U.S. at 612–13.

5. *Wallace v. Jaffree,* 472 U.S. at 60.

6. Ibid., at 71–74 (Justice O'Connor concurring).

7. *Abington School District v. Schempp,* 374 U.S. at 203, 281 (Justice Brennan concurring).

8. *Brown v. Gilmore,* 258 F.3d 265, 276 (U.S. Court of Appeals for the Fourth Circuit 2001).

9. *Lee v. Weisman,* 505 U.S. 577, 641 (1992; Justice Scalia dissenting).

10. *Weisman,* at 587.

11. Ibid., at 632, 643 (Justice Scalia dissenting).

12. Ibid., at 642.

13. *Weisman,* 505 U.S. at 593–94.

14. *McCollum,* 333 U.S. at 227 (Justice Frankfurter concurring).

15. Michael W. McConnell, "Religious Participation in Public Programs: Religious Freedom at the Crossroads," *University of Chicago Law Review* 59 (winter 1992): 115, 158–59.

16. Michael W. McConnell, "Religion and the State: The Origins of the Religion Clauses of the Constitution; Coercion, the Lost Element of Establishment," *William and Mary Law Review* 27 (summer 1986): 933, 935–36.

17. *Schempp,* 374 U.S. at 316 (Justice Stewart dissenting).

18. *Widmar v. Vincent,* 454 U.S. 263, 271–74 (1981).

19. Ibid., at 284 (Justice White dissenting).

20. Equal Access Act, *U.S. Code* 20, 4071–74.

21. *Westside Community Board of Education v. Mergens,* 496 U.S. 226, 247–50 (1990).

22. *Rosenberger v. Rector of the University of Virginia,* 515 U.S. 819 (1995).

23. *Santa Fe Independent School District v. Doe,* 530 U.S. 290 (2000).

24. Ibid., at 324 (Chief Justice Rehnquist dissenting).

25. *Jones v. Clear Creek Independent School District,* 977 F.2d 963 (U.S. Court of Appeals for the Fifth Circuit 1992).

26. Ibid., at 969.

27. Ibid., at 971–72.

28. *Ingebretsen v. Jackson Public School District,* 88 F.3d 274 (U.S. Court of Appeals for the Fifth Circuit 1996).

29. *Herdahl v. Pontotoc County Board of Education,* 933 F. Supp. 582 (U.S. District Court for the Northern District of Mississippi 1996).

30. *Wallace v. Jaffree,* 472 U.S. at 92 (Chief Justice Rehnquist dissenting).

31. Ibid., at 94.

32. Ibid., at 95.

33. Ibid., at 99.

34. Ibid., at 113.

35. Douglas Laycock, "Religion and the State: The Origins of the Religion Clauses of the Constitution; 'Nonpreferential' Aid to Religion; A False Claim About Original Intent," *William and Mary Law Review* 27 (summer 1986): 875, 879–82.

36. Ibid., 913.

37. James Madison to Edward Livingston, July 10, 1822, in *James Madison: Writings* (New York: Library of America, 1999), 788.

38. Eck, *A New Religious America,* 152.

39. Finke and Stark, *Churching of America,* 15.

40. *Yearbook of American Churches,* ed. Benson Y. Landis, 32nd issue (New York: National Council of the Churches of Christ in the USA, 1964), 252, 254, 257.

41. Madison to Livingston, July 10, 1822, in *Writings,* 789.

EPILOGUE

1. Le Beau, *The Atheist,* 260–62.

2. Ibid., 281.

3. Ibid., 307–21.

4. Ellery Schempp, discussion, April 17, 2003.

5. Abington Senior High School, Hall of Fame, http://www.abington.k12.pa.us/senior/hall_of_fame/main.html (accessed November 24, 2006).

Index

Abernathy, Thomas, 261

Abington Friends School, 102–3

Abington school district: Bible reading practices in, 131; Brennan on promoting moral values and discipline in, 299–300; considers appeal to Supreme Court on *Schempp* case, 203–4; as defendant in *Schempp* case, 67; dismantling of public school devotionals in, 309–10; historical account of subjects taught in, 103

Abington School District v. Schempp: constitutional amendments on school prayer proposed after, 262, 309, 315–17; court-stripping tactics after, 317–18; debate on coercion and, 330–31; defiance against, 310–13; establishment clause shifts after, 338–43; Frankfurter on conformity pressures on children and, 332–33; free exercise issues in *Chamberlin* and, 333–34; McConnell on coercion and, 333; moments of silence tests after, 325–28; more conservative Supreme Court and, 324–25; Protestant acceptance of, 320–23; resistance to, 307–9; Roman Catholic acceptance of, 319–20; Scalia on coercion after, 328,

330–31; student-initiated prayers and, 334–38. See also *Schempp* case

Abington Senior High School: alumni honors for Schempp by, 348; conformity in, 11–12; construction of, 2–3; new building for, 19; student council, 18–19; teacher requirements on devotional exercises at, 22–23. See also Karam, Irvin A.; Stull, W. Eugene

Abington Township: commissioner on *Schempp* opinion, 202–3; description of, 1–2; Penn's charter from King George and, 101–2; settlers, churches, meetinghouses, and schools in, 102–3

abstention doctrine, 230, 266

Ahlstrom, Sydney E., 82

Alabama, moment of silence case from, 326–27, 339–41

Alito, Samuel, A., Jr., 325

American Civil Liberties Union (ACLU): debates filing *Schempp* in federal or state courts, 57–58; Ellery asks for help from, 30; on Gideon Bible distribution in public schools as sectarian, 145–46; in Miami, *Chamberlin* and, 190, 191; New York chapter

383

234–35; Sawyer's argument at Supreme Court, 271, 277, 278–79; Third Circuit opinion in, 197–98; U.S. Supreme Court remands to Biggs, 231; Ward prepares for Supreme Court hearing, 268–70; Ward's arguments at Supreme Court on, 275–77; Weigle on moral value of Bible reading to children, 166; Weigle on sectarian nature of various versions of the Bible, 164–65; Weigle on various versions of the Bible, 163–64; Wolfman resigns from, 41

Schiffler, George, 115

school prayer: Brennan on difficulties with decisions on, 281–82; conservative justices on, 6–7; defenders of, on coercion in, 329–30; in Florida public schools, 190, 213; as free speech, litigation on, 337–38; at high school football games, 336. *See also* devotional exercises; Lord's Prayer recitations; religion in schools; *Schempp* case

school superintendents, interpretation of *Schempp* by, 312

schools: in American colonies, 4–5; Brennan reviews historical changes in, 298; colonial, rules on teaching religion in, 100–101; colonial and early nineteenth-century, 98–100; conservative justices on prayer in, 6–7; evolution from private to public in U.S., 71; financial assistance for religious publications by, 336; history of religion in, periods of, 96–97; Hughes pushes for Catholic parochial system in New York, 121; Pan-Protes-

tantism in, 108; public, development of, 108–13; teaching American values of self-governance in, 125. *See also* common religion for common schools; religion in schools; textbooks

Scott, John M., 117–18

Second Great Awakening, 91–92

Sedition Act of 1798, 343

Senate Judiciary Committee, 262

sermons, fundamentalist, in Miami Beach public schools, 189

Shannon, Charles Kenneth, 103, 107–8

Sheen, Fulton J., 320

silent generation, 8–9

Simon, Tobias, 256

Simple Justice (Kluger), 290

Sissel, H. B., 202–3

Smith, Adam, 90

Smith, Charles, 204

Society of Friends, 78–79. *See also* Quakers

South Carolina: church and state relations in, 76; colonial, religious diversity in, 81; colonial, statutes on schools in, 99

Speer, David, 129

spellers, as early American textbooks, 104

Spellman, Francis Cardinal, 263, 319–20

Squibb, Alva M., 23

Stein, A. C., 129

Stern, Philip, 215

Stewart, Potter: dissent in *Schempp* and *Murray cases*, 295, 302–4, 339; early processing of *Schempp* and *Murray* cases and, 267; *Engel v. Vitale* decision and, 261; on free exercise clause in *Murray*, 302–4; on free exercise clause in *Schempp*, 302–4, 334; opinion on